On
Philology

Of
Art and
Wisdom

DAVID ROOCHNIK

OF
ART AND
WISDOM

PLATO'S UNDERSTANDING OF TECHNE

THE PENNSYLVANIA STATE UNIVERSITY PRESS
UNIVERSITY PARK, PENNSYLVANIA

David Roochnik is Associate Professor of Philosophy at Boston University. He is the author of *The Tragedy of Reason* (Routledge, 1990).

Library of Congress Cataloging-in-Publication Data

Roochnik, David.
    Of art and wisdom : Plato's understanding of techne / David Roochnik.

        p.   cm.
    Includes bibliographical references and index.
    ISBN-13: 978-0-271-03273-3
    1. Plato—Contributions in concept of techne.   2. Techne (Philosophy)   I. Title.
    B398.T4R66   1996
    184—dc20   95-40452
                                                                                    CIP

Published by The Pennsylvania State University Press,
University Park, PA 16802-1003

It is the policy of The Pennsylvania State University Press to use acid-free paper for the first printing of all clothbound books. Publications on uncoated stock satisfy the minimum requirements of American National Standard for Information Sciences—Permanence of Paper for Printed Library Materials, ANSI Z39.48-1992.

To Gina

CONTENTS

Oh, you people who, with such great futility, get it all wrong! Why do you teach your myriad kinds of technical knowledge (*technas*), why do you invent and devise all manner of things, but still not know a single way to teach wisdom to those who lack intelligence? Worse, you're not even trying to hunt one down.

—Euripides, *Hippolytus*, 916–920

ACKNOWLEDGMENTS

The *American Journal of Philology, Arethusa, Interpretation, Journal of the History of Philosophy, Phoenix,* and *Rhetorica* kindly allowed me to reprint small portions of previously published work.

I wish to thank my teacher Stanley Rosen, who some fifteen years ago put me on the trail of the techne question. To Rosen I was introduced by my first teacher, Drew Hyland, with whom I have worked closely for twenty-five years (and who commented on a draft of this book). If my work has any merit, it is due to the composite influence of these two very different kinds of men.

Jacob Howland read a version of this book and offered valuable suggestions. Sandy Thatcher was helpful and supportive from the start. To both I am grateful.

I spent a year teaching at Williams College, where I tried out some of the ideas basic to this book. That the wonderful students there, as well as my friends and colleagues Alan White and Dan O'Connor, did not toss me out on my ear encouraged me to continue.

Charles Griswold has been my best critic for a long time. Without him my philosophical life would have been far lonelier than it has been.

My daughters, Lena and Shana, have been a fountain of energy. Their voices ring constantly through my home, reminding me always to think small. A good service that.

My wife, Gina Crandell, has been a warm and loving presence for years. She believes my ideas have value, and for this, and so much else, I am grateful. This book is dedicated to Gina.

PREFACE

Technē—skill, art, craft, expertise, profession, science, knowledge, technical knowledge—is a crucial term in the Platonic dialogues. Indeed, it has been crucial in the development of Western culture itself, for we, following the Greeks for centuries, now use its descendants to describe ourselves: we live with "technology," reward the "technocrats," admire the "technical," covet the "high-tech."

We live surrounded by the works of techne and are amazed by their extraordinary power, speed, cleverness, and ability to insinuate themselves into our daily lives. Most of our intellectual capital is spent in their pursuit, and we are convinced that in techne our future lies.

And yet some still ask: How are these technical wonders to be used? What sort of life is there to be lived in a world gone technical?

The ancient Greeks had little technology to boast. Yet, by having "techne" in their vocabulary they gave themselves the occasion to reflect on it and its human consequences. And their reflections ran deep, so much so that they are worth being unearthed even at this late date.

This book treats the concept of techne as it appears and is used by Plato. That techne plays a significant role in the dialogues has long been noted by scholars. But never has it been systematically analyzed, located within the context of its historical antecedents, and made the focus of a full-length study (in English, at least). This book does that. I do not address the spe-

cifics of modern Western technology, or its relationship to its Greek ancestor. The category of this book is strictly Plato, and neither the Philosophy
nor the History of Technology. Still, I can think of no better source than
these dialogues from which to philosophize and wonder about technology.
If I make but few connections between now and then, I nonetheless believe
many are there to be made. Why else bother with dead Plato?

In writing this book I take up themes that have long preoccupied me.
For better or worse, and whatever my intentions, all my writings have,
from a variety of angles, approached, elaborated, and tried to hammer out
a single thought. As a result, the present book covers some of the same
ground as my first, *The Tragedy of Reason*. In both I try to articulate
Plato's conception of reason or moral knowledge. In the first book, I do so
via the lens of tragedy; in this the second, of techne. The connection is
straightforward enough: for Plato reason is tragic because it cannot
achieve a moral techne, a stable body of reliable knowledge able to tell us,
in fixed terms readily teachable to others, how we ought to live. In both
books I try to uncover the wonderfully elusive, the live and crackling sense
of reason/knowledge animating the dialogues. Again, I do so because of
my conviction that the dialogues can benefit us in these hypertechnical
times.

INTRODUCTION

By the Gods, you simply (ἀτεχνῶς) do not stop speaking about shoemakers, fullers, cooks, and doctors, as if our discussion were about them.

—Callicles to Socrates, *Gorgias* 491a

Callicles is right: Socrates does talk repeatedly about shoemakers, fullers, cooks, and doctors; in short, about men who possess a *technē*—an "art" (or "craft," "skill," "expertise," "profession," or even, as it is sometimes translated, a "science")—a thorough, masterful knowledge of a specific field that typically issues in a useful result, can be taught to others, and can be recognized, certified, and rewarded.[1] This is true, at least, in the *Apology, Laches, Charmides, Euthyphro, Republic* (book 1), *Euthydemus, Ion, Hippias Minor, Protagoras,* and *Gorgias;* that is, in what are standardly described as Plato's "early" dialogues.[2] In several of the most significant and richest passages in these works, techne plays a critical role, usually as part of analogical arguments. This book is a thorough documentation of Socrates' use of the techne analogy, as well as an examination of its philosophical implications.

1. Just how frequently Socrates does talk about the *technai* can be gleaned from the catalogue in Brumbaugh 1976. Since it soon becomes part of my standard vocabulary, I will neither underline nor include a diacritical mark on "techne" or "technai." For a good discussion of these criteria of techne, see Heinimann 1961. Unless otherwise noted, all citations from Plato are my own translations of Burnet's Oxford edition. For a comment similar to the statement by Callicles used as my epigraph, see *Symposium* 221e. See Appendix 2 for a discussion of ἀτεχνῶς.

2. This standard list conforms with Vlastos 1991, 46, with only one exception: he calls the *Euthydemus* "transitional." For the latest, and most technical, update on chronology, see Ledger 1989.

To gain a sense of why this is a project worth undertaking—and not just for Plato scholars—consider the following passage from the *Laches*. Lysimachus, who hopes to educate his son and make him into an excellent man, asks two well-known generals, Laches and Nicias, for advice. Do they think that armor fighting is a good vehicle for teaching excellence (*aretē*)? Laches says no, Nicias yes. In the face of such disagreement Lysimachus asks Socrates to cast the deciding vote. Socrates is appalled at the prospect of so serious a question being settled by a vote. In order to convince Lysimachus that he is being wrongheaded, Socrates argues thus: if there were a debate about what exercise Lysimachus's son should perform, he would consult an expert in the field, a well-educated and highly regarded trainer. The question would be decided, not by the principle of majority rule, but by someone knowledgeable (*technikos:* 185a1), by an "expert" or *technitēs,* a man who has a techne. Similarly, the present question—whether Lysimachus's son should learn armor fighting in order to become excellent—should be decided, not by a vote, but by someone knowledgeable about arete.

Socrates seems to assume this analogy: as the expert, or technical trainer, is to the excellence of the body, so X, a *technitēs,* is to the excellence of the "soul" (*psuchē:* 185e2).

Or consider *Apology* 20a–c, Socrates' account of his conversation with Callias. If Callias's two sons were colts or calves, he would hire a horse trainer or farmer as their "overseer" (*epistatēs:* 20a8) to train them in their specific excellence. His sons, however, are men. Who, then, is knowledgeable (*epistēmōn*) about the specifically human, that is, the political, excellence (20b4–5)? Callias responds that Evenus of Paros, a Sophist, has this techne (20b8). Socrates' irony makes it certain he disagrees. Furthermore, he denies having it himself. Therefore, the analogy is left as this: as the horse trainer is to the specific excellence of colts, so X is to the excellence of human beings. If *hippikē,* the techne of horse training, is substituted for the horse trainer, X refers to a kind of knowledge.[3]

These passages are critical, for they seem to answer a fundamental question permeating Plato's early dialogues, and perhaps all of them: What is "moral knowledge," knowledge of the arete of the *psuchē,* of how to live an excellent life? It seems to be analogous to a techne. However it is ulti-

3. Lyons (1967, 143) says "the form in *-ikē* may be used indifferently with or without *technē* and in either case it will be picked up by *technē* with equal readiness."

mately translated, "techne" signifies clear, reliable, specialized, and authoritative knowledge. Commenting on *Laches* 185a, Gould says, "*[T]echnikos* in this passage clearly enough denotes what we would call an 'expert,' the sort of man in any particular field whose opinion one would trust unreservedly. Such a man is likely to go about his tasks in a rational and dependable manner." He continues, "These characteristics—rational procedure, comparative rarity and dependability—are all attributes of technical ability in general. Socrates hoped that they would attach also to the moral ability which he established as his ideal."[4]

If Gould is right, then Socrates' use of the techne analogy is pivotal in shaping, or at least expressing, a conception of the nature of human life itself. For if arete were to become the province of a *technitēs,* then dependable, rational procedures would become available to determine how an excellent life could be achieved. On such a view, arete could be reliably taught, and human life would be rendered stable and "manageable." If Plato truly believes moral knowledge is analogous to a techne, then, even if he himself denies being a proper *technitēs,* he would fit well the description of him offered by Nietzsche over a century ago and echoed repeatedly since (notably by Nussbaum): he would be a "theoretical optimist" who (wrongly) identifies knowledge—specifically, technical knowledge—as the essential condition of human flourishing.[5] He would be an elitist maintaining that a "comparatively rare" human being, the moral *technitēs,* knows what is best for "laypersons," who, in turn, should submit to the *technitēs'* authoritative judgments. He would be the supreme intellectualist despising the somatic messiness of everyday life.

Gould is hardly alone in attributing to Plato the "hope" of moral knowledge becoming technical. Indeed, there is such widespread agreement among Plato scholars concerning the philosophical significance of Socrates' use of the analogy that it is fair to refer to a "standard account of techne" (SAT). Irwin represents the SAT when he says about Socrates, "[H]e has good reasons for thinking that real virtue . . . will be a craft; for a craft will clearly satisfy some of his basic demands of virtue and moral knowledge." According to Irwin, such demands include being able to give a rational account, having a definite subject matter, being teachable, and granting its possessor the status of an authority. Commenting specifically

4. Gould 1955, 34.
5. See Nietzsche 1967, 97, and Nussbaum 1986.

about *Laches* 185a, he bluntly states, "[Socrates] demands an expert craftsman in moral training."[6]

In broad strokes, then, the SAT holds that in the early dialogues Socrates' use of the techne analogy represents Plato's assertion of a serious theoretical model of moral knowledge as a guide and telos of his philosophizing. On this reading, Plato hopes for and desires a techne whose subject matter is arete. Nussbaum exemplifies the SAT when she states, "Socrates argues that really decisive progress in human social life will be made only when we have developed a new techne," a "science of practical reasoning."[7] So too does Penner: "The Socratic [early] dialogues treat of virtue as an expertise (science, art, craft) like any other expertise."[8]

The SAT, as sketched above, is sufficiently broad to allow for considerable disagreement among its proponents. There is, for example, sharp dispute about how Plato's views on techne changed as he developed. Irwin argues that in dialogues such as the *Apology, Laches, Euthyphro,* and *Charmides,* Plato, in thrall to the historical Socrates, holds strictly to the techne analogy. As he matures, however, he gradually liberates himself from the influence of his master and begins to criticize the analogy. Irwin's Plato raises his first questions about the techne analogy as early as the *Gorgias.* He elaborates and expands these questions into full-fledged objections in the *Meno* and the *Symposium,* two "middle dialogues." Finally, in the *Republic,* "Plato rejects those Socratic principles which supported the [techne analogy]."[9] Reeve is in substantial agreement.[10]

Woodruff tells a similar story. About the *Meno*'s theory of recollection he says, "A consequence of these developments is that the techne model for knowledge is abandoned, for here Socrates considers a sort of knowledge that is always present in the knower and so never taught."[11]

Sprague's view is quite different. While she agrees that the techne analogy sets the theoretical stage in the early dialogues, she argues, unlike Irwin, Reeve, and Woodruff, that in later dialogues techne continues to provide a positive model for moral knowledge. An early work like the *Ion,* in which the techne analogy figures prominently, is thus continuous with the *Republic* and its doctrine of the philosopher-king because, Sprague argues,

---

6. Irwin 1977, 75 and 71.
7. Nussbaum 1986, 89–90. "Science of Practical Reasoning" is actually a chapter title.
8. Penner 1992a, 125.
9. Irwin 1977, 177.
10. Reeve 1988, 26.
11. Woodruff 1992, 81.

"The philosopher-king, for Plato, is a man of art or science; he has a *technē*."[12] Graham holds a similar view, for he finds the techne model operative even in the *Timaeus,* a late work.[13]

If commentators such as Irwin and Woodruff hold a "discontinuity thesis," arguing that Plato turned away from the techne model at some point in his career, then Graham and Sprague's is a "continuity thesis." (There are ample representatives of both these versions of the SAT.)[14] Even in the midst of this sort of disagreement, however, there is yet broad agreement in both camps regarding the role techne plays in the early dialogues.[15] According to the commentators mentioned above, the young Plato was animated by a serious theoretical project and had his Socrates hold strictly to the terms of the techne analogy in order to establish a positive model of moral knowledge.

A second point of disagreement among proponents of the SAT concerns the meaning of "techne" itself. Nussbaum has criticized Irwin on this score: "In *Plato's Moral Theory,* Irwin has claimed that '*technē*,' like English 'craft,' includes as a part of its meaning the notion of an external end or product, identifiable and specifiable independently of the craft and its activities." She objects: "[I]n fact the evidence about the ordinary conception of techne gives no support to Irwin's claim." In other words, Nussbaum challenges Irwin's identification of "techne" with "craft," that is, with productive knowledge that has an end, an *ergon,* distinct from its producer. She argues (I think correctly) that the meaning of "techne" is broader and embraces within it forms of knowledge that do not have an external end specifiable apart from the "art activities" themselves.[16]

Regardless of who is right in this debate, it is obvious that, if the young Plato believes moral knowledge is analogous to techne—and Nussbaum would certainly agree he does—then the meaning of "techne" must be understood in order to understand fully the nature of moral knowledge. Again, while the Irwin/Nussbaum disagreement is significant, it must be located within the larger context of their agreement: they share a concep-

12. Sprague 1976, 9.
13. Graham 1991.
14. The literature is vast. Lesses (1982) provides a good general description of the SAT. Among the continuists I would include Graham, Kato, Kübe, O'Brien, Thomsen, Parry, Sprague, Warren. Discontinuists are Gould, Irwin, Penner, Reeve, Woodruff. Hirschberger's view is probably closest to my own.
15. An interesting exception is Hirschberger (1932). He describes Plato's project as being "die Emanzipation der Ethik von der Technik" (3).
16. Nussbaum 1986, 74. See also Vlastos 1978 and Roochnik 1986.

tion of the early dialogues in which Plato hopes for, and works toward, a techne whose subject matter is arete.

A third point of disagreement among proponents of the SAT concerns how strictly the techne analogy should be taken. Consider Reeve, who holds a view similar to Irwin's: "Socrates routinely makes . . . the following assumption . . . the virtues are, or are exactly analogous to, crafts such as medicine and shepherding."[17] Vlastos demurs: "For though Socrates certainly wants moral knowledge to be in *some* respects like that of carpenters and the like—for example, in being honest knowledge, free of rhetorician's humbug—he knows that it is radically different in others."[18] This is a critical point of divergence. If, for example, moral knowledge is analogous to a techne only insofar as both are purposeful and desirable, then the analogy would not reveal much about the structure of moral knowledge.

To summarize: Even if they disagree concerning the development of Plato's thinking, the meaning of "techne," or the exact level of strictness implied in Socrates' use of the techne analogy, commentators such as Nussbaum, Woodruff, Graham, Sprague, Reeve, and Irwin all find that the analogy in the early dialogues provides a serious, positive theoretical model for the moral knowledge Socrates seeks. It is this general thesis I call the standard account of techne. And it is this thesis I dispute. In the "early" dialogues *Plato rejects techne as a model of moral knowledge.* These dialogues do frame a philosophical project, for Socrates does indeed hope to achieve knowledge of arete, but such knowledge is not best modeled by a techne. Instead, the goal of these dialogues is *nontechnical knowledge.* I explicate and substantiate this statement through a detailed analysis of Socrates' use of the techne analogy in the dialogues I have listed above. My conclusion can be expressed schematically: if moral knowledge were a techne, then insuperable difficulties would result, and moral knowledge would become impossible; since it is not impossible, it is not a techne.

To reiterate: taking a stand on the techne question in Plato's early dialogues is of philosophical, and not merely philological, significance. This book, like my first, argues against the Nietzschean interpretation of Plato as a theoretical optimist, that is, as one who conceives of human life as amenable to technical treatment and therefore as rationally manageable.

17. Reeve 1988, 4.
18. Vlastos 1978.

INTRODUCTION 7

On my reading, nontechnical knowledge is the goal and animating impulse of the Platonic dialogues. Plato understands well what Nussbaum calls "the fragility of goodness" and the consequent need for a comparably fragile, and hence nontechnical, conception of moral knowledge. As I have argued before, contrary to what is very much a standard story, Plato is surprisingly similar to those who, like Nussbaum and Nietzsche, recoil at the notion that human excellence can be taught, controlled, or produced by technical knowledge.[19]

A caveat concerning my use of "early," "middle," and "late" to categorize the dialogues: at least in the English-speaking world of Plato scholarship, this is now standard terminology. It has become an article of faith among such scholars that Plato's views changed significantly as he matured. Again speaking generally, the chronologists find the early Plato deeply influenced by and philosophically close to the historical Socrates. For them, only in his middle period does Plato begin to engage in independent, genuinely "Platonic," thinking. It is probably Vlastos who has definitively articulated this position: "In different segments of Plato's corpus two philosophers bear that name [Socrates]. The individual remains the same. But in different sets of dialogues he pursues philosophies so different that they could not have been depicted as cohabiting the same brain throughout unless it had been the brain of a schizophrenic."[20]

To avoid the diagnosis of schizophrenia, Vlastos offers the distinction between Socrates$_E$, the character expressing the views of the early Plato, and Socrates$_M$, the one who represents the decisively changed philosophical position of the Plato working in the middle of his career.

Even though stylometric arguments can support the division of the dialogues into chronological periods, the significant distinctions between Vlastos's Socrates$_E$ and Socrates$_M$ are thematic and philosophical. Vlastos himself does not target techne as a principal theme with which to divide the dialogues, but many commentators following his lead, that is, ones who would largely agree with the previous citation, have. Several, notably Irwin but also Woodruff and Reeve, have made techne the centerpiece of their developmental readings. They argue that the young Plato was captivated by the model of techne, whereas the middle Plato realized the conceptual limitations of a moral philosophy framed by the techne analogy

19. See Roochnik 1990.
20. Vlastos 1991, 46.

and broke from it in order to work through doctrines such as recollection and the separability of forms.[21]

The story these "discontinuists" tell, then, is roughly this: the young Plato used the techne model to accomplish certain theoretical tasks. As he matured, however, he saw the intrinsic difficulties with the model and therefore sought other means to accomplish those tasks. But—and this is the key point—those tasks remained quite the same. In other words, even if these commentators find Plato changing his views, they assume he retained a general conception of what he hoped to accomplish throughout his career. And this, to borrow from Irwin, might be called a "moral theory." To borrow from Nussbaum: it is "a science of practical reasoning."

Woodruff offers one way for a discontinuist to connect the early and middle dialogues. He argues that there is a "bridge from early Plato's theory of *Technē* to later Plato's theory of Forms: if you have a *Technē*, you know the essential nature of your product; essential natures will turn out in the middle dialogues to be Forms, entities so special that you must be oriented in a special direction in order to know them."[22] Woodruff implies that the basic philosophical project or ideal structuring the early dialogues remains intact in later works. Even if, by the time of the *Meno*, Plato has realized the conceptual limitations of the techne model, he nonetheless was guided by the same desire for rigorous, theoretically satisfying moral knowledge that animated his earlier works. Because the "continuist" branch of the SAT, exemplified by Sprague, finds Plato pursuing the same goal, namely, the achievement of a moral techne, throughout his career, its adherents obviously share this view.

I challenge this position. Taking my bearings from the techne analogy in the early dialogues, I argue that *from the outset* Plato is not a "theoretical optimist." Two advantages follow from my approach. First, my interpretation of specific passages, I believe, explains more than that offered by the SAT. Second, it mitigates the need for constructing a complex chronological story to explain Plato's development. As mentioned, chronology is invoked, especially by the discontinuists, to explain what appear to be discrepancies. So, for example, that Socrates in the *Meno* speaks about recollection, a "theory" incompatible with the (putative) philosophical implications of the techne analogy, is taken by Irwin and Woodruff to be a problem explicable by the author's having changed his mind about his

21. An excellent summary of the chronological approach to the dialogues can be found in Tigerstedt 1977. See also Xenophon *Memorabilia* 3.5 for his version of Socrates on techne.
22. Woodruff 1992, 97.

most basic doctrines concerning moral knowledge. If, however, Socrates' use of the analogy does *not* imply techne is the model of moral knowledge, then at least one significant motivation for telling an elaborate, and highly speculative, chronological story will have been removed.

The following chapters discuss issues concerning chronology in more detail. At this point suffice it to say that chronological development plays no role in my interpretation of the dialogues. For the sake of convenience and to conform to scholarly convention, I retain the phrase "early dialogues," but I could just as easily, and perhaps more appropriately, have spoken of "dialogues in which the techne analogy plays a significant role." Since I do not assume the younger Plato was in thrall to the historical Socrates (and the techne model), whereas the mature Plato liberated himself from his master's tutelage, when I use the name "Socrates," I refer *only* to the character appearing in these works and make no claim whatsoever about the historical figure.[23]

A final way to formulate my quarrel with the SAT: Plato scholars come equipped with expectations. A prevalent one is, as mentioned above, that a "moral theory" can and should be elicited from the dialogues. Probably more than any commentator of the past twenty-five years, Irwin has systematically generated a theory he takes to be implicit in the early dialogues. He introduces his work with these remarks:

> The following chapters are meant to be an exposition of Plato's views. I cite textual evidence as fully as I can, to show that I am discussing some views he really holds. But I do not claim that the arguments for or against a particular view, or the consequences I draw from it, are always to be found in Plato, or even that he would accept them if he were asked. This way of "reading into" the text is hard to avoid in discussing any philosopher, if we want to raise the most interesting questions about him, and to discuss him critically, instead of merely reporting what he says. With Plato it is essential.

Later, Irwin says, "What I say about Plato will sometimes sound excessively charitable, in so far as I sometimes discount flaws or obscurities in his arguments, or in his defences of his claims; and in general I try to

---

23. For an overt attack on the chronological thesis, see Howland 1991.

discuss those parts of his doctrine which I think are more plausible in more detail than the parts I think less plausible."[24]

Irwin seeks an "interesting" and "plausible" moral theory, and these criteria effect his selection of textual material to analyze. So, for example, he chooses to concentrate on the specifics of Socrates' arguments much more than, say, their dramatic context.

In one sense, Irwin's methodology is unassailable because it is inevitable. All commentators begin somewhere, and no one can take everything into account. The interpretation I offer is no exception. But on one score there is a great difference between this book and *Plato's Moral Theory*. Irwin thinks a specific brand of philosophy, that resulting in a rigorously argued, self-contained moral theory (or techne), is "plausible" and "interesting." This belief contributes directly to his reading of the techne analogy and his strict adherence to the SAT. Even if he takes an extreme position on the techne question, he is far from alone in his general orientation. Indeed, it is precisely because Irwin's general presuppositions are so widespread among Plato scholars that I dare to classify his view as one of the many that are "standard." Such a classification, however, should hardly be surprising: we do, after all, live in a world thoroughly enamored by the technical. My expectations differ. In particular, they do not commit me in advance to a technical conception of moral knowledge. In the case of the techne question, this becomes an interpretive advantage because, from a philosophical perspective, there is an inherent *indeterminacy* in Socrates' use of the analogy, which my approach is able to address appropriately and to explain. To clarify, recall the *Laches* passage (185a) cited above. Socrates says to Lysimachus that if he wished to obtain for his son an education in the excellence of his body, he would consult a *technitēs*, the expert trainer. Similarly, to educate one's son in psychic excellence, one should find someone knowledgeable. Irwin infers from this remark that Socrates "demands an expert craftsman in moral training," a demand that in turn becomes a basic ingredient of an implicit moral theory. But the text, in itself, does not warrant such an inference. Irwin may be right; in other words, his view is coherent and plausible. But that Socrates uses the analogy as he does against Lysimachus in fact implies very little. Perhaps he cites the familiar example of the "technical trainer," not because he himself champions technical knowledge, but simply because its familiarity will be effective in persuading Lysimachus to seek knowledge. In other words, it is possible that

24. Irwin 1977, 3. I criticize Irwin in Griswold 1988, 183–94.

the moral knowledge toward which Socrates urges Lysimachus bears only slight resemblance to a techne. Perhaps Socrates believes that, yes, one ought to pursue such knowledge but that, unlike a techne, moral knowledge cannot be authoritatively mastered, unambiguously possessed, and straightforwardly taught. Again, such beliefs are compatible with his use of the techne analogy to dissuade Lysimachus from taking a vote on the value of armor fighting.

To clarify further, consider a contemporary version of the techne analogy. In a recent essay, Searle argues against "postmodernism" and on behalf of "realism," or the "Western Rationalistic Tradition." The latter includes the following tenets: reality exists independently of human representations; language can sometimes successfully, that is, accurately, represent objects and states of affairs of that reality, and when it does so, the result is truth; knowledge is objective, and so "intellectual standards are not up for grabs. There are both objectively and intersubjectively valid criteria of intellectual achievement and excellence."[25]

The many critics of Western rationalism, that is, the postmodernists, deny these views. To persuade them they are being wrongheaded, Searle argues thus:

> Suppose I call my car mechanic to find out if the carburetor is fixed; or I call the doctor to get the report of my medical examination. Now, suppose I have reached a deconstructionist car mechanic and he tries to explain to me that a carburetor is just a text anyway, and that there is nothing to talk about except the textuality of the text. Or suppose I have reached a postmodernist doctor who explains to me that disease is essentially a metaphorical construct. Whatever else one can say about such situations, one thing is clear: communication has broken down. (81)

Searle appeals to our ordinary practices and our customary reliance on the technai to demonstrate the possibility of objective knowledge of reality. In other words, he thinks realism is presupposed by such practices. Searle's appeal to the auto mechanic is strikingly similar to the strategy Socrates employs against Lysimachus, a man who, like the postmodernist, is willing to abandon the search for objective knowledge. Searle's appeal is also similarly indeterminate. In other words, even if we grant his contentions about ordinary language and realism, Searle's examples of auto me-

25. Searle, 1993, 68. What Searle calls "postmodernism" I call "rhetoric."

chanics and medicine do not comprehensively dictate the criteria of the objective knowledge he advocates. Such knowledge must be objective, true about a mind-independent reality, and communicable in language. But within these constraints, there is ample room for maneuver. One could well believe that, yes, objective knowledge is possible and desirable, but some forms of it, unlike the technical knowledge of the auto mechanic or the physician, are *not* readily mastered, clearly teachable, useful, and easily measured. Perhaps such knowledge can only be partially or provisionally attained. Perhaps, unlike auto mechanics, its presence can be measured only with difficulty. Perhaps it cannot be attained at all and, at best, functions only as a regulative ideal. These negative characteristics are compatible with Searle's use of technical examples to argue against the postmodernist. In this sense, his invocation, like Socrates', of the techne analogy is indeterminate; the characteristics of the knowledge that is prescribed by the analogy require further definition in the bigger story Searle has to tell.

In a similar vein, from Socrates' use of the techne analogy itself very little can be confidently inferred concerning the positive characteristics of moral knowledge. Irwin, armed as he is with his goal of achieving a plausible moral theory, derives much—too much, as I argue. By contrast, my own focus, which does not commit me in advance to a technical conception of philosophy, requires me to examine not only the logical implications of the analogy but what Socrates *does* with it in the specific dialogical situations in which he brings it to bear. The philosophical conclusions I generate from this approach are dramatically different from, as well as more modest and less optimistic than, those achieved by proponents of the SAT. I offer no Platonic version of a moral theory or techne. On the other hand, my account does justice to the text. I show that Plato is more cognizant of the limits of technical knowledge than is typically thought. For me, this is finally what makes him "interesting" and "plausible"—and important.

The following, then, are the tasks of this book. First, as is obvious (or, if it is not, then as the Irwin/Nussbaum debate shows), it is imperative to understand what "techne" means. What was the "ordinary" Greek understanding of this all-important term? Is "craft" the right translation? Is techne always productive knowledge? In Chapter 1, I examine the pre-Platonic meaning of "techne" and the development of the word from the Homeric poems to Plato's contemporary Isocrates. Chapter 1 is more than a word study, however. I indeed investigate the word's meaning, but by examining Homer, Solon, Aeschylus, Sophocles, "Hippocrates," Protagoras, Gorgias, and Isocrates, I also, and more significantly, generate a philosophical discussion concerning the nature of techne.

To prefigure my story: many of the extraordinary intellectual developments of the fifth- and fourth-century Greek "enlightenment" can be encapsulated by the "techne question." Simply put, this asks, Is X *really* a techne? In the Hippocratic writing, "On Techne," for example, the X is medicine; in Isocrates' *Against the Sophists,* it is rhetoric.

Führmann has shown that during this period "techne" became an independent genre with a distinct epistemic self-conception and attendant criteria. Beginning with Antisthenes' fourth-century rhetorical techne and moving through centuries and works with subject matters as diverse as grammar and architecture, he documents how durable and consistent the conception of a "techne" actually was throughout antiquity. (It "zeigt eine erstaunliche Gleichförmigkeit des Typus," he says.)[26] As a stock question often appearing in the introductions to these works, an author would ask of his subject, Is it really a techne? To cite two telling examples: Longinus begins his second chapter by saying, "First of all, we must raise the question of whether there is such a thing as a techne of the sublime or lofty."[27] Varro puts it this way: "[T]ell us whether the knowledge of those things used in agriculture is an art (*ars*) or not."[28] (How stock this question really was can be gleaned from the fact that Lucian satirized it in his *Parasite* [2]: "Well then, Simon, is Parasitic [*parasitikē*] a techne?")[29]

I show how philosophically rich this apparently innocuous question actually is. When an author asks of his own work, Is it a techne? he engages in a self-reflection that forces him to raise epistemological questions about both the nature of his subject matter and his cognitive access to it. As a result, these writings broach, with varying degrees of explicitness, many of the same issues that surface when the X becomes moral knowledge, as it does in the early Platonic dialogues. This is especially true when the subject matter is logoi, specifically political and ethical speeches (or arete itself), that is, when the putative techne is sophistic rhetoric. As Socrates, who is expressing a widely held view (with which he strongly disagrees), says to Anytus in the *Meno* (91b), the Athenian who seeks to learn arete

26. Führmann, 1960, 122.
27. *On the Sublime* 2.23 (trans. W. Roberts [New York: Garland, 1987]).
28. *On Agriculture* 1.3 (trans. W. Hooper [Cambridge, Mass.: Harvard University Press, Loeb Classical Library, 1934]).
29. Trans. A. Harmon (Cambridge, Mass.: Harvard University Press, Loeb Classical Library, 1960).

probably should approach those who profess to be teachers of it and who charge tuition accordingly: the Sophists. Because rhetoric claims to have achieved technical mastery over the very same subject matter to which Socrates is devoted, I discuss, in a major section of Chapter 1, the techne question in rhetoric.

Chapter 1 culminates with Isocrates' *Against the Sophists,* in which the question, Is rhetoric a techne? is treated with enormous self-consciousness and care. This work, written at approximately the same time as Plato's *Gorgias* and *Protagoras,* raises many of the same issues concerning moral knowledge as do these dialogues. Furthermore, it does so in a way deeply challenging to, as well as illuminating of, Plato's own philosophical response to the techne question.

In Chapter 2, I analyze the techne analogy in the *Laches, Charmides, Euthyphro, Republic* (bk. 1), and *Euthydemus.* I argue that Plato has Socrates deploy the analogy for one basic reason: to *point* to a "nontechnical" conception of moral knowledge. As the phrase indicates, my characterization of this knowledge initially is negative: I show what it is not. From the outset of the chapter, however, I allude to, and then progressively develop, a more positive characterization.

Chapter 3, which makes frequent reference to the discussion of rhetoric (especially Isocrates) in Chapter 1, treats the *Gorgias* and the *Protagoras.* These two works, in which the techne analogy is crucial, reenact the "old quarrel" between Socrates and the rhetoricians/Sophists. I argue that, given Plato's conception of techne, rhetoric is not one. In this sense, however, it actually resembles the nontechnical knowledge I claim is the goal of the early dialogues. Finally, however, rhetoric is different indeed from philosophy; even if it is nontechnical, it is not the nontechnical moral knowledge Plato thinks can be achieved by the philosopher. It is in the working out of these similarities and differences between rhetoric and philosophy, in the examination of the old quarrel through the lens of the techne question, that I hope to articulate what Platonic moral knowledge really is.

Chapter 4, building on the results of Chapter 3 and addressing specifically the work of Vlastos, describes Plato's nontechnical conception of moral knowledge.

This book concludes with a series of four appendixes in which I summarize much of the textual support for my position. The first three treat Plato's use of the words "techne" and *atechnōs;* the fourth shows how "techne" appears in Isocrates. The purpose of these appendixes is to provide a philological background to the philosophical argument that is at the heart of my work. In addition, Appendixes 1, 2, and 3 briefly comment on passages from several dialogues not mentioned in Chapters 2, 3, and 4.

Techne is important to Plato, to the rhetoricians, to us. It is paradigmatic of knowledge that gives us control, that offers us stability. Because techne can be effectively, perhaps even systematically, taught, its possession can be certified. Because it so often treats subjects of pressing concern and apparent usefulness, those who do possess it are well regarded, and frequently well rewarded, by their communities. The *technitēs* is, quite literally, a professor: he avows publicly that he knows.

Moral knowledge for Plato is far more precarious and difficult to recognize, far less systematic and professorial, than this. It is nontechnical, and it is a problem. To the articulation of this problem, the following pages are devoted.

CHAPTER ONE

THE PRE-PLATONIC MEANING OF "TECHNE"

This chapter relates how the meaning of "techne" developed before Plato wrote his dialogues in the fourth century. This historical preface is necessary because Plato wrote largely in an ordinary language whose terms naturally tended to retain, at least on the surface, the standard meanings they had inherited over years of use. His understanding of "techne" was, of course, not simply ordinary. Indeed, Plato's philosophical treatment of "techne" complicated the ordinary meaning of the word considerably. Nevertheless, a systematic examination of the word and the concept of "techne" in the dialogues requires as its first step a study of Plato's predecessors.

As mentioned in the Introduction, there is a second reason to begin with the pre-Platonic past. By studying the implicit treatment afforded to "techne" by poets such as Homer, Solon, Aeschylus, and Sophocles, as well as the explicit and, at times, highly sophisticated account of it found in the Hippocratic and rhetorical writings, a set of philosophical questions emerge. By the fourth century, the "techne question" had already been pursued in earnest by a wide variety of writers. When Plato raised a version of it by asking, Is moral knowledge, knowledge of the arete of the human psyche, a techne? he entered into what was then a vigorous and ongoing discussion. By articulating the issues and terms of that discussion, this chapter contributes to an understanding of the Platonic treatment of "techne," not only on a philological level but on a philosophical one as well.

Before beginning, two brief warnings: First, even without being precise about its meaning, it is safe to say that "techne" was an important term used by the Greeks to refer to knowledge. As a result, a thorough tracking of its development would require a comprehensive analysis of how the concept of knowledge itself evolved in Greece. This sort of intellectual history has been offered many times, with Jaeger's *Paideia* perhaps remaining the best-known.[1] Compared to encyclopedic works such as *Paideia*, the following chapter is no more than a sketch, one concentrating only on those pivotal moments in the development of "techne" germane to a study of Plato's understanding of the term.

Second, the account to follow is not strictly chronological. But the (minor) liberties I take with chronology (e.g., Sophocles is discussed after the Hippocratic writings) are justifiable in that my ultimate goal is to tell a philosophical, rather than a historical, story.[2] Furthermore, I allow myself several historical digressions. Two examples: In discussing Isocrates, I refer to Quintilian, who, because he was influenced by his Greek predecessor, is invoked to amplify important themes that receive only compressed treatment in *Against the Sophists*. And I call upon Philolaus, the fifth-century Pythagorean, to help explicate an important line in Aeschylus's *Prometheus Bound*.

The Homeric Poems

The literary tradition begins with the Homeric poems, in which "techne" has a variety of meanings. It names the "skill" of the shipbuilder who works with wood; the "craft" of Hephaestus, who forges metal bonds to hold even the mighty Ares; the "craftiness" of Proteus, who is able to change his form at will; and the "plan," or "stratagem," Aegisthus devises to murder Agamemnon. In short, the meaning of the word in the Homeric poems is multifaceted. Kübe, however, argues that Homer already represents a "relatively late point in the development of techne." He therefore

1. See Jaeger 1967. Shorter versions of the techne story, especially as it applies to Plato, can be found in Hirschberger 1932, Isnardi Parente 1966, Joos 1955, Kübe 1969, and O'Brien 1967.
2. The dating of the Hippocratic writings is controversial in any event.

feels justified in delving into the precarious world of etymology in order to uncover a more primitive meaning of the word.[3]

"Techne" derives from the Indo-European root "tek," which, according to Porkorny, means "to fit together the woodwork of a woven house."[4] Kübe concludes that "in its original form techne probably means the building of a house which was woven together from trunks and twigs and was erected by the family or tribe in a communal effort."[5] As social life became more settled, the need for building skills increased. As the division of labor progressed, the work of building houses was no longer left to families. It became the province of a specialized (in Gould's words, a "comparatively rare") individual: the *tektōn*, the "woodworker." "Techne," in its pre-Homeric meaning, came to refer to the knowledge or skill of the *tektōn*, he who *produces* something from wood.[6]

The original, preliterate meaning of "techne," then, is specific. As the word developed, however, its meaning broadened considerably, and eventually, as in the Homeric poems, it came to embrace other productive activities. (This is also true of *tektōn*, which, in Homer, is not restricted to woodworking.)[7] Kübe speculates why it is that woodworking, rather than a comparably important activity such as smithing, gave rise to the more generalized "techne": "The activity of the carpenter is distinguished from that of the smith by its more 'rational' character. It demands a capacity for intellectual solution of determinate tasks, some rudimentary knowledge of geometry or statics, in general an ability to combine and improvise, which if explained to the layman is also sensible and comprehensible. But to be able to coordinate its individual elements systematically towards a determinate goal remains the privilege of the expert."[8]

Socrates, in Plato's *Philebus*, lends support to Kübe's contention that woodworking was paradigmatic of all technical activities. He says, "The

3. Kübe 1969, 9. In general, this is a most helpful book, which covers many of the same sources as I do in this chapter. I refer to it often; translations from the German are my own.
4. Porkorny 1967, s.v. "techne."
5. Kübe 1969, 13.
6. Liddell, Scott, and Jones cite *tek* as the root of both "techne" and *tektōn*, referring both back to *tiktō*, "to give birth." In other words, "techne" is originally productive. As Heidegger (1977, 13) puts it, "Techne belongs to bringing-forth, to poiēsis." He is right, but only regarding the earliest meaning of the word. On the principle of specialization in the technai, see Xenophon *Cyropaedia* 8.2.5.
7. Cunliffe (1963, 376) on *tektōn* in Homer: "a skilled worker in wood, a joiner, carpenter, or shipwright. . . . With a qualifying word indicating another material in which a man works."
8. Kübe 1969, 14.

techne of building (*tektonikē*), I think, uses the greatest number of measures and tools which make it more technical (*technikoteran*) than most other forms of knowledge (*epistēmē*: 56b)." Kübe's account, however, cannot be proven. Still, it is provocative, and by suggesting a conception of "techne" it usefully prepares for much that is to follow. The following list of criteria is provoked by Kübe's remarks and meant to characterize a "primitive" conception of "techne," one understood as an etymological offspring of the *tektōn*, the "woodworker."

(The following is the first in a series of lists of criteria that must be met for a knowledge claim to qualify as a techne. Criteria of some sort are obviously necessary in order to answer the "techne question," which, as mentioned in the Introduction, is critical in many of the writings studied below. These lists, however, do not claim to determine the essential attributes of the concept of "techne." Instead, they are meant only to be informal, suggestive, and a convenient device by which to organize the material of this chapter.)

List of Criteria 1: The Primitive Meaning of "Techne"

1. Techne is knowledge of a specific field: its subject matter is *determinate*. The knowledge of the *tektōn*, to cite the key example, is restricted to working in wood; the *tektōn* does not know how to forge metal.
2. It is oriented to a specific goal and *produces something useful*: the *tektōn* builds houses for the members of the community.
3. It is reliable. The *tektōn* can be counted on to perform his tasks correctly.
4. It is knowledge recognized, and rewarded, by other members of the community. It is agreed that the expert knows what he is doing; the proof is in the product, the houses he builds. The expert is "comparatively rare" and is counted as an authority to whose judgments "laypersons" ought to defer.
5. Techne can be certified. The houses of the *tektōn* serve as his credentials. They give evidence that he actually has the knowledge he claims.
6. It can be taught. Unlike someone who merely has accumulated experience, the *tektōn* can explain something about woodworking to those who wish to learn about it; he can help to transform a layman into a fellow expert. This implies some set of rational principles, some sort of logos, governing the field, the subject matter, in question. The capacity to communicate these principles becomes another mode of certification:

because he can explain or teach what he is doing, the *tektōn* merits the special status he has as an expert.[9]

With these informal and suggestive criteria, extracted from and elaborating upon Kübe's speculations, I address not only the historical origin of "techne" but its phenomenological character as well.[10] This explains why the list seems anachronistic: surely there was no "certification" process three thousand years ago. Nonetheless, I include item 5 because it addresses a crucial dimension of techne. Whether the *technitēs* is a Mycenean slave, an itinerant craftsman, a free but lowly citizen of fifth-century Athens, or a member of a medieval guild, he is in all instances someone with expertise. Within a more or less limited, more or less respected realm of expertise, the *technitēs* is authoritative. His work can be certified, if not literally by a board of examiners, then simply by the good things the *technitēs* has made. Even within the primitive meaning of the word, this attribute can be felt, and so I include it above.

I also include these criteria because, frankly, I wish to prefigure later definitions. Consider Sextus Empiricus (writing around 200 C.E.): "Every techne is a body [*sustēma*] consisting of items of knowledge which are mutually cohesive [*ek katalepseōn suggegumnasmenōn*] and having reference to one of the ends which are useful in life."[11]

Even though formulated in specifically Stoic terminology, this definition probably reflects a widely held view, for, as Barnes notes, it "can be found in a dozen other texts." Its key features are similar to those suggested in List 1: a techne, Barnes continues, is "an organised system of knowledge"; that is, it must itself be determinate, a consequence of its subject matter (e.g., woodworking) itself being specific and restricted. It must "refer to some end," that is, be useful. Because of these features, it is knowledge that can be recognized and rewarded by others. There is little doubt that the *tektōn* knows something; one need only look at the houses he has built for proof. The *technitēs* is authoritative; he is an "answer man" whom we consult when concerned with his specific field of expertise.

---

9. Heinimann (1961, 105–6) lists four criteria of the "pre-Platonic" conception of techne: (1) a useful product, (2) a determinate task, (3) a firm knowledge base, (4) being teachable.

10. Hirschberger (1932, 17–33) discusses "der Techne-Begriff." In a different sense, so too does Heidegger (1977). A good source of Plato's own "phenomenology" of techne is *Gorgias* 503e. For the historical background, that is, the actual role of techne in this and later periods, see Bolkestein 1958 and Finley 1978.

11. This translation is from Barnes 1986, 5.

The first meaning of "techne," understood as closely related to *tektōn*, is "productive knowledge," or "craft." It is knowledge of a determinate field (or subject matter), knowledge of how to shape specific material into a useful product. By the time of the Homer epics, however, the meaning of the word has already widened.

"Techne" appears only once in the *Iliad*, where it hearkens back to its (putative) origin in woodworking. Paris, acknowledging that Hektor rebukes him "right, not beyond measure," says to his brother, "[S]till, your heart forever is weariless, like an axe-blade, driven by a man's strength through the timber, one who, with [techne], hews a piece for a ship" (3.60–63).[12] Obviously, the word here resonates with its primitive meaning of working in wood. In addition, as Schaerer notes, this line invokes the related notions of exactitude and inflexibility. Like the shipbuilder who knows exactly the right measure at which to cut his wood, Hektor's relentless criticism hits the mark as he accurately censures his wayward brother.[13]

Odyssey 5.259 finds a similar meaning, although the noun is transformed into a verb. Under the guidance of Calypso, Odysseus builds sails for a raft: "and he built (*technēsato*) these well."

"Techne" is found eight times in the *Odyssey* (3.433, 4.455, 4.529, 6.234, 8.327, 8.332, 11.614, 23.161). Six of these usages refer to smithing, and several quite naturally are affiliated with Hephaestus, the god of anvil and metal, who is *klutotechnēs*, "famed for his [techne]." (See *Iliad* 1.571, 18.143, 18.391, and *Odyssey* 8.286.) Perhaps the best-known story of Hephaestus is that told by Demodikus of the revenge wrought by the lame god on his wife, Aphrodite, and her lover Ares. With his techne (*Odyssey* 8.327) the ingenious Hephaestus forges a trap whose "artful" (*technēentes:* 8.297) bonds snare the adulterers in bed. Once they are rendered immobile, Hephaestus invites the rest of the gods to laugh at his victims. By means of his techne (8.332) the slowest and least physical of the gods has rendered the most beautiful as well as the most aggressive altogether ludicrous.

In addition to Hephaestus, Athene, born from the head of Zeus (whose head, in some stories and visual images, is chopped open by Hephaestus) and responsible for the crafts of war, weaving, and the cultivation of the olive, is identified with techne. Thus, a "master craftsman," one who can

---

12. For Homer, I follow Lattimore's translations (New York: Harper & Row, 1975 [*The Iliad*] and 1979 [*The Odyssey*]), substituting only "techne" for his English translations.
13. Schaerer 1930, 2.

overlay gold on silver and whose works are graceful, is "taught by Hephaestus and Pallas Athene in [techne] complete" (6.234, repeated at 23.159–61).

Two derivatives of "techne," one an adjective, the other an adverb, express related meanings. The Phaiacian women are "skilled" (*technēssai:* 7.110) at weaving, and Odysseus "skillfully" (*technēentēs:* 5.270) guides a ship. Both of these usages clearly derive from "techne" understood as productive skill or craft.

The two remaining usages of "techne" are quite different, for they do not refer to a specific craft, like woodworking or smithing, which has a tangible product. Of Proteus, the old man of the sea, it is said, "[He] did not forget the subtlety of his [techne]" (*doliēs . . . technēs:* 4.455). Proteus knows how to do, rather than make, something: he can change his form at will. But his unique skill has no definite product analogous to a house or a shield. In this sense, the knowledge or ability Proteus does have is more ambiguous, and less tangible, than a typical craft.

The last of Homer's usages of the word to be discussed employs the identical phrase cited above. It requires, however, a different translation: "Aegisthus devised a treacherous stratagem" (*doliēn . . . technēn:* 4.529). Here the word does not refer to a craft at all. Instead, it is a plan, a purely intellectual object that has not yet been, but will be, actualized in practice. A similar meaning is found in the verbal derivative used by Antilochus regarding his plans to win the chariot race: I shall "contrive (*technēsomai*) it, so that we get by in the narrow place" (*Iliad* 23.415).

This meaning of "techne" predominates in Hesiod's *Theogony*. To combat the viciousness of Sky, "Earth devises a crafty wile" (line 160). Prometheus, with *doliēn technē,* covers the bones with fat and gives them to Zeus (540, 547, 555, 560). Zeus and his mother, Rhea, vanquish Cronus by means of a ruse, a "techne" (496). Cerberus has an evil "techne" (770): he pretends to welcome those who enter Hades, but then refuses to let them out.

Why is this meaning of "techne" connected to wiles and trickery? Demodikus's Hephaestus story is a clue: the most "intellectual" of the gods is capable of overpowering the most physical through his craft. The mind is capable of mastering the body, of influencing its course of events. Techne as "crafty wile" reveals the epic poet's acknowledgment of the power of intellectual ability; with it one can defeat opponents of superior physical force or higher social status. Like a craft, which issues in a tangible item, craftiness bears palpable fruit: Hephaestus overpowers the stronger Ares; Aegisthus murders the king Agamemnon; Prometheus tricks Zeus.[14]

In sum, "techne" in the most ancient of poets is primarily related to basic crafts and productive skills that are highly developed, needed, recognized, and rewarded, namely, smithing and woodworking. That the word is not applied to, say, the leather cutter or the potter is (according to Kübe) largely an accident. In other words, since they are both similarly productive of useful items, it well could have been applied.[15] Again, one might question why it is reserved for smithing and woodworking. Both are valuable to the community, and the value of their products is immediately visible. The products of the smith literally shine; they stand as testimony to the skill of their producer. Perhaps woodworking receives special notice as a techne because of its reliance on the rudiments of applied mathematics. Techne has a useful, a visible product, which is produced through the application of rational and clearly communicable means. Smithing and woodworking, rather than leather cutting and pottery, are the most readily identifiable paradigms.

Although it is not an identity, the connection between techne and productive craft is extremely strong in the Homeric poems. This is the reason why the word is not used when the poet mentions the prophet, doctor, singer, or herald who (along with the *tektōn dourōn*) are said to be the *dēmiourgoi*, those who work for the *dēmos* rather than for themselves, and who are "the men who all over the endless earth are invited" (see *Odyssey* 17.381–84 and 19.135). As Kübe puts it, "The representation of craft production is still too narrowly bound up with the concept [of techne]" for the word to refer to these highly useful, but not explicitly productive, skills.[16]

This seems quite right, but it must be noted that already in Homer (and more markedly in Hesiod), the meaning of the word includes abstract but as yet unactualized plans and purely intellectual "craftiness," such as that of Proteus. As a result, even if "techne" is largely restricted to productive craft in the Homeric poems, it has the potential, which can already be felt in several of its usages, for expansion.

14. Detienne and Vernant (1978) discuss *mētis*, "the wiles of cunning." Their analysis is most interesting, and their connection of *mētis* with techne is helpful in explaining these lines from Hesiod. What they fail to take into account is how the meaning of "techne" evolves and eventually, as this chapter shows, refers to a kind of knowledge much more stable and rigid than the flexible shrewdness of *mētis*.

15. Kübe 1969, 14.

16. Kübe 1969, 15.

This potential is explicitly actualized in the Homeric Hymns (probably written soon after the epics). Consider, for example, that in the "Hymn to Hermes" the ability to play the lyre and the pipe is described as a "techne" (see 445, 465, 483, and 511). Again following Kübe, this reflects the tendency in literature subsequent to the epics to embrace the knowledge of the Homeric *dēmiourgos* under the single rubric of "techne." By the time of Plato's *Laches* the two terms have virtually been conflated, and so Laches can say, "[A]ll the rest of the *dēmiourgoi* know what is to be feared and what is to be dared in their own technai" (195b8–9).

The transition, then, from the knowledge possessed by the *dēmiourgos* in Homer to "techne" in later writers, is a natural one given the potential for expansion latent in the meaning of the latter in the Homeric poems. Soon after Homer, "techne" names skills, knowledges, both those like woodworking and smithing, which have tangible products, and those like lyre playing or the wiles of Prometheus, which do not.

The passage from the *Odyssey* (17.381–89) describing the *dēmiourgoi* has been much studied by social historians.[17] It is not obvious who these men were. Were they independent craftsmen from within (or without) the community? Were they protoprofessionals? Fortunately, for my purposes this does not matter greatly. My emphasis is on the fact that the *dēmiourgoi* could be *invited* (*klētoi:* 17.386). To be able to invite someone, say a doctor, presupposes that he can be recognized as a doctor. In other words, the doctor, and the knowledge the doctor possesses, are visible, recognizable, accessible to the community. His previous technical accomplishments stand as evidence that, if called upon, he will again do good work. The doctor has an "address" to which the invitation can be "mailed." The doctor has hung a "shingle" to advertise his profession.[18]

Again, this sounds anachronistic. I do not imply that the Homeric *dēmiourgoi* actually hung up shingles. They may or may not have been protoprofessionals. They were, however, "invited," and this presupposes that they could be reached. Only a shingle, even a metaphorical one, makes such invitations possible. It is precisely this sort of accessibility that comes (and continues) to characterize a "techne."

To summarize: A set of criteria similar to List 1 can be extracted from

17. See Murakawa 1957 and Finley 1978, 55–56.
18. Nehamas and Woodruff translate "techne" as "profession" (*Symposium* [Indianapolis, Ind.: Hackett, 1989]). A great deal of sociological ink has been spilled on the issue of professionalism. Starr (1982) discusses the specific case of medicine. Larson (1979) writes generally about professionalism.

the Homeric poems. But the Homeric conception differs somewhat, for it must express a sense of the word's emerging flexibility and range. List 2, although titled "The Homeric Conception," reflects not only the explicit usage found in the Homeric epics but also the word's potential for expansion in later works.

List of Criteria 2: The Homeric Conception

1. A techne has a determinate task or field. The various technai—wood-working, smithing, weaving—are directed to the achievement of something specific.
2. It is usually, but not necessarily, productive. Ships, houses, and metal-work are examples of products. A skill like piloting a ship, while not explicitly called a "techne" in the poems, is nonetheless described by using a derivative of "techne." Soon after the Homeric poems, the prophet, doctor, singer, and herald are be said to possess a techne.
3. It has to be applied in order to be complete. The shipbuilder who does not build a ship is not a complete shipbuilder.
4. Its results are beneficial and are "for the people." The technai, even if they are not explicitly called such in the poems, belong to the *dēmiourgoi,* those whose works benefit, can be shared and admired by, the *dēmos.* As a result, the *technitēs* can be recognized, certified, and re-warded by ordinary people. He has earned the right to "hang a shingle," and thereby be "invited" to do his work.
5. Techne requires mastery of rational principles that can be explained, and therefore taught. The woodworker and the pilot, for example, employ rudimentary applied mathematics.

I add item 3, the need for a techne to be applied in order to be complete, in order to emphasize that, even though the Homeric meaning is not re-stricted to productive knowledge, it shares a basic feature of it. If, for example, I know how to build a ship but do not build one (or teach some-one else how to do it), then I am indistinguishable from one who does not know anything about shipbuilding. Similarly, Aegisthus has a "techne," a plan, to ambush Agamemnon. This is not productive knowledge, but it must be analogously actualized, that is, put into action, in order to be fully realized as knowledge. Homeric techne, even if not identified with produc-tion, is nonetheless bound to the notion of application. The man with a techne must do something, usually make something, with his knowledge. Although the word in Homer clearly favors production, it does not ex-clude other possibilities.

Solon

Solon (writing around 600 B.C.E.) uses "techne" only once, to describe Hephaestus as "master of many crafts" (*polutechneo:* 13.49).[19] Still, even without explicitly naming them as such, not only does he discuss the technai, but he prefigures issues that prove to be decisive in the history of this word, and to the basic questions of this book. Specifically, while it is clear from Lists 1 and 2 that the oldest meaning of "techne" includes its having a useful product, and therefore its being useful or good, Solon offers an ethical reflection on the extent and nature of its goodness, one whose reverberations will long be felt.

In his "Prayer to the Muses," Solon asks for "happiness at the hands of the blessed gods, and good fame at the hands of men" (13.3–4). But his poem does not merely ask for human happiness, it is also protreptic. Solon urges his audience to reflect: if their actions are unjust, they, or their descendants, will suffer grievously the vengeance of Zeus. Yes, Solon says, "Wealth I desire to possess"; but he warns against gaining wealth "unjustly" (*adikōs:* 13.7) or by "lawless violence" (*hubris:* 13.11). Immoral gain is seen by the all-seeing Zeus, and punishment is certain.

(A terminological point: I translate Solon's *olbon* as "happiness." The Greek word usually refers to accumulation of wealth and can also be translated as "prosperity." I choose "happiness" because with it I can look forward to what later writers will call *eudaimonia*, the state of "flourishing," "success," or "well-being" that accompanies a person's achievement of arete. Solon's prayer is not simply for material prosperity; his ethical poem concerns the nature of human happiness in general.)[20]

There is something of a counterpoint to the initial, protreptic side of Solon's "Prayer to the Muses," for the poet reminds his listeners that human happiness ultimately depends on factors beyond their control. He is acutely aware of how human beings delude themselves concerning the efficacy of their actions. We evaluate our lives more positively than we should; we hope for the best, when the best is not forthcoming; and we act with the expectation, one regularly thwarted, that our actions, if well done, will secure success for us. In expressing this more fatalistic dimension of his thinking, techne plays a significant role.

19. The Greek text is West 1980. My translations are clumsy, but somewhat literal.
20. On *olbon*, see Anhalt 1993, 22–26.

We mortal men, whether good or bad, think like this: each of us keeps that *doxa* of himself which he has until he suffers something. Then straightaway he grieves. Until this point, open-mouthed we enjoy empty hopes, and whoever is squeezed by painful diseases thinks that he will be healthy. One man, really a wretch, thinks he is good; another thinks himself beautiful, even though he doesn't have a fine shape. And if a man is penniless and constrained by the force of poverty, he thinks that he will soon possess a great deal of wealth.

Everybody is eager for something: one man on the sea sails in his ship and desires to bring home gain by fishing, even though he is buffeted by grievous winds and doesn't spare his life a bit. Another man working the well-planted earth throughout the year serves those who work with the curved plow. Another man, who has learned the works (*erga*) of Athena and Hepheastus, master of many crafts, gets his living with his hands. Another having been taught his gifts by the Olympian Muses is knowledgeable (*epistamenos*) in the measure of lovely wisdom.

Others are doctors, having the work (*ergon*) of the Healer who has many remedies. And to these there is no end because often from a little pain comes great distress and a doctor cannot relieve it by dispensing soothing remedies; but sometimes he quickly makes the man suffering grievous and painful illness healthy by touching him with his hand.

Another man the farseeing Apollo makes a seer; he whom the gods attend knows the far-off evil that approaches a man—for no augury or offering will ward off what is destined to be.

Indeed, it is *moira* that brings evil and good to mortals, and the gifts that the immortal gods give are inescapable. Surely there is risk in every activity, and no one knows, when a situation begins, how it will turn out. (13.33–66)

Six technai are mentioned in the passage: fishing, farming, smithing (i.e., "the works of Athena and Hephaestus"), poetry ("taught by the Olympian Muse"), medicine, and prophecy. Smithing is obviously a productive craft and thus easily meets the criteria established on List 1. The productiveness of farming and fishing are, however, less obvious. The latter acquires, rather than produces, a natural being.[21] Farming is somewhere between production and acquisition. It requires the human intervention into natural

21. As I show in detail in Chapter 2 and Appendix 3, acquisition becomes an important metaphor in Plato's discussion of techne.

processes and results in the production of crops that would not have existed if there were no human desire for them. Since both fishing and farming have a determinate field of expertise, require rational method, can be taught, and have a useful (even if not produced) result, they are covered by the expanded sense of "techne" expressed in List 2. The last three technai—poetry, medicine, and prophecy—are each described by Homer as belonging to a *dēmiourgos,* and therefore, as suggested above, they too can be embraced under the rubric of "techne" as the word expands in post-Homeric literature.

Solon does not significantly advance the meaning of "techne," nor is his list of six items particularly interesting. Instead, what is striking in this poem is its "ethical" reflection on the nature and the limits of techne itself. As Jaeger puts it, the poem teaches that "*Moira,* Fate, makes all human effort fundamentally insecure, however earnest and logical it may seem to be; and this *Moira* cannot be averted by foreknowledge."[22] The six technai Solon mentions, I propose, are used as paradigm cases of "logical effort." They are cases in which men think they are in rational control of the outcome of their actions, when in fact they are not. Men think they have the answers, when in fact their lives are shot through with questions: "there is risk in every activity."

Three of Solon's examples—smithing, poetry, and prophecy—are described as gifts of the gods, and so their very possession is beyond human control.[23] The other three represent "foreknowledge," the ability to achieve a goal in a systematic and explicable manner. Solon insists that even in these activities in which human beings are most knowledgeable, we run the risk of deluding ourselves about the extent to which we control our lives. Moira, and not technical expertise, brings evil and good to mortals, and finally determines whether a human project fully succeeds or not.

The juxtaposition of moira with the technai is richly provocative because, even if implicitly, it circumscribes and thereby calls into question what might be termed the "technical realm" (i.e., both techne itself and the immediate results of its application). The technical realm is not self-sufficient for Solon: it is but a small portion of a larger world, whose course human agency cannot influence. For this reason, the degree to which human beings—even those with techne—can mandate and achieve their own happiness is severely limited. Whether the final outcome of even a well-executed techne is successful depends on more than the skills of the techni-

22. Jaeger 1967, 145.
23. Schaerer 1930, 2.

cian. The doctor, for example, may rightly apply the "soothing remedy" that has regularly cured a given disease in the past, but on any specific occasion a small pain may surprisingly lead to a terrible illness. The ultimate success of a human project is thoroughly qualified by external conditions. What Solon's poem discloses is thus a *gap* between techne and its ultimate consequences. A fisherman may fish well and to the best of his considerable knowledge, but an unexpected storm may wreck him yet.

This sense of the grave limitations of human efficacy stands in some tension with the first, protreptic section of the poem (13.1–33). There Solon seems to assume the viability of moral agency: our pursuit of wealth should not be done *adikōs* or with hubris. Presumably, then, our moral stance, unlike our technical relationship to the world, is within our control. It is we, not moira, who dictate whether we will act with hubris and therefore meet with Zeus's retribution. This sense of responsibility for our own happiness contrasts with, and thus illuminates, the nature of techne. The fisherman may be a technical master of his trade; although he cannot alter the course of the unexpected storm, he can decide whether to sell his catch at an inflated price or give it away to those who are starving. In this sense, he can determine whether he will feel the vengeance of Zeus.

It is not entirely clear whether Solon's poem emphasizes "human responsibility and sanity of mind" or "fatalism [and] jealous gods."[24] To the extent that avoiding hubris is within our control, we are capable of enhancing our prospects for happiness by averting the vengeance of Zeus. On the other hand, there are limits even to the effects of our well-intended moral actions: "Sometimes the man who strives to do good falls unknowingly (*ou phrononēsas*) into great ruin (*atē*) and difficulty, while god gives good fortune to the one who does badly in everything, and deliverance from his lack of good judgment (*aphrosunēs*)" (13.67–70).

The cumulative effect of the poem on our understanding of techne, then, is this: the technical realm is independent of the "moral," that sphere of human values, meanings, and prospects for happiness in which the ultimate outcomes of techne and all other human enterprises are felt. In this sense, and to speak anachronistically, Solon has identified the *"value-neutrality"* of techne: its possession does not guarantee its good application. The technical fisherman may perform an act of hubris, steal his competitor's net, and subsequently meet with disaster. There is nothing within the epistemic content of his techne itself either to prohibit or to

---

24. Greene 1963, 38. As Greene puts it, Solon does not achieve "absolute consistency . . . but a faith in spite of misgivings" (37).

encourage him to act morally. Simply qua *technitēs*, the fisherman knows nothing about *dikē*.

The issue implicit here, to digress briefly, concerns the use- or value-neutrality of techne. Aristotle puts this point succinctly by describing techne as a "rational *dunamis*" that can produce contrary results; for example, "medicine can produce disease and health" (*Metaphysics*, 1046b2–5). Whether it produces the one or the other depends upon the character of the physician and how he chooses to *use* his technical knowledge. And this, the physician's "disposition" (*hexis*), is, if he is excellent, fixed and stable and "does not also produce the contrary result" (*Nicomachean Ethics* 1129a14).[25] In short, it is in the using of things technical that ethical value becomes visible.

As Chapters 2 and 3 demonstrate, this is a theme of great significance in the Platonic dialogues as well, for Socrates regularly raises the question, How should the results of a techne be used? He does so because, again, it is in the use of the techne, not simply in the techne itself, that ethical value resides. This importation of ethical weight into "use" is reflected in the Greek word *chrēstos*. A verbal adjective derived from *chraomai*, "to use," it means not only "useful" but also "good." Ethical evaluation in general, then, takes place within the realm of "use."

Solon's poem, while hardly explicit, prefigures such a point, for we might well imagine him urging the fisherman to ask questions such as, *Should* I give my fish away to hungry children? that is, How should I use the results of my techne? Even allowing for lines 67–70 and their suggestion of fatalism concerning the ultimate consequences of well-intended moral actions, Solon seems to hold that in some fashion these questions can be answered and that it is possible for the fisherman to choose to behave properly. Again, if he does, it will not be qua fisherman. Possession of a techne leads only to a successful execution of a set of rational procedures; it does not lead to happiness or true human flourishing. As a result, a new item is suggested on our list of criteria for a techne.

List of Criteria 3: The Solonic Conception

1.–6.: The same as List 2.
  7. A techne is use- or value-neutral and cannot in itself bring happiness.

25. Aristotle makes a related distinction between ethical virtue and techne when he insists that the value of the latter is measured solely by the quality of the work produced, whereas determining the value of an ethical action requires the more difficult task of evaluating the motives and character of the agent (*Nicomachean Ethics* 1105a25–31).

If a techne is value-neutral, how is it possible for *technitēs,* or anyone else, to make a correct choice concerning ethical behavior? Solon does not elaborate, and perhaps is ultimately pessimistic about this prospect, but the most straightforward way, implied in his other poems and by his career as *archōn* of Athens, is to obey the nomoi, the laws or customs, of the polis. But the nomoi do not cover every situation, nor is it obvious that they themselves are always good. How, then, does one know how to be just or fair or good? Can one have anything like "moral knowledge?" If so, how would such knowledge compare to the technai, which seem to be for Solon the best examples of ordinary, and usually effective, human knowledge? Would moral knowledge be as limited and as subject to the vagaries of moira as the technai? Or would it differ in kind?

What remains of Solon's work of course neither asks nor answers questions such as these. His "Prayer to the Muses" does, however, provoke them; it projects an ethical or practical realm of human values and happiness, which "surrounds" the technical realm. Techne seems to represent for Solon the paradigmatic case of the human effort to gain rational control over life's contingencies. As such, to him it may well be counted a good. But if so, it is a highly conditional good, covering as it does only a limited dimension of experience. Beyond techne stands, first of all, chance and moira, which by definition are impervious to human effort. Second, and for my purposes more significant, Solon's poem postulates, however cautiously, an ethical realm, one governed by human agency, in which human happiness can be felt or missed and which has no direct relationship to the possession of a techne.

Too often, Solon seems to say, people become confused about the boundaries separating these realms. They falsely think that by exhibiting technical mastery they are ensured success in the quest for happiness. Socrates makes a similar point in the *Apology* (22d): he grants that the "technicians" (*cheirotechnas*) do indeed know many fine things. But they delude themselves, are seduced by their own expertise; because they have mastered their technai, they think themselves wise in matters of the "greatest" human significance. About this, however, they are severely mistaken, for, qua technicians, they are ignorant about human excellence and happiness.[26]

Even if it does not do so explicitly, Solon's protreptic poem thus provides the elements of a question to play so large a role during the next 250 years: what can be known about the ethical realm? Because the poem jux-

---

26. A similar point is made at *Republic* 495d.

taposes the technai, which it seems to adopt as exemplars of knowledge, with both moira and moral action, it provides the terms with which to ask a more specific question: can the ethical realm be known by means of a techne? To use language soon to emerge, can there be a techne whose subject matter is arete? Solon himself does not ask this question, but those who followed him do.

Aeschylus

A more optimistic, less constricted view of techne is found in Aeschylus's *Prometheus Bound* (probably written around 460).[27] Prometheus, chained to a cliff by Zeus in punishment for the assistance he has given to humanity, attempts to persuade the chorus of his record as a "philanthropist."

PROMETHEUS: Instead, hear what wretched lives people used to lead, how babyish they were—until I gave them intelligence, I made them masters of their own thought. . . .

Men and women looking saw nothing, they listened and did not hear, but like shapes in a dream dragging out their long lives bewildered they make hodgepodge of everything, they knew nothing of making brick-knitted houses the sun warms, nor how to work in wood. They swarmed like bitty ants in dugouts in sunless cave. They hadn't any sure signs of winter nor spring flowering nor later summer when the crops came in. All their work was work without thought, until I taught them to see what had been hard to see: where and when the stars rise and set.

What's more, for them I invented Number [*arithmon*], wisdom above all other. And the painstaking, putting together of Letters: to be their memory of everything, to be their Muses' mother, their handmaid.

And I was the first to put brute beasts under the yoke, fit them out with pack saddles, so they could take the heaviest burdens off the backs of human beings. Horses I broke and harnessed to the chariot shaft so that they loved their reins, they showed off the pride and wealth of their owners.

27. I follow the translation by Herrington and Scully (New York: Oxford University Press, 1989), substituting only my own "techne."

I, I alone invented the sea wandering linen winged chariots for sails.
All these devices I invented for human beings. Yet now in my own
misery, I can't devise one single trick to free myself from this agony.

CHORUS: You've been tortured, humiliated, so that your mind wanders
driven to distraction. Like a bad doctor fallen sick you grope, desperate for what you can't find: the drugs that will make you well.

PROMETHEUS: But hear the rest, you'll be more amazed: what [technai],
what resources, I worked out! And then greatest was this. . . . If someone fell sick there was nothing for it: nothing to eat, drink nor rub
into the skin. Without drugs people wasted away, until I showed them
how to mix soothing herbs to ward off every sort of disease.

I marked out the many ways men might see into the future. . . .

So much for these. As for the benefits to humankind hid under the
earth (the copper the iron the silver the gold) who but I could claim he
discovered them. No one, except a babbling idiot.

In a word: listen!

All the [technai] that mortals have come from Prometheus. (441–
506)

Since the last line is summary, each of the nine items mentioned by
Prometheus—housebuilding (or woodworking), astronomy (or meteorol-
ogy), arithmetic, writing, animal husbandry, shipbuilding, medicine,
prophecy, and metallurgy—is fairly called a techne.[28]

Several items are already familiar: housebuilding and shipbuilding are
clear examples of productive craft; medicine and prophecy belong to the
Homeric *dēmiourgoi*; animal husbandry and metallurgy, like Solon's fishing and agriculture, are acquisitive and methodical. What is strikingly new
on this list is "Number [*arithmon*], wisdom above all other," and writing
("the painstaking, putting together of Letters"). In what sense are these
technai? Is the written word a product analogous to a house or a ship? In
some attenuated sense, yes: it is a visible object produced by, and distinct
from, a knowledgeable human being. But this is not, I suggest, the significant reason why Prometheus includes writing on his list of technai.

Writing is a techne because it requires mastery of a determinate subject
matter: namely, a fixed set of elements (letters) and the specific rules for
their proper combination (orthography and grammar). Indeed, as Isocrates
will soon point out, the subject matter of writing makes it not only a

28. For a commentary on the specific items of the list, see Joos 1955, 329–31.

techne but almost emblematic of the technai in general. More so than the wood of the woodworker or the techniques of the fisherman, how to spell a word correctly is clearly determined and then fixed by the rules of orthography.[29] As a result, teaching someone to spell or write is a highly systematic, almost mechanical task whose success rate is easily measured and typically very high. Failure to learn to write is exceptional, and is usually explained by some defect in the student rather than the teacher. The latter is thus readily identified, certified, and employed. Not surprisingly, then, the basic reason why boys went to school in ancient Greece was, according to Xenophon at least, in order to learn to read and write (*grammata mathēsomenoi*).[30]

There is, however, another sense in which writing is unique. Unlike a "typical" techne, whose field is sharply delimited, the province of writing spans the entirety of language itself. It can thus be used by any number of citizens and technicians. Even in Aeschylus's time the person who could write was hardly a "comparatively rare" expert or specialist.[31] The product of writing is useful, but in a way quite different from a house or a ship. Although like the other technai it is field-specific—it requires the mastery of a fixed subject matter—its arena of application is indefinite. Prometheus, for example, describes writing as an aid to the memory. In this capacity, it supplements all other intellectual activities, rather than being a self-sufficient activity in itself. A century later Aristotle states in the *Politics* (1338a15–17) that there are four basic uses of writing: business, household management, political activity, and, broadest of all, "learning" (*mathēsin*).

Such indefiniteness distinguishes writing. Its inclusion on Prometheus's list therefore demonstrates how far the meaning of "techne" has advanced from that described by List 1, where it was inextricably tied to productive craft. Since "techne" now includes writing, it no longer simply means "craft"; instead, and even though the crafts still provide most of its examples, it refers to "knowledge" in some as-yet-unspecified sense.

Prometheus says that he invented (*exhēuron:* 460) letters "to be [hu-

29. I do not imply that the rules for spelling were uniform or codifed. As Thomas (1989, 47) puts it, "[I]t is a comparatively recent development in modern Europe for a country to try to maintain a single sytem of correct spelling, and dictionaries are an essential tool for that." Still, as she points out, there was a concept, however shaky, of orthography. Bad spelling in graffiti, for example, was "often taken to show that the writer was particuarly ill-educated." For the role of orthography at Pompeii, see Harris 1989, 264.

30. Xenophon *Cyropaedia* 1.2.6. See also Marrou 1956, 72.

31. See Harris 1989 for the literacy rates of antiquity.

manity's] memory of everything, to be their Muses' mother." In other
words, before becoming literate, people needed divine assistance to pursue
the intellectual work that required memory. With the advent of writing,
however, the need for the Muses disappeared, and humanity became more
self-sufficient. This Promethean declaration of independence stands in contrast to Solon's cautious reminder that human success is always contingent
upon chance and the divine and never fully within human grasp. While
Aeschylus's Prometheus is hardly the figure revered by nineteenth-century
Romantics, and while a real interpretation of this passage would of course
require an analysis of the entire play, it is clear that writing tokens some
measure of liberation from the gods and fate; with this techne, human
beings become their own Muse.

Prometheus describes Number as "wisdom above all other" (*exochon
sophismatōn*). Why? Unlike the typical technai, arithmos, which means
both number (the study of which is arithmetic) and counting, is not an
overtly productive enterprise. On an immediate level, at least, it does not
even seem to be useful. Indeed, within a hundred years or so, arithmetic
will be conceived of as purely "theoretical" knowledge, i.e., one with no
practical application at all. (I refer to Aristotle's *Metaphysics* 6.1, where
mathematics is a prime example of a "theoretical episteme," that is, one
whose sole value and purpose is to "see" [*theōrein*] rather than to do or
make.) Since most of the technai listed by Prometheus are productive and
useful in the "traditional" manner—they are, after all, given to humans to
facilitate their survival—it seems likely that because of the indirect but
significant practical benefit of even a rudimentary knowledge of arithmetic, Prometheus praises arithmos. (Recall what Kübe has to say about the
role of mathematics in the work of the *tektōn*.) Mathematical knowledge
can be applied in many fields and thus aids in the human quest to overcome chance and natural scarcity.

Still, the prominence Prometheus accords number needs a further explanation. Perhaps it is this: as I suggested by making it item 1 on my first list
of criteria, having a *determinate* field or subject matter is paramount in
characterizing a techne. The *technitēs* is an "expert," and no one can be an
expert in everything. Instead, he or she achieves epistemic mastery of this
or that particular, highly delimited subject matter. From this first criterion
all others follow. In other words, because the subject matter is determinate
and thus can be mastered, a *technitēs* can be recognized and certified as
authoritative. As Chapter 2 shows, when Socrates appeals to the technai in
his analogical arguments, he looks toward their clarity and authority, both

of which follow from the determinacy, the "masterability," of their subject matters.

These considerations may suggest why Prometheus called arithmos "wisdom above all others." Arithmetic is the most clear and authoritative, and its subject matter is the epitome of determinacy. To elaborate, I must digress considerably: first, to a passage from Plato's *Republic* and, second, to two fragments by the Pythagorean Philolaus (who was a contemporary of the historical Socrates). I do so for reasons of convenience and to prepare for later discussion: the passage from Plato illuminates what I think is implicit in Aeschylus, whereas Philolaus succinctly treats what I take to be the basic philosophical issue underlying the citation from the *Republic*.[32]

Consider the following statement Socrates makes in the *Republic:* "The trivial business of distinguishing the one, the two, and the three. In sum, I mean counting (arithmos) and calculation (*logismon*). Or isn't it the case concerning these that every techne and episteme is forced to participate in them?" (522c5–8).

Socrates does not explain in what exact sense techne must "participate" in arithmos. Does he mean that every techne is some version of applied mathematics? Perhaps. But this statement could also be taken in a more general, almost metaphorical sense. On this reading, a techne must have a determinate subject matter, some *one* area of expertise. And arithmos, of which the one is the principle (*archē:* see Aristotle's *Metaphysics* 5.15.5), is the paradigm case of, and indeed what makes possible, such determinacy.

Consider these two fragments of Philolaus.

> For there will not even be an object of apprehension at all if everything is indeterminate. (3)

> And indeed all objects of apprehension have [*arithmos*], for it is not possible for us to think of or apprehend anything without this. (4)[33]

Even allowing for their ambiguity, these statements seem to imply two propositions: (1) determinacy is the necessary condition of intelligibility (and thus knowledge), and (2) the necessary condition of determinacy is arithmos. How exactly arithmos supplies this condition is not clear. Nussbaum finds Philolaus making a kind of transcendental argument. It is

---

32. It has been conjectured that Philolaus influenced Socrates, but such a historical connection is irrelevant for my purposes.

33. I borrow the translation by Nussbaum (1979), leaving *arithmos* untranslated.

given that the world is intelligible to us; we can apprehend or recognize (*gignōskein*) things. And the condition of the possibility of such apprehension is our ability to distinguish "this" from "that." Making such distinctions necessarily requires delimiting the boundaries of "this" and thereby treating it as a countable unit separate from "that."

Huffman argues somewhat similarly, although he disagrees concerning *gignōskein,* which for him refers to secure knowledge and not merely to "apprehension" or "recognition." He says, "Philolaus accepts Parmenides' claim that the object of knowledge must be a determinate state of affairs but wants to preserve a plurality. The bold step he takes is to argue that numerical relationships and mathematical relationships in general solve the problem." In turn, what this means is "that we only really understand something when we understand the structure of and relationship between its various parts."[34]

For the purpose of this chapter, it is not necessary to determine exactly the meaning of Philolaus's fragments, but only to use them to illustrate Socrates' comment in the *Republic* (and Prometheus's description of arithmos as a "wisdom above all others"). Even if he does not explain it in precise conceptual terms, Socrates explicitly mentions an intimate, perhaps even a foundational, relationship between arithmos and techne. Because of its mastery of a determinate subject matter, the latter is a good, perhaps the best, example of a sustained intelligibility (or knowledge of *one* subject matter). At the least, the former is a good, perhaps the best, example of the latter.

Of course, the philosophical treatment of techne offered by Plato and Philolaus is beyond anything conceived in Aeschylus's poetry. Nevertheless, latent within Prometheus's praise of arithmos may well be a similar point. Arithmos is "wisdom above all others" because it is both constitutive and paradigmatic of techne in general. Again, woodworking is about *one* subject only: the production of useful artifacts from wood. The woodworker, qua woodworker, knows nothing about metalwork or agriculture, for these are distinct "units" to be studied. Arithmetic is about number, the basis of determinateness itself. In other words, the very notion of specific fields of study, that is, subject X as a self-contained unit of study distinct from subject Y, is a "protoarithmetical" concept. Number, the subject matter of arithmetic, is what makes such distinction possible. This, perhaps, is one reason why arithmos receives such praise from Prometheus.

A second is this: all technai must attain a certain level of precision, of

34. Huffman 1988, 22 and 28.

akribeia.[35] When a *technitēs* is asked a question about his work, he must be able to answer clearly in order to validate the authority "techne" implies. Arithmetic is the most precise of all subjects, for in it, more than in any other, when one solves a problem, the resulting answer and explanation are certain, clear, and definitive. In the strongest possible way, then, we can count on arithmetic.[36] In this sense, it functions as a paradigm of all technai, which, as item 3 on List 1 indicates, must be reliable.

It is impossible to prove that Aeschylus had in mind considerations such as these when he had Prometheus describe arithmos as "wisdom above all others." Indeed, Prometheus offers no explanation at all for granting arithmos such a privileged position on his list. But his silence is itself telling. Precisely because there is no explanation why, his praise of arithmos must have sounded reasonable to his audience. In other words, arithmos must already have been associated with techne, and with intelligibility in general, in their minds. Nussbaum believes this was the case: "[F]rom the earliest texts (and fifth-century texts are fully consistent with these) we see the use of arithmos to mean that which is counted, and a close association between . . . numerability and knowability."[37]

This association is further reflected in the mythic figure of Palamedes who, as described in Gorgias's *Palamedes* (30) and like Prometheus, benefited the human race by providing various technai as well as "arithmos" (see *Republic* 522d). Or consider what Aristotle, who no doubt expresses a widely held belief, says about the "periodic style" in his *Rhetoric*: it is easy to learn because it is easy to remember, and this, in turn, is because it "has arithmos, which of all things is the easiest to remember" (1409b3–4). In sum, arithmos is closely linked with intelligibility. To count requires the ability to identify an intelligible unit making the count possible. An analogous identification of subject matter makes a techne, a sustained form of intelligibility, possible.

This digression should cast doubt on the standard identification of techne as a strictly practical or applied knowledge. Even if during the period of the *Prometheus Bound* and earlier these senses of "techne" predominate, its meaning nonetheless has the potential for expansion. By including arithmos, which is characterized more by its high level of intelligibility than by its immediate practicality, "techne" seems to veer closer to "knowledge," conceived in a rather broad sense.[38]

35. See Kurz 1970.
36. See Roochnik 1990 and 1994a.
37. Nussbaum 1979, 69.
38. For a contrary view, see Gould (1972, 3–31), who invokes Ryle's distinction between knowing how and knowing that.

So too with "writing." Like arithmos, it does not have the immediate usefulness traditionally associated with a craft. Both it and arithmos are, however, indirectly very useful, and this surely explains the prominence Prometheus accords them. In addition, however, both seem to exemplify *intellectual* attributes illuminating of the very notion of techne itself. Their subject matters are formal, can be analyzed into elements and rules, and can thus be mastered and explained with precision. Both are reliably taught, and the rate of success of their teaching can readily be measured. Both writing and arithmetic exemplify the principle suggested by Huffman's interpretation of Philolaus: "[W]e only really understand something when we understand the structure of and relationship between its various parts." In other words, both are consummately intelligible. It is precisely this feature that, as the chapters below show, later writers will draw upon in their own confrontations with the techne question.

Aeschylus's *Prometheus* is not a self-conscious philosophical work. Nonetheless, this poem lays the groundwork for, because it provides the elements of, what will soon become decisive philosophical questions. To prefigure: Prometheus declares knowledge in the form of techne to be essential for human survival. But how far can knowledge extend? Since survival is a precondition for human flourishing, for living a life of excellence, of arete, and so achieving "happiness," a question emerges: can a techne take human beings beyond survival and help them achieve arete and thus happiness? Or is techne, as Solon implies, mute on the questions of value, that is, value-neutral? Aeschylus does not explicitly raise this question. But because Prometheus so pointedly conceives of techne as central to human life, Aeschylus's poem invites us to ask the basic question of this book: *is there a techne of arete?*

If the speculations and digressions offered above were appropriate, more specific questions emerge: if arithmetic is paradigmatic of a techne, is the knowledge of arete like arithmetic? If techne is the consummate form of sustained intelligibility, and if human happiness can be conceived as a subject matter of a techne, is human life like arithmos? If writing is an exemplar of technical knowing, then is human life, the ethical realm of happiness, like *ta grammata*? Does arete have parts that can be known individually and in terms of their interrelationships? Is there a grammar of happiness, mastery of which will lead to arete? Again, these are precisely the sorts of questions soon to be taken up by later writers.

Regardless of Aeschylus's unspoken thoughts on arithmetic and writing, Prometheus's list encompasses virtually every aspect of intellectual activity. From straightforward craft production to arithmos, to writing, the items on this list comprise a huge catalogue of intellectual achievements. The breadth of the list has led many commentators to describe Prometheus's gift as human culture itself. Herrington and Scully, for example, actually use this phrase to translate "technai" at the end of the passage. On the one hand, their translation is misleading: "technai" is plural and is meant to refer summarily to the items just listed, each of which should thus be called a "techne." On the other hand, they are surely right: the technai cumulatively represent an ever-increasing ability to confront the world with reason, independence from the gods, distinction from the animals, the ability to survive and flourish by means of human resources alone. And the principal human resource is knowledge. "Techne no longer means this or that particular ability, but in general human practical intelligence."[39]

List 4 summarizes:

List of Criteria 4: The Promethean Conception

1. A techne (with the possible exception of writing) has a determinate subject matter or field.
2. It has a useful result, either directly, as in the case of the shipbuilder, or indirectly, as in the case of writing and arithmetic, whose knowledge can be used to supplement and assist the process of production.
3. It promotes human independence from gods, nature, and chance.
4. It must be applied, either directly or indirectly, in order to become useful.
5. It is easily recognized. Because each item on his list is readily identified by the chorus as real and valuable knowledge, Prometheus succeeds in persuading them that he is humanity's friend.
6. The technai are teachable. Prometheus, after all, transmitted them to humanity, and men could presumably do the same by teaching them to others. Prometheus uses verbs like "show" (458, 482), "discover" (460, 468, 503), "invent" (477), "mark out" (487), and "lead into [techne]" (497–98), to describe how he brought techne to humanity. All could be used to describe teaching. A techne, then, has a rational content, a logos, that can be communicated.
7. Perhaps because of its exemplary intelligibility, arithmetic is paradigmatic. Perhaps for similar reasons, writing is included.

In Aeschylus there is an openness to, even an optimism about, technical possibilities that is missing in Solon. (This is the reason I omit "value-neutrality" from List 4.) Since *Prometheus Bound* was but one-third of a

39. Kübe 1969, 36–37.

trilogy whose remainder is now missing, this statement must be asserted with caution. What is most important here is that Aeschylus reflects a broadened conception of techne, one in which the tantalizing possibility that arithmetic is somehow paradigmatic is offered, one on which writing is included, and finally one which implies an essential relationship between humanity itself and techne.

One techne described in strikingly hopeful terms by Prometheus is medicine. It is, he says, the "greatest" (*megiston:* 478). Presumably, the health of the body is a great good, and only the advent of medical knowledge enables men to restore it reliably. Indeed, there is probably no other techne that does better work for the people. For this reason, then, I turn next to the medical writings themselves and their conception of a techne.

The Hippocratic Writings

If Solon represents the first moment of reflection on the ethical character of techne, the Hippocratic response to the question, Is medicine really a techne and, if so, why? is the first thoroughly self-conscious treatment of its epistemic nature. The Hippocratic writings not only address the question in medical terms, they also raise epistemological issues at a highly general level. As a result, they influenced subsequent writers of all stripes who themselves took up the techne question. Their influence seems particularly strong on Plato. Consider Jaeger's comment:

> Plato speaks of doctors and medicine in such high terms that, even if the early medical literature of Greece were entirely lost, we should need no further evidence to infer that, during the late fifth and the fourth centuries before Christ, the social and intellectual prestige of the Greek medical profession was very high indeed. Plato thinks of the doctor as the representative of a highly specialized and refined department of knowledge; and also as the embodiment of a professional code which is rigorous enough to be a perfect model of the proper relation between knowledge and its purpose in practical conduct. . . . It is no exaggeration to say that Socrates' doctrine of ethical knowledge, on which so many of the arguments in Plato's dialogues turn, would be unthinkable without that model, medical science, to which he so often refers. Of all the

branches of human knowledge then existing (including mathematics and natural science) medicine is the most closely akin to the ethical science of Socrates.[40]

With this statement Jaeger offers one version of the standard account of techne: he describes the "science" of medicine as a "highly specialized . . . department of knowledge," which provides a theoretical "model" for Plato's conception of "ethical science." He is not alone in holding such views.[41] Before evaluating them, it is first necessary to determine just what the medical techne actually was. Given the diversity and size of the Hippocratic corpus, this is no easy task. What follows does not address the numerous philological questions plaguing the corpus (e.g., of authorship and date), nor will it make any attempt to be comprehensive. It is only a sketch designed to delineate what "techne" means for the medical writers and to guide future attempts to understand how Plato used this term to explicate his own conception of knowledge.

The two texts directly bearing on my question are "On Techne" and "On Ancient Medicine" (VM).[42] The former defends medicine against a hypothetical critic who argues that medicine is *not* a techne. Perhaps this is puzzling: the physician had been described by Homer as a *dēmiourgos,* Solon included medicine in his "Prayer to the Muses," and Prometheus praised it as "greatest." Who, then, would such a critic be, and why would he direct the techne question at medicine in the first place?

The answer must be that during the late fifth and early fourth centuries a wide-ranging debate was taking place about the nature, limits, and epistemic character of techne. In this age of "the Greek enlightenment," when the notion of a genuine "professional" was developing, the very word "techne" had become a prized appellation that could confer credibility on a subject and its practitioner. It is precisely such credibility at which the Hippocratic writings seem to aim. The physicians were eager to promote their developing "science," to put it on firm epistemic ground, and thereby to distinguish themselves from "those in the temples of Asclepius or the itinerant purifiers," that is, from the nontechnical quacks.[43] To do this,

40. Jaeger 1967, 3.
41. See Kato 1986, O'Brien 1963, Wehrli 1951, and Edelstein 1952 (who offers a divergent view).
42. My text and translation of the Hippocratic writings come from Jones's translation (Cambridge, Mass.: Harvard University Press, Loeb Classical Library, 1956), except that I regularly substitute "techne" for Jones's "art."
43. Lloyd 1987, 89.

they needed to meet the challenge posed by the techne question and convince their audience that medicine satisfied those criteria belonging to a techne. They confronted what was probably a standard set of objections to their claims by offering an epistemological apologia. This is exactly the task of "On Techne," which indeed has been titled by Gomperz *Die Apologie der Heilkunst.*[44]

The author of this work initially responds to his critic in extremely general terms. First, he criticizes him as one who pointlessly vilifies knowledge, is showing off his disputational skill and, because he disparages the good work of the intellect, inadvertently reveals his own base nature and "want of art" (*atechniē:* 1.14). Second, the author argues in an almost Eleatic fashion for the absurdity of saying that something, in this case the medical techne, does not exist (2). Both of these initial arguments are highly rhetorical, and in them the author reveals himself as a "streitlustiger und streitgewohnter Kampe," as a "Meister der Rede" who is conversant with the issues of his day.[45] As suggested above, the techne question is in the air; it is a hot item on the debaters' circuit and one with which the author of "On Techne" is apparently familiar.

After this initial line of defense, the author responds to a set of related objections specifically directed at medicine:

1. The results of medicine are not entirely reliable; some patients who are treated are not cured (see 4 and 7). The carpenter, by contrast, does not fail to produce a house when called upon to do so.[46] As a result, when a patient does recover, the cause is not the physician's techne, but chance (*tuchē:* 4).
2. Many people who fall ill get better without a physician's help at all (5).
3. Physicians "refuse to undertake desperate cases," and the critic complains "that while physicians undertake cases which would cure themselves, they do not touch those where great help is necessary; whereas if the [techne] exists, it ought to cure all alike" (8.2–6).

Clearly, the critic's argument presupposes a definite conception of techne, articulated by the following criteria:

List of Criteria 5: The Critic of "On Techne"

1. A techne has a determinate subject matter and task. In the case of medicine, that task, that subject matter, is health.

44. Gomperz 1910.
45. Gomperz 1910, 86.
46. I formulate this point in my own terms, but it is implied in 12.

2. A techne effects a useful result that would not appear without the active intervention of the technician. Without the carpenter there would be no house; assuming it is a techne, without medicine there would be no cure of a disease.
3. It is teachable.
4. It is extremely reliable. It can be counted on to perform its task. Its function is identical to its end.
5. It is universal; that is, all particulars putatively under its purview can be handled with equal competence.
6. A techne "is a deliberate application of human intelligence to some part of the world, yielding some control over *tuchē*."[47]

The notion of techne formed by this list of criteria extends, intensifies, and makes more explicit what was implicit in previous conceptions. Criterion 1, for example, has remained largely the same on each of the four lists. As discussed in the previous section, determinateness of subject matter not only is a necessary condition for being a techne, but is the one characteristic from which all the others derive. Criterion 2, the usefulness of its result, has also been a constant, as has (3), being teachable, that is, being based on rational principles that can be communicated. In (4), (5), and (6), however, the critic significantly extends the conception of techne held by his predecessors.

Although reliability (4) is present in its primitive meaning (see List 1), techne is conceived by the critic as extremely, indeed almost perfectly, reliable: it simply does not fail. (Compare Thrasymachus's view at *Republic* 340e.) The point seems to be this: a shipbuilder is recognized by the community as a *technitēs*. If someone hires him, that someone can reasonably expect a ship to be built. If, however, the ship should sink upon its first sailing, then its builder would be stripped of his title. The technician, qua technician, does not fail. Alternatively formulated, in this conception of techne, function is identical to end. The function of the shipbuilder is to make ships; when he performs his function, his end is achieved and ships are made. If they are not made, the maker has failed to execute his function and therefore can legitimately be deemed a fraud.[48]

Criterion 6 moves us beyond, although it is obviously related to, the Promethean conception wherein human beings gain a significant portion of independence through techne. For the critic, a technically equipped humanity is capable of mastering the ravages of *tuchē*. Again, consider the

47. Nussbaum 1986, 95. See also Joos 1955.
48. See Allen 1989, 4.

shipbuilder: he has no excuses for failure. If, for example, the wood he chooses for the hull is not sufficiently supple, he cannot (qua technician) legitimately appeal to bad luck, for as a technician he should be able to make his own luck.

Precisely because medicine does not satisfy these criteria, that is, because it regularly meets with failure and seems vulnerable to chance, the critic levels his charge against it.

To respond, the author of "On Techne" deploys a twofold strategy. First, even though he remains cautious, he does attempt to refute directly his critic's specific objections. Second, the author grants the critic's contention that medicine does not satisfy all the rigorous criteria listed above. He argues, however, that these are the wrong criteria. In other words, he denies his critic's rigorous conception is the sole model of techne. As "On Ancient Medicine" helps to show, the Hippocratic strategy is to bifurcate techne into two kinds, into what I term techne$_1$ and techne$_2$. The first, belonging to the critic and explicated on Lists 5 and 6, refines and intensifies the traditional view. The second, claimed and practiced by the Hippocratic physician (articulated on List 7 below), significantly alters the traditional view.

In response to his critic's first objection, that medicine is not perfectly reliable and that *tuchē*, and not techne, is responsible for the healing of the patient, the author of "On Techne" rejoins: "How is it possible for patients to attribute their recoveries to anything else except the [techne], seeing that it was by using it and serving it that they recovered. For in that they committed themselves to the [techne] they showed their unwillingness to behold nothing but the reality of luck" (4).

This is not much of an argument, for it relies only on the observation that medicine seems actually to work and on the naïve belief, perhaps even faith, of those patients who come to the physician for treatment. While patients may well reject the role of *tuchē* in explaining their recovery, this implies nothing about the actual cause of their recovery. Fortunately, the author does not hinge his status as a professional on arguments such as these. Instead, the full force of his defense is best felt in the second phase of his strategy.

The author *agrees* with his critic that "many, even without calling in a physician, have been cured" (5). He denies, however, that this is sufficient evidence to discredit medicine's claim to be a techne. Those who do get better on their own, he argues, typically have altered their normal routines. They may have fasted or changed their diet, abstained from drinking, or taken additional rest. If they got better, then what they did was correct. Medicine is a direct extension of this ordinary experience of trial and error, for the layman often stumbles upon the correct way to treat a disease. "Now where correctness (*to orthon*) and incorrectness each have a defined limit, surely there must be a [techne]" (5). In other words, medicine originates in and remains continuous with pretechnical experience. In the latter, the correct response to a disease can be distinguished from the incorrect response. Medicine systematically generalizes and rises from such humble origins.

The author of "On Ancient Medicine" develops this point. For him, medicine emerged from the ordinary desire to find a nutritious diet and from the kind of experimentation with different foods that most people perform. (Indeed, this is what "ancient medicine" was: see VM 3.) From this he concludes that the difference between the physician with a techne and the "ancient" layman who experimented with his diet is not an essential one.

> What difference then can be seen between the purpose of him we call physician, who is an acknowledged handicraftsman (*cheirotechnēs*), the discoverer of the mode of life and of the nourishment suitable for the sick, and him who discovered and prepared originally nourishment for all men, which we now use, instead of the old savage and brutish mode of living? My own view is that their reasoning was identical and the discovery one and the same. . . . How do the two pursuits differ, except in their scope and in that the latter is more complex and requires the greater application, while the former is the starting point and came first in time. (VM 7)

This author goes even further in emphasizing the continuity between medicine and ordinary life. He insists that the language of medicine must be "ordinary": "But it is particularly necessary, in my opinion, for one who discusses this [techne] to discuss things familiar to ordinary folk. . . . But if you miss being understood by laymen, and fail to put your hearers in this condition, you will miss reality" (VM 2).

Having said this, the author is aware of a potentially crippling objection: if the line dividing medicine and pretechnical experience, in terms of both their language and reasoning, should become too porous, there would be no way of distinguishing the technical physician from the layman. This would be a serious problem because, as early as Homer, the *technitēs* has been someone "comparatively rare" who deserves a reward for his uniquely useful knowledge. "That it [medicine] is not commonly considered a [techne] is not surprising, for it is inappropriate to call anyone a technician in a [techne] in which none are laymen, but all possess knowledge through being compelled to use it" (VM 4).

There are two reasons why the Hippocratic author is confident that, even though medicine originates in and does not essentially differ from ordinary pretechnical experience, it is yet a techne. The first has already been mentioned: the medical techne systematically generalizes what is correctly stumbled upon in pretechnical experience. In doing so, the technical physician, unlike the layman, can give a general account, a logos or explanation, why a specific treatment works for a particular disease. This is, of course, what makes a techne teachable (and teachability has been a criterion since the "primitive" conception of techne given in List 1): "It is not sufficient to learn simply that cheese is a bad food, as it gives a pain to one who eats a surfeit of it; we must know what the pain is, the reasons for it, and which constituent of man is harmfully affected" (VM 20).[49]

The second reason is equally important. The author insists medicine should not be judged by an excessive standard of precision, one achievable *only* by a form of reasoning that sharply breaks with the messiness of ordinary life. In seeking treatments for complex diseases,

> [i]t is necessary to aim at some measure. But no measure, neither number nor weight, by reference to which knowledge can be made exact, can be found except bodily feeling. Wherefore it is laborious to make knowledge so exact that only small mistakes are made here and there. And that physician who makes only small mistakes would win my hearty praise. Perfectly exact truth [*to atrekes*] is but rarely to be seen. (VM 9)

> [I]t is difficult always to attain perfect accuracy. . . . I declare, however, that we ought not to reject the ancient techne as non-existent, or on the ground that its method of inquiry is faulty, just because it has not attained exactness in every detail, but much rather, because it has been able by reasoning to rise from deep ignorance to approximately perfect accuracy, I think we ought to admire the dis-

---

49. This statement prefigures Aristotle's discussion of a techne in *Metaphysics* 1.1.

coveries as the work, not of chance, but of inquiry rightly and correctly conducted. (VM 12)

In much the same fashion as in "On Techne," the author here responds to a critic who, because he holds a very rigorous conception of techne, criticizes medicine on the grounds of its imprecision and its continuity with the jumbles of ordinary experience. As the mention of "number" and "weight" in the first passage above suggests, the paradigm of techne held by the critic seems to be mathematics. In questions about strictly quantitative matters, there is no dispute, no imprecision. By contrast, the Hippocratic author objects to arithmos as an excessive and, for reasons he will delineate, an inappropriate standard of rigor.

The author of "On Ancient Medicine" defends himself against another charge, that coming from critics who insist medicine break entirely with its past and model itself on fifth-century natural science. They want medicine to be like a deductive system emanating from a single unambiguous "postulate" (*hupothesis*): "All who, on attempting to speak or to write on medicine have assumed for themselves a postulate (*hupothesin*) as a basis for their discussion—heat, cold, moisture, dryness, or anything else that they may fancy—who narrow down the causal principle of diseases and of death among men, and make it the same in all cases, postulating one thing or two, all these obviously blunder in many points of their statement, but they are most open to censure because they blunder in what is a techne" (VM 1).

Those attacking medicine on the grounds of insufficient precision and the failure to reduce itself to a clear and distinct principle simply do not understand what a techne is. They invoke the wrong paradigm and therefore inappropriately demand that medicine become a certain type of deductive theory. To repeat: the unnamed critic here seems to have Ionian natural science in mind. "There can be no doubt," Lloyd argues, "that the *hupotheseis* referred to in VM are postulates or assumptions used as the basis of philosophical and medical theories." Lloyd further speculates that the target of the Hippocratic criticism is Philolaus, and the basic postulate is that of the "hot and the cold."[50]

The very notion of a "postulate," however, should bring mathematics to mind as well because, as Jones puts it, "the best example of hupotheseis are the axioms and postulates of geometry."[51] Lloyd acknowledges the

50. Lloyd 1963, 111 and 124.
51. Jones 1956, 7 n. 42.

plausibility of this view: "[I]t seems at least as likely that the term was introduced into medicine from geometry."[52] If so, then the critic is making explicit what was implicit in Prometheus's praise of arithmos (see criterion 7 on List 4), namely, that mathematics, because of its extreme reliability and rigor, is paradigmatic of techne. Against this view the Hippocratic author argues.

List of Criteria 6: The Critic of "On Ancient Medicine"

1.–6.: The same as on List 5.
   7. A techne is precise. It requires complete mastery of clearly stated basic principles from which the body of knowledge is derived.
   8. The paradigm of a techne is mathematics.

This conception of a techne$_1$, advocated by the critic and explicated in Lists 5 and 6, is precise knowledge that is clearly differentiated from ordinary experience. Because it is expressed in language reducible to a "postulate," it is accessible only to a few. It is knowledge that can resist *tuchē* and offer its possessor a strong measure of control over the portion of reality it studies. In turn, the Hippocratic authors resist this conception of techne, and in response offer a mode of knowledge limited in its expertise, imperfectly reliable, expressible in and therefore continuous with ordinary language, subject to the vagaries of *tuchē*, and *not* best modeled by either mathematics or a natural science derived from a single *hupothesis*. Later writers developed this conception into "medical empiricism," a school of thought often linked with skepticism.[53] "On Ancient Medicine," however, is not skeptical. Instead, what it offers is a techne$_2$, a fallibilistic or "stochastic" form of knowledge. To elaborate, I return briefly to "On Techne."

The occasional failures of medicine are explained by the author in various ways: Sometimes it is just bad luck (*atuchia:* 7). Sometimes (and this becomes an important point below) it is because "the sick cannot follow out the orders" issued by their physicians (7). And sometimes the disease is simply impossible to detect or cure (8). Medicine, in other words, has limits determined by the nature of its subject matter, and "if a man demand from a [techne] a power over what does not belong to the [techne] . . . his ignorance is more allied to madness than to lack of knowledge" (8).

52. Lloyd 1963, 111.
53. Frede 1985, xxii and xxiii.

This is why the physician is justified in refusing to treat desperate cases where the disease is too serious or has progressed beyond the possibility of cure.

In the following passage, the author gives examples of technai in which, unlike in medicine, failure is unacceptable. In so doing he suggests what it is about subject matter that makes for the different powers of the different technai: "And the [technai] that are worked in materials easy to shape aright, using in some cases wood, in others leather, in others—these form the great majority—paint, bronze, iron and similar substances—the articles wrought, I say, through these [technai] and with the substances are easily shaped aright" (12).

If in some technai the materials are "easy to shape aright" (*euepanorthōtoisi:* 12) and in other technai the materials are not, then (so the implicit argument would go) the standards used to evaluate the former should not be applied to the latter. The study of the human body is a prime example of the latter for three reasons. First, because the body is a living organism of great complexity, the source of many of its breakdowns lies hidden from observation. Since medicine is (according to this author) a strictly empirical affair, it is "limited only by the capacity of the sick to be examined" (11). These limits are determined by the specific structure of the body.

Second, the level of variety in individual human beings is high. This is due to both their physiological differences (e.g., some people have strong constitutions, others do not) as well as their widely divergent habits (see 11 and 12). Diseases run various and sometimes unpredictable courses in these many different bodies. Because of this the doctor, unlike the mathematician (who treats only of abstract and invariable objects), must exhibit "a sensitivity to the peculiar features of particular situations."[54] "The physician must know when the right moment (*kairos*) has come to act."[55] In other words, unlike a techne$_1$, which demands a universal command of its subject (see criterion 5 on List 5), medicine requires a flexibility in treating particulars.[56]

Finally, and for my purposes most interesting, because the body being treated is *human,* it is animated by intelligence and a "free will." Frequently, a patient "knows neither what he is suffering from, nor the cause thereof." As a result, he will often be "fearful of the future" and perhaps

54. Allen 1989, 5.
55. Edelstein 1967, 109.
56. It is precisely this kind of thinking that Detienne and Vernant call *mētis.*

be "wishful of treatment rather to enjoy immediate alleviation of his sick-ness than to recover his health" (7). In such a condition, a patient may well become obstinate and refuse to obey his doctor's orders.

In sum, the subject matter of medicine is neither an abstract formal ob-ject, such as number, nor a passive, malleable material, such as wood. Instead, it is a living, willful, extremely complex, and unpredictable human being. The power of medicine is therefore limited, and to expect otherwise is madness. As a result, it would a "blunder" to expect from medicine the success rate achieved by shipbuilding. If the shipbuilder fails, he is stripped of the title *technitēs*. A physician, by contrast, can fail, can even refuse to treat certain cases, and nonetheless be entitled to hang his shingle, for his is a techne$_2$, a stochastic techne. The following list of criteria explicates further.

List of Criteria 7: Techne$_2$

1. A techne$_2$ has a determinate but not a rigidly fixed or invariable subject matter. For example, the human body, like wood or number, is a unit of epistemic content distinguishable from other such units. Because it is complex, alive, and willful, however, it is not as fixed or invariable as the subject matters of other technai.
2. It effects a useful result, for example, health.
3. It is reliable, but not totally so. It offers "rules of thumb," rather than rigid rules.[57] It is stochastic, requires appropriate responses to particular occasions, and is compatible with failure.
4. It is precise, but does not measure up to the standard provided by mathematics.
5. Its end is distinct from its function.[58] The function of medicine is to do everything possible to save the patient; since saving the patient is its end, it is possible for medicine to succeed in exercising its function but fail to achieve its end.
6. It is certifiable and recognizable by the community, but not infallibly so. It is, for example, more difficult to distinguish a layman from a technical physician than to distinguish a layman from a professional shipbuilder.
7. Its language is ordinary, not technical. It can give a logos, but not one of unimpeachable clarity. It is not a theory derived from an originating "postulate."
8. It is teachable but not infallibly so.

57. This is a phrase I borrow from Fish 1990, 316. I cite it here to prepare for my discus-sion of rhetoric.
58. See Allen 1989, 6.

Consider (8): since the subject matter of medicine is not a fixed, invariable object but is instead the human body and its innumerable particularities, the content of its teaching, its logos, is not absolutely precise or governed by abstract rules. As a result, the physician not only must master the basic principles that govern the workings of the body in general, but also must develop a sensitivity to the particulars of any given case. Such sensitivity cannot be mechanically transmitted from teacher to student. This dimension of a medical education is thus a precarious affair.[59]

Furthermore, since the physician treats patients with whom he must discuss urgent problems, he should be able to use ordinary language effectively. He should, for example, know how to persuade a frightened patient that taking a painful medicine will ultimately be advantageous.[60] Because it requires the ability to respond appropriately to irremediably particularized situations, this sort of rhetorical effectiveness, like the "sensitivity" mentioned above, cannot be mechanically transmitted to the student by the teacher. There are no hard-and-fast rules on how to speak to patients, only rules of thumb. And the ability to follow these must be inculcated, refined, nurtured through a long apprenticeship wherein the student somehow absorbs the wisdom of the master physician. The teaching of medicine thus requires a sustained personal relationship between teacher and student. This is reflected, for example, by the Hippocratic Oath, in which the student pledges utter allegiance to his teacher.

In short, the teaching of a stochastic techne, a techne$_2$, is a messy, less determinate, more personally engaging affair than that of a techne$_1$.

In Plato's *Philebus* Socrates hints at a distinction between techne$_1$ and techne$_2$. He divides the technai into those that "have less precision in their works, and those which, like building, have more" (56c). The former he calls "stochastic" (55e) and, in a manner similar to the Hippocratic author, distinguishes from the latter on the basis of their being less mathematical, that is, less precise. Aristotle too makes this distinction. It is not, however, until Alexander of Aphrodisias that the distinction becomes explicitly codified. Consider his commentary on Aristotle's *Topics*, whose lines 101b5–8, cited below, compare dialectic to rhetoric and medicine:

> We shall possess the method completely when we are in a position similar to that in which we are with regard to rhetoric and medicine and other such faculties; that is to say, when we carry out our pur-

59. See Cole 1991, 86–87, for these points. See also Frede 1985, xxvi, 4, and 25, for a discussion of *autopsia* in Galen.
60. Plato's *Gorgias* claims he can do this better than his brother the doctor: *Gorgias* 456b.

pose with every available means. For neither will the rhetorician seek to persuade nor the physician to heal by every expedient; but if he omits none of the available means, we shall say that he possesses the science (*epistēmē*) in an adequate degree.

Alexander comments thus:

> For the function (*ergon*) of the physician is to use all the possible means of saving, but it is not saving. For if someone were to say that this is the function of the physician, then he who is not a physician would be a physician, for often those who are not physicians save those who are ill, having with good fortune applied something to them. And it is also possible that physicians may fail to save. (32.27–33.4)[61]

To paraphrase: in a techne$_1$, end is identical to function; in a techne$_2$, it is not. The function of rhetoric is to use all the available means of persuasion. It is not to persuade, for if it were, then failure to do so would disqualify even a good orator from having a techne. Since it is often the case that two well-trained orators square off against each other and one fails, failure must be compatible with possession of the rhetorical techne. And this is possible only if function is differentiated from end.

Medicine is analogous. Its function is not to save patients but to use all the available means for doing so. Laypeople frequently effect, in a haphazard fashion, a cure and thereby achieve the end at which the physicians aim. This does not make them physicians. Similarly, the physician often fails to save. This does not disqualify him as a *technitēs*, since he is defined only as one who exercises his function correctly. Once again, such compatibility with failure would not be tolerated in a techne$_1$.

Alexander officially labels this more flexible and generous notion a "stochastic techne." After first stating that "the same logos" that had described medicine applies to rhetoric and dialectic (33.6–7), he goes on to speak generally about the different kinds of techne.

> For in these kinds of technai [techne$_2$] judgment (*krisis*) does not emerge on the basis of the ends achieved, as it does in building and

61. The translation of Aristotle is by E. S. Forster (Cambridge, Mass.: Harvard University Press, Loeb Classical Library, 1976). The translation of Alexander of Aphrodisias is my own; for the Greek, see Alexandri Aphrodisiensis, *In Aristotelis Topicorum*, ed. M. Wallies (Berlin: Reimer, 1891).

weaving and the rest of the productive technai. In these production (*energeia*) occurs in all cases according to the same well-defined and fixed methods, and it is not possible for their result to come about by chance. . . .

By contrast, in stochastic technai things do not entirely come about according to what the techne is for the sake of. And the cause of this is that they come about by chance and the methods through which the things coming about from these technai actually come about are not well defined. Therefore, that which comes about from these kind of technai is not the end of the technai, as is the case in those technai which come to be through well-defined methods and which, apart from these methods, would not exist. For as I said, in this type of techne [techne$_1$] the function is the end and the sign that something has happened according to techne. (33.10–23)

This passage, inspired of course by Aristotle, offers a full-blown distinction between techne$_1$ and techne$_2$.[62] In the former "the procedures through which, and only through which, their aims are achieved are themselves determined; if the procedures are carried out correctly the end aimed at must result."[63] There is no interference from chance. By contrast, the material of the stochastic techne$_2$ is not as fixed and determinate, and as a result, rigid procedures invariably attaining correct results cannot be established. Some measure of chance may interfere with the workings of a stochastic techne, and proper exercise of its function is compatible with failure.[64]

I close this section with a speculation about the authorship of "On Techne" and an indication of how the discussion it has provoked figures in later chapters of this book. The affinity between the medicine described in "On Techne" and rhetoric is manifest. The Hippocratic treatise discusses the techne question in general terms and itself operates on a highly rhetorical level. As a result, some scholars have concluded that it was not written by a physician at all, but by a Sophist. Gomperz has identified the author as a student of Protagoras.[65] Even without plunging into a detailed philological argument to prove (or disprove) such a claim, it is illuminating at least to consider it.

62. Compare Aristotle *Rhetoric* 1.1.2 and 1.2.12.
63. Allen 1989, 6.
64. See Edelstein 1967, 107.
65. Gomperz 1910, 72. See also Edelstein 1967, 101.

Assume the author of "On Techne" was in fact a Sophist. He has written a highly rhetorical work in which he has created a hypothetical critic who holds to a very rigorous conception of techne. He does so precisely in order to take this critic, and his conception of techne, to task. By overcoming the challenge presented to him by his critic, the author can carve out an "epistemic space" into which he can fit medicine, which, as a techne$_2$, he admits cannot achieve the level of rigor demanded by a techne$_1$. In a subsequent section, I show that Isocrates' epistemic conception of rhetoric is quite similar to such a techne$_2$. Therefore, if the author of "On Techne" is a Sophist, then medicine functions as a placeholder for his own subject in this treatise. In other words, many of the same arguments made about medicine can be usefully applied to rhetoric as well.

Why would a Sophist substitute medicine for rhetoric? Precisely because, as Prometheus had said, medicine is "greatest." Unlike the newly emergent and deeply controversial subject of the Sophists, the physician had long been acknowledged as *dēmiourgos*. A debate may have been raging concerning the nature of medicine as a science, but the sad fact of human sickness remained constant, and those who were ill were eager to become "patients." If the stochastic character of medicine could be successfully defended, it would become easier for the sophistic author to defend his own subject of rhetoric, which was epistemically isomorphic with medicine.

Nothing in this chapter hinges on these speculations concerning the author of "On Techne" and his putative strategy for defending rhetoric. Instead, I have elaborated Gomperz's view only in order to offer a transition to my discussion of the rhetorical techne (which in turn broaches some of the basic issues awaiting Plato). Before turning to the Sophists, however, I must take a historical step backward. In the next section I briefly discuss one passage from Sophocles' *Antigone,* the famous "ode to human being" (written around 441 B.C.E.; the Hippocratic writings are probably later). It continues the process that begins with the Hippocratic writings, namely, complicating the conception of techne.

The Hippocratic authors acknowledge their techne is not typical. Their subject matter is alive and, even worse, equipped with an unpredictable and freely operating human will. They realize that as a result their techne cannot achieve, and should not aim for, the sort of clarity, precision, and reliability achieved by other technai. Their subject cannot fairly be measured by the rigor of mathematics, nor should the physician expect to attain the success rate of the shipbuilder. In short, when the human body is the object of study, the expectations and the discussion of the techne have to be compromised, and the conception of techne has to be bifurcated.

Sophocles complicates matters even further. In a manner reminiscent of Solon's "Prayer to the Muses," he adopts an ethical or practical, a reflexive or uniquely human point of view, from which techne is seen as problematic and potentially quite delusory. As does Solon, the tragedian makes possible the asking of the sorts of questions soon to inform the Platonic project: What sort of knowledge can reasonably be expected to govern human activity? What is "moral knowledge"? Can there be a techne whose subject matter is human arete?

Sophocles' *Antigone*

In this section I analyze a single choral ode found in Sophocles' *Antigone*. After having witnessed Creon interrogate the hapless guard who had been responsible for the corpse of Polyneices, the chorus sings of the "wonders" of being human:

> There are many *deinon* things, but not one of them is more *deinon* than the human being. This thing crosses the gray sea in the winter storm-wind, making its path along the troughs of the swelling waves. And the loftiest of goddesses, Earth, deathless and unwearied, it wears away, turning up the soil with the offspring of horses, as the ploughs go back and forth from year to year.
>
> And the race of light-headed birds, and the tribes of savage beasts, and the sea-dwelling brood of the deep, he snares with the meshes of his twisted net and leads captive, cunning man. He masters with his arts [*mechanai*] the beasts of the open air, walkers on hills. The horse with his shaggy mane he tames, yoking him about the neck, and the tireless mountain bull.
>
> Speech, too, and thought (*phronēma*) swift as the wind, and the temper (*orgas*) that builds cities, he has taught himself; and how to escape the arrows of the frost that makes hard lodging under a clear sky, and the arrows of the rain. He has a resource for everything; without resource he comes to nothing in the future. Only against death can he procure no escape; but he has devised escapes from hopeless diseases.

Clever beyond hope is the inventive [techne] he possesses. It brings him now to ill, now to good. When he fulfills the laws of the land and the oath-sworn justice of the gods, he is a man of lofty city; citiless the person who lives with what is not noble in his rash daring. May he never share my hearth, may he never think as I do, the one who does these things. (332–75)[66]

As in Prometheus's catalogue of his technical gifts to humanity, the appearance of "techne" (366) in a summary line suggests the pervading theme of the passage: the role technical knowledge plays in human life.

The following technai, in paraphrase, are mentioned by the chorus: sailing, agriculture, hunting (of birds, land animals, fish), horsemanship, speech, thought, "city-building," housebuilding, and medicine. Several of these are by now familiar: housebuilding dates back to the primitive meaning of "techne"; shipbuilding, back to Homer; and fishing, farming, and medicine were mentioned by Solon. It is not clear what "the temper that builds cities" means. This does not refer to "city planning" or architecture; instead it seems to point to the spiritual precondition of social life. As such, it has no overtly tangible product. The same is true of speech and thought. Both, like Prometheus's mention of "Letters," are intellectual activities whose inclusion on this list shows how extensively the meaning of the word has broadened by the fifth century.

What receives the most emphasis in this passage is the human ability, described as *deinon* (a notoriously ambiguous word meaning both "wonderful" and "terrible"), to use techne to master the world in which we live. The chorus's language expresses an adversarial, at times almost a violent, relationship to nature. A man can make a path across the stormy and forbidding sea. He can "wear away" (*apotruetai:* 339) the great goddess earth, "snare" (*agrei:* 343) birds and fish, "master" (*kratei:* 348) the animals, "yoke" and thereby bring under his power (*hupaxemen:* 351) the wild horse, "escape" (*pheugein:* 357) the rain by building houses, and devise "escapes" (*phugas:* 363) from hopeless disease.

This passage seems to celebrate the human, technical power to control nature. Indeed, nothing is "more *deinon*" than a human being who can perform these feats. But as many commentators have noted, Sophocles seriously qualifies, even undercuts, this appearance of celebration in several ways. Consider, for example, his frequent use of the "alpha privative" (a negative prefix in Greek). The earth is described as "deathless" (*aphthiton:*

66. I follow the translation by Nussbaum (1986, 72–73), only substituting "techne" for "craft."

339) and "unwearied" (*akamatan:* 339), the mountain bull is "tireless" (*akmēta:* 352), and diseases are "hopeless" (*amachanōn* [or "irresistible"]: 363). In each word, the alpha privative stands near a verb that expresses a human intention or aspiration almost directly antithetical to the negative adjective. The earth is "unwearied," yet the farmers *wear* it away. The mountain bull is "tireless," but can be made tired by being yoked to work in service of man. In the sharpest contrast, diseases are "irresistible," but medicine is somehow able to resist them by providing an escape.

This is puzzling. Are diseases irresistible or not? If they are, then presumably medicine is powerless to resist them. If the earth truly cannot be tired out, then farmers cannot wear it away. These peculiar juxtapositions culminate at 360, where, in an almost Heraclitean fashion, the polar opposites "[having] a resource for everything" and "without resource" (*pantoporos aporos*) stand next to each other. Are human beings truly resourceful in facing future contingencies? If so, there would be reason to celebrate our riches. But if not—and the sureness of death would seem to suggest not—then we are at once *pantoporos aporos* and possessed of a resourcefulness that is qualified, conditioned, even mocked by the certainty of our failures. On this reading we are ambiguously *deinon:* our technical abilities are wonderful to behold, but since the earth is tireless and diseases are irresistible, they are also profoundly limited. The ode does not celebrate techne. Instead, like Solon's poem, it warns against infatuation with our instruments of power.

As Nussbaum has argued, this reading of the ode is compatible with the rest of the *Antigone*. Creon, for example, conceives of himself as a pilot who can knowledgeably guide the ship of state through the "great seastorm" of civil strife plaguing Thebes.[67] He, like Oedipus in the play to be written some twenty years later, is confident about his ability to understand and manage the vicissitudes of his world. His confidence, which pushes him to the disastrous act of eliminating Antigone, is terribly ill conceived. Creon thinks he knows, believes he is in control of, his city's destiny, when he is not. Only at the end of the play does he realize this: "O crimes of my wicked heart, harshness bringing death. You see the killer, you see the kin he killed. My planning was all unblest" (1261–65). When the chorus says to him, "You have learned justice (*dikēn idein*), though it comes too late," he agrees: "Yes, I have learned (*mathōn*) in sorrow" (1270–72).

The "ode to human being" presages this final, tragic recognition. As

67. Nussbaum 1986, 74.

such, it stands in the tradition, established by Solon, of the protreptic warning. Nussbaum puts it thus: "[T]he statement of human triumphs through reason turns out to be also a compressed document of reason's limitations, transgressions and conflict."[68] Or, as Segal has it, "Sophocles sees in reason and technical control not simply a source of human freedom, as Aeschylus did, but also a potential source of human bondage."[69]

The final lines of the passage state this theme in sharp and provocative terms. "Clever beyond hope" (*sophon . . . huper elpida*) is the techne man possesses. What does this mean? How can something's cleverness, its intellectual merit, be "beyond hope"? Perhaps *elpis* should be translated as "expectation." This would mean that human techne is surprising. It is that. But more to the point is that its effects are unpredictable, and on this note the chorus closes: techne can bring its possessor either to ill (*kakon*) or to good (*esthlon*: 367). In other words, in and of itself it is neither. Only the application of techne, how it is *used,* determines its value. In itself it is "value-neutral." Clever, yes; but in its value-neutrality, *deinon* too.

The earth will not be wearied by the plow, the bull ultimately cannot be yoked, diseases are irresistible, for against death there is no escape. If technical mastery is limited in this manner, what then determines a successful outcome? Again, the answer is Solonic: following the laws of the land and those pertaining to *dikē.* When a man does both, he is "of lofty city." If he does neither, he is "citiless." In other words, the space between just and unjust, right and wrong, is the final arena in which a techne's value is determined.

By juxtaposing the technical and the ethical realms, by holding them near one another, the *Antigone* supplies the ingredients with which to ask a fundamental question: What is the relationship between techne and human happiness? Can there be a techne to teach us to live a good life and use our technical instruments for good ends? Techne is the clear instance of knowledge that is useful, widely recognized, and (within limits) powerful. But can such knowledge look inward, toward the *technitēs* himself? Can it become morally reflexive? Can a techne of arete be attained? It seems not: techne looks outward, toward regions it can master, and in this sense is value-neutral. Does this imply there is no knowledge of justice and the correct way of acting? Only if techne is the sole model of knowledge.

68. Nussbaum 1986, 65.
69. Segal 1986, 154.

And whether this is the case remains to be seen. The *Antigone* provokes the question, Can there be knowledge of arete? If so, what sort of knowledge would it be?

The Hippocratic authors open the possibility of a techne$_2$, a stochastic techne. They do so in order to accommodate their subject matter, namely, the living human body. Medicine cannot achieve the high level of precision or rate of success expected of a techne$_1$. The introduction of a techne$_2$ self-consciously treats the question, How can knowledge take up an atypical, that is, a human, object? How can it sustain failure, preserve indeterminacy, be subject to chance, and yet be knowledge? The knowledge proposed by the physicians is flexible, "empirical," requires sensitivity to the particular "occasion" (the *kairos*), and thus rejects both mathematics and natural science as paradigms.

If these are epistemological "complications," generated by the Hippocratic concern for welfare of the human body, the "ode to human being" adds an ethical dimension to the controversy. It provokes the question, If the object of study is not merely the human body but the human soul in its life as a potentially valuable member of a polis, then what sort of moral knowledge is forthcoming? A techne$_1$, a techne$_2$, or some other form of knowledge altogether?

Questions such as these were no doubt debated during the late fifth and early fourth centuries, and they were encapsulated by asking, Can arete be taught? Since techne is the paradigmatic form of teachable knowledge, this question implies the primary issue of this book: is there a techne of arete? Consider, for example, the following speech by Hecuba in the play of that name by Euripides (probably written in 424):

> But how strange (*deinon*) it seems:
> Even worthless ground, given a gentle push from heaven, will harvest well, while fertile soil, starved of what it needs, bears badly. But human nature never seems to change; evil stays itself, evil to the end, and goodness good, tis nature uncorrupted by any shock or blow, always the same, enduring excellence.
> Is it in our blood or something we acquire? But goodness can be taught, and any man who knows what goodness is knows evil too, because he judges from the good. But all this is the rambling nothing of despair. (592–603)[70]

70. I follow Arrowsmith in his translation of *Hecuba* for the University of Chicago series.

The passage begins with *deinon*. There is something terribly ambiguous about being good or evil. Hecuba seems to think that unlike the growth of crops in the field, which finally are dependent on the chance occurrence of rain and sun (*tuchousa:* 593; *tuchein:* 594), the goodness of human beings can reliably be molded. She is not sure why this is the case. Is it nature or nurture? she asks. And then she answers her own question: men become *esthlon* (597, 601) or excellent (*chrēstos:* 598) through learning. Her confidence in this notion may well be undermined by the end of the play, even by the end of the passage, but these lines suggest one view concerning the teaching of arete current at this time.

Adrastus in Euripides' *Suppliant Women* speaks directly to this issue: "Virtue is teachable" (*euandria didaktos:* 913–14), he boldly declares. Theseus, in the *Hippolytus*, is far less sanguine and sounds Solonic/Sophoclean when he says, "Oh, human beings who err with such great futility; why have you taught thousands of technai and invented and devised everything, but you do not know nor have you hunted out a single way to teach wisdom (*phronein*) to those who lack intelligence (*nous*)" (916–920). Hippolytus replies, "You have uttered a *deinon sophistēn*."

Consider also the following lines by Democritus (written probably close to the time of the *Hecuba*): "Good things come to us from the very same things by which we can partake in bad things. Or we can remain outside of the bad things. For example, deep water is useful for many purposes, but on the other hand, it's bad. For there is the risk of drowning. But a technique (*mēchanē*) has been devised: swimming instruction."[71]

This too bespeaks some optimism. Just as knowing how to swim can guide us through deep waters, so too knowing how to live seemingly can guide us through our lives.[72]

The *Dissoi Logoi*, probably published around 400, summarizes both sides of the question. Can excellence be taught? No. If it could, "there would have been acknowledged teachers of it," and there are not. The excellent would have transmitted excellence to their friends, and they have not. Even if there are men who claim to teach arete and wisdom—the "Sophists"—the students who attend their classes "derived no benefit from them." Furthermore, students who have never once taken a course in excellence seem to turn out fine. (This is parallel to an argument raised against the Hippocratic physician: those who are ill often recover without the benefit of medicine, whereas those who are treated frequently die.)

---

71. My translation of DK 68b15.
72. Compare Thucydides 1.71.3, where he compares political activity to techne.

The author also offers several reasons why excellence can be taught. The Sophists do in fact teach it. So too did Anaxagoras and Pythagoras. Even if some men succeed in attaining excellence without attending the classes of the Sophists, this does not invalidate the claim that such knowledge is teachable. After all, some people fail to learn their "letters" (*ta grammata*), but no one would say letters are unteachable. Also, people learn how to speak, not from studying with a teacher, but simply by being raised in a linguistic community. Presumably, learning excellence is similarly attainable.[73]

What even this scant review of a few sources reveals is that the notion of arete being teachable and of reliable knowledge guiding human life was seriously considered by a variety of writers during the Athenian "enlightenment."[74] Sophocles' "ode to human being," in echoing Solonic themes, is perhaps a reactionary, or at least cautionary, warning against too quickly and unreflectively accepting the positive claims for knowledge and techne. (Aristophanes is Sophocles' comrade on this score at least.)[75] But there were those who did indeed believe that, since it is teachable, arete could become the subject matter of a techne. And these were the "Sophists."

The Rhetorical Techne of the Sophists

The Rhetorical Handbook

Speaking (ironically) to Anytus in the *Meno*, Socrates uses the techne analogy to identify those who might qualify as "teachers of arete." If we wanted Meno to become a good physician, he says, we would send him to study with physicians. They, after all, are professionals; they "profess" (*antipoioumenous:* 90d2) a techne and correspondingly charge a fee. So too with professional flautists; they "promise" to teach their techne and therefore also feel justified in charging tuition. Meno wishes to have the "wisdom and arete by which men manage well their houses and cities." To whom, then, should we send him? According to the analogy, he should go to those who profess to teach arete, who charge a fee and are available to any Greek who wants to learn. These men are the Sophists (90c–91b).

"Sophist" covers a wide variety of professional teachers who first ap-

---

73. Sprague 1972, 289–90.
74. See Kübe 1969, 48–51, and Shorey 1909 for further discussion of this issue.
75. I think in particular of the *Clouds*.

peared in the fifth century. For reasons to become apparent, I concentrate on those whose explicit, that is, written, claim was to teach rhetoric. Some of these writings literally advertised *the techne of rhetoric:* they were "textbooks," "handbooks" or "manuals" of instruction with the title "Techne" (later to be translated by Latin authors as *Ars.*) According to Quintilian, "the earliest writers of arts (*artium scriptores*) were the Sicilians, Corax and Tisias. They were followed by a man from the same island, named Gorgias of Leontini, said to have been a pupil of Empedocles" (3.1.8).

In this section, I briefly examine the structure of one such "Techne," that by Anaximenes of Lampsacus. More to the point, however, I consider in some detail the philosophical implications of using "techne" to title a work of rhetoric. Far from being a small matter of a conventional label, the consequences are significant and directly relate to the question sparked by the *Meno* passage cited above: Is there a techne whose subject matter is arete? If so, who possesses it, and how can we find them?

Corax and Tisias lived in fifth-century Sicily and became prominent after the death of the tyrant Hiero. Scholars have suggested that rhetoric as a distinct discipline began to flourish during this period precisely because tyranny was giving way to democracy. Whether or not this actually was the historical cause, it is obvious that democracy and rhetoric are closely related. If power is gained through the approval of citizens, rather than through force, then the ability to win votes by *persuasion* becomes a tremendous political asset. According to one story, "Corax by his rhetorical art was able to sway the new assembly and direct the democratic state. This art he formulated in rules, and undertook to teach for a fee."[76]

According to Quintilian, Corax published these rules in a handbook of rhetorical instruction. Little is known about the actual content of this work except that its "principal part . . . is the celebrated doctrine of *eikos* or argument from probabilities."[77] Despite such ignorance, it is still useful to ask why Corax, and then his many descendants, titled their manuals "Techne." One reason, at least, is that these fledgling rhetoricians were seeking social as well as epistemic legitimation. As argued previously, "techne" connotes a respected mode of knowledge that can be recognized by its useful results, and confers upon its possessor the status of an authority in his field. The shipbuilder, for example, stands out clearly in his com-

---

76. Hinks 1940, 62. Cole (1991) offers a contrasting view. Various portions of this section are elaborated in Roochnik 1994b.

77. Hinks 1940, 63.

munity as a *technitēs*. People know whom to "invite" when they want a ship built. Because of his expertise, and "certified" by his past productions, the shipbuilder has hung a "shingle" and is ready to work. His clients can reasonably expect a successful outcome, and so he is justified in charging a fee.

The early rhetoricians sought just this sort of validation, for theirs was a new and, at least to those who held traditional seats of power, controversial subject. As Cahn puts it, the title "of *technē* confers upon a discipline a certain professional quality, an honorific degree of knowledge, and a superior rank in the scale of knowledge as a whole. Its opposite is . . . pseudo-art and sham knowledge."[78]

But what exactly is rhetoric? In the broadest sense, it is the ability, perhaps the techne, of speaking well in a public, political, or practical arena. Whether it is specifically deliberative, forensic, or epideictic, rhetoric is able to make good use of language, of logos, which aims to achieve some practical purpose for a specific audience. To clarify this extremely broad description, consider the following two discussions of logos, the first by Aristotle, the second by Isocrates.

> For nature, as we declare, does nothing without purpose. And human being alone of the animals possesses logos. The mere voice, it is true, can indicate pain and pleasure, and therefore it is possessed by other animals as well . . . but logos is for the indication of what is advantageous and what is harmful, and therefore also of what is right and wrong. For it is the unique property of human beings in distinction to the other animals that they alone have perception of good and bad and right and wrong and other such things, and it is partnership in these things that makes a household and a polis. (*Politics* 1253a)

> For in the other powers . . . we are in no respect superior to other living creatures; nay, we are inferior to many in swiftness and in strength and in other resources; but, because there has been implanted in us the power to persuade each other and to make clear to each other whatever we desire, not only have we escaped the life of wild beasts, but we have come together and founded cities and laws and invented technai; and, generally speaking, there is no institu-

78. Cahn 1993, 70. For *atechnia*, see Aristotle *Nicomachean Ethics* 1140a20 and Quintilian 2.15.2, 2.20.2, 2.23.

tion devised by man which the power of speech has not helped us to
establish. For this it is which has laid down laws concerning things
just and unjust, and things honourable and base; and if it were not
for the ordinances we should not be able to live with one another.
By speech we refute the wicked and praise the good. By speech we
educate the ignorant and inform the wise. We regard the ability to
speak properly as the best sign of intelligence, and truthful legal,
and just speech is the reflection of a good and trustworthy soul. . . .
If I must sum up on this subject, we shall find that nothing done
with intelligence is done without speech, but speech is the marshall
of all actions and of thought and those must use it who have the
greatest wisdom. (*Antidosis* 254)[79]

Both statements describe logos as virtually coextensive with being human. Aristotle puts this point in characteristically teleological terms. What
makes human beings unique among the animals is the ability not only to
indicate what hurts or feels good by means of the voice but to discuss what
is right and wrong. This ability to evaluate and to discuss such evaluations
makes a polis possible. Logos, according to Aristotle, is thus the essential
constituent, as well as the medium, of political life.

Isocrates begins by noting the human ability to persuade, and closes by
taking Aristotle's point even further. For him, all "cultural" achievements
are permeated by logos, and everything intelligent is "logical." Logos, specifically the attempt to persuade about values, is not only the medium of
political life, it is the lifeblood of all human institutions; it saturates every
uniquely human action. In short, logos is for Isocrates coextensive with the
moral realm, the human world of value, meaning, and well-being.

If logos is as Aristotle and Isocrates describe, then to assert a techne of
rhetoric, as the title of the handbooks implicitly did, is to make, however
unreflectively, a much larger claim, namely, to have a moral techne.[80] The
artium scriptores thus seem to have overcome Solon's and Sophocles' wor-
ries about the scope of techne. They are confident they understand the
deinon human animal who speaks. These rhetoricians assert the right to
hang up a shingle and ask for a fee from those who wish to learn how to
become excellent speakers, indeed excellent men.

According to Kennedy, written "instruction in rhetoric in the fifth cen-

79. The translation is from Kennedy 1963, 9.
80. Note that Quintilian describes rhetoric as a "practical art" (2.18.5).

tury was given in two rather different ways."[81] The first was via a collection of "commonplaces," examples of basic argument patterns that could be memorized and then used as needed. Gorgias's "Defense of Palamedes" was (perhaps) such a work. It presents a series of arguments defending Palamedes against the charge of murder. None, however, are case specific. Consider one example: "I wish next to address the accuser. . . . Do you accuse me, knowing accurately what you say, or imagining it? If it is with knowledge, you know either from seeing or participating or learning from someone. If then you saw, tell these judges the place, the time, when and where, how you saw."[82]

Clearly, such an "argument" is generic and could be used in any trial in which the outcome is uncertain (a *status coniecturalis*). Therefore, if the student memorizes the "Palamedes," he can later extract its various arguments when occasion demands. As Cole suggests, the "Palamedes" is a "practice and demonstration" text that was "designed to show off the master's skill to admiring amateurs as well as illustrate its workings to prospective professionals."[83]

Aristotle is contemptuous of this kind of written collection:

> He [Gorgias] . . . assigned rhetorical discourse to be learned by heart. . . . It was presumed for the most part that these discourses included the arguments on both sides of the issue. As a result, the teaching was quick, but unsystematic. The teachers thought they could educate by imparting not techne, but the products of techne, just as if someone were to claim to furnish knowledge for the prevention of sore feet and then did not teach shoemaking nor how suitable shoes could be procured, but offered many varieties of all sorts of foot gear. (*Sophistical Refutations* 1836b)

According to this account, the teacher would mechanically impart the "commonplaces or specimens of oratory," the "building blocks from which a speech could be constructed," and the student could then choose from the list as future occasions demanded.[84] But such instruction is like having a collection of shoes. Since different shoes will be useful on different occasions, a large collection is of some value. But if the use of the shoes

81. Kennedy 1963, 52.
82. The translation is from Sprague 1972, 59.
83. Cole 1991, 75.
84. Kennedy 1963, 52. The translation of the *Sophistical Refutations* is also on this page.

is not guided by knowledge, and if the possessor of the shoes does not know how to make new ones, then the value of such a collection is severely limited. The commonplaces that were collected and transmitted mechanically are treated by Aristotle with contempt, for they do not represent the serious achievement of real knowledge.

The second method of (written) rhetorical instruction consisted of "[a]n exposition of precepts, not a collection of examples. . . . When the ancient sources speak of techne or *ars* they always mean theoretical instruction and usually a written theoretical exposition or handbook, never collections of commonplaces."[85]

What were these theoretical expositions of rhetorical precepts? Führmann, who has collected and analyzed numerous examples of ancient "Technai" is helpful here. He begins with Anaximenes of Lampsachos, author of *Techne Rhetorikē* (which has come down under the erroneous title, *Rhetorica ad Alexandrum* and was wrongly attributed to Aristotle), and ends with such Roman works as Varro's *On Agriculture*. These "Technai/Artes," Führmann shows, share a basic method and self-conception. Anaximenes' work, even if uninspired in content, is nevertheless illuminating, for as an early, perhaps the earliest, surviving "Techne," it exemplifies "better than anything else the tradition of sophistic rhetoric."[86]

The *Techne Rhetorikē* begins by dividing its subject matter, political speeches, into three kinds: the "parliamentary" (*demegorikon*), the "ceremonial" (*epideiktikon*), and the "forensic" (*dikanikon*). The author then further subdivides these into species: exhortation, dissuasion, eulogy, vituperation, accusation, defense, and investigation (1421b8–12).[87] His passion for division continues, as he divides the speeches themselves into their parts: prooimium (1436a), exposition (1438a), proof (1438b), and epilogue (or appeal to feeling: 1439b).

When the basic subject matter has been thoroughly analyzed into its elements, the author states that he will take up each of these parts and "enumerate" their "qualities" (*dunameis*), "uses," and "arrangement" (1421b17). The result is a series of definitions: for example, "exhortation is an attempt to urge people to some line of speech or action." These, in turn, are refined even further. The orator who is exhorting, to continue the example, must show that "the courses to which he exhorts are just" (1421b24–25). There then follows a definition of justice: "the unwritten

85. Kennedy 1963, 75. Cole (1991, 168) disagrees.
86. Kennedy 1963, 115. See also 115–23.
87. The text of the *Rhetorica ad Alexandrum,* treated as an Aristotelian work, is from the Loeb Classical Library.

custom of the whole or the greatest part of mankind, distinguishing honourable actions from base ones" (1421b37–38). And then comes a list of
honorable actions.

Such detailed information, the author believes, results in set of *rules*
providing specific advice to the prospective orator. For example, he asserts
there are seven "topics" about which political speeches are made. One is
alliances with other states (1423a25): "It is necessary (*anangkaion*) to secure allies on occasions when people by themselves are weak or when a
war is expected, or to make an alliance with one nation because it is
thought that this will deter another nation from war. These and a number
of additional similar reasons are the grounds for making allies; and when
one wishes to support the formation of an alliance *one must* (*dei*) show
that the situation is of this nature" (1424b29–36).

The details of Anaximenes' system matter not at all to the argument of
this chapter. What does matter is the general character of this work, and
this is conceptual division (*diaeresis*) issuing in rule-governed synthesis.
The *Techne Rhetorikē* systematically analyzes its subject, public speeches,
into its parts, defines these parts, and then orders them hierarchically. The
presupposition guiding this project is that such a thorough grasp of the
structure of logos will yield both theoretical and practical results. Not only
will the student understand the parts of logos, but he will learn how to
produce effectively his own speeches in any given political or practical
situation. Mastery of these classifications and subdivision, of this "kind of
logical and rhetorical atomism . . . would be what provided the greatest
flexibility and variety when it came to generating actual speeches through
a process of recombination."[88] There would be a set of rules (expressed by
dei and *anangkaion*) by which the world of logos could be restructured to
meet the exigencies of a particular situation.

Führmann explicates the methodology shared by a wide variety of ancient "Technai." These books attempt to delineate a comprehensive "view
over the entirety of a discipline." The "organizational and presentational
forms" they employ to accomplish this hinge on conceptual division, "the
motive power of system building." *Diaeresis* produces a "conceptual pyra-
mid" that demarcates the relationships of super- and subordination that
obtain between the various parts of the system. Grasping the system, therefore, implies mastery of the entirety of the subject matter.[89]

A "Techne" whose goal is this type of precise conceptual clarification

88. Cole 1991, 85.
89. Führmann 1960, 7.

presupposes a specific sort of subject matter. Minimally, it must be determinate, that is, have clear and distinct boundaries. This, of course, has been a requirement of a techne since its earliest usage. But in the case of a systematic "handbook," or "Techne," not only must the subject matter be determinate, it must also be amenable to analysis; it must be able to be broken down into constituent elements, which in turn can be synthesized into meaningful wholes without distortion of the original subject matter. One paradigm of this sort of subject matter, already mentioned by Prometheus and soon to play a crucial role for Isocrates, is *ta grammata*, the mastery of which is "orthography," or correct spelling.[90]

The alphabet represents a determinate subject matter each of whose constituent parts can stand as a discrete, intelligible individual. The alphabet can thus be analyzed, and then its parts synthesized; that is, words can be correctly spelled, according to the strict rules of orthography. As a model of a techne, then, orthography bespeaks total mastery of its subject matter, the ready ability to discriminate between a successful and an unsuccessful outcome, and ease of teaching. Indeed, teaching correct spelling is a mechanical process, learned virtually by all, in which failure is typically attributed to the student rather than to the teacher or to the difficulty of the subject. Orthography thus illustrates the criteria required by a systematic techne.

List of Criteria 8: The "Systematic Handbook"

1. The techne must have a determinate subject matter.
2. It aims to effect a useful result; in the case of rhetoric, successful public speech making.
3. Its subject matter, or content, is a complex conceptual whole that can be analyzed into discrete parts, the recombination of which is clearly delineated by a set of rules.
4. The recombination of its parts does not distort the original whole.
5. It achieves maximal precision. Its paradigm is orthography.
6. Possession of this techne yields complete mastery of the subject matter.
7. It is mechanically teachable.

This rigorous conception of "Techne" develops further the notion of a "techne₁" held by the critic found in the Hippocratic writings. It is also

90. And, of course, the letters are an important metaphor for Plato as well. See, for example, *Philebus* 17b and *Theaetetus*.

clear that because arithmetic shares many of the same features, it could easily substitute for orthography.

Like orthography, Anaximenes' rhetorical techne breaks down logos into parts and then allows the student/reader to reconstitute them into well-formulated wholes, that is, successful orations. Because of the close connection between logos and the moral realm, Anaximenes' "Techne" thus implies the possibility of an orthography of morality. A problem, however, lurks, and it is that raised by Sophocles' "ode to human being": if techne is value-neutral, if it can be used for good or ill, indeed if it needs to be *used* before it actually attains value, then how can there be a techne whose subject matter is value itself? Anaximenes, who is intent on churning out his system, does not pause to consider this question. But Plato will. Indeed, he will become obsessed with this question, and his being so will trigger a fundamental philosophical question of his dialogues, namely, is there a techne of "use"?

Gorgias

As the above citation from Aristotle's *Sophistical Refutations* indicates, Gorgias himself did not write a systematic "Techne" like Anaximenes'. Nevertheless, he did (apparently) write a "techne" of some sort.[91] While it is not possible to be specific, his *Encomium of Helen* suggests clues to what a Gorgian conception of a rhetorical techne would be.

Gorgias defends Helen by listing all the possible reasons why she went to Troy and then systematically showing that she can be exonerated on all counts. One explanation is that she was persuaded by Paris. But "if it was speech (logos) which persuaded her and deceived her heart, not even to this is it difficult to make an answer and to banish blame as follows. Speech is a powerful lord" (8).[92] For example, Gorgias continues, logos in the form of poetry (whose only unique characteristic is meter) is capable of having an enormous, even irresistible, impact on people. It can create "fearful shuddering and tearful pity and grievous longing" (9). Logos, then, is like magic, capable of insinuating itself into the human heart and then working its will from afar (see 10).

Note that when Gorgias compares logos to magic, he calls the latter a

91. Kennedy (1963, 62) disagrees.
92. I follow the translation in Sprague 1972. References to the *Encomium to Helen* are by section number.

techne (10). De Romilly makes this comparison central to her interpretation: "Gorgias' magic is technical. He wants to emulate the power of the
magician by a scientific analysis of language and of its influence. He is the
theoretician of the magic spell of words." She goes on: "Gorgias, while
emulating the magician, had a completely different approach. He knew
well enough that, with all the pride of a fifth-century man, he was deliberately shifting magic into something rational. And it should be noticed that
even his simile does not hold to the irrational nature of magic. He speaks
of magic as a techne."[93]

For de Romilly, then, Gorgias conceives of a techne of rhetoric (whether
or not he wrote a "Techne"), a systematic account of how logos could
effect human beings. The following passage from the *Helen* suggests what
this might be: "The effect of speech upon the condition of the soul is
comparable to the power of drugs over the nature of bodies. For just as
different drugs dispel different secretions from the body, and some bring
an end to disease and others to life, so also in the case of speeches, some
distress, others delight, some cause fear, others make the hearers bold, and
some drug and bewitch the soul with a kind of evil persuasion" (14).

Gorgias here outlines, albeit indirectly, a program for rhetoric. If
speeches-as-drugs and their effects can be systematically categorized, then
the rhetorician, armed with his catalogue, would become a "logical physician," able to intervene effectively in any given practical difficulty or crisis.
No details are provided regarding what sort of epistemic characteristics
this techne would have (would it be a $techne_1$ or, as the Hippocratic authors argued for their own subject, a $techne_2$?). But like Anaximenes'
Techne Rhetorikē it would offer mastery of logos, understood as a specific
subject matter.

One dimension of Gorgias's work may seem to contradict what has just
been stated: his skepticism. This is most directly stated in the thesis of his
On the Nonexistent (as reported by Sextus Empiricus): "first and foremost, that nothing exists; second, that even if it exists it is incomprehens-
ible to man; third, that even if it is comprehensible, still it is without doubt
incapable of being expressed or explained to the next man."[94]

Gorgias's skepticism is announced in the *Helen* as well: "All who have
and do persuade people of things do so by molding a false argument. . . .
So that on most subjects most men take opinion (*doxa*) as counselor to

93. De Romilly 1975, 20.
94. Sprague 1972, 42.

their soul, but since opinion is slippery and insecure it casts those employing it into slippery and insecure successes" (11). He goes on to say that even astronomers (*meteorologoi*) substitute "opinion for opinion, taking away one but creating another, making what is incredible and unclear true to the eyes of opinion" (13).

If knowledge is inaccessible, if *doxa* guides human behavior, then truth is but an "adornment" (*kosmos:* 1) of logos. In other words, the articulation of an abiding Truth that structures all of reality is neither a reasonable telos nor a characteristic of a good logos. Instead, for Gorgias the best logos can do is mold the psyche and create a variety of *doxai*. As result, given the traditional conception of Truth, according to Gorgias there is none.[95] In the absence of Truth, rhetoric, understood as the medicine/magic of logos, can mold the *doxai* constituting moral life, and so becomes the fundamental "logical" activity. By contrast, if there were a Truth, rhetoric would become devalued, and "mere" would be added before "persuasion."

Since he offers both a defense of skepticism and what seems to be an indirect claim to possess a techne, Gorgias may well fall prey to the problem of self-reference, that is, of internal inconsistency. On the other hand, he may be entirely consistent in the sense that, like so many contemporary thinkers, he simply rejects the value of Truth in the first place and then conceives of rhetoric, not as a replacement for Truth, but as the ability to manipulate opinions in its absence. There is not enough textual material— nor is the issue concerning Gorgias sufficiently interesting—to make this question worth pursuing. What does matter here is that, whether it took the form of a collection of commonplaces, a treatise more like the *Techne Rhetorikē,* or some other, less formal catalogue of speeches and their effects, the goal of the (putative) Gorgian techne was to master logos/praxis and to do so in the absence of Truth.

The handbook, or "Techne," tradition of rhetoric is open to a powerful criticism: its conception of knowledge is too rigid and mechanical to address adequately its subject matter, namely, logos, the realm of human evaluation and meaning. The moral realm is flexible, highly variable, subject to the vagaries of chance, and therefore impossible to "pin down" with epistemic force. To claim a systematic mastery of logos, as Anaximenes does, reifies and so distorts the essential character of its subject

95. See MacDowell 1982, 10–16, for a different view.

matter. Kennedy voices a similar criticism: A work such as that by Anaximenes "means that oratory can be reduced to rule. . . . By the second half
of the fourth-century B.C. there were probably few educated men in Greece
who would deny this. . . . The acceptance of rules of art, of right and
wrong answers, meant the beginning of that process of ossification which
overtook all of ancient creativity. Practice within the art was controlled
more and more by strict rules."[96]

To reformulate in terms shortly to be elaborated: logos, human life in all
its contingent variability, is simply not analogous to the alphabet.[97] The
latter represents a paradigmatically fixed conceptual content, which is
amenable to division, whereas the former is not. Logos cannot be so
cleanly analyzed into parts. As a result, there are no rules for its correct
synthesis. The Sophist, if he wishes to address his subject matter adequately, should thus follow the lead of the Hippocratic authors, who reject
techne$_1$ in favor of a more flexibly stochastic form of knowledge. The
thinker who most effectively accomplished this was Isocrates.

Isocrates

In his *Against the Sophists* (probably written around 390), Isocrates directly addresses the nature of rhetoric's subject matter and his own conception of what it is he teaches. To begin, he criticizes those Sophists who
make exaggerated claims for themselves.

> I am amazed whenever I see these [Sophists], who fail to understand
> that they are applying the paradigm (*paradeigma*) of a fixed (*tetag-
> menē*) techne to a creative process, setting themselves up as instruc-
> tors of youth. For who except them does not know that, on the one
> hand, correct spelling is stable and remains unchanged, so that we
> continually and always use the same letters for the same purpose,
> whereas, on the other hand, when it comes to speeches (*logoi*), the
> situation is exactly the opposite. (12)[98]

96. Kennedy 1963, 124.
97. Marcus Aurelius (6.26) would disagree. Note also his use of *arithmos* in this passage.
98. My Greek text is from Norlin's bilingual edition (Cambridge, Mass.: Harvard University Press, Loeb Classical Library, 1982). Translations are my own. References are by section
number.

Isocrates uses precisely the example discussed above, namely, orthography, to illustrate what he calls a "fixed techne," that is, one with hard-and-fast rules and rigorous definitions. The correct spelling of a word allows of no variation or interpretation, and therefore its teaching is a mechanical process. By contrast—and this is the first of numerous *men . . . de* oppositions (all of which I translate as "on the one hand . . . on the other hand")[99] dominating the passage—Isocrates' own subject matter is entirely different. It is "creative," since the good speaker must be novel in his response to the many subjects and occasions he faces. "This speaker, who speaks in a way that is worthy of his subject, seems to be the most skillful (*technikōtatos*) and is able to discover a unique way of approaching the subject" (12).

The use of *technikōtatos* here is striking, for it echoes the phrase *tetagmenēn* ("fixed") *technēn* found in the first sentence of section 12.[100] Isocrates distances himself from those Sophists who believe their subject matter is analogous to the fixity of a correct spelling.[101] But he also thinks it is possible for someone to become (or at least to *seem* to become) "most skillful" in speaking. Is this a contradiction? If not, it is either because being (or seeming to be) *technikōtatos* does not require possession of a techne or because Isocrates believes that his own subject is a techne$_2$ and is not "fixed." Isocrates does not explicitly pursue the second possibility; indeed, he is largely silent about what sort of knowledge he has in mind here. As a result, all we can say (so far) about making someone "skillful" in speaking is negative: such instruction would not be mechanical and analogous to teaching someone to spell correctly. It would not be a techne$_1$.

Isocrates explains why his subject matter is not fixed and stable. A good speech responds appropriately to the occasion and is novel. A good orator has some impact on the course of events, and the course of events is unpredictable. The orator must, therefore, be flexible enough to respond to the contingencies and particularities of the moment, and there are no hard and fast rules to explain how this is done. The question is, can this capacity be taught, and if so, how? (Compare *Antidosis* 141.)

After criticizing his competitors' teaching methods, as well as their inappropriate selection of a paradigm, Isocrates explains his own conception of rhetorical education. He admits that some men have become clever in speaking without formal training.

99. This is an overly rigid translation, but one I deem necessary in order to make apparent in the English what I claim transpires in the Greek.
100. Compare the use of *tetagmenē* at *Republic* 500c2.
101. Quintilian (2.8) makes a similar point. See also Cole 1991, 81.

For ability, on the one hand, in both speeches and all other activities, is found in those who have good natures and who have been trained by experience. On the other hand, education, on the one hand, makes such young men more skillful (*technikōterous*) and more resourceful in discovery, for it teaches them to take from a readier source those things which they now chance upon in a haphazard fashion. On the other hand, [education] cannot, on the one hand, make those who are inferior in nature good debaters or makers of speeches; it can, on the other hand, lead them to self-improvement and to a greater degree of intelligence on many matters. (14–15)

First, Isocrates admits that there are those who, on their own, are naturally inclined toward success in speech making. With such an admission he seems to degrade his own pedagogical prowess; he admits that he is not always needed. This may seem self-defeating, especially in a work often thought to be a "prospectus" for his own school.[102] Indeed, Isocrates here states what later becomes a standard objection to rhetoric, namely, that (in the words of Sextus Empiricus) "it is possible to make a speech quite successfully and well without having studied rhetoric. . . . Hence, rhetoric is not a techne."[103]

Immediately following such a disavowal, however, comes a strong positive claim: rhetorical education does make students more "skillful." (Note that he does not say "seem" here.) More specifically, it can improve those who have good natures by systematically organizing what they intuitively, and hence unreliably, know. This would make Isocrates the teacher valuable indeed.

There is, however, more disavowal: even the best teacher cannot transform a student with a poor nature into a good debater or speech maker. And then comes yet another antithetical response: with some education even such poor students can at least improve. The passage is all but dizzying in its vacillation. Negation is followed by affirmation in an almost strophe/antistrophe rhythm. What exact claim does Isocrates the teacher of rhetoric make?

Isocrates does grant that some portion of his educational program is "fixed": "For I state that, on the one hand, grasping the knowledge (*epis-*

---

102. See Jaeger 1967, 55.
103. "Against the Rhetoricians," 2.16. See also Shorey 1909 on this issue.

tēmē) of the "forms" (*ideai*) from which we articulate and compose all speeches is not terribly difficult" (16).

It is not obvious what *ideai* means in this passage. Jaeger suggests "basic forms of oratory," Taylor "Gorgianic figures," Hubbel "commonplace arguments," and Lidov "thought elements."[104] Fortunately, it is not necessary here to decide this issue. What is sufficient for my purposes is to note that Isocrates does describe some dimension of his teaching as "fixed," systematically, even mechanically, communicable to virtually anyone. Not surprisingly, however, he follows this assertion with a disavowal: "On the other hand, to choose [from the *ideai*] those which should be chosen for each subject and to arrange and order (*taxai*) them properly, and furthermore not to miss the occasion (*kairos*) but appropriately to adorn the whole speech with striking thoughts and to clothe it in flowing and melodious phrases—these things require much practice and are the work of a manly and intuitive mind" (16–17).

To summarize: On the one hand, it is not difficult to receive the fixed portion of the knowledge Isocrates professes to teach. On the other hand, such a claim extends only to the "forms," the fixed content of his teaching, whatever that might be. The ability to combine and order (*taxai*) these forms properly, that is, to apply creatively what has been learned mechanically, is reserved only for the student with a "manly and intuitive soul." In other words, to *use* the fixed portion of the discipline discerningly requires a kind of knowledge, a sensitivity to the *kairos,* not formally contained within the discipline. Clearly, however, this reliance on such "sensitivity" calls into question the disciplinary status of rhetoric itself. "*Kairos* brings the discipline which always strove for the autonomy of *technē* to the verge of its dissolution as an independent authority . . . art engages in a vehement, self-undermining polemic against the codification of art."[105]

The use of *taxai* in section 16 is striking because it is related to *tetagmenē* (the perfect participle of the same verb). Isocrates denies his subject is fixed and fully ordered, but this is not to imply that it is devoid of order or stable epistemic content. Indeed, it is the mark of a good student to be able to order the "forms" properly. This ability, however, can only be "taught" in a qualified way.

> The student, on the one hand, not only must have the right kind of nature, but he must also, on the one hand, learn the forms of

104. Lidov (1983) summarizes this material well.
105. Cahn 1993, 68.

speeches and, on the other hand, exercise himself in their use. On the other hand, the teacher must, on the one hand, be able to go through [the forms] with such accuracy as to leave nothing out that can be taught and, on the other hand, concerning that which remains, must supply himself as such a paradigm (*paradeigma*) that those students who have been formed by him and are able to imitate him will straightaway show in their speaking more grace and charm than the rest. On the one hand, if all these things fall together, those philosophizing will achieve complete success; on the other hand, if one of the things I have discussed is lacking, then the followers must of necessity be worse in this respect. (17–18)

After having thoroughly gone through what can be straightforwardly taught, that is, the fixed portion of the curriculum, the teacher should make himself a "paradigm" for his students to imitate.[106] Since formal instruction does not exhaust the content of rhetoric, since it in no way would prepare the student to become sensitive to the *kairos* or teach him to respond "appropriately" to the moment, a different, more indeterminate mode of instruction is needed. As Cahn puts it, since "rhetorical knowledge ceases to exist in the shape of independent technical formulations," its method of instruction becomes highly personal and intimate.[107] Isocrates, the highly successful teacher, became a paradigm who made a lasting impression on the lives of his students.

This use of *paradeigma* in section 17 recalls Isocrates' first objection to his competitors in section 12: they think their subject has hard-and-fast rules, that is, is a techne₁, or "Techne" ("handbook"). In doing so, they invoke the inappropriate *paradeigma* of orthography to explicate, and perhaps advertise, their teaching of rhetoric. Only the contingent presence of the teacher himself can communicate the ultimate Isocratean lesson. Only by exhibiting, rather than systematically expounding, the ability to be clever, to be novel, and to engage a particular audience by responding appropriately to their needs does the successful Isocratean teacher teach. A human paradigm replaces the abstract and purely formal one.

Isocrates ends section 18 with yet another *men . . . de* construction. Only if, on the one hand, all these factors—the character and practice of the student, the thorough treatment of the fixed aspect of the curriculum by the teacher, and the exhibition of a good paradigm by the teacher—

106. Socrates describes himself as a kind of paradigm at *Apology* 23b1.
107. Cahn 1989, 135. See also Cahn 1993, 69.

"fall together" will the outcome be successful and Isocrates' student turn
out to be a genuine "philosopher."[108] If, on the other hand, one of these
ingredients is missing, the result will be seriously flawed. Using the verb
"fall together" (*sumpiptō*) is a bold admission of the role *tuchē* plays in
the whole educational process. Unlike teaching a child how to spell, this is
a lesson that may well not be learned (compare *Panegyricus* 48).

Such moderate pedagogical claims are characteristic of Isocrates. He frequently acknowledges that compared to the nature and experience of his
student, instruction falls short in its power to determine success, and that
it is perfectly possible for someone to be clever at speaking and acting
without the benefit of formal training (see *Antidosis* 271, 184). Even
though his ultimate pedagogical goal is thoroughly laden with ethical concerns, Isocrates admits that no techne can "produce sobriety and justice in
depraved natures" (21).

Isocrates is very much a teacher, however, and so he also makes quite
positive claims for himself. In *Antidosis* (199), for example, he responds
extensively to the charge that *paideia* is a "sham," and in *To Nicocles* (12)
he asserts that practice and, by extension, education are useful in becoming more intelligent. There thus might seem to be two contradictory
strands running through Isocrates' self-description. Not so. Instead, what
Isocrates is offering, even without being explicit about it, is what I term a
techne$_2$.

I defend this assertion by first addressing a historical question that has
been raised since antiquity: did Isocrates himself publish a "Techne," a
formal rhetorical treatise or systematic set of instructions? Barwick and
Cahn are confident that "Isocrates did, in fact, never compose an art of
rhetoric."[109] Without entering into the philological argument needed to
substantiate this purely historical claim, it should be clear that my reading
of *Against the Sophists* would favor such a view. What I have shown is
that the conception of Isocrates' subject matter implicit in *Against the
Sophists* is similar to the stochastic techne articulated by the Hippocratic
authors, and therefore ill suited to become a standard rhetorical techne.

To substantiate this similarity, consider first that the Hippocratic author
of "Ancient Medicine" admits that patients get better on their own. This is
analogous to Isocrates admitting that some students achieve the end of
rhetoric, effective public speaking, without the assistance of the rhetorical

---

108. *Philosophia* for Isocrates does not mean what it does for Plato and Aristotle. See
Schiappa 1993.

109. See Barwick 1963 and Cahn 1989.

techne. The Hippocratic author sees medicine as generalizing from and refining ordinary pretechnical experience. Isocrates says this is exactly what rhetoric does: it offers an orderly presentation of what the gifted student would stumble upon haphazardly. The Hippocratic physician is straightforward about not treating a "hopeless case" and believes that his refusal to do so is entirely compatible with his claim to a techne. Likewise, Isocrates admits some students simply cannot be made into good speakers. In general, and as Aristotle points out, there is a basic similarity between rhetoric and medicine: since both are stochastic, function and end are not identical. "It does not belong to medicine to produce health, but only to promote it as much as is possible . . . it belongs to rhetoric to discover the real and apparent means of persuasion" (*Rhetoric* 1355b12). In other words, these technai are compatible with failure.

As described above, medicine is continuous with and must employ the language of ordinary, pretechnical experience. Since the audience to whom rhetoric directs its speeches is the general body of citizens, this is obviously true of rhetoric as well. Since the formal aspect of rhetorical instruction does not exhaust the content of the teaching, a personal, verbal relationship is needed between student and teacher. As reflected in the Hippocratic Oath, the relationship between student and teacher must be intimate: in order to convey the kind of sensitivity to the medical version of the *kairos,* the student must spend time with the master. It is similar with Isocrates, the paradigm who, like a stamp on a seal of wax, makes a lasting impression of the soul of a student.

Even though Isocrates never directly claims a techne, he certainly has a subject to teach. He may indeed avoid the word "techne" in order to distance himself from the "Techne" tradition he criticizes.[110] Unlike the *artium scriptores,* Isocrates realizes his subject is indeterminate and susceptible to the vagaries of chance; he must have students who are already good if he is to succeed in teaching; his is a personal, rather than a technical/formal, mode of presentation; his subject is not analogous to orthography (or to mathematics). Instead, it meets the criteria of List 7. Even further, since it deals with logos, understood as political or even cultural activity, it is constituted by a series of unpredictable *kairoi,* occasions. The best rhetorician, then, is one who is flexible, able to sniff out what is appropriate and respond accordingly.[111]

110. This is an important point in Cahn 1989 and the theme of Appendix 4 below.
111. Again, Detienne and Vernant categorize and discuss this mode of thought under the rubric *mētis.*

Isocrates expresses all of this by using the *men . . . de* construction in the fashion noted above. Is rhetoric a techne? On the one hand, yes, on the other, no. Yes: it is a teachable subject, is reasonably reliable, has a subject matter, and merits payment. Its possessor is a *technitēs* who deserves his shingle. But no: rhetoric is not like a typical techne. Success is not guaranteed, function differs from end, chance intrudes, an informal kind of sensitivity is required, and therefore teaching it is a personal, and precarious, business. In short, rhetoric is not a techne$_1$, the most rigorous and obvious form of techne.

Against the Sophists concludes:[112] "And yet those who wish to obey the prescriptions of this 'philosophy' may be benefited more quickly with respect to their goodness (*epieikeian*) than to their rhetorical ability. But let no one think that I assert that justice can be taught; for, on the one hand, in general I think that there does not exist a techne that can implant sobriety and justice in depraved natures. On the other hand, I do think that the study of political logoi can especially help to stimulate and exercise such qualities of character" (21).

Unlike Gorgias, Isocrates' project is thoroughly value-laden. He is committed to moral education, and so he insists upon making his students into good men who will work for the betterment of Greece. Consider, for example, his encomium to arete in "On the Peace": "Nothing contributes as much toward the achievement of wealth or of reputation or of doing the right thing or in general of happiness (*eudaimonia*) as does arete" (32). Norlin rightly compares this passage to Plato's *Apology* 30a–b, and it is probably just this commitment to arete that led Plato to mention him favorably in the *Phaedrus* (279a–b).

On the other hand, Isocrates is adamant that whatever moral knowledge he has is not a typically productive techne: he cannot implant arete in the souls of those who are not already equipped with it. He is not like the shipbuilder, who can take his wood and make his ship.

To reiterate: Isocrates' views on rhetoric are of more than historical interest. His self-reflective analysis in *Against the Sophists,* operating as it does through the lens of the techne question, takes up, with its own kind of consistency, the relationship between knowledge and moral action/ logos, knowledge and life. Yes, it is possible to know something about how to live, about how to talk. Yes, there is a subject to be taught,

---

112. The work is typically thought to be fragmentary. Cahn (1989) questions this assumption.

namely, rhetoric, that will enable the student to function excellently in the polis. But, no, such knowledge is neither formal nor reducible to a set of elements with rules for their synthesis. No, such knowledge is not teachable in a mechanical sense, because it requires for its successful application a sensitivity to the *kairos* available only to a few. Yes, there is knowledge, but it cannot be fully abstracted from its human practitioners; it is located within human life. And it is only the paradigmatic status of a living, breathing teacher that can communicate what needs to be known.

Isocrates' views are not only coherent and accessible, they are also alive and well today. (I think of Fish and Rorty, writers whose "postmodernism" is manifestly akin to this conception of rhetoric.)[113] Furthermore, Isocrates was tremendously influential in the history of rhetoric itself. I digress briefly in the next section in order to show that this is the case and, more important, to explicate further the position I have ascribed to him above.

Back to the Future: Isocrates' Influence

Later rhetoricians followed Isocrates' lead when responding to the question, Is rhetoric a techne? Consider Philodemus (100–40 B.C.E.). As did Alexander of Aphrodisias, he treats the character of stochastic techne in general, as well as of rhetoric in particular. In a format reminiscent of that used by the Hippocratic writers, Philodemus defends rhetoric against the charge of not being a techne. He presents his work as a series of responses to objections. The critic objects: "An untrained person should not be able to excel one who has been trained in [a techne], but in rhetoric this sometimes occurs." The response: "[T]he untrained man may excel the trained man at times in a [stochastic] (*stochastikē*) [techne], but never in an exact science" (1.20; 269).[114]

Philodemus adduces the examples of piloting and medicine to illustrate the stochastic techne, the type of knowledge compatible with failure: "The captain sometimes loses his ship, the physician kills his patient. We must

113. Fish (1990) would support, and is useful in unpacking, this assertion. I criticize Fish in Roochnik 1991.

114. I follow the translation by Hubbell (*The Rhetorica of Philodemus* [New Haven: Connecticut Academy of Arts and Sciences, 1920]). The Greek text comes from Philodemi, *Volumina Rhetorica*, ed. S. Sudhaus (Leipzig: Teubner, 1892), whose numbering I cite first, followed by a corresponding page in Hubbell. As always, I substitute "techne" for "art." I also substitute "stochastic" for Hubbell's "conjectural."

either deny that navigation and medicine are arts, or abandon the demand that all arts must always be beneficial" (1.19; 269).

He then offers an explicit comparison between rhetoric and medicine: "Those are wrong who claim that rhetoric is not [a techne] on the assumption that [a techne] must have method (*to methodikon*) and a transmission of definite knowledge (*hestēkeos paradosin*), if on the other hand they allow medicine which is [stochastic] to be [a techne]" (1.53; 274). Next, he offers a definition of a techne:

> [A techne], as the term is commonly used, is a state or condition resulting from the observation of certain common and elementary principles, which apply to the majority of cases, accomplishing such a result as cannot be attained by one who has studied it, and this regularly and certainly and not by conjecture. . . . This definition applies both to the exact sciences like grammar and music which have certain definite rules and to the [stochastic technai] which are in possession of certain common elements affecting individual cases, although these common elements may not have been completely mastered and the result may not be accomplished always but only more frequently than those who do not possess the [techne]. (1.69–70; 276–77)

Like Alexander, Philodemus divides techne into two principal branches, the exact and the stochastic. Rhetoric belongs in the latter. It is reliable, unified knowledge, capable of being "packaged" and "sold," but it is not exact, not like "grammar." By qualifying the technical status of rhetoric in this manner, Philodemus brings to the surface what is implicit in Isocrates' ambivalent treatment of the techne question.

This treatment of the technical status of rhetoric is even more elaborate in Quintilian (writing around 95 C.E.). He devotes a substantial passage to the question, "Is rhetoric an art?" (2.17–21), within which he treats what will prove to be the issue decisive to his response: the subject matter (*materia*) of rhetoric.

Quintilian admits the subject matter of rhetoric is essentially different from that of a typical *ars*: "I hold that the subject matter of rhetoric is composed of everything that may be placed before it as a subject for speech" (2.21). But what can be placed before an orator as a subject? Everything about which we talk. But "everything" cannot be the subject of a single techne. As I have shown from the outset, a techne requires a deter-

minate object, a something, not everything, as its field of expertise. One
who possesses a techne is a *technitēs,* an expert, and no one can be an
expert in everything.

Quintilian anticipates this line of objection: "[B]ut this subject matter,
as we call it, that is to say the things brought before [rhetoric], has been
criticized by some, at times on the ground that it is indeterminate (*infinita*), and sometimes on the ground that it is not peculiar to oratory
(2.21.7)." On the one hand, he is willing to accede to this criticism. However, like Isocrates, who also grants the indeterminacy of his subject matter
and his consequent inability to exhaust the teaching of it via formal instruction, he does not think the objection damages his claim to possess or
teach an *ars.* This is because his subject matter is not *infinita,* but "multifold" (*multiplex*). He illustrates through an analogy between rhetoric and
four "minor" arts.

Architecture embraces within it everything that is useful for the purpose
of building; engraving and sculpture work in different media: gold, silver,
ivory, and so forth; medicine deals with exercise, normally conceived as
the field of the expert trainer, and diet, the province of the cook (2.21.8–
11). The point seems to be that each of these four arts is like rhetoric in
not having a determinate and unique subject matter. But surely if this is
the point, then Quintilian fails to make his case with these four examples.
While it is true that architecture is "architectonic" and that so to it other
building arts are subordinated, and even if the subject matter of architecture, building, is complex, it is nonetheless determinate. Engraving and
sculpture represent the mastery of basic techniques that can be executed in
various media. But the fact that media differ in no way compromises the
unity of these basic techniques. Even if medicine infringes on the provinces
of the trainer and the cook, its subject matter is still restricted to the health
of the body.

In sum, each of these four arts is radically different from rhetoric,
which, unlike them, can treat of everything, and so Quintilian's argument
by analogy does not seem to work. There is, however, a more charitable
sense in which this argument can be read. There are several ancillary arts
about which architecture must be knowledgeable. The architect must, for
example, know something about masonry. He need not be an expert mason, but he must *know enough* about masonry to be able to converse with
and direct the mason who works for him. This reading of Quintilian's
argument by analogy may be more defensible.

Quintilian asks, if the orator can talk knowledgeably about everything, does it follow that he "must be the master of all arts?" (2.21.14). Surely this is an impossibly encyclopedic demand, although one that seems to have been made by Hippias and Cicero.[115] Quintilian, at least, rejects the notion that the orator has to know all the arts; "I . . . regard it as sufficient that an orator should not be actually ignorant of the subject on which he has to speak. For he cannot have knowledge of all causes, and yet he should be able to speak on all. On what then will he speak? On those which he has studied. Similarly as regards the arts, he will study those concerning which he has to speak, as occasion may demand, and will speak on those which he has studied" (2.21.15).

This is the key passage. What the orator should know is not everything, but *what to study and when to study it*. So, for example, if the debate in the Senate is about foreign policy, then the orator should know something about, say, naval technology. First of all, having such knowledge is required to meet the goal of persuasion. If the debate focuses on whether to expand the fleet, the orator should learn enough to be able to speak effectively about shipbuilding. But how much is enough? What it takes to avoid being "actually ignorant" and to get the job done. But will not the expert speak better about shipbuilding than the orator? Only if the orator has not done his homework. If he has studied the subject at hand, he will do a better job representing the position than the shipbuilder himself (compare *Gorgias,* 456b). Only if a specific technical point arises should the ship-builder himself speak (2.21.16–17).

The orator must know how to take up any subject and quickly learn its rudiments, at least those relevant to presenting his case. Of course, this requires being able to distinguish what is relevant from what is not. In this sense the orator is like the architect, who masters what needs to be known about the ancillary art of masonry. Again, the orator must do this not only to understand properly the issue at hand but also to speak effectively. He should know how much technical information to incorporate into his speech. Too much will alienate the audience; too little will impress them with the speaker's ignorance. The orator should thus be prepared to study any subject:. "For my part I hold that practically all subjects are under circumstances liable to come up for treatment by the orator. If the circumstances do not occur the subjects will not concern him" (2.21.19).

The *officium* of the orator is almost everything; it is indefinite, for he

---

115. Hippias is described in Plato's *Hippias Major* 368b. Cicero outlines similar views in *De Oratore* 2.32 (although he does not do so in his own voice).

should be able to respond appropriately to any number of circumstances, to learn enough about any given subject in order to speak effectively about it. Only in this sense, namely, knowing what to study and when, can it be said that the orator can talk knowledgeably about everything.

Quintilian struggles with the techne question and then, like Isocrates, compromises. Achieving technical mastery of everything is surely impossible. But everything is what the orator must be able to address. This means that he must know what to study and when, what is appropriate and relevant, and how to get the job done.

Implicit within this ambiguous response to the techne question is a conception of moral/political life itself. No, it cannot be rendered fully determinate. It cannot become a matter of hard-and-fast rules (see 2.13). There are, however, "rules of thumb" that can be communicated, and if supplemented by a sensitive awareness of what is needed at the moment, they will be effective in guiding the orator. Yes, human life can be treated with reason; but, no, reason, at least not as manifested in a techne$_1$, is not sufficient to master it.

Quintilian's response to the techne question, then, is fundamentally similar to Isocrates'. When he begins his discussion of it he says this: "Indeed, I will confess that I had doubts as to whether I should discuss this inquiry, for there is no one, I will not say so unlearned, but so devoid of ordinary sense, as to hold that building, weaving or moulding vessels from clay are arts, and at the same time to consider that rhetoric . . . has reached such a lofty eminence without the assistance of art" (2.17.3).

It is obvious to Quintilian that someone can learn rhetoric and that it is a subject worth paying for. There are, after all, schools out there that have been in business for years. But what exactly is the content of rhetoric? Anything that can be placed before the orator as a subject for a speech. To explicate this assertion he states that the subject matter of rhetoric is not unlimited, but multifold. What this means, however, is that the orator needs to know what to study and when, what is relevant and what is not. He should, in other words, know how to respond appropriately to the *kairos*. And this unique sensitivity—as Isocrates knows well—cannot be taught; at least not in a technical or formal manner.

Cicero, who preceded Quintilian by about a century, had made the same point. In *De Oratore*, his character Crassus says:

> I think there is no art of speaking at all or a very thin (*pertenuem*) one. . . . For if, as Antonius just now explained, an art is defined as

consisting in things thoroughly examined and clearly apprehended, and which are also outside the control of mere opinion, and within the grasp of exact knowledge (*scientia*), then to me there seems to be no such thing as an art of oratory. For all the kinds of language we ourselves use in public speaking are changeable matter (*varia*) and adapted to the general understanding of the crowd. If however the actual things noticed in the practice and conduct of speaking have been heeded and recorded by means of skill and experience, if they have been defined in terms illuminated by classification, and distributed under sub-divisions . . . I do not understand why this should not be regarded as an art, perhaps not in the precise (*subtili*) sense of the term, but at any rate according to the other and popular estimate. (1.107–9)

This conception of the technical status of rhetoric again echoes much in Isocrates. Rhetoric is an *ars,* but not a typical one. This is because the indeterminate nature of its subject matter, human political life or logos, does not offer its student a fixed and stable object to be studied.

If the first rhetoricians were *artium scriptores,* writers of "Technai," then Isocrates and his descendants offered a techne$_2$, or stochastic form of knowledge. As James Allen has argued, because this epistemic conception is far from typical, it requires special justification. As indicated by Lists 1–7, the traditional sense of techne implies reliable knowledge. When, for example, we go to the shipbuilder, we expect the ship to get built. If it is not, his shingle is revoked. But when we go to the physician, and when we evaluate the orator, we must be willing to accept failure, for with these kinds of knowledge, function is not identical to end. As a result, a "special" justification of stochastic knowledge is required. "Defenders of the stochastic arts need to give us a reason to concede that the stochastic arts involve artistic knowledge, albeit knowledge of a special kind, instead of concluding that the precepts they rely on, though not entirely valueless, do not amount to a body of knowledge. In other words, we need to see how the introduction of a type of knowledge with special stochastic characteristics can be justified."[116]

The rhetoricians themselves do not supply such a justification. Allen argues, rightly I think, that only Aristotle does this. But the rhetorical writings are profoundly important because, located within the frequently re-

116. Allen 1989, 9.

peated and apparently innocuous question, Is rhetoric a techne? is a set of philosophical questions of the highest order. Can the realm of politics and public speeches, of morality and logos, be rendered fixed and stable? Is there anything in this world of human affairs that can be counted upon, that can be known with reliability? Is the political world in any way analogous to the alphabet, whose subject matter is the paradigm of analyticity and determinacy? Do we have access to stable values and standards? Is there something to be known that can regulate our political lives? If so, should not a hierarchy be drawn in which the person having such knowledge is situated at the top, and perhaps even granted political rule? If not, then should not the question of rule be decided by public debate in a democratic forum?

These are among the most basic questions of what we know as moral or political philosophy. The rhetoricians' ambivalent response to the techne question itself expresses a coherent and enduring response to them (one which, again, is much in favor in these postmodern times.) These same questions will soon by asked by Plato, who, for reasons I hope are now apparent, was deeply concerned, perhaps even obsessed, with his rhetorical competitors and whose conception of moral knowledge, like theirs, can best be seen by looking through the lens of the techne question.

CHAPTER TWO

TECHNE AND THE VIRTUES IN THE PLATONIC DIALOGUES

The purpose of Chapter 1, a selective examination of pre-Platonic writings, was to prepare for a study of the role techne plays in the early dialogues. As explained in the Introduction, among scholars there is broad agreement concerning the philosophical implications of Socrates' use of the techne analogy. The purpose of this chapter is to challenge conventional wisdom, that is, the standard view that techne in the "early" dialogues is meant to function as a positive theoretical model for moral knowledge.

From discussion of passages from five dialogues—the *Laches, Charmides, Euthyphro, Republic,* and *Euthydemus*—a common pattern emerges: Socrates examines an interlocutor who offers an answer to his famous question, *ti esti,* "what is it"? The "it" in each of the dialogues is a specific virtue: courage, moderation, piety, justice, and wisdom. Two assumptions govern these examinations: (1) the virtue in question is in some way identified with knowledge; (2) the model of such knowledge is techne. Ultimately, each of the five discussions terminates in *aporia,* conceptual "impasse." These *aporiai* force a choice upon the reader: either virtue is not knowledge, or knowledge is not best modeled by a techne. The first choice is unacceptable, for without the assumption of virtue being knowledge, the early dialogues become unintelligible. Therefore, the aporiai are generated by Socrates' second assumption, that knowledge is exclusively modeled by techne. While the Socratic version of virtue *is* knowledge, it is therefore *not a techne.*

Courage in the *Laches*

The *Laches* opens with Lysimachus asking two well-regarded generals, Nicias and Laches, how his and Melesias's sons can become "excellent" (*aristoi:* 179b2). "By learning or doing what," he asks, "would they become excellent?" (179d6–7). Someone had recommended to Lysimachus the very activity he is currently observing, namely, armor fighting, as a method of inculcating excellence. Do Nicias and Laches agree? Before answering, Laches suggests that Socrates be consulted. After all, he spends much of his time investigating just these sorts of questions. Socrates, however, defers to his elders and urges Nicias to answer Lysimachus's question (181c–d).

Nicias straightforwardly defends the study and practice of armor fighting. It is, he argues, strenuous physical exercise and therefore beneficial to the young. Like horsemanship, it is particularly fitting for free citizens, since it helps to prepare them for the noble business of war. It is especially useful when the lines are broken and there is man-to-man fighting. Furthermore, learning how to fight will excite the desire for another fine subject, that which "comes next" in the sequential training of a military man, namely, "tactics." Learning this will, in turn, inspire the student to pursue generalship itself. Since Nicias is convinced of the intrinsic value of military activity, he thinks it obvious that a young man ought to study armor fighting. His reasoning (from 181e to 182c) is straightforward and probably reflective of the standard training of an Athenian military man. But there is more: "Let's add to this list an addition that's not trivial, namely, that this episteme can make every man much more daring and courageous in war than he was before" (182c5–7).

Learning the subject of armor fighting will, according to Nicias, have a positive "moral" effect on the student. A young man will become better, specifically braver, if he gains this knowledge. The word translated as "knowledge" here is *epistēmē,* which, as I document throughout this chapter and as has been widely acknowledged by other scholars, is synonymous with "techne" in the early dialogues.[1] As a result, with his addition, Nicias brings to the foreground the question lurking in the background of the *Laches* from the outset: *what is the relationship between techne and arete?* Can a specifically technical subject have a beneficial moral effect on the student?

---

1. "Socrates uses *technē* . . . and *epistēmē* . . . interchangeably. 'Expertise' seems to me the best word for the single conception Socrates has in mind . . . and 'science' next best." Penner 1992a, 149. Hirschberger (1932, 24) calls the two words a "hendiadys."

Laches does not share his colleague's enthusiasm for armor fighting. After raising several pragmatic criticisms of it (e.g., if it were truly valuable, then the Spartans would teach it, and they do not), Laches turns to what proves to be a critical argument: even if a young man learns the subject of armor fighting, there is no guarantee that in actual warfare he will exercise the subject well and to his advantage. To illustrate his point, Laches tells the story of Stesilaos, the expert in armor fighting Lysimachus has just observed. In an actual battle, Stesilaos's armor got tangled up in the rigging of a ship; he was pulled along by it and, despite his professed mastery of the techne, made a fool of himself (183d–e).

The moral of Laches' story is this: the quality of one's character *precedes* and is not formed by the possession of a techne. As a result, learning a given techne cannot in and of itself inculcate arete. Socrates makes a similar point in the *Meno*. Pericles taught his sons horsemanship, gymnastics, and "all else that comes under the head of techne" (94b6), but failed to make them excellent. In short, and as Solon and Sophocles knew well, there is a gap between a technical and a moral education. Laches is hardly explicit on this point, but he seems to be onto it:

> For it seems to me that if a man who was cowardly should believe that he knew it [the techne of armor fighting], he would become more rash on account of it, and so it would become quite clear what sort of man he really was. If he should be brave, he would be closely watched by other men; and if he should make the smallest mistake, he would be heavily criticized. This is because pretending to such knowledge (*epistēmē*) would create envy, and so unless the man was distinguished in arete to an extraordinary degree, he could not escape the mockery of others. (184b–c)

If a cowardly man learns this techne, he gains only in rashness, a gain that ultimately will do him harm: since he is a coward, he will not be able to fend off the attacks his too venturesome attitude will invite. Similarly, if the soldier is of average bravery, then knowing a specialized techne will only draw undeserved attention to him. Only the man *already* excellent will truly benefit from learning armor fighting.

With these comments Laches expresses, albeit indirectly, the central problem concerning the value of techne. His objection recalls Solon's "Prayer to the Muses": techne seduces the *technitēs* into a false hope of success, even happiness. It appears, but in fact fails, to offer the prospect of some control over the contingencies of human life. Even if it is good, techne is of only limited value in creating the conditions for human happiness, for this requires not only a good character and obedience to the dictates of *dikē,* but good luck as well.

Laches' objections to armor fighting also suggest a caution reminiscent of the "ode to human being" of the *Antigone.* Techne is value-neutral; it can be applied for good or ill, and the quality of the application is independent of the techne itself. Sophocles seems to be properly skeptical about the intrinsic benefit of any given techne; what finally matters is whether a man is law-abiding and decent or not. However indirectly he puts the point, Laches seems to be thinking along similar lines: what matters is not whether a soldier masters the latest technical advances in warfare, but how brave he is.[2]

Finally, a parallel might also be drawn between Laches' objection to armor fighting and Isocrates' criticism of the "Techne" tradition of rhetoric. Isocrates criticizes his competitors for wrongly conceiving of their work as a *tetagmenē* techne, a fixed, determinate, and mechanically teachable form of knowledge. Given his conception of the epistemic limits of rhetoric, as well as his demand that rhetorical instruction be morally responsible, Isocrates admits he is unable to produce a good soul in all his students. In terms of his own curriculum, learning the *ideai,* the fixed and structured content of his teaching, is not enough to become a good orator, for no techne, Isocrates says, produces "justice and sobriety in depraved natures" (21). In other words, having a good character is a necessary precondition for becoming a good orator, and this cannot be engendered by technical means.

Laches' point seems to be that even if studying a subject like armor fighting will no doubt benefit some young men, it cannot actually make them excellent. If they are already good, then the discipline will help to organize and perfect their goodness; it will not produce it. If the boy is a coward, learning a techne will not help.

To summarize: At this point Nicias seems to be a naïve advocate of the blanket goodness of the technai, while Laches is more (and appropriately) concerned with the difficult task of applying techne in the realm of human actions. As a result, he is far more cautious in judging the value of armor fighting. For this reason, and as other evidence (including the title of the

---

2. Also, recall *Apology* 22d7: his knowledge seduces the technician into believing that he understands the "greatest" of matters.

dialogue) shows, Laches is the favored interlocutor throughout this dialogue.[3] He consistently shows real insight into the issues being discussed and, through both his words and his deeds, provides the best clues in this first attempt to come to terms with Plato's understanding of techne.

From Lysimachus's point of view, the conversation has reached an impasse. To the question, Should a young man learn armor fighting in order to become excellent? Nicias has answered in the affirmative, Laches in the negative. Lysimachus, unable to reach a decision, or even think seriously, on his own, asks Socrates to cast the deciding vote. Socrates refuses. He is appalled at the prospect of so urgent a subject—namely, education in arete—being decided by the principle of majority rule (184d). In order to convince Lysimachus (and Melesias) that they are being entirely wrongheaded in relying on a vote, he uses the techne analogy: "What if your deliberation was about what sort of gymnastic exercise your son should practice, would you be persuaded by the majority of us, or by that man who actually has been educated and has practiced under a good trainer?" (184e).

Melesias answers, the latter. Why? Because this is a clear case where deciding a question well requires episteme and where majority opinion is, or should be, irrelevant. Socrates continues: "Therefore, it is necessary now to examine this very question: is one of us knowledgeable (*technikos*) about the subject we are considering? And if one of us is, then we should abide by what he says, even though he is just one, and ignore everybody else. If none of us is [knowledgeable], then we should search for someone who is" (185a).

As mentioned in the Introduction, this passage seems to imply the following: as the technical trainer is to the excellence of the body, so X, a person who is *technikos,* is to the excellence of the *psuchē* (185a3). Proponents of the standard account of techne (SAT) such as Irwin and Gould have interpreted this passage as a straightforward statement of Plato's theoretical intentions. To reiterate Irwin's comment on 185a: "[Socrates] demands an expert craftsman in moral training."[4] In other words, he attributes to Socrates the view that there is (or should be) an X who is *technikos,* who has moral knowledge strictly analogous to that of the expert trainer.

The evidence for Irwin's reading is slim. Socrates' use of the analogy

---

3. Nothing in my argument hinges on the title of the *Laches.* For an alternative, and excellent, discussion of Laches, indeed of all the characters in the dialogue, see Schmid 1992.
4. Irwin 1977, 71.

here may well imply only that there is some sort of knowledge of arete that should be sought. In other words, what sort of knowledge this might be is left open. Socrates' use of the *paidotribēs*, the technical trainer or coach, as an example is readily explained by its being an ordinary example of knowledge, one Lysimachus will easily recognize. Recall that Socrates' specific purpose in this passage is to *exhort*, to persuade Lysimachus not to capitulate to the lure of majority rule but to seek knowledge instead. As argued throughout the previous chapter, because it is straightforwardly identified, techne is certifiable knowledge and typically is rewarded as such. Members of the community agree that to prepare a boy for athletic excellence, one should consult the trainer who has hung a shingle testifying to his previous successes, rather than solicit random opinions or take a vote. By citing the trainer in the analogy, Socrates thus invokes an accessible and compelling example of knowledge for the manifestly non-philosophical Lysimachus.[5] He may well use the analogy between the trainer and X, the person with knowledge of arete, not because he thinks X has technical knowledge, but because he thinks X simply has knowledge.

And what would this knowledge be? Perhaps it would indeed be a techne, although simply to say this does not yet delineate exactly what sort of knowledge it is. This "moral knowledge" could, after all, be either a $techne_1$ or a $techne_2$. Socrates' use of the analogy also leaves open the possibility that the knowledge possessed by X would be neither a $techne_1$ nor a $techne_2$, but some form of nontechnical knowledge instead. Finally, Socrates' use of the techne analogy at *Laches* 185a allows for the possibility that knowledge of arete, whatever it turns out to be, might never be possessed. Recall that Socrates uses the analogy in order to urge Lysimachus to seek knowledge. He does not promise that Lysimachus will succeed.

The basic point is this: pertaining to what Socrates *does* with the analogy in the dialogue itself—namely, exhort Lysimachus to pursue knowledge—we learn precious little about what he thinks moral knowledge actually is. It is clear only that he thinks it is desirable and should be sought. As a result, Irwin's confident assertion—"[Socrates] demands an expert craftsman in moral training"—is unwarranted.

To return to the text: the participants agree that someone with knowl-

---

5. For a similarly protreptic use of the analogy, which also invokes the *paidotribēs*, see *Crito* 46c–47d.

edge should be sought to adjudicate the question, What should a young man study in order to become excellent? Socrates explains that if we want to discover who is most "knowledgeable" (*technikōtatos*: 185b) about gymnastics, we will look for the person who has "studied and practiced it, and who had good teachers" (185b). In other words, he reiterates the techne analogy and seems to recommend searching for someone with the kinds of credentials attainable and demanded by a techne. There is, however, a problem. The participants, Socrates says, have not yet agreed what it is they are deliberating about (185b). As should be (but is not) obvious, the issue is not fighting in armor but the excellence of the human psyche. "Therefore, it is necessary to investigate whether any of us is *technikos* about the treatment (*therapeia*) of the psyche and is able to treat it well, and whether he has had good teachers" (185e). Laches, however, interjects, "What about this, Socrates: haven't you noticed that in some matters men become more knowledgeable (*technikōterous*) without teachers than with teachers?" (185e).

With this remark, Laches raises a standard objection to a techne claim. The hypothetical critic found in the Hippocratic writings, for example, objects to the technical pretensions of medicine because often a patient gets well without the efforts of a physician. A similar objection is traditionally made against rhetoric: "[I]t is possible to make a speech quite successfully and well without having studied rhetoric. . . . Hence, rhetoric is not a techne."[6] Laches' simple observation—in some matters men become knowledgeable without teachers—expresses a similar thought.

The subject under consideration in the *Laches,* namely, human arete, is, like the subjects of medicine and rhetoric, suspect. Whether it is amenable to technical treatment, or can even be taught, is not obvious. As they consistently have been, Laches' remarks about teaching raise the larger issue shaping the dialogue, for they force the reader to consider the unique character of human excellence and, once again, prepare for the principal theme of the dialogue: the relationship between techne and arete.

Socrates himself has had no teacher of arete: "First of all, Lysimachus and Melesias, I say about myself that I have never had a teacher concerning this subject. I have, however, desired one since I was a young man. But I have not been able to pay the tuition charged by the Sophists, who alone claim to be able to make men 'fine and good.' I myself, on the other hand, even now have been unable to discover this techne" (186c).

6. Sextus Empiricus, "Against the Rhetoricians," 2.16.

With manifest irony, Socrates identifies the Sophists, professors of the rhetorical techne, as the teachers being sought. But his irony should not be construed as easy dismissal. The Sophists are Socrates' prime competitors, for they tread upon his turf, namely, the "moral realm" of human excellence (opened up by the reflections of Solon and Sophocles). *Laches* 186c discloses a basic point of divergence to which I return frequently: *unlike the Sophists, Socrates professes no techne.*

Socrates assumes that, in one sense, Nicias and Laches must be like the Sophists: since they so confidently answer the question about the value of armor fighting, they must "have discovered or learned" the techne whose subject matter is arete. The *technitēs*, after all, is the "answer man," to whose authoritative judgments laypeople should defer. Socrates advises Lysimachus to examine the two generals by asking them to show either their "diplomas" (i.e., cite their teachers) or examples of those they have actually made better (186c–e). True to form, Lysimachus would rather have Socrates do this for him (187d).

Nicias seems to welcome such an examination, for he claims to know Socrates and his style of discussion well. A Socratic dialogue, he says, is never confined to its initial topic, in this case the education of Lysimachus's son. Instead, the interlocutor is "ceaselessly turned around by him in the logos until he is forced to give an account of himself and whatever way he is presently living and whatever sort of past life he has lived" (187e–188a).

Laches, however, is not as sure. This is because he is of two minds when it comes to logos.

> My attitude toward speeches (*logos*) is simple or, if you wish, not simple but complex. For it's possible that I could appear to someone as both a lover of speeches (*philologos*) and a hater of speeches (*misologos*). For whenever I hear a man discussing excellence or some other part of wisdom as if he really is a man and worthy of the speeches he is speaking, I am completely delighted to see if the man speaking and the things he is saying are appropriate to and fit together with each other. And such a man seems to me to be altogether musical, for he has prepared a most beautiful harmony, not on the lyre or any other instrument, but in reality he himself has harmonized his life, his actions (*erga*) with his words (*logoi*). And he has done this not in the Ionic or the Phrygian or the Lydian mode, but in the only mode that is truly a Greek harmony, the Doric. (188c–d)

Laches admires the "Doric harmony" of logos and *ergon,* word and deed. He is not interested in those who just talk; he wants actions to harmonize with the words. So, in this discussion, he wants not only to learn what arete is, but to learn it from someone who is actively excellent, who practices what he preaches. He is willing to listen to Socrates, but only because he, as Laches himself witnessed, was an excellent soldier at Delium (188e).

Laches' demand to blend word and deed represents a very old sentiment among the Greeks, dating back at least to the Homeric poems. It is also an important philosophical component of the *Laches,* for, as was the case with his comments about the limited value of armor fighting and his observation that teachers are not always required in the learning of some subjects, Laches' demand for a Doric harmony of word and deed discloses much concerning the fundamental issue of the early dialogues: the relationship between techne and arete.

The great worry about techne, alluded to by Solon and Sophocles, is that in one sense logos and *ergon* need not harmonize. Criterion 3 on List 2 is meant to express this: a techne must be applied in order to be complete. The shipbuilder knows how to build a ship—in this sense, he has the logos—but he need not do so. If he does not, if no *ergon* is forthcoming, then his techne is not fully actualized. Even more important is the moral dimension of the Solonic and Sophoclean worry. The shipbuilder may build a ship, and do so well, but use it for the wrong purpose, to supply the Persians, say, rather than the Greeks. In this sense, it is possible for the *technites* to have the right logos, that is, to know what to do in order to execute his technical task well, but to misdirect the *erga* that issue from his successful execution of the techne. Despite the obvious "practical" connotations of the word "techne," it is implicit in its very nature to allow for a gap, a disharmony, between logos and *ergon.*[7]

Laches' praise of the Doric harmony implicitly raises these issues and when placed within the context of the dialogue as a whole provides an important clue to what "nontechnical" knowledge means for Plato. The knowledge of arete, that is, the goal of the early dialogues, is not a techne; it cannot suffer a gap between logos and *ergon.* The possession of it as a logos must entail its rightful actualization. What this means is not yet clear but will become more so as the analysis proceeds.

To return again to the text: according to Socrates, his interlocutors need

---

7. For "techne" (and "episteme") as a form of "knowing how," see Gould (1972, 3–31), who offers an alternative view.

to know what arete, the subject of their discussion, is, before they can adequately find a teacher of it. By saying this, he reiterates an essential criterion of a techne: having a determinate, and hence readily identifiable, subject matter, a *ti,* an intelligible "something," about which one may fairly ask, What is it? Before they go further in looking for teachers or evaluating claims to be able to teach, the discussants have to know what their subject is. It is arete. But what does this mean? Answering such a question, Socrates says, would be too big a job. In order to facilitate the discussion, he proposes limiting the investigation to a "part" (*meros:* 190c9) of arete. The question, which is generated by the questionable assumption that arete has parts, now becomes, What is courage? Laches ventures the first answer: "If someone is willing to defend against his enemies and stay in formation and not run away, you'd better believe that he would be courageous" (190e).

This is, for Socrates, hardly satisfying as a definition, for it does not achieve a sufficient level of generality and is thus easily dismissed by a counterexample: it is possible to be courageous while retreating (191c), as Socrates was at Delium. Laches understands the objection and quickly revises his proposal. Courage, he says, is "endurance of the soul" (*karteria . . . tēs psuchēs:* 192b9). This definition turns out to be too general. "Endurance of the soul" would include foolish endurance, which the participants agree cannot be good at all. Since they agree that courage is good (192c), the definition must be revised again.

Laches' third definition is "intelligent (*phronimos*) endurance" (192d10). This is a promising move, for with it knowledge, at least in the form of "intelligence," is wedded to excellence. And this, as mentioned earlier, is an assumption basic to the early dialogues. As Kahn and several other commentators have pointed out, further evidence of its promise is that "it is never directly refuted."[8] Instead, Socrates demands only that the meaning of "intelligent" be specified. To accomplish this, he asks for an analysis of the following example: "If someone shows intelligent endurance in the spending of money, knowing (*eidōs*) that if he spends more, he will possess more, would you call this man courageous?" (192e).

In other words, if a man has the money-making techne and calculates correctly that a certain investment will be profitable, it takes no courage to invest. Other examples cited to make the same point are a doctor who

---

8. Kahn 1986, 12. The assumption that definitions not refuted can be attributed to Plato, sometimes called the "Bonitz principle," is, however, questionable. See Schmidt 1992, 42–45.

does not relent when a sick patient demands water, which the doctor *knows* will harm him, a general who *knows* his troops are superior in battle, those who enter battle *knowing* horsemanship or archery, and a technically proficient well diver.

Each example is of a kind of knowledge that significantly reduces the ill effects of chance, of *tuchē,* to its possessor. Diving into wells is a risky business for most of us, but not for one who has mastered the techne of well diving. Therefore, although it might take courage for an untrained layman to dive into a well, it does not for a technical well diver (compare *Protagoras* 349e, where this example is invoked for different reasons).

This inverse relationship between techne and *tuchē* is of long standing. Recall Aeschylus's Prometheus: human beings, he asserts, will become masters of their own destiny, manage the winds of fortune, and greatly enhance their chance of survival once they possess the technai. This point (which appears as criterion 3 on List 4) becomes prominent in later discussions. As Nussbaum puts it (see criterion 6 on List 5), "[A] techne is a deliberate application of human intelligence to some part of the world, yielding some control over tuchē." The critic of the Hippocratic physicians accepts such a view, and so denounces medicine as nontechnical precisely because it fails to guarantee success in controlling illness. Some patients die, and the cause of recovery in others, the critic argues, may well be a matter of luck.

Socrates' examination of Laches' definition seems to assume this conception of techne. If "intelligent endurance" is modeled by techne, which in turn is assumed to mitigate the ill effects of *tuchē,* and if courage requires facing the dangers *tuchē* implies, then courage cannot be "intelligent endurance." Is courage, then, "foolish endurance"? No, since knowledge has already been wedded to excellence and since foolish endurance would be shameful (see 192d). The quest for a definition has thus reached an impasse. It must be noted, however, that Laches' actual definition, "intelligent endurance," has not itself been refuted, for Socrates has only demonstrated the difficulties of understanding what *phronimos,* "intelligent," means. *If* the model for intelligence is a $techne_1$, then the definition fails, for courage requires the presence of risk. Such a failure, however, does not imply that courage is "foolish endurance." That would be true *only if* $techne_1$ were the exclusive model for "intelligence." And as Chapter 1 indicates, this is not the case. Perhaps the intelligence that is courage is more like a $techne_2$, or perhaps it is nontechnical knowledge (whatever that means).

Unlike Socrates' first use of the techne analogy with Lysimachus, which was for the purpose of *exhortation,* against Laches' definitions it is for *critique.* His arguments expose the difficulties generated by employing the most obvious sense of techne to model moral knowledge/courage. This argument, then, can be of little assistance to proponents of the SAT. It is not surprising, therefore, that neither Irwin nor Nussbaum refer to it. (This omission is particularly egregious in Nussbaum's case, since her book is subtitled *Luck and Ethics in Greek Tragedy and Philosophy.*)

Nicias takes over the conversation. (I omit discussion of 194a–b, a passage of great importance, but return to it shortly.) Echoing what he has heard from Socrates, he defines courage as "a kind of wisdom" (194d9). Socrates, with Laches' encouragement, demands that "wisdom" be specified. He asks, "Surely it would not be skill at playing the flute?" (194e); in other words, surely it would not be knowledge analogous to a specific techne. As he did with Laches' "intelligent," Socrates uses the techne analogy to expose the ambiguities in "wisdom."

Nicias grants that courage as wisdom is not analogous to a typical techne, and he proceeds to specify his definition in the fashion requested by Socrates. Courage, Nicias says, "is knowledge (*epistēmē*) of what is to be feared and what is to be dared in war and in everything else" (194e11–195a1).[9] This time Laches leads the attack, and does so in a Socratic fashion. Doctors know what is to be feared or dared in the matter of disease. Farmers know what is to be feared or dared in the case of agriculture. In general, those who have a techne know what is to be feared and what dared "in their own technai" (195b9). But surely, Laches concludes, this does not make them courageous.

Like Socrates, Laches has identified the episteme mentioned by Nicias with techne, and then on the basis of this identification shown the weakness of the definition. In other words, *if* the knowledge that is courage is modeled by techne, then courage cannot be knowledge. Nicias, however, rebuts: "[Laches] . . . believes that doctors know more about those who are sick than they are able to explain what health and sickness are. But doctors know only this much. Do you think, Laches, that when a man's recovery is more fearful than his being sick, doctors know this? Or don't you think that for many people it is better not to recover from a disease than to recover from it?" (195c).

Nicias argues that a techne such as medicine is, to use the term invoked

<hr/>

9. Compare *Protagoras* 360d, Aristotle, *Nicomachean Ethics* 3.7–8, and Thucydides 2.40.

in Chapter 1, "value-neutral." The doctor qua doctor knows only what health and disease are, and can thereby intervene in order to produce one or the other. He does not, however, know whether he *should* apply or withhold his knowledge. He does not know, for example, whether it is better or worse for a given patient to die. Laches and Nicias agree that in some cases it is indeed better for a patient to die. But the doctor qua doctor does not know in which cases this would be so. Only a man who is courageous and therefore knowledgeable about what should be feared and what dared, would know this.[10]

By showing that courage as knowledge is *not* like an ordinary techne, Nicias fends off Laches' attack. But Laches presses forward: by defining courage as knowledge of what should be feared or dared, Nicias must think courageous men are prophets, for who else would know whether it is better for a man to live or to die? No, says Nicias, prophecy too is a typical, that is, value-neutral, techne: it knows something about the future, but not whether what is coming is good or bad and therefore should be welcomed or dreaded (195e).

Again, Nicias seems to understand that courage as knowledge cannot be a typical techne. By definition, courage must be value-laden, whereas (in this dialogue at least) techne is conceived as value-neutral. By making this distinction he defends himself against Laches' use of the techne analogy. But he pays a price: he fails to describe positively what the "moral knowledge" he recommends actually is. Laches gets frustrated: "But, Socrates, I don't understand what he means. For it is clear that neither a prophet nor a doctor nor anybody else whom he has mentioned is the courageous man, unless he means that he is a god" (196a).

This remark again reveals Laches' considerable insight. He understands, as Nicias does not, what a dilemma the latter faces. Nicias defines courage as a kind of wisdom, or knowledge. But what kind? It is not one of the technai, for these are value-neutral. But they are also the most ordinary, easily recognizable forms of knowledge. Courage, then, must be an *extraordinary* kind of knowledge; such, at least, is suggested by the phrase "unless he means that he [the possessor of this knowledge] is a god." In other words, Laches' frustration is insightful, for it tokens his understanding of the difference between moral knowledge and a typical techne. Nicias, despite his professed sympathy for Socratic discourse, unreflectively assumes that courage as knowledge is accessible and straightfor-

---

10. Hemmenway (1993), Tiles (1984), and Warren (1985) each argue that for Plato techne is not value-neutral (not a "two-way" *dunamis*).

ward. He is unaware of the extraordinary character of moral knowledge and the resulting difficulty in identifying it. In other words, the task of doing so *should* be frustrating. Perhaps such knowledge would be a techne$_2$, the type of knowledge, represented by Isocrates and the Hippocratics, that, precisely because it is not a typical techne, requires a "special" justification. Perhaps, as I argue, courage as knowledge is nontechnical. If so, the difficulties in defining it will be even more pressing.

Socrates continues the refutation of Nicias. He attacks the definition—courage is a kind of wisdom/episteme—for contradicting common sense. We typically identify various men and even some animals (like the lion) as courageous. If Nicias's definition holds, then all such apparently courageous beings would be stripped of their virtue (196d–e). Laches enthusiastically endorses Socrates' attack: "By the gods, Socrates, well said! Nicias, answer this honestly for us, whether you say that these animals, which everybody agrees are courageous, are wiser than we, or do you dare to oppose everybody and refuse to call them courageous?" (197a).

Nicias is indeed willing to oppose commonsense and ordinary *doxa*. He explains that when we call certain animals or people (such as children) "courageous," we do so wrongly. They are fearless, not courageous, because courage is a kind of wisdom. Again, Laches' exasperation and his unwillingness to abandon the ordinary meaning of "courage" are instructive. Nicias's definition of courage, a wisdom allowing us to discriminate between what is fearful and what is not, cannot be a techne. A typical techne has a specific subject matter securely identifying it. Medicine, for example, is about the health and disease of the human body; farming is about the production of crops from the earth. Techne is knowledge ordinarily identified and typically rewarded with a fee. Since, however, it is value-neutral, it is an illegitimate model for arete. Thus, when Nicias glibly identifies courage with knowledge and then casually denies it is technical, he reveals his unreflectiveness. He does not understand the depths of the difficulties attending his own logos. Nevertheless, he is willing to sacrifice the ordinary conception of courage for his ill-conceived definition. It is a bad trade, and Laches knows it.

The conclusion of the dialogue contains Socrates' final refutation of Nicias. I schematize the argument, which runs from 198a to 199e, as follows:

1. Courage is a part of arete. (This was agreed to at the outset of the argument: 190c6.)

2. Courage is defined by Nicias as episteme of what is to be feared, what is to be dared.
3. Fear is the expectation of future evil.
4. Therefore, knowledge of what is to be feared and what not is knowledge of future goods and evils.
5. Knowledge (based on the models of medicine and farming at 198e) cannot be restricted to the future. Its purview must span past, present, and future alike.
6. Therefore, there can be no knowledge of future evils and goods; there can only be knowledge of good and evil *simpliciter*.
7. Knowledge of good and evil *simpliciter* would be the whole (*sumpasa*), and not a part, of arete. He who possessed such knowledge would not lack in courage, moderation, piety, or justice.
8. Therefore, Nicias's definition is self-contradictory: courage is defined as both a part of, and as the whole of, arete (198a–199e).

This refutation succeeds only because of the contradiction generated by the assumption, *first proposed by Socrates,* that courage is a part of arete. As a result, the refutation does not seriously challenge the central tenet of Nicias's definition, courage as a kind of wisdom, or knowledge. As was the case with the previous definitions, this one is not directly refuted. It is therefore reasonable to conclude that for Socrates, in the *Laches* at least, courage is a kind of wisdom. But what kind of wisdom? Since no specific answer is given and accepted, the *Laches* ends in aporia. But even if the various attempts to define courage do not succeed, they do not entirely fail. By using the parts of the definitions not directly refuted or dismissed by Socrates, we can extract a rough outline of what courage is. It *is* a "kind of wisdom." If (and this is a controversial move) we want to include an emotion component, we can say it is "intelligent endurance." (This is controversial because Socratic ethics are usually said to be thoroughly "intellectualistic.")[11] Griswold performs this extraction nicely: "[C]ourage is an endurance of the soul, in a situation containing risk to oneself, endurance accompanied by knowledge (which is not a techne), of goods and evils hoped for and feared."[12]

Of course, such a definition provokes the question, *what is nontechnical knowledge?* To which I make two suggestions. The first emerges from the last argument of the *Laches,* concerning the unity of virtue. Socrates' refutation seems to imply that the supposedly individual virtues lose their

11. See Gould 1987.
12. Griswold 1986a, 189.

independent status because they are each subsumed under the single definition of knowledge of good and evil. The unity of the virtues is one of the
famous Socratic paradoxes—for to declare that courage is not distinct
from justice and wisdom seems to contravene common sense—and large
quantities of ink have been spilled in its discussion.[13] Does Socrates believe
that excellence, because it is knowledge of good and evil, is a simple unity,
or does he think that it has parts that mutually imply one another? If the
former, as seems to be the case in the final refutation of Nicias, then why
does he begin his examination of Laches and Nicias with the assumption
that courage is but a part of arete? I contend, with Penner, that Socrates
does believe that excellence is a unity and that he himself offers what turns
out to be (by his own lights) a false assumption as a kind of teaching device
with which to demonstrate what courage is not.[14] What is most important to
my analysis, however, is its ramifications for the techne question.

Socrates' refutation of Nicias suggests that arete, understood as knowledge of good and evil, cannot be broken down into parts. As a result, it
cannot meet the criteria of the most rigorous form of techne discussed in
Chapter 1, namely, that represented by the "Techne" tradition in rhetoric
and outlined on List 8. Given this conception, in order to achieve maximal
clarity and precision, the subject matter of a techne must be analyzable
into component parts, and a series of rules must be generated by which to
govern the reconstitution of those parts into well-ordered wholes. The
paradigm of such a subject matter was the alphabet, the study of which
issues in orthography.

If arete cannot be broken down into parts, if it is not like the alphabet,
then virtue as knowledge is not like orthography. As a result, it cannot be
systematically taught; there is no "handbook," no "Techne," of rules to
assure its mastery. These negative comments are reminiscent of Isocrates'
objection to his competitors who invoke orthography as a paradigm in the
mistaken belief that their subject is sufficiently *tetagmenē* to be purchased
and easily learned. For Isocrates, logos is fundamentally different from the
alphabet, since it cannot be broken down into constituent parts and then
synthesized flawlessly. Instead, logos comprises an indefinite field, to become excellent in which requires years of personal communication with a
master. It is a precarious venture requiring a student with natural talents
and a gifted teacher.

13. A recent example is Penner 1992b.
14. Penner 1992c.

Socrates' refutation of Nicias suggests a similar conception, namely, that arete is some sort of unanalyzable whole. On the one hand, such a view does indeed seem paradoxical: people typically think that someone can be courageous without being just or wise. On the other hand, this view is commonsensical in that, as Laches has already noted, many would agree that teaching excellence is a peculiar, even extraordinary, task. It is easy to imagine learning how to fight in armor or become a shipbuilder. These are typical technai and hence can be taught. By contrast, it is difficult to understand how one teaches excellence. Is it even possible? If so, why is learning it so difficult? Why do virtuous parents regularly fail to transmit it to their children? Why can there not be a moral *technitēs* who hangs a shingle and can be hired as a consultant? Perhaps because arete as knowledge of good and evil is some sort of whole incapable of being broken down into the constituent parts of courage, justice, and so forth. As a result, it cannot become the object of a *tetagmenē* techne, a fixed and mechanically communicable set of rules.

My second suggestion concerning "nontechnical knowledge" is, once again, to focus on the eponymous character of the dialogue. I refer in particular to two critical passages. (1) At 188d Laches praises the "Doric harmony" and describes himself as a *philologos* only if a man's logoi harmonize with his *erga*. This passage is important because, to reiterate, it shows that techne fails as a model of moral knowledge because it implies a gap between knowledge of the subject matter, which can be construed as having a logos, and its correct use, that is, its *ergon*. In other words, a techne is value- or use-neutral. A doctor knows how to heal a patient of a given disease, but he does not know if it would be better for the patient to die. Since courage is specifically described as knowledge of good and evil, it cannot be a techne. The person with the moral knowledge Socrates seeks will suffer no gap between the possession and the good application of such knowledge. He will, in this sense, exhibit a Doric harmony of word and deed. He will have a practical knowledge; he who possesses knowledge of good will be good. Since this knowledge is not a techne, it will not necessarily effect any control over *tuchē*. Even if the possessor acts and knows well, bad luck may impinge and wreak havoc. The possessor will achieve a Doric harmony, an appropriate fit, of word and deed, a complete whole. The knowledge will be the good life well lived.

This is vague. I clarify with three words that might appear to digress but in fact disclose a central argument of this entire book: *Plato wrote dialogues.* A dialogue is a kind of drama, an imitation of praxis, of characters acting. Plato chose the dialogue form, I propose, because it is the ideal vehicle with which to express nontechnical knowledge. The dialogue is a logos inseparable from deeds. To illustrate: consider the second passage that features Laches. (2) After his final attempt to define courage has failed, he responds: "I am ready, Socrates, not to give up. Although I am unaccustomed to these sorts of discussions, a passion for victory (*philonikia*) has grabbed me concerning what has been said, and I'm really irritated that I cannot articulate what it is I think. On the one hand, I believe that I can think about what courage is. On the other hand, I do not know how it just now has escaped me so that I can't comprehend it in a definition and state what it is" (194a–b).

This statement captures the tension between having an intuition and being able to give an account of same. Laches believes he can reliably identify a courageous man. He trusts his intuitions and consequently believes he knows what courage is. When pressed by Socrates, however, he is unable to define it adequately. Contrary to O'Brien's comment that he "quickly gives in," Laches is eager to carry on the search.[15] Indeed, he says that a *philonikia* has grabbed him and that he wants to push on.[16]

It is crucial to note that the issue at hand is of more than abstract or passing interest to Laches. He is a professional soldier, and as such, his basic moral "worldview" depends on his ability to distinguish between courage and cowardice. If he cannot define courage, then how can he distinguish between courage and cowardice, between good and bad soldiers? How can he effectively judge himself? And if he cannot do this, then his worldview is seriously jeopardized. That Laches pushes forward in the face of such risk is evidence of what can be termed "philosophical courage," which Socrates alludes to when he says, "Let us too be steadfast and enduring in our inquiry, so as not to be ridiculed by courage herself for failing to be courageous in our search for her" (194a).[17]

In his exhibition of "philosophical courage" Laches exemplifies the Doric harmony of word and deed. He does something: endure in the face of a potentially risky situation, namely, the destruction of his moral worldview. Laches also says something: in essence, "I don't know what courage is, but I want to find out." As a character in the dialogue he harmonizes word and deed. He exhibits philosophical courage. He exhibits nontechnical knowledge.

15. O'Brien 1963, 141.
16. The joke is that Nicias fails to exhibit *philonikia*.
17. This theme is the focus of Griswold 1986a.

Nontechnical knowledge is the Doric harmony of word and deed. It is knowledge that can be lived. It is not an abstract techne like mathematics or a productive one like shipbuilding; it is not like medicine, in which a gap exists between knowledge and use. Instead, this knowledge, as Plato portrays it, reveals a deep awareness of and sympathy with the kinds of objections to techne offered by Solon and Sophocles. The moral knowledge Plato advocates can accommodate these objections. The moral knowledge he recommends, then, is best exemplified by living dialogue, of which Plato's writings are imitations. As written works they attempt to reflect or exhibit or reveal the nontechnical knowledge that is arete.

My account is unsatisfying, for to "turn" to the drama of the dialogue, rather than to an analysis of specific arguments or the construction of "Plato's Moral Theory," offers no explicit definition of courage. This, however, is a crippling objection only if it is assumed that techne (the most satisfying form of knowledge) is the appropriate model for moral knowledge. In the *Laches* this assumption is problematic. As such, my turn to the drama is plausible and accomplishes something the standard account of techne cannot: namely, it gives an account of why Plato wrote dialogues. On my reading, the literary form Plato chooses is essentially related to the philosophical content he wishes to express. The dialogue is not merely a pedagogical device, nor is it meant to conceal a positive, nondialogical teaching. It is not provisional in the sense that Plato hopes someday to be able to replace it with a treatise or a techne. Instead, it is essential to the Platonic teaching. Moral knowledge is nontechnical. It is not reducible to a set of true propositions. It must embrace word and deed. And only the dialogue form can adequately explain it.[18]

This attempt to flesh out the character of nontechnical knowledge is far from complete. At the least, however, this section has shown what difficulties ensue if moral knowledge is modeled on a techne. The dialogue, I conclude, points to or suggests the possibility of some sort of nontechnical knowledge, which acknowledges the power of *tuchē*, does not have a determinate and analyzable subject matter, suffers no gap between logos and *ergon*, cannot be readily or mechanically taught, and is thoroughly precarious. Obviously, these negative descriptions call for further explication. A study of the *Charmides*, in which the question, What is *sōphrosunē?* becomes paramount, will offer just this.

18. Much has recently been written on the dialogue form. See Griswold 1988, for a thorough discussion.

Sōphrosunē in the *Charmides*

The techne analogy is prominent in Socrates' refutation of Critias's definition of *sōphrosunē* ("moderation" or "temperance"). He uses it in much the same fashion as he did when examining the two basic definitions of courage in the *Laches*—"intelligent endurance" and "a kind of wisdom"—namely, to disclose the kind of knowledge that arete is not. The analogy thus leaves the reader with the following conditional: if knowledge is best modeled by a techne, then arete cannot be knowledge. Since it is essential to the Platonic dialogues that the consequent be false, it follows that arete cannot be a techne. Such, at least, is the argument of this chapter.

The background to the central argument of the *Charmides* is this: upon returning from the Athenian defeat at Potidea, Socrates goes to the gymnasium. Showing virtually no reaction to the bloody battle, he asks who among the young men are distinguished in "wisdom or beauty or both" (153d4). Critias answers that Charmides surpasses all. To test this boast, Socrates wishes to examine the boy. Critias agrees, but deems it necessary to lie to Charmides, telling him that Socrates knows a cure for the morning headaches he has recently suffered.[19] Socrates plays along. Yes, he says, he does know the cure: a certain leaf whose application is accompanied by the singing of a charm (155b–e).

In his guise as a physician, Socrates seems to "practice" a form of holistic medicine, for he stipulates that the charm cannot cure the head in isolation from the rest of the body.[20] Indeed, having studied with the Thracians, Socrates applies this principle to the psyche as well, "for if this [the psyche] is out of order it is impossible for any part to be in order" (156e5–6). To be free from his headaches, then, Charmides requires *therapeia* of the *psuchē* (two terms prominent in the *Laches*; see 185e4).

Because Socrates *pretends* to be a physician, it is fair to infer that, just as he admitted in the *Laches* (186c), he in fact does not have the psychotherapeutic techne. Perhaps his description of the charm, an essential ingredient in the proposed cure of Charmides, helps to explain why. True medicine, at least as practiced by the Thracians and espoused here by Soc

---

19. Hyland (1981, 41) speculates that Charmides' morning headaches are actually hangovers. In general, this is a superb analysis of the dramatic aspect of the *Charmides*. In what follows, my translations are based on those by Lamb (Cambridge, Mass.: Harvard University Press, Loeb Classical Library, 1974).

20. See Coolidge 1993 for a good discussion of this entire scene.

rates, refuses to separate and then treat the parts of a human being in isolation from the whole. Since, as stated in Chapter 1, a rigorous techne$_1$ requires that parts can be so separated (see criterion 3, List 8), then Socrates, if the Thracian principle holds, cannot be a technical psychotherapist (at least not in the sense of a techne$_1$). Thracian, or holistic, therapy treats the entire psychosomatic unity of the human being. Three options therefore remain: Socrates is a technical psychotherapist, but has a techne$_2$; he has no knowledge of psychotherapy at all; or finally, he has some mode of nontechnical knowledge. I argue that, like the *Laches,* the *Charmides* points to a conception of nontechnical knowledge.

The charm to cure Charmides consists of "beautiful words," for by these "*sōphrosunē* is engendered in the psyche" (157a5–6). Does the boy lack *sōphrosunē,* the source of health for the head and everything else? Critias says no (157d). Socrates examines him to find out: "Now, it is clear that, if *sōphrosunē* is present in you, you can form some opinion of it. For if it is within you, as I assume it is, it is necessary that it supply some perception (*aisthēsin*) from which you can form some opinion of what *sōphrosunē* is, and what kind of thing it is. Don't you think so?" (158e7–159a4).

Charmides agrees: if someone is *sōphron,* the virtue of *sōphrosunē* is somehow "in" him, and he should then be able to "look within himself" (160d6), gain an *aisthēsis* of *sōphrosunē,* and as a result be able to offer some answer to the question, What is it? Since he understands and can speak Greek, Charmides should thus make himself available for the Socratic *ti esti* style examination. He is cooperative and to the question, What is *sōphrosunē*? answers, "[D]oing everything in an orderly fashion and quietly . . . what may be called quietness" (159b3–5).

His answer is on a level of particularity similar to Laches' first effort to define courage (staying at one's post: *Laches* 190e), and is likewise dismissed by a counterexample. Since it is a virtue, *sōphrosunē* is always good. Sometimes, however, it is not good to do things quietly (or slowly, as Socrates changes terms). With all sorts of examples, both bodily and psychic, Socrates shows that often quickness, and not quietness, is good. Therefore, *sōphrosunē* cannot be quietness (159c–160c).

Charmides' second try is "modesty" (*aidōs:* 160e4), which is again refuted on the grounds of insufficient generality. *Sōphrosunē* is always good, and as Homer attests, modesty is "no good mate for a needy man" (161a4). The definition is abandoned.

In the third definition the discussion begins to shift toward Critias, for

Charmides, in a move Socrates strongly condemns, borrows from his cousin the proposition "doing one's own business" (161b6). Socrates rebukes Charmides in extremely strong language—"you vile polluter," he says at 161b8—because the young man has, at this dramatic moment, failed "to look within himself" in order to find *sōphrosunē*. In other words, he has ceased to think for himself and instead (like Nicias) has borrowed from Critias and unreflectively repeated an impressive sounding answer. Quite unlike Laches, who at a similar moment admitted that he did not know the answer to Socrates' question, Charmides exhibits philosophical cowardice. He fears the admission of ignorance, falls back on a borrowed answer, and thereby betrays the very project of philosophical inquiry.

Aiming his remarks at the still silent Critias, Socrates begins the refutation of "doing one's own business": scribes do the business of others, that is, they are hired to write for others. This is true of other *techniteis* as well, "for in healing, and building, and weaving and the production of results by some techne from some techne" (161e6–8) the producer does someone else's business. Socrates seems to interpret Charmides' definition—literally, "doing (*prattein*) the things of oneself (*ta heautou*)"—as follows: "*Prattein*" embraces within it virtually all activities, including those of the technai, and so would best be translated by the equally broad "doing." "Oneself" connotes an almost material sense of "self." By writing a letter for a customer, for example, a scribe does the work of someone else. This simply means that he writes a letter belonging to another person, and so the "oneself" connotes almost tangible boundaries; the scribe reaches out beyond his own body to do the work of another. On this reading, if I hire a housebuilder and he builds a house for me, he is doing my business.

Socrates repeats the outline of his argument: all "craftsmen" (*dēmiourgoi*) make (*poiein*) something, and not just for themselves but for others as well. There is no reason to suppose that a craftsman cannot be *sōphron* in doing so. Therefore, the definition, "doing one's own business," is wrongheaded. Critias squirms at what he takes to be the mishandling of his ideas by his protégé and finally enters the dialogue himself. Socrates, Critias says, confuses *poiein* and *prattein*. Basing his remarks on a line from Hesiod's *Works and Days*—"work (*ergon*) is no reproach"— he argues that "[m]aking (*poiēsis*) is different from doing (*prattein*) and working (*ergasia*), and that while a thing made might be a reproach if it had no connexion with what is fine (*kalon*), work could never be a reproach. For things finely and usefully made [Hesiod] called works, and such makings he called working and doings" (163c).

As Socrates correctly points out, such Prodicean wordplay does not address the serious questions attending the definition (such as, What is the difference between making and doing, and what really does "oneself" mean?). He encapsulates Critias's objection by asking, "Do you say that this doing or making, or whatever you want to call it, of good things, is *sōphrosunē*?" (163e1–2).

Critias agrees, choosing "the doing (*praxis*) of good things" (163e4) as his official formulation. After remarking that perhaps Critias's definition is true, Socrates changes tack entirely and asks, "[B]ut still I wonder, whether you judge that *sōphron* people are ignorant of the fact that they are *sōphron*" (164a2–3). A physician, for example, performs what is apparently a beneficial service, namely, making someone healthy. As such, his work conforms to the definition of *sōphrosunē* as "doing good things." But does the physician know when his application of the medical techne is beneficial (*ōphelimōs*) and when not? No, agrees Critias, he does not (164a–b).

Socrates' abrupt objection to Critias expresses a familiar point: a *technitēs* such as the physician is generally assumed to do good works and, given Critias's definition, thereby to be *sōphron*. But the physician himself does not know that he is virtuous, for the medical techne is itself value- or use-neutral. The physician may apply the correct bandages to save a patient's life, but if the patient is a tyrant, perhaps it would have been better to let him die. As Solon and Sophocles, and perhaps even Laches, have warned, techne is blind to the fate and ultimate value of its applications.

This use of the *technitēs* to exemplify the *sōphron* man forces Critias to revise his definition radically. In order to accommodate Socrates' objections, he shifts from "doing good things" to "self-knowledge" (*to gignōskein heauton*: 164d4). It is as if Socrates' examination had triggered a "Solonic" recognition in Critias, namely, that techne, as typically conceived, is limited to the production of an object external to the *technitēs* himself and knows nothing beyond that object. In other words, techne is object-oriented rather than self-reflexive. And this implies it is neutral on the question of use or value, for to understand use requires reflection, not on the object conceived as distinct from the subject, but on the object as part of an expanded context including the object and the subject (the *technitēs* himself).

Critias's definition of *sōphrosunē* as "self-knowledge" is a direct response to Socrates' demand that the *sōphron* man *know* he is doing something good. It is a turning point of the dialogue, for (as does Laches' definition of courage as "intelligent endurance") it bonds arete to knowledge.

No defense is given of this bond; nonetheless, it functions as a guiding theme for the remainder of the dialogue. At this point in the analysis, I draw only one conclusion: techne (in the form of the physician; see 164b) is rejected as a possible model for this explicitly value-laden conception of knowledge.

As a result of the above, Socrates' next question, which initiates his examination of "self-knowledge," may seem difficult to explain. He asks: "[I]f *sōphrosunē* is some sort of knowing (*gignōskein*), it is clear that it would be an episteme and of something (*tinos*). Right?" (165c5–6). As in the *Laches*, "episteme" is used synonymously with "techne" (although in the *Charmides* the former is more common than the latter), and so the second of the two operative assumptions, namely, the techne analogy itself, is now in place. But this is puzzling: techne has *already* been (provisionally) rejected, on the grounds of lacking self-reflection, as a model through which to explicate self-knowledge. Even if he does good things, the doctor qua doctor does not, indeed cannot, know he is doing good. But if this is the case, then why would Socrates, in his initial effort to explicate "self-knowledge," assume it is a techne?

The reason is similar to that found in the *Laches*. Recall Socrates' use of the analogy with the technical *paidotribēs* to convince Lysimachus not to rely on the opinion of the majority, but rather to seek someone knowledgeable concerning arete (184e). This use does not in itself imply that moral knowledge is a techne; instead, it can be explained via the character of Lysimachus. He is a nonphilosopher for whom the technai are readily identified examples of reliable and authoritative knowledge. Socrates understands his interlocutor's beliefs and is able to exhort him accordingly. What can thus be safely inferred from Socrates' use of the analogy is only the belief that, like a techne, moral knowledge is knowledge and should be sought.

Similarly in the *Charmides:* Socrates invokes a familiar kind of knowledge in order to clarify the otherwise obscure notion of "self-knowledge." *Sōphrosunē* as self-knowledge "sounds good" to its advocate, Critias, and does respond, albeit too broadly, to the Socratic demand that self-reflection be a component of virtue-as-knowledge. But what exactly it means is hardly obvious. Socrates' explication of it via the techne analogy (pace Irwin and other proponents of the SAT) need not imply that "[i]n the *Charmides* [Socrates] . . . considers what kind of craft [*sōphrosunē*] must be . . . he must assume it is no more than a craft."[21] Instead, Socrates

21. Irwin 1977, 31.

invokes this familiar kind of knowledge as a negative contrast by which to identify the value-laden knowledge that is *sōphrosunē*.[22]

Back to the text: *sōphrosunē* as "self-knowledge" is assumed to be an episteme (or techne) of something (*tinos*). To determine what this "something" is, Socrates applies the following analogy: medicine is the episteme of health, which is its useful (*chrēsimē*: 165c11) result; the analogous *ergon* of housebuilding is houses; since "it would be similar in the rest of the technai" (165d4–5), self-knowledge must stand in a similar relation to a determinate, useful object.[23]

Medicine and housebuilding are traditional, productive forms of techne. However, even if productive knowledge (or craft) is the oldest and most common meaning of techne, this is not, as was demonstrated in Chapter 1, its only meaning (especially after the fifth century). Critias immediately points this out: "But, Socrates, you are not inquiring correctly. For in its nature it [self-knowledge] is not like the other epistemai, any more than any of them is like any other; whereas you make your inquiry as though they were all alike. For tell me, he said, what ergon is there of the technai of calculation or geometry that is like a house is to housebuilding or cloak is to weaving, or other such erga of the sort that one might point to in many of the technai?" (165e).

This is an effective rejoinder: in demanding that self-knowledge have a discernible *ergon*, Socrates has too narrowly construed the meaning of "techne" (or "episteme" or *gignōskein*). He has, says Critias, falsely homogenized the technai, for they are not all productive crafts. The surest piece of evidence for this comes from mathematics. Geometry has no product. It is, to use language later made standard by Aristotle, "theoretical" (*Metaphysics* 6.2.8–10); rather than make or even change geometry's object, the geometrician simply "looks at" it, that is, knows an object existing independently of the knower. The technai, in short, are of at least two kinds, the productive and the theoretical (a notion badly damaging Irwin's translation of "techne" as "craft" and his performance in his debate with Nussbaum; see Appendix 3 for elaboration).

Socrates readily grants Critias's objection, for his refutation does not require techne to be exclusively productive. What it does require, not surprisingly, is that all technai have a determinate object other than them-

---

22. Hyland (1981, 96) believes that the "Right?" (*ē ou*) of 165c6 is meant to offer Critias (and the reader) a chance to say no; that is, *sōphrosunē* is not like a typical episteme/techne. This is a rich suggestion, even if *ē ou* regularly meets with an affirmative response in the dialogues.

23. Note the seamless transition from "episteme" to "techne."

selves, an *ergon* (which would then be translated not as "product" but "result"). An episteme, Socrates says, is an episteme *tinos* (166a): a specific branch of knowledge is of some object, it has a subject matter distinct from the subject, that is, the knowledge itself (and the knower). So, for example, in calculation (*logistikē*), the subject matter is the odd and the even; the object of statics is the heavy and the light (166a–b). In terms of the present argument, mathematics is the "worst" case; that is, it is knowledge at furthest remove from production. If even it exemplifies the subject (knower)-object (subject matter) structure of a techne, the principle should, a fortiori, be binding in all cases. Socrates therefore asks: "So tell me, *sōphrosunē* is episteme of what object (*tinos*) that happens to be different from *sōphrosunē* itself?" (166b5–6).

Critias again accuses Socrates of unfairly homogenizing the epistemai: "There you are, Socrates: you push your investigation up to the real issue, in what *sōphrosunē* differs from all epistemai, but you then proceed to seek some similarity between it and the rest of them. It doesn't work this way, because the rest of the epistemai have something other than themselves as their subject matter, this one alone is an episteme of the rest of the epistemai and itself is of itself" (166b–c).

Socrates then reformulates Critias's remarks: *sōphrosunē* is "the episteme of itself and of the other epistemai." As such, he infers, it will also be the episteme of "the lack of episteme" (*anepistēmosunēs*: 166e7).[24] To use a phrase to be discussed at length below: *sōphrosunē* appears to be a "second-order" form of knowledge, one whose subject matter is other instances of knowledge. Presumably, if someone is *sōphron*, he will know how to distinguish what he really knows from what he does not. In short, *sōphrosunē* as self-knowledge means "knowing what one knows and what one does not know" (167a6–7).

This definition is, of course, reminiscent of Socrates' description of his own "human wisdom" in the *Apology*, namely, his understanding that he himself is not wise (see 21d, 29b). But how does one know what one does not know? Without plunging into the difficulties quite yet, this can be said with confidence: knowledge of what one knows and what one does not cannot be a typical techne, for it would defy the subject-object structure basic to the technai. Can it then be a "second-order" techne? I argue not, for as the refutation of Critias progresses, the argument points further away from techne as a possible model for this increasingly *strange* notion of self-knowledge.

---

24. This is a much-discussed notion. See Dyson 1974.

Socrates attacks Critias's definition, "knowing what one knows and what one does not," by offering a series of examples: seeing is a seeing of something visible, and not a seeing of seeing. Hearing is hearing something audible, not hearing itself. Desire is of the pleasurable, wishing is for something good, love is of the beautiful, fear is of something fearful, and not of fear itself. Opinion too is of something other than itself (167d–168a). This rather unwieldy list of examples is meant, I think, to show that human activities, from simple sensations to complex emotions, are "intentional." When we see, hear, fear, love, and so forth, we are directed toward something other than ourselves. Because episteme, or techne, is an ordinary form of knowledge, it fits into this, the most familiar relationship of subject to object. Since it is self-reflexive, self-knowledge would not.

Socrates gives other examples to suggest the impossibility of self-knowledge. He says, "[T]his episteme is an episteme of something, that is, it has a certain faculty (*dunamis*) whereby it can be of something, isn't that so?" (168b2–3). Critias agrees. Socrates then lists various examples of other "faculties." He mentions the "greater," which he says has the *dunamis* of being greater than something. So too with the smaller, the double, the more, the heavier, and the older. If any of these *dunameis* are applied to themselves, a contradiction ensues: the more, if applied to itself, would be more than itself and so would, while being more, also be less (168b–c).

In sum, given this whole gamut of human activities—seeing and hearing and various *dunameis* such as being greater than—a basic pattern emerges. Sight sees the visible, which is not itself sight; X is greater than Y, which is not X. Even if Socrates has regularly been criticized for confusion here (in particular, for conflating the objective and comparative genitives), his point is commonsensical: self-reflection seems to be atypical. His argument perhaps is no more than a loose assembly of examples, but his point, if taken informally, seems plausible. In addition, Socrates does not categorically reject the possibility of self-reflection:

> Then do you see, Critias, that in the various cases we have gone through, how some of them strike us as absolutely impossible, while others raise serious doubts as to the faculty of the thing being ever applicable to itself. For with magnitudes, quantities and the like it is absolutely impossible, is it not?
> Certainly.
> But again, with hearing and sight, or in the further case of motion moving itself and heat burning itself, and all other actions of

the sort, the fact must appear incredible to some, but perhaps not to
others. So what we want, my friend, is some great man who will
determine to our satisfaction in every respect whether there is nothing in nature so constituted as to have it its own faculty applicable
to itself. (168e–169a)

This passage should soften the objection that Socrates' list is too motley
to secure the strong conclusion that self-reflection, and hence *sōphrosunē*
as self-knowledge, are impossible. One might, for example, fear the onrush
of fear, or love being in love. Socrates' examples, therefore, only suggest
that self-reflection, if possible, is exceptional or is, to use a word to play an
increasingly important role in this discussion, "strange" (*atopos*). To discover whether self-knowledge or any other form of self-reflexivity actually
exists would thus require "some great man (*megalos*)."

This comment should recall *Laches* 196a, the point at which Laches
becomes frustrated by Nicias's failure to clarify his definition of courage as
the episteme of what is to be feared and what is to be dared in war and in
everything else (195a). Laches does not understand what such an episteme
could possibly be. It cannot be a typical techne, such as medicine or agriculture, for surely farmers and physicians do not have courage as a result
of being knowledgeable in their areas. Nicias agrees that courage as
knowledge is not like the typical technai; these, after all, are value-neutral,
and the knowledge he has in mind is value-laden. But what is it? Prophecy? No, for the seer only knows what is coming in the future, and not
whether what is coming is good or bad and therefore should be welcomed
or feared. Except for distinguishing courage from the technai, Nicias cannot specify what this knowledge is. Again, this is the reason why the following remarks of Laches are instructive: "But, Socrates, I don't understand what he means. For it is clear that neither a prophet nor a doctor
nor anybody else whom he has mentioned is the courageous man, *unless
he means that he is a god*" (196a).

Socrates' allusion in the *Charmides* to "some great man" tokens a similar
notion as the "god" mentioned here by Laches: the possibility of extraordinary knowledge.[25] The question in the *Charmides* is, Is self-knowledge possible? If so, then it must violate the basic pattern of a typical techne, and
indeed of most human activities: it would be self-reflexive. As such, to explain or articulate it would require somebody "great." Laches makes much

25. See Hirschberger 1932, 18.

the same point: because courage as knowledge is value-laden and therefore not a typical techne, the episteme Nicias carelessly proffers as a definition of courage is intrinsically difficult to comprehend. In both the *Laches* and the *Charmides,* then, virtue as knowledge is extraordinary, is nontechnical.

Socrates, at *Charmides* 168e6, insists that it is "absolutely impossible" (*pantapasin adunaton*) for relations of "magnitudes and quantities" to be self-reflexive. If X is "more than," it must be more than some Y that is less than and thus not equal to X. As a result, mathematics cannot provide the model for self-knowledge. (This, of course, eliminates self-knowledge from consideration as a techne$_1$: see Lists 4 and 6 in Chapter 1.) He does, however, leave open the possibility of self-reflection in some of the cases he has mentioned. Perhaps the most alluring of these, as Klein thinks, is "motion moving itself." Klein notes that "self motion [is] precisely that which characterizes soul as described in the palinode of the *Phaedrus.*"[26] If the psyche is self-motion, then it is neither a "thing" nor a stable object passively waiting to be apprehended and mastered. Knowing it, therefore, would be a matter altogether different from knowing magnitudes or quantities. The question then arises, How can the psyche, or the "self," be known at all? Can it become the subject matter of a techne? Not of a techne$_1$, surely, for the psyche as so conceived is not a fixed and determinate entity. Can it become the subject matter of a techne$_2$? Possibly. Can it become the object of some sort of nontechnical knowledge? If so, what would this be?

Ultimately, Socrates declares the question of the possibility of self-knowledge intractable. He suggests, however, that he and Critias simply assume, contrary to the evidence, that it is possible (169d). If so, he asks, what good or benefit would it bring? The only answer he offers is the ability "to determine that of two things, one is episteme, and the other is not episteme" (170a7–8). This description leads to serious problems. Medicine, for example, is of health. Presumably, the person with self-knowledge would know that medicine is knowledge, while not knowing anything about health. The person would only know *that* he or someone else knows, but not *what* he knows (170c). However, to determine whether Hippocrates is a real doctor or a quack, one must know something substantial about medicine. *Sōphrosunē,* defined as episteme of episteme, does not provide for such substantial knowledge. Indeed, it has no determinate content at all (at least none analogous to an ordinary techne), and this is why it is so difficult to conceive. Socrates asks:

26. Klein 1975, 25.

Is not each episteme defined, not only as an episteme, but as a particular episteme by this, by being about something particular?
By this to be sure.
And medicine is defined as different from the other epistemai by
being episteme of health and disease.
Yes.
And so anyone who wishes to investigate medicine must investigate the subject matter of medicine (*en hois pot' estin*), and not
anything that lies outside of it. (171a5–b2)

The *sōphron* man as so defined is unable to distinguish one who knows
"the content of his techne" (*ta tēs technēs*) from one who does not, for
only someone *homotechnon* (171c8), who shares the techne and has mastered its content, can do this. Of what benefit, then, is *sōphrosunē*? Furthermore, to reiterate the earlier question, is it even possible? *Sōphrosunē*,
like courage and arete in the *Laches*, even like the psyche itself, does not
seem to fulfill the fundamental criterion of having a subject matter distinct
from itself, and so is not amenable to technical treatment. It is, therefore,
either beyond the pale of human knowledge or accessible only to a kind of
nontechnical knowledge. Socrates suggests as much when he says, "Perhaps our examining has resulted in nothing useful. I think this because in
my view such strange (*atopa*) things have appeared concerning
sōphrosunē" (172c4–5).
Critias, quite reasonably, is surprised Socrates would question the benefit of *sōphrosunē* understood as episteme of episteme: "[T]ruly Socrates,
what you are saying is strange indeed (*atopa:* 172e3)." Swearing by the
dog, Socrates agrees: *there is something strange* about this discussion, and
Socrates relates a dream to explain what:

Suppose that *sōphrosunē* were such as we now define her, that she
had entire control of us: must it not be that every act would be
done according to the epistemai, and no one professing to be a pilot
when he was not would deceive us, nor would a doctor, nor a general, nor anyone else pretending to know something he did know,
go undetected; and would not these conditions result in our having
greater bodily health than we have now, safety in perils of the sea
and war, and skillful (*technikos*) workmanship in all our utensils,
our clothes, our shoes, nay, everything about us, and various things

besides, because we should be employing genuine craftsmen (*dēmi-ourgoi*)? (173b–c)

Equipped with *sōphrosunē* to guard against ignorance, the human race "would live knowledgeably" (173d1). But, Socrates asks, would such knowledge provide for a good life? Would it result in *eudaimonia*? (173d4). This is doubtful. Even with several charitable assumptions—including (1) the possibility of self-knowledge defined as episteme of episteme, (2) the ability of someone with self-knowledge in fact to distinguish between a quack and a genuine *technitēs,* and (3) the ability of such a man to gain control of an entire polis and thereby ensure that only legitimate *techniteis* work in their claimed fields of expertise—the benefit of this knowledge would *still* be in doubt.

Socrates asks of his dreamlike vision of a *sōphrosunē,* which knows all other forms of technai: "[A]bout what is it knowledgeable?" (173d7–8). Surely it is not the making of shoes or the working in brass, wool, or wood. Surely it is not, in other words, a typical techne. Is *sōphrosunē,* then, the prophet's knowledge of the future? No. To attain to the dream vision of a world governed by knowledge, the governing knowledge cannot be restricted to the future, but must include the past and present as well (compare to *Laches* 199b–c). Perhaps it is draught playing or calculation or medicine? No. In each case, Socrates concludes, no ordinary form of knowledge will make a man happy (173d–174b).

If knowledge is to achieve *eudaimonia,* and if the techne analogy is in force, then such knowledge must have a determinate subject matter. As a result, the subject matter of *sōphrosunē* must be the good and the evil (*agathon, kakon:* 174b10). Using exactly the same phrase with which he had earlier condemned Charmides, Socrates explodes at Critias: "Vile polluter! You have all this time been dragging me round and round, while concealing the fact that the life according to episteme does not make us do well and be happy, not even if it be knowledge of all the other knowledges together, but only if it is of this single one concerning good and evil" (174c).

In terms Solon and Sophocles might have welcomed, Socrates explains to Critias that without knowledge of the good, even if the physician makes his patients healthy and the shoemaker makes his shoes, the results of these technai will not come to be "well and usefully" done (174c).

Critias responds: if *sōphrosunē* is the episteme of the other epistemai, and if the good is the object of a single episteme, then in just the same fashion that *sōphrosunē* would have shoemaking under its purview, so too would it have the good (174e). Of course, this gambit does not work, for Socrates can simply repeat the same objection: since *sōphrosunē* so defined knows only that, for example, medicine is knowledge, knows nothing about health, it cannot produce health. Similarly with the good. In sum, *sōphrosunē* still has no definite content.

Through a circuitous series of steps, then, the dialogue has reached aporia. The conception of *sōphrosunē* as value-laden self-knowledge cannot be identified. To review briefly: Beginning with the assumption that if a person is virtuous, he can explain what virtue is, the question has been, What is *sōphrosunē?* By shifting from "doing good things" to "self-knowledge" Critias makes the critical move to bond arete to knowledge. His introduction of self-reflexivity aims to make possible the kind of understanding of use that is absent in a typical, object-oriented and hence value-neutral techne. Self-knowledge, however, meets with terrible difficulties throughout the dialogue. It does not seem possible, for it has no unique content. Even if its possibility is assumed and we dream the Socratic dream of a world governed by knowledge, the problem yet remains: without knowledge of the good, there is no benefit, no *eudaimonia.*

As in the *Laches,* the aporia of the *Charmides* allows for several interpretations. First, perhaps it tokens the impossibility of self-knowledge and the error of the dialogue's guiding assumption, that is, the bonding of arete and knowledge. This reading leads to the uncomfortable conclusion that Socrates' apparent commitment to moral philosophy is a sham. Perhaps, then, the assumption is not faulty, and self-knowledge is both possible and a virtue, but *is not a techne.* This, of course, is the option I favor. There is, however, a third possibility, one figuring prominently in the "continuist" branch of the SAT; namely, that *sōphrosunē* as self-knowledge is a techne, but a "second-order" rather than a typical, or "first-order," one.

The continuists argue that Plato progressively developed, rather than abandoned, the techne model of moral knowledge. Consider Sprague's view. First, she describes a first-order "art." It is knowledge *peri tinos,* about something specific (17); that is, it has "its own special field upon which no other art encroaches" (11).[27] It is confined to that restricted field through which both the art itself and the "artist" are defined. It is exemplified by arithmeticians and doctors (8).

The key move in Sprague's analysis is to insist that "not all arts occupy

---

27. All page citations in parentheses are from Sprague 1976.

the same level"; a second-order art has no specific field, but instead is "about other arts" (7). Critias's proposed episteme of episteme would be an example. In the *Charmides* (and other early dialogues), "[t]he second-order arts, because they have no recognizable scope, appear parasitic and empty." Sprague, however, argues against such a negative conclusion: "It will turn out in fact to be the case that the art which Plato values most (that of the statesman and the philosopher: the kingly art) will have just this characteristic property of lack of specific scope" (29).

Her interpretation hinges on later works, such as the *Euthydemus*, *Republic*, and *Statesman*. I would thus get too far ahead of myself were I to argue here against her reading of those dialogues. Instead, my question is, What evidence in the *Charmides* itself shows that Plato is preparing for the establishment of a second-order art?

Sprague's Socrates believes that "the art of temperance" has the following characteristics: "[I]ts subject matter consists of (a) itself, (b) the other sciences, (c) the absence of science" (36). As noted above, this definition sounds strikingly similar to the description Socrates offers of his own "human wisdom" in the *Apology*. Sprague makes much of this similarity and argues that because of it, "Plato intends to accept the definition of temperance as a self-knowing science of sciences" (38). It turns out, of course, that because Socrates fails to articulate the structure of *sōphrosunē*, the *Charmides* ends in aporia. This does not deter Sprague from arguing that, because the self-knowledge described in the *Charmides* is similar to Socrates' self-description in the *Apology*, this *is* the kind of knowledge Plato attributes to Socrates. Furthermore, "because it also seems probable that Plato regarded Socrates as a man possessing temperance . . . we should not be too quick to . . . acquiesce in Socrates' defeat" (42).

In short, Sprague believes that the *Apology* warrants her reading of the *Charmides*, whose aporia she reads as a projection of a theoretical task, namely, the actualization of a second-order techne. There is, however, a serious problem. While the definition of *sōphrosunē* in the *Charmides* and Socrates' self-description in the *Apology* are similar, there is one enormous difference between them: the latter is not described as a techne. Indeed, in the *Apology* Socrates denies he has a techne. Recall 20a–c, his account of his conversation with Callias. If Callias's two sons were colts or calves, he would hire a horse trainer or farmer as their "overseer" (*epistatēs*: 20a8) to make them excellent in their specific virtue. His sons, however, are men. Who, then, is knowledgeable (*epistēmon*) about the human, the political virtue (20b4–5)? Callias responds that Evenus of Paros, a Sophist, has this techne (20c1). Socrates' irony makes it certain he thinks Evenus has no such knowledge, and he is explicit in saying that he himself does not possess it.

Determining what Socrates claims to know, and of what to be ignorant, in the *Apology* is crucial to an understanding of the early dialogues. As a result, my Chapter 4 is devoted to this question. What is clear now is only this: Sprague may well be right in noting a similarity between *sōphrosunē* as self-knowledge and Socrates' wisdom in the *Apology*. Even so, the *Apology* supplies no evidence that a second-order techne is the implicit goal of the *Charmides,* for it offers no notion of a Socratic techne at all.

Sprague's second-order techne not only would have in its purview the other technai but, because it is a virtue, would know how those technai *should* be used: "Plato really did intend to describe temperance as a science of sciences. Not only that, but it seems likely that he meant to identify the science of sciences with the science of good and evil—not simply to subsume the latter under the former, as Critias tried to do. (The result, of course, is that the science of good and evil becomes a second-order techne.) But the really positive evidence for this is in the *Statesman* and the *Republic,* not in the *Charmides*" (42).

This is a telling remark. Sprague uses not only the *Apology* to warrant her interpretation of the *Charmides,* but the *Republic* as well.[28] In her view, since the *Republic* actually displays a second-order, value-laden techne, it must be the case that the *Charmides* points to it: "The chief difficulties connected with the second-order arts are as follows: they have no content, they are useless, and they generate regresses. The knowledge of the good, as expounded by Plato, avoids all of these difficulties, while still retaining its second-order character" (91).

What is startling about this assertion is how little Sprague says about the subject matter of the putative second-order techne that she finds in the *Republic,* namely, the Idea of the Good. "In the images of the sun, line and cave are mingled metaphysics, logic, ethics and politics, but all are pointing in the same direction" (91). This direction is, again, toward a second-order techne. On the one hand, she is surely right in saying that the dialogues point to knowledge of the good, which in turn cannot be a typical first-order techne. On the other hand, Sprague does not squarely face the question, What sort of knowledge is it? Does the *Republic* really communicate a techne? Is it anything like the *Rhetorica ad Alexandrum* or

---

28. I do not here discuss the *Statesman.* But do see 304c.

even a Hippocratic text? Does it, like a "textbook," contain a set of rules, or even rules of thumb, concerning the practice of justice? If so, what are they?

Crudely put, the *Republic* looks nothing like a "Techne." It is a dialogue, filled with imagery and interruption, digression and obscurity. If it did "contain" a techne, it should be possible to articulate the structure of the Idea of the Good, its putative subject matter. And because Socrates largely expresses his views through images, this would be, to state the obvious, an immensely problematic task. In short, Sprague too easily assumes the possibility of a second-order art and blithely ignores the conceptual difficulties inherent in it.

I get ahead of myself. This book does not treat the middle dialogues, and so the question whether the *Republic* conceives of moral knowledge as a techne must be left open. Despite the intrinsic implausibility of her thesis, that is, despite the difficulties intrinsic to the notion of a second-order techne, it is possible Sprague is right. If, however, we attend only to the *Charmides* and other early dialogues, and not to Plato's "future," it is far from obvious what moral knowledge would be. The early dialogues should not be read through the lens of the later ones. (And the later ones should not be read through the lens of the SAT's reading of the early ones.) Instead, one question should dominate: What exactly is Socrates doing with the techne analogy in the early dialogues? Focusing only on this, the results are indeterminate. Socrates uses the analogy to expose the problems with Critias's definition of self-knowledge. From this, however, it does not follow that techne, whether first- or second-order, becomes the paradigm of moral knowledge.

Woodruff argues somewhat similarly as Sprague. He distinguishes between "a class of technai that ought to be subordinate to a ruling Techne. Subordinate technai are ones you can master without knowing exactly when it is good to apply them, or how their products are best used," while the ruling or adequate Techne "in the final analysis will turn out to be essentially the same as expert knowledge of the good." Like Sprague, Woodruff detects in the early dialogues a projection of a theoretical need, namely, the actualization of the one adequate Techne. He differs in arguing that finally Plato turned away from the techne model altogether by the time of the *Meno*. Woodruff thus combines discontinuist and continuist strands of the SAT. He aligns himself with the latter in believing that the techne project propels Plato into the middle dialogues: Socrates' demand that an adequate Techne be expert knowledge of the good is, according to

Woodruff, "the feature of Techne that will be carried most significantly into Plato's middle epistemology (e.g., *Republic* Vi 508e)."[29] Because he finds a break in the *Meno* and later dialogues, he is, of course, a discontinuist.

The distinction between subordinate and adequate, first- and second-order technai, should recall the notion of a techne$_1$ and a techne$_2$ developed in Chapter 1. The form of knowledge proper to a techne$_2$ does not have a fixed and stable subject matter that can be mastered with epistemic authority. Especially in the case of rhetoric, it is knowledge of what is contingent and indefinite. The subject matter of rhetoric, to quote Quintilian (who follows Isocrates and Gorgias), is "everything" everybody discusses. Because of the Isocratean demand that it be value-laden, rhetoric as a techne$_2$ would be quite similar to Woodruff's adequate, Sprague's second-order, techne. It would be knowledge at a different level, embracing within it other knowledges and able to answer the question of how they *should* be used.

In one important sense, however, Isocrates' discussion of rhetoric is superior to Sprague's treatment of second-order techne: simply put, he appreciates how "strange" the knowledge he claims really is. Unlike a "normal" techne, rhetoric cannot be taught systematically: it is not best modeled by a *tetagmenē* subject like orthography. It is value-laden and requires years of personal instruction in which an already well-disposed soul is molded. In sum, Isocrates appreciates why his stochastic techne$_2$, precisely because it is "strange," requires a "special justification."

"Strange" (*atopos*) is a word used several times in the *Charmides* (see 168a10), and it captures perfectly what Isocratean knowledge, as well as the self-knowledge Socrates recommends, does not have: a *topos*, a specific topic, a determinate subject matter with fixed boundaries. Does this imply that Socratic knowledge is a techne$_2$? Although the similarities between the two are indeed real, a major purpose of the final chapter of this book is to demonstrate their significant differences. To prefigure: Socrates does not possess technical knowledge, either in the form of a techne$_1$ or a techne$_2$, at all. His knowledge, which I dare call wisdom, is "nontechnical."

To summarize: In both the *Charmides* and *Laches* a particular virtue is affiliated with knowledge. Laches, responding to Socrates' prodding, defines courage as "intelligent endurance"; Nicias, explicitly citing Socrates as his source, defines it as "a kind of wisdom"; and Critias, also replying

29. Woodruff 1992, 96.

to a Socratic attack, shifts from "doing good things" to "self-knowledge" in his definition of *sōphrosunē*. These three moves are neither defended nor called into question. They reflect, therefore, a basic assumption governing these dialogues. Socrates offers a second assumption operative in both dialogues: the knowledge associated with the virtue in question is modeled on techne. The consequence in both cases is aporia.

In the *Laches*, if courage is a techne, three problems ensue: First, it would eliminate the possibility of risk taking (an essential ingredient of courage), for techne masters *tuchē*. Second, and more important, techne is value-neutral: it only knows "that" and not "should." Third, since a techne requires application for its completion, it allows for a gap between "theory" and "practice," between logos and *ergon*. By contrast, virtue as knowledge would be more like a Doric harmony of word and deed.

In the case of *sōphrosunē*, if self-knowledge defined as episteme of episteme is modeled on techne, then no determinate object can be located as its epistemic content. This is part of a broader problem concerning self-knowledge. For it to be rendered technical, the self would have to be reified or stabilized, in order to function as a proper object. The self, however, is not such an object, for it is capable of self-reflection (i.e., it moves itself). In both dialogues, then, the assumption of techne as the proper model of knowledge generates the aporia. Why Plato would have Socrates foist this model upon the dialogues has already been explained: techne is the most ordinary, the easiest to recognize form of reliable knowledge. Socrates invokes it in order to address his interlocutors appropriately, that is, at their level. He uses it not to furnish a positive theoretical model but to explain by contrast what moral knowledge is not. The techne analogy in the *Charmides* is used to expose the lack of clarity in the "strange" notion of self-knowledge. In the *Laches* it performs this function concerning "intelligent endurance" and "a kind of wisdom." By means of the analogy Plato offers the reader a lens through which the problem of moral knowledge can be reviewed.

The techne analogy has a second function. Socrates uses it to exhort Lysimachus to pursue moral knowledge. It is effective because Lysimachus will readily acknowledge the authority of a typical techne. As a result, he might be led to pursue moral knowledge.

Criticism, refutation, and protreptic, then, are purposes for which Socrates applies the techne analogy. Providing a strict paradigm for moral knowledge is not. Consequently, the standard account of techne, which in both its continuist and discontinuist branches identifies techne as the positive theoretical model for Plato's early conception of moral knowledge, is wrongheaded. Consider again Irwin's comment about *Charmides* 165c4–e3: "In the *Charmides* he [Socrates] argues that temperance is not modesty; he does not ask if it is wise modesty, but considers what kind of craft it must be . . . he must assume it is no more than a craft." On what Irwin bases this assertion is unclear. Klosko is thus on target when he says, "Exactly what the *Charmides* establishes is not clear, but it seems to damage [Irwin's reading of the techne analogy] more than support it."[30]

A final observation: Socrates describes his search for *sōphrosunē* as circular. Critias had begun with the definition "doing good things." Socrates then insisted some component of knowledge, specifically self-knowledge, be added to the definition. Critias agreed. Then Socrates proceeded to dismantle the very notion of self-knowledge and returned to the beginning of his conversation with Critias: *sōphrosunē* is knowledge of the good. Such circularity is made thematic and explicit in a dialogue soon to be discussed, namely, the *Euthydemus*. Suffice it to say here that techne implies a "linear" concept of knowledge: there is the subject, the knower, who takes up the object, or subject matter. Because it is self-reflexive, self-knowledge, like the dialogue itself, is circular: the self knows itself knowing itself. As such, it is entirely reasonable to expect this sort of knowledge to be "nonlinear," and hence to be "nontechnical."

Piety in the *Euthyphro*

Socrates meets Euthyphro, who is in the process of filing a charge against his own father for (unintentionally) killing a workman (a man who himself had murdered one of the house slaves: 4c–d). He describes Euthyphro as "far advanced in wisdom": who else would unhesitatingly perform an action so obviously problematic on religious and moral grounds? "By Zeus, Euthyphro, do you think that your knowledge of how it stands with the gods, and of the holy things (*hōsia*) and the unholy ones (*anōsia*), is so precise that, with these actions being performed as you describe, you need not be afraid that in prosecuting your father you yourself happen to be doing something unholy?" (4e)

Socrates assumes, as he does in the *Laches*, that if an interlocutor takes a strong stand on a controversial issue (as Nicias does in advocating the

30. Klosko 1981, 102.

study of armor fighting) or gives a "precise" answer to a difficult question, he must believe he is knowledgeable. In fact, the interlocutor must believe, however unreflectively, that he has something like a techne, that is, the mode of knowledge best at providing clear answers to questions (and thereby making the *technitēs* confident). Euthyphro fits the bill. Concerning religious matters he thinks himself an expert, with "clear" (5c8) knowledge. In response, Socrates expresses (ironically) a desire to become his student (5a4) in order to prepare for his forthcoming defense against Meletus's charge of impiety (*asebeia:* 5c7).

Since Euthyphro is knowledgeable, and because piety is assumed to be a self-identical universal instantiated in all pious acts (i.e., to have a single *idea*), Euthyphro should be able to answer the relevant *ti esti* question, What are the holy (*hosion*) and the unholy (*anosion:* 5d5)?

Again, even though the techne analogy has yet to be invoked, already it is implicit in the dialogue, for at least three reasons: (1) The manner in which Euthyphro's knowledge is described—it is "precise," "clear," authoritative, able to give answers—could obviously be applied to a techne. (2) Socrates' profession, however ironic, of wanting to become Euthyphro's student recalls the teachability of a techne. (3) The famous Socratic demand to answer the *ti esti* question is parallel to the demand that a techne have a determinate subject matter: it is *peri tinos,* about some *ti* that, if masterfully known by the *technitēs,* can be identified. In short, Socrates treats Euthyphro as a *technitēs.*

As were Laches' and Charmides' first responses to Socrates' *ti esti* question, Euthyphro's is too particular; "Holiness is just what I am now doing, namely, prosecuting someone who is guilty of an offense, either of murder or stealing from a temple or some other action, whether he is your father or your mother or anyone else" (5d).

Socrates rejects the answer. He wants no truck with particular examples, only a definition to articulate the "very form (*eidos*) by which all holy things are holy" (6d). Euthyphro tries to comply: "What the gods love (*prosphiles*) is holy, and what they do not love is unholy" (7a). While Socrates is pleased at the properly broad scope of the answer, he doubts it is true. The gods frequently quarrel with one another when what one loves is hateful to another. In other words, situations arise where the same thing is both holy and unholy. Since the holy and the unholy are assumed to be strict opposites, the definition falls (7a–8a). But it is soon revised: "What *all* the gods hate is unholy, and what they love is holy" (9d).

Before this revision, however, Socrates makes an important distinction.

Presumably, the gods disagree about many issues, but only concerning some does hostility (i.e., disagreement about what is loved) result. "My good man, disagreement about what creates hostility and anger? Look at it this way: if you and I disagree about number (*arithmos*), which [of two numbers] is larger, would the disagreement about this make us hostile and angry with one another, or would we settle it quickly by turning to calculation (*logismon*)" (7b6–c1).

Socrates elaborates. If there is disagreement about what is greater and what lesser, the dispute can quickly be put to rest by turning to "measurement" (*metrein:* 7c4); if the disagreement is about what is heavier and what lighter, the decision is easily made by turning to "weighing" (*histanai:* 7c7).[31] Since each of these areas of potential dispute can be studied and thoroughly mastered using a specific mathematical techne that can authoritatively adjudicate any disagreements within that area, disputants need not get angry with one another. By contrast, when disagreement occurs about what is "right and wrong, fine and shameful, and good and evil," that is, about moral issues, there is real trouble: for these no straightforward and satisfactory solution (*hikanēn krisin*) seems forthcoming. As a result, in such areas hostility between disputants is likely (7d1–5). As possible objects of inquiry, then, arithmos and morality seem fundamentally different.

Euthyphro 7a–8a highlights a familiar and important point. Recall that in the *Prometheus Bound* arithmos is cited as a decisive example of a techne. Perhaps, as Kübe suggests, even in its primitive conception, some elementary form of applied mathematics was required for a subject to qualify as a techne (see List 1 in Chapter 1). Because it supplies definitive answers, arithmos ("number" and "counting") is a paradigmatic case of techne.[32] There is, for example, no reason to get angry over the question, How many olive trees are there in this field? The answer can readily be achieved by making a count. In *Euthyphro* 7a–8a, at least, Socrates seems pessimistic about an analogously straightforward decision being reached on the question, What is the good?

Socrates proceeds to investigate the definition "what all the gods love is holy." The refutation, finally, is based upon a famous ambiguity: Is what is loved by the gods loved (and so holy) *because* it is holy, or is it holy *because* it is loved? The answer, Socrates insists, must be the former (10e).

31. See Lloyd 1987, 247–56, for a discussion of "weighing."
32. For the relationship between *arithmos* and *logismos* in Plato, see Klein 1968, 17–26, and Heath 1981, 1:13–16. See also Roochnik 1994a.

In other words, he assumes gods love for a reason, that the object of their love is worth loving, that is, is holy. But if so, then the definition is uninformative: if the holy is loved because it is holy, then the holy cannot be defined as what is loved. At best, being loved by the gods can be counted a *pathos* or attribute of the holy, but not its "essence" (11a).

The investigation reaches an impasse, and so Socrates changes tack. At his behest, Euthyphro defines piety and holiness as "the part of the right (*dikaion*) concerning 'attention' (*therapeia*) to the gods" (12e5–7). Socrates is impressed, and he praises the answer (12e9). Still, clarification is needed: What does *therapeia* mean?

> For surely you don't mean that we pay the same kind of attention to the gods as we pay to other things. We say, for example, that not everyone knows how (*epistatai*) to attend to horses, but only the man trained in horsemanship (*hippikos*). Right?
> Of course.
> The techne of horsemanship (*hippikē*) is [knowledge of] attending to horses. (13a)

Further examples of proper, that is, knowledgeable, *therapeia* are the technai of hunting (*kunēgetikē*) and ox herding (*boēlatikē*). With these remarks, two assumptions are put into play by Socrates. First, after praising "*therapeia* to the gods," he insists that, since piety is a virtue, it must be coupled with knowledge. Not everyone, but only the "relatively rare" man, knows properly "how to pay attention." Second is the techne analogy: as horsemanship (knowledgeable *therapeia*) is to horses, and ox herding to oxen, so piety is to the gods.

Given the techne analogy, however, the definition collapses. A techne, as described in the *Charmides,* is oriented to an object other than itself. If *therapeia* is modeled on a techne, then it must benefit the object of its "attention." The problem, of course, is that unlike horses and oxen, which are benefited by the attention paid to them by a human *technitēs,* the gods (by definition) are not enhanced by human ministration (13c).

The definition—which, to reiterate, Socrates praises—*fails because techne is the model of knowledge used to articulate it.* It is clear, therefore, that Irwin misrepresents this passage: "In the *Euthyphro* [Socrates] asks how piety is parallel with other crafts, what its product is."[33] Yes, Socrates

33. Irwin 1977, 72.

does ask this question, but only to demonstrate that piety, if it is in fact *therapeia* to the gods, is not a techne.

Euthyphro readily agrees that, unlike the relationship between the horse and the technical horseman, the gods cannot be enhanced by human *therapeia*. He changes his definition to "a kind of service (*hupēretikē*) to the gods" (13d7). Socrates attacks: "Now, would you say that the techne that serves the physicians happens to be a service that issues in some result (*ergon*)? And don't you think this result is health?" (13d9–11).

However convoluted its formulation, the point is familiar: a techne is *peri tinos*, about something specific; it issues in a determinate *ergon* by which it can identify itself. There is a techne, Socrates continues, serving the shipbuilder in the production of ships, and the housebuilder in making houses (13d–e). Given the strictures of the analogy, piety should be a techne serving the gods in the production of what "altogether beautiful *ergon*?" (13e10). Euthyphro dodges: these are, he says, "many beautiful things." Socrates is unrelenting: generals also can claim a plurality of fine results issuing from their techne. These, however, can readily be summarized under a single "heading" (*kephalaion*: 14a1), namely, "victory in war." So too the farmer: "the production of crops from the earth" (14a6–7). What is the analogous *ergon* of gods who are served by piety-as-techne? Euthyphro dodges again: "If someone knows how to say and do, by means of prayer and sacrifice, what is gratifying to the gods, such things are holy" (14b2–4).

Socrates reformulates: piety is "knowledge (*epistēmē*) of sacrifice and prayer." Since sacrificing is giving to the gods and praying is asking from them, piety is really "knowledge of asking from and giving to the gods." The right way of asking is to ask for what is needed from the gods. Correspondingly, the right way of giving is to give them what they need: "For it would not be technical (*technikon*: 14e3) gift giving to give someone what is not needed." Piety, therefore, is *emporikē* (14e6), the techne of commercial trading with the gods.

There is a problem. Although the gain humans receive from the gods is (supposedly) obvious, what benefit accrues to the gods in trading with us? Euthyphro answers: worship, gifts of honor, and gratitude (*charis*). Human beings can appreciate the gods' gifts and in doing so somehow benefit the gods. But why would this be a benefit? Because, Euthyphro concludes, such appreciation is dear to (or loved by, *philon*) the gods. Saying this, however, returns Euthyphro to his earlier definition, for now piety seems, once again, to be what is dear to the gods (15a–b).

The *Euthyphro* thus ends in aporia (and like the *Charmides* has a circular structure), and Euthyphro's vacillation is likened to Daedalus and Proteus (15b). Socrates closes by reiterating a basic principle: since Euthyphro boldly prosecutes his father, that is, gives an unequivocal answer to a controversial moral question, he makes a strong claim to knowledge. Conversely, should Euthyphro (like Laches) acknowledge his ignorance of what his putative virtue is—and his experience with Socrates should have led him to this conclusion—then he would not prosecute his father. Perhaps Euthyphro understands this, for he leaves the court *before* he has filed the charge against his father. Of course, he may well plan on returning as soon as Socrates finishes his business.

This indeterminate, this dramatic, ending of Plato's dialogue, forces the reader to ask, Does Euthyphro leave simply to get away from the annoying Socrates, with the intention of returning to the court tomorrow, or does he do so because he is genuinely perplexed and realizes his moral confidence is unwarranted? The reader is left to wonder.

To close: Socrates describes Euthyphro's definition of piety—part of the *dikaion* that concerns the *therapeia* to the gods—as "well said." He assumes such *therapeia*, because it is a virtue, must be connected to knowledge. The problem, however, is that, upon being modeled by techne, it becomes impossible to articulate piety as knowledge. The reader is faced with various options: Taking an "anticonstructivist" line, one may conclude that Socrates does not believe piety is the *therapeia* to the gods.[34] Or perhaps Socrates does believe this. If so, then techne must be the wrong model of that knowledge.

Perhaps the very wonder with which the reader is left concerning the departing Euthyphro is itself an important clue. If he leaves the court because he has realized his ignorance, then he has gained a kind of knowledge, one better expressed in *aporia* and through a *dialogue* than in a techne.

Justice in *Republic,* Book 1

Book 1 of *Republic* has long troubled Plato's chronologically minded commentators, to whom it seems markedly different, in tone and substance, from books 2–10. Vlastos speaks for many. Book 1, he says, is concerned

34. See McPherran 1992.

with "the way we ought to live"; there is no allusion to either a theory of separable forms or a tripartite psyche; it is elenctic in method; it ends in aporia. Therefore, he concludes, "the content of the dialogue leaves no doubt that it displays conspicuously the characteristics of Plato's earlier dialogues."[35]

As mentioned in the Introduction, Vlastos virtually ignores the techne question. However, because techne figures so prominently in book 1 (the word appears more than once per page: see Appendix 1), his position is echoed by many proponents of the discontinuist branch of the SAT. Book 1 has, for example, been read as an early work embracing the techne model of justice, a work that was added as an introduction to Plato's mature teaching found in books 2–10, in which such a model was rejected. As Irwin rightly notes, "[T]his solution still leaves us with the question why Plato should have retained [book 1], if he rejected the [craft-analogy]."[36]

In response, chronologists have constructed a subtler version of the discontinuist thesis. Consider Reeve: "Book 1 emerges as a brilliant critique of Socrates, every aspect of which is designed to reveal a flaw in his theories." So, to cite the prime example, when Plato had his Socrates use the techne analogy in early dialogues like the *Laches, Charmides,* or *Euthyphro,* he did so because he actually considered it a good model for moral knowledge. Book 1 of the *Republic,* by contrast, "exposes a crippling defect in the craft analogy." For Reeve, book 1 is an introduction to books 2–10 that prepares for a "Platonic moral theory" free from "Socratic" assumptions. After having criticized his earlier views in book 1, Plato begins book 2 by creating a Socrates "stripped of the elenchus and the craft analogy, and transformed into a positive theorist, who, having learned the lessons of [book 1], goes on to offer a much stronger response to Thrasymachus' arguments."[37]

I contend that the problems inherent in the techne analogy disclosed in book 1 are isomorphic with those *already* uncovered in the *Laches, Charmides,* and *Euthyphro.* In other words, Plato understood the basic "flaw" of the analogy *from the beginning:* if arete is assumed to be knowl-

---

35. Vlastos 1991, 248–50. Several commentators consider book 1 of the *Republic* critical to Plato's view on techne. See Kato 1986, 15–36, and Thomsen 1990, 124–35. For readings different from my own, see Hemmenway 1993, Salkever 1994, Tiles 1984, and Warren 1985 and 1989.

36. Irwin 1977, 324.

37. Reeve 1988, 22–23.

edge, and if techne is the model of moral knowledge, an unacceptable consequence—namely, arete is not knowledge—ensues. As a result, on Platonic grounds, techne is not the proper model of moral knowledge. This is the basic conclusion to which the "early" dialogues point, and it is fully compatible with book 1 of the *Republic* as well.

Even if I am correct, it is still possible to argue that in books 2–10, as well as "later" works, Plato rejects the notion of nontechnical knowledge and, as Vlastos, Reeve, Irwin, Woodruff, and other discontinuists (indeed, most English-speaking scholars) believe, forges an innovative and technical moral theory. As stated several times, this book is devoted only to the "early" dialogues. Consequently, it provides scant proof that Plato does *not* offer a new, substantial, moral theory in his "middle" works. I confess, however, to trying to derail such a reading at its onset (and to dissuade commentators from speculating about Plato's developing psyche). My strategy is to remove at least one inspiration for the discontinuist branch of the SAT, namely, the interpretation of Socrates' use of the techne analogy in the "early" dialogues as a prototype of, or a badly conceived first stab at, the kind of moral theory only coming to fruition in later works. In other words, if I succeed in showing the nontechnical character of the "early" dialogues' conception of arete, then the reader should be less disposed to *expect* a moral theory that, even if not explicitly modeled on techne, is nonetheless "technical" in the "middle" works.

This book is not a comprehensive interpretation of the Platonic corpus, and so will largely remain quiet on the "later" dialogues. Still, in order to illustrate the kind of interpretation I would welcome, in this section I make one suggestion. Through an analysis of the "ship-of-state" image in book 6 and a critique of a representative commentary, I show why, even here in the heart of the middle dialogues, Plato is not obviously a theoretical optimist espousing a technical moral theory.

Cephalus, the owner of the house in which the action of the *Republic* takes place, is conversing with Socrates about the benefits of having wealth in one's old age: "The possession of money contributes a great deal to not having to cheat or lie to any man against one's will and, moreover, to not having to depart for that other place frightened because one owes some sacrifices to a god or money to a human being" (331b).[38]

___

38. Throughout, I follow the translation of Bloom (New York: Basic, 1968). Bloom's introduction, which is heavily indebted to the work of Leo Strauss, should also be consulted for a good overview of the dramatic context. See also Howland 1993 for a good reading of the *Republic*.

From this statement Socrates (probably to Cephalus's surprise) extracts a definition of justice. He operates, therefore, with the same assumption governing the three dialogues previously discussed: a claim to virtue (such as Charmides makes or about which Euthyphro is so bold) or to knowledge of how to inculcate it (as Nicias asserts) implies the ability to define the virtue. The definition of justice Socrates extracts, almost forcibly, from Cephalus is "speaking the truth and giving back what one takes" (331d2–3).

At this point, Polemarchus takes over the defense of his father's position and gives Cephalus a welcome opportunity to leave the conversation. He agrees with his father (and Simonides) that "it is just to give to each what is owed" (331e3). Such a definition is easily rebuffed upon consideration of the case of a man asked to return a weapon borrowed from someone who subsequently has gone mad (331e–332a). The definition is therefore modified to "friends owe it to friends to do some good and nothing bad" (332a10). Later it is added that one also owes one's enemy something bad (332b8). Socrates summarizes: "[I]t is just to give to everyone what is fitting" (332c2).

At this juncture Socrates makes a critical move (underlining its importance, perhaps, with an oath to Zeus): he assimilates Polemarchus's definition under the rubric of techne. The techne (332c7) of medicine, he says, gives what is fitting (drugs, food) to bodies; the techne (332c10) of cooking gives what is fitting (seasoning) to meats. If justice is analogous to medicine and cooking (and there is no argument given to suggest why it should be), it must be a techne (332d1) and give what is fitting, namely, benefits and injuries, to friends and enemies.

Socrates has introduced twin assumptions: first, justice, as a virtue, requires or simply is a form of knowledge; second, justice as knowledge is best exemplified or modeled by techne. The ease with which Polemarchus accepts the second indicates either Socrates' ability to foist his own views on a witless interlocutor or the broad and attractive connotations of "techne" that cause it to be so easily welcomed into the conversation. (Chapter 1 is, of course, designed to support the latter.) In any case, Socrates next poses the following examples: Doctors do the most good or harm to friends or enemies with respect to (*pros:* 332c11) health and disease. Pilots do so with respect to the dangers of the sea. With respect to what *ergon* (332e3) would the just man be able to do good and harm?

A familiar point: if justice is interpreted on the model of a techne, it must have a determinate subject matter, a restricted field in which it can be exercised, and it should be recognizably useful within the confines of that field. Polemarchus dutifully obeys the mandate of the analogy and identifies war as the area with respect to which the just man can do benefit and harm. Socrates quickly dismisses this answer: the doctor is useless to someone with a healthy body; the pilot is useless on land. Given the analogy, is the just man useless in peacetime? Yes, if the analogy is held to strictly, for apart from its special field a techne is useless (332e5).

Since this description of the just man is patently ludicrous, what is needed next is identification of the particular kind of useful result justice provides in peacetime. Farming is useful for the acquisition of food, shoemaking for making shoes. Justice, Polemarchus suggests, is similarly useful for making contracts and partnerships (333a12). But Socrates relentlessly pushes for further specification. A contract is an agreement between two parties concerning some mutually decided upon item, for example, the playing of draughts or the making of bricks. With what particular type of contract, with what analogously specific item, is justice concerned?

Polemarchus offers "money matters" (333b10). Socrates challenges: "[E]xcept perhaps in using (chrēsthai) money," he says (333b11). In other words, since money must be used before it takes on actual value, no one enters into a contract concerning money not to be used; and when money is used, it is always "with respect to" something other than money. If one enters a contract hoping to profit concerning horses, he should do business with someone equipped with hippikē, the techne of horsemanship; to make money concerning ships requires someone with knowledge of shipbuilding. It is difficult to find an analogous item, a readily identifiable area of expertise, in which the just man would be useful in making contracts.

Perhaps, then, the just man becomes useful when money is deposited solely for safekeeping. But such deposits represent money not being used. When a pruning hook is used, a farmer uses it; when it is "deposited" and thus useless, a just man is useful. So too with a shield. The general conclusion: "[J]ustice is useless in the use of each thing and useful in its uselessness" (333d7). In everyday life, usefulness or value is particularized: this or that is useful. Consequently, it is the technitēs, the master of this or that, who can be counted on to be of use. But justice, at least as defined by Polemarchus, is not similarly particularized; in this argument at least, it is cloaked in a kind of indeterminacy rendering it useless.

This argument should recall the kinds of objections raised by Socrates against sōphrosunē understood as an episteme of epistemai in the Charmides. A physician understands the health of the human body. What analogous item does the man with *sōphrosunē* understand? The difficulty in answering this question raises doubts about both its possibility and benefit (see 171a–c). Socrates' analysis of his "dream" (see 173c–e) reiterates that even if there were a techne that knew all the other technai, because it would yet have no determinate content or specific value, it would be unable to make its possessor happy. Value is a matter of use, which is manifested via a particular item other than the techne itself. *Sōphrosunē* in the *Charmides,* like justice in the argument against Polemarchus, is indeterminate and hence seems useless.

Socrates next asks, would not the man most clever (*deinos*) at landing a blow in boxing also be most clever at guarding against being struck?[39] The doctor most adept at guarding against disease can also produce disease. The general who can effectively safeguard the security of his army can also become an effective spy (333e). Yet again, techne is value- or use-neutral. Plato articulates this point as "early" as the *Laches:* the doctor knows *only* what health and disease are, not whether they are fearful or welcome, that is, whether they are good or bad (see 195c). As a result, Reeve is mistaken in asserting that this passage from the *Republic* shows Plato for the first time criticizing his old Socratic self and trying to "point to [the techne analogy's] greatest flaw."[40] On his reading, the author of the *Laches, Charmides,* and *Euthyphro* had no understanding of this characteristic of techne. If I am correct, then the value-neutrality of techne has consistently been well understood by Plato; indeed, he has woven this insight into the essential fabric of his early dialogues.

In any case, if justice is interpreted as an ordinary value-neutral techne, and if its determinate field is useless money, then the just man should be both a good guard and a good thief. The quest for justice has traversed a mocking path and culminates in its being called the techne of stealing (*kleptikē:* 334b4). For my purposes, the key point is that the definition collapses into absurdity because of its initial assumption: justice is a techne.

"Socrates v. Polemarchus" is similar to a much discussed passage in the *Hippias Minor* in which the paradoxical notion that the voluntary wrongdoer is superior to the involuntary wrongdoer is seemingly defended. The question is, Who is the better man, and in respect to what, Achilles or Odysseus? The latter is the "most wily" (*polytropōtaton:* 364c6). In other

39. This same example is found at *Gorgias* 456d. (Compare Aristophanes *Clouds* 1330–40.)
40. Reeve 1988, 8.

words, Odysseus is "false." But what does this mean? Those who are false have the power to deceive. They are intelligent (*phronimoi:* 365e5) and knowledgeable about those matters in which they are deceitful. As such, they are analogous to men like Hippias, who is knowledgeable, is powerful, wise, and best concerning "calculation" (*logistikē:* 366c6). As such, he cannot only tell the truth about these matters but lie about them as well. So, for example, if someone were to ask Hippias how much three times seven hundred is, he would unfailingly be able to give either the right or wrong answer. By contrast, the man ignorant in *logistikē* might inadvertently tell the truth. The "calculator," then, has the most power to state truth and falsity with respect to calculations. Since he is "best" concerning calculations, he exemplifies the good man who becomes "false" while at the same time being true.

Socrates draws the same conclusion from the examples of geometry and astronomy. In other words, the mathematical *technai*, he clearly implies, are value- or use-neutral. A "calculator" knows three times seven hundred is twenty-one hundred, but there is nothing in *logistikē* itself to inform him how he *should* answer the question if it is posed. Since he knows the right answer, he is best equipped to answer it incorrectly. As such, he, the "true" man—as interpreted via the techne analogy—is identical to the "false" (366c–369b).

This *reductio*, this exposure of the character of technical knowledge, is aimed at Hippias, for he is famous as "the wisest of all men concerning the most technai" (368b2). He is fluent in mathematics; he makes his own clothes, sandals, and jewelry; he produces poetry; he knows music and "orthography" (*grammatōn orthotētos:* 368d4).

The argument continues. Unlike Achilles, Odysseus lies willfully. Surprisingly, this leads Socrates to describe him as better than Achilles and to generalize that those who voluntarily do wrong are better than those who do so involuntarily (371e–372a). His reasoning is familiar. In running, speed is good, slowness bad. But if someone is fast, he can run slowly, whereas the slow runner cannot run fast. The good runner who voluntarily runs badly (slowly) is thus superior to the bad/slow runner who does so involuntarily. The same pattern obtains in wrestling and every other bodily exercise. So too when it comes to physical beauty: he who is graceless voluntarily can also be graceful and so is superior to those who are involuntarily graceless.

Further examples include steering a ship, playing the lyre, and shooting arrows—in general, the technai. "Concerning all the technai and epistemai, that psyche is better which does bad and shameful things and errs voluntarily, whereas that psyche is worse which does so involuntarily" (375b8–c3). Socrates includes justice on this list. Whether it is construed as having a power or an episteme, the just psyche, when it does shameful things, does so voluntarily "on account of its power and techne" (376a3). "Therefore, it is characteristic of a good man to do wrong voluntarily, and of a bad man to do so involuntarily" (376b2–3). Of course, this conclusion is reached only because, as in book 1 of the *Republic*, justice is included among the value-neutral technai. I thus agree with Shorey: "Plato uses, but is not himself confused by, the Socratic analogy between the virtues and the arts." The paradox of the *Hippias Minor*, Shorey continues, demonstrates that "Plato 'already' in the Socratic period does not take [the techne analogy] seriously, but merely uses it for dramatic or propadeutic purposes."[41] (I object, of course, to Shorey's "merely.")

In "Socrates v. Polemarchus" the just man is said to be a good thief. In the *Hippias Minor* the just man who errs voluntarily is superior to the one who errs involuntarily. Both paradoxes leave the reader with options: perhaps justice really is useless and value-neutral; more likely, techne is inappropriately used to model or illustrate it.

Socrates engages in two more arguments with Polemarchus, which I do not discuss. Instead, consider next his battle against Thrasymachus, where the issue of techne is pivotal once again.

After witnessing Socrates thoroughly dominate Polemarchus, Thrasymachus, a professional teacher of rhetoric (and thus a "shingled" *technitēs*), can restrain himself no longer and bursts into the conversation. After some wrangling he is persuaded to offer his own definition of justice. He boldly asserts, "[T]he just is nothing other than the advantage of the stronger" (338c2). By "stronger" Thrasymachus means the politically stronger, that is, those in power, and so his definition implies some version of political relativism or conventionalism. Socrates offers the following series of arguments, which I paraphrase below, against this position.[42]

Argument 1 (338c4–339e8)

1. Justice is the advantage of the stronger, that is, of the ruling body.
2. It is just to obey the ruling body.
3. The ruling body sometimes makes mistakes; it makes incorrect laws.

41. Shorey 1968, 10.
42. Here I repeat an argument I presented in different form in Roochnik 1991, 89–91.

4. An incorrect law is disadvantageous to the ruling body.
5. It is just to obey all laws, correct and incorrect.
6. Therefore, it is just to do what is disadvantageous to the ruling body.

Statements 1 and 6 contradict one another, and so the definition is reduced to absurdity. At this point Polemarchus enthusiastically proclaims Socrates' victory. By contrast, another character, Cleitophon, is not convinced. Cleitophon understands, I suggest, that Socrates' refutation of Thrasymachus requires acceptance of (3) and (4), and Thrasymachus could, and therefore should, have rejected these statements. If it is true that the ruling body makes mistakes, that is, makes incorrect laws disadvantageous to itself, and if it is necessary to obey all laws, then doing what is disadvantageous to the ruling body can be just. But why should Thrasymachus accept (3) and (4)? Since these statements affirm the possibility of incorrectness, they presuppose some standard of correctness. They assume a distinction between what *really is* and what *only seems to be* advantageous to the ruling body. And this is precisely an assumption that Thrasymachus, as "some sort of" relativist, could reasonably be expected to reject. Cleitophon says this: "[Thrasymachus] said that the advantage of the stronger is what the stronger believes to be his advantage. This is what must be done by the weaker, and this is what he set down as the just" (340b6–8).

In fact, Thrasymachus did not say this. He described justice as the advantage, not what seems to be the advantage, of the stronger. Cleitophon, then, offers Thrasymachus a way out of the refutation. He proposes rejecting (3) and (4), which together make possible the distinction between correct and incorrect law, between real and apparent advantage. Cleitophon is a radical relativist who admits of no objective standards whatsoever. Socrates asks Thrasymachus which of the formulations he prefers: "Now tell me, Thrasymachus, was this what you wanted to say the just is, what seems to the stronger to be the advantage of the stronger, whether it is advantageous or not?" (340c2–5).

Socrates' question highlights the distinction between being and seeming. Cleitophon's rejection of this distinction would guarantee the safety of Thrasymachus's definition. If radical relativism obtains, then justice is simply the successful attainment of the self-interested desire of the strongest, to which there is no possibility of rational objection. Thrasymachus, however, refuses Cleitophon's offer of assistance. This is because he conceives of himself as *technitēs,* a professional teacher of rhetoric, and this requires him to affirm some objective epistemic content that he, as a knowledgeable professional, has mastered. ("Neoptolemus of Paros says . . . that the following epitaph is inscribed on the memorial to the sophist Thrasymachus: 'Name: Thrasymachus. Birthplace: Chalcedon. Techne: *Sophia.*'")[43]

As I argue in Chapter 1, the title of *technitēs*, with its promise of both epistemic and social status, that is, a "shingle" by which to advertise oneself and charge tuition, was coveted by fifth-century rhetoricians. Socrates exploits this feature of the rhetorician's conception of himself. He will hoist Thrasymachus on his own petard, that is, his claim to a techne.

According to Thrasymachus, a man who makes mistakes is not stronger at the moment he makes them (340c6–7). If one uses the term precisely, a doctor ceases to be a doctor when making mistakes; one who has mastered the techne of calculation is no longer *logistikos* (340c3) at the moment of erring. In precise language, "no craftsman (*dēmiourgos*), wise man or ruler makes a mistake at the moment when he is ruling" (340e5).

Thrasymachus has himself declared that ruling and techne are analogous. (He uses *dēmiourgos,* but his examples—medicine, *logistikē,* and grammar—clearly refer to technai.) Against his would-be ally Cleitophon, he insists there is some standard of correct rule to which the real ruler can appeal and which then forms the distinction between knowledge and error. For Thrasymachus only the man with knowledge should rule, and knowledge does not err.

Three points: First, it is in Thrasymachus's short-term interest to make this claim. Since he conceives of himself as a *technitēs*, he needs to present himself as a knowledgeable professional in order to ply his trade, which includes teaching others for a fee. Second, he models his knowledge on a $techne_1$: it is virtually infallible (see criterion 4 on List 5, and contrast it to criterion 3 on List 7). Third, Thrasymachus has given Socrates the weapons he needs to refute him. Given his use of the techne analogy in the *Laches, Charmides,* and *Euthyphro* to criticize a definition, Socrates' next move is predictable:

Argument 2 (341c5–342e8)

1. The doctor (the one in "precise" speech, i.e., the one who does not err) cares for the sick.
2. The pilot rules the sailors.

43. Sprague 1972, 88.

3. Therefore, all the technai (341d7) are directed toward the advantage of their objects.
4. Therefore, no techne considers its own advantage.
5. Justice is a techne.
6. Therefore, neither justice nor the just man (qua *technitēs*) consider their own advantage.

The point here is similar to one made in the *Charmides:* techne (like most other activities and relations) does not seem self-reflexive. Instead, it is structured by the basic subject (knower)–object (known, subject matter) relationship. If justice is assumed to be a techne, it must "aim" at the benefit of an object other than itself and cannot be self-reflexive. It therefore cannot be defined as the advantage of the stronger or the ruling body. Thrasymachus has been defeated by his adamant claim to a techne.

It must be made clear that, pace Warren, Socrates has not shifted to a value-laden conception of techne in this argument. Yes, Socrates describes techne as directed toward the *sumpheron* (341d8) of its object. The physician, for example, is a *therapeutēs* of those who are ill. (By contrast, the pilot is an *archōn* [341c9] of his sailors.) What is emphasized in this passage, however, is not the morality but the intentionality of techne: it aims at something other than itself. In this sense, techne might even be described as purposive. As Warren puts it, "A techne is designed to bring its object to its excellence or good."[44] Even so, the excellence (or the "advantage") of the object is "technical." The physician knows how to treat the patient. When he does so, the patient is benefited. Qua physician, however, he does not know whether or to what extent *he* should treat any given patient, and he knows nothing of the value of, but simply how to produce, health.

A similar point should be made about an earlier passage, 335c–e. To Polemarchus, Socrates argues thus: the man with *musikē* makes unmusical men musical, that is, teaches or benefits them; the man with the techne of *hippikē* makes incompetent riders skilled in horsemanship; since justice is assumed to be like such technai, it must always work in an analogous

---

44. Warren 1989, 105. Hemmenway (1993) makes a similarly challenging point. Warren notes Socrates' shift in the argument from the craftsman to the craft (a shift I do not express in my own paraphrases). The former may well choose not to execute his craft; the latter by definition is its execution. Warren (1989, 107) states: "Because of this difficulty Socrates' argument abandoned the craftsman for the craft." In my terms, Warren sees craft qua craft as resolving the potential gap between logos and *ergon*. This, however, requires a major abstraction: there is no craft without a craftsman, and no craftsman capable of making judgments concerning the value of his work. The *Charmides,* indeed the very nature of Platonic *dialogue* itself, should, I think, speak against such a move.

fashion, that is, to benefit and make better, rather than harm, other men. According to Warren, this tokens a shift in Socrates' understanding of a techne: "[T]he value-neutral notion of the craft is ignored [in this passage] ... craftsmen *qua* craftsmen, by practicing their crafts, make things better, not worse."[45]

This is not quite right. Justice, interpreted on the model of a techne, is intentionally directed at an object, namely, other human beings. As a techne, it aims for the advantage of that object. In this sense, yes, it does aim "to make things better." Again, however, the sense of "better" here is technical. The car mechanic makes the engine better, not worse. But he or she knows how to make it worse, and there is nothing in the expertise to prevent the mechanic from doing so or from refusing to treat a given car. Like the mechanic, the just man does not harm other men, but makes them better. But should he practice justice all the time? In fact, why should he be just at all? The answers to such questions he, qua *technitēs*, would not know. In short, even if technical knowledge does have its own sense of "better," it still is unsatisfying as a model of justice.

To begin his next argument, Socrates asks, "Do you think that the rulers in the cities, those who truly rule, rule willingly?" (345e1–2). Naturally, Thrasymachus says yes. If so, why do they ask for wages? If ruling were truly for the advantage of the ruler, it would not need to be supplemented by wages. According to Socrates, each techne provides "some peculiar benefit (*ophelian idian*)." Medicine, for example, provides health. Getting wages is a benefit provided by the wage earner's techne (*misthōtikē*: 346b1). Given this assumption, the next argument proceeds as follows:

Argument 3 (345e8–347a4)

1. Every *technitēs* actually has two technai: his own and the "wage-earning techne."
2. The wage-earning techne furnishes wages and is for the advantage of the *technitēs*.
3. The techne unique to the individual *technitēs* is for the advantage of its specific object (from statement 3 in Argument 2).
4. Those who rule get paid wages.
5. Therefore, those who rule have two technai.
6. Therefore, the unique techne of the ruler, namely, justice, is for the advantage not of the ruler but of its object.

45. Warren 1985, 6.

From Argument 2 we learn techne is not self-reflexive but directed toward the advantage of its object. For the *technitēs* to gain advantage for himself, he must possess the supplementary and extraordinary techne of *mistharnetikē*. Therefore, those who rule and get paid wages do not, qua possessors of the ruling techne, rule for their own benefit.

This wage-earning techne is strange. First, it would be common to all technai in which wages are paid, and as such would not have its own field of expertise. As Bloom puts it, "The wage earner's art is ubiquitous. It accompanies all the other arts and directs their action. It is thus an architectonic art."[46] For Bloom, in other words, it is a "second-order" art. But this is not quite right. The wage-earning art surely does not "direct" the action of the other technai. Wages are a by-product of the other technai, and to earn them a technician needs neither to know nor to practice anything other than his own techne. Since it does not require any special knowledge, indeed any knowledge at all, how can wage earning be conceived as a techne?

Despite this problem, wage earning is conceptually alluring. It is ubiquitous and has no determinate field of its own. As such, it resembles a second-order techne or a full-fledged techne of arete that would be able to direct the use of the other technai. Bloom puts this point boldly, but overstates it considerably: "The wage earner's art is a kind of political substitute for philosophy. The intention of philosophy is to understand the nature of the arts and order them towards the production of human happiness and to educate men to desire those things which most conduce to happiness. It can claim to rule all the other arts for it alone tries to know the whole."[47]

Bloom thinks philosophy is an architectonic, or "second-order," techne embracing the other technai and represented, or at least suggested, by the wage earner's techne. As such, he follows the continuist line of the SAT (as exemplified by Sprague). Bloom's version of the philosopher-king would be a man whose techne results in a happy and just polis. Like Sprague, Bloom mentions none of the intrinsic difficulties attending such a notion, the most pressing of which would be, What exactly is the subject matter of the wage earner's, and thus the philosopher's, techne? What exactly would he know, and how would such knowledge overcome the epistemological objections raised in the *Charmides?*

46. Bloom 1968, 333.
47. Bloom 1968, 333.

Bloom has neglected the dramatic context in which Socrates here invokes the techne analogy. He uses it to *refute* Thrasymachus, a professional teacher according to whom justice is a techne *and* for the benefit of the ruler. From this "dialogical fact," however, it does not follow that Plato actually believes a wage earner's techne is possible and a "substitute" for a higher-order, value-laden form of technical knowledge. Indeed, the intrinsic problems infecting such a notion would surely suggest he does not.

A fourth argument against Thrasymachus also makes use of the analogy. After much prodding, the rhetorician asserts, "[P]erfect injustice is more profitable than justice" (348b). As a result, he puts "injustice in the camp of arete and wisdom, and justice among their opposites" (348e). The argument then commences:

Argument 4 (349b–350c)

1. The just man wants to "get the better of" the unjust man who is unlike him, not a just man who is like him.
2. The unjust man wants to get the better of both the like (the unjust man) and the unlike (the just man).
3. The man with the musical techne wants to get the better only of the unlike (the unmusical) man.
4. The physician wants to get the better only of the unlike man (who is ignorant of medicine).
5. Therefore (from [3] and [4]), only the ignorant man wants to "get the better of both the man who knows and the man who does not" (350b2).
6. The man who knows is wise and good.
7. Therefore, he "who is both good and wise will not want to get the better of the like, but of the unlike and opposite" (350b6).
8. Therefore, the unjust man is ignorant, and not like the good and wise man.

If justice is like a techne, as (3) and (4) state, then justice, not injustice, is more like wisdom and arete. This conclusion contradicts Thrasymachus's initial statement that injustice is arete and wisdom. The *technitēs* "does not try to 'outdo' his fellow Craftsmen in that he does not try to go beyond the principles of his (and their) Craft." As many commentators point out, however, the argument seems fallacious. To mention only one objection: those with the technai of generalship or boxing try to outdo their fellows all the time.[48] Therefore, the best to be said of Argument 4 is that by likening justice to a techne it manages, whether legitimately or not, to refute Thrasymachus: he blushes at his apparent defeat (350d3).

I have discussed only four of the arguments Socrates employs against Thrasymachus, in the last three of which techne is central. Argument 2 reiterates the basic point made in the discussion of the *Charmides:* a self-reflexive techne is impossible. If arete requires some dimension of self-reflexivity, then techne, even if it aims for the "advantage" of its object, cannot be its model. The "wage-earning" techne used in Argument 3 appears (to Bloom at least) to suggest the possibility of a reflexive or second-order techne. This appearance could become reality *only if* a wage-earning techne were itself epistemologically intelligible. And it is not: wages are simply a by-product of a "first-order" techne.

Argument 4 seems to show, not the weakness of techne as a model for justice, but its strength. Presumably, like music and medicine, justice qua techne wants to get the better only of the unlike, that is, the unjust/ignorant. But does Socrates' use of the analogy in Argument 4 thus give credence to the SAT?[49] Perhaps, although the reader must be cautious. What this argument implies—and does so problematically—is only that justice is *similar* to techne in its relationship to the like and the unlike. From this it does not necessarily follow that justice as knowledge is a techne.

To reformulate: there does indeed seem to be something good about techne. It aims for the advantage of, or to "better," its object (see 335c–e). According to Socrates, it attempts to "outdo" only its opposite, that is, the ignorant, and so is admirable. Again, however, a conclusion such as Warren's is misleading: "Plato uses two forms of the craft argument, one which sees the craft as value-neutral and as technique and a second which sees the craft as intrinsically connected to a good."[50] First of all, it is Socrates, not Plato, who uses the techne analogy. In other words, any given appearance of the analogy is located in a specific dramatic context. Second, while techne may have positive features, for example, being a form of reliable, intentional, and purposive knowledge, this does not mean Plato shifts to a value-laden conception of techne. Like Solon and Sophocles, he may well believe techne is a qualified or potential good, which must be *used* properly before it attains its full value. And use is not itself within its epistemic domain.

48. Reeve 1988, 20.
49. Sprague (1976, 54) thinks so. For her, this is a radically new deployment of the analogy.
50. Warren 1989, 103.

Book 1 of the *Republic* ends in aporia and provokes the question, Is justice a techne? If, like Sprague and Warren, one embraces a continuist line, the answer is yes, and in the later books of the *Republic* justice becomes a techne whose specific object is the Idea of the Good. If one chooses the discontinuist line, then, like Reeve, book 1 signals the problems with the techne analogy and the advent of a new Platonic theory of justice. But if the reader attends mainly to what Socrates actually does with the techne analogy—namely, expose the weaknesses of Polemarchus's and Thrasymachus's definitions of justice—and then examines the logical implications of the analogy, there is no reason to agree with either reading of book 1. Even if Socrates operates with his two familiar assumptions— justice is a kind of knowledge, and knowledge is exemplified by techne—it does not follow that justice *is* a kind of techne. Indeed, because the aporia is generated by the second assumption (at least in the arguments against Polemarchus as well as in Arguments 2 and 3, and perhaps in 4, against Thrasymachus), there is good reason to think it is not.

If my reading is attractive, it should alter the expectations a reader brings to books 2–10. In other words, if in book 1 and his early works Plato was pointing to a conception of nontechnical moral knowledge, it becomes increasing likely that in his middle works he also eschewed a technical moral theory. (This is, at least, more plausible than the SAT's contention that the early dialogues hold strictly to the techne analogy in order to postulate a serious model of moral knowledge.) I cannot prove such an assertion and instead offer only a suggestion concerning a single passage from book 6, one that calls into question the confidence with which commentators (of all stripes) attribute "theoretical optimism" to Plato's middle dialogues. I turn next to the "ship-of-state" image (487e7– 489a2) and to an instructive commentary on it by Bambrough.[51]

Socrates likens the polis to a ship whose owner is strong and large, but deaf, shortsighted, and ignorant of seamanship. The sailors on board quarrel over who will rule: each believes he ought to be the pilot. None of them, however, has the techne (488b5) of piloting, and they even deny piloting can be taught. (In fact, they "are ready to cut to pieces the man who says it is teachable.")[52] The sailors try to persuade the shipowner and are willing even to kill their competitors in order to get control of the

51. Page numbers in parentheses that follow refer to Bambrough 1971. See Tiles 1984 for a critique of Bambrough's conception of a techne.

52. This extraordinary reaction to what seems to be an innocuous proposition—piloting can be taught—discloses the centrality of teachability to the conception of a techne.

ship's rudder. Finally, the shipowner is bound and drugged, and one of the sailors is declared pilot. This man, clever only at figuring out how to gain rule of the ship, is falsely praised as "knowledgeable" (*epistamenon*: 488d1) about seamanship. By contrast, the true pilot, who understands the seasons, the sky, the winds, that is, who has the genuine techne of piloting, is dismissed by the sailors as useless. He does not know how to win the battle for the rudder, only how to guide the ship. The ship, therefore, sails without the benefit of techne, for the true *technitēs* is despised as one who partakes in idle chatter and useless skygazing.

The implications of the image seem clear: the city is the "ship of state" and typically is not ruled by a techne that knowledgeably produces well-being for the citizens. In a democracy, for example, power flows to those who win the rudder, that is, win the debates and get the votes. This image seems to encapsulate the major theme of the *Republic*: rule by the ignorant is intolerable, by a *technitēs* desirable. Bambrough, at least, reads the passage this way and finds within it the essence of Plato's political teaching: "The doctrine that political wisdom is analogous to a special skill is nowhere more clearly and succinctly expressed than in the Parable of the Ship" (192).

As a proponent of the "continuist" branch of the SAT, he describes Platonic justice as "a techne like medicine, mathematics, music or agriculture" (189), and to those possessing it the rule of cities should be entrusted. Bambrough's Plato is an extreme aristocrat for whom rule belongs in the hands of a knowledgeable elite. For these reasons, he is harshly critical and aims to expose "the fatal limitation" and the "radically misleading" nature of the analogy. Briefly, his argument is this: it is not the technically proficient pilot who sets the course of the ship, but the passengers or the shipowner. The technical pilot only knows the means to achieve some pregiven destination. In other words, technical reasoning is only about the means to an end. As Annas puts it, "A skill has a determinate end and finds means and methods of attaining it; the reasoning involved is means-end reasoning. It is no part of [a techne] to question what its own end is."[53]

Plato, according to Bambrough, fails to realize that if a ruler were really like a pilot, he would know only how to sail the ship of state to pregiven destinations, not in what direction it should sail. If the ruler/pilot were to attempt to determine the actual course of the ship, he would be "going

53. Annas 1981, 26.

beyond his professional scope by prescribing the route and the destination as well as the course by which the route can best be traversed and the destination most suitably reached" (195). As a result, the ruler/pilot analogy, according to Bambrough, fundamentally distorts the actual character of political life, which is precisely about ends.

> Ethical and political disagreement is different in logical kind from medical disagreement or disagreement among navigators. Ethical and political disagreement is radical and interminable in a sense in which scientific disagreement, or disagreement about the means for achieving an agreed end, is terminable by recognized procedures; such disagreement remains terminable in principle even when it is not terminated in fact. But ethical and political disagreement in its most characteristic forms is interminable, because it is not about means, but about ends. (198)

The great statesman or moralist knows "by wide knowledge, long experience, clear thought, and above all the tolerant recognition that the search for a right solution to a practical problem can never be ended by a Q.E.D." (205). In other words, he knows mathematics is the wrong paradigm for moral knowledge. In my terms, political life is not a legitimate object of a techne$_1$. Although the techne analogy has the positive value of teaching us that "there is scope for sustained rational discussion about the choice of ends and purposes" (199), Bambrough accuses it of being grossly misleading. The "Platonic error" (199) is to look for technical certainty and rigorous solutions to practical problems. It is to embrace the paradigm of mathematics where it is inappropriate.

Bambrough brings a "Sophoclean" objection against Plato, accusing him of being too enamored of the power of techne and having forgotten its intrinsic limitations. He reiterates Isocrates' basic conception of logos (understood as coextensive with political activity). Recall that in *Against the Sophists* Isocrates strongly objects to the description of rhetoric, the study of logos, as a *tetagmenē* techne best exemplified by orthography (see 13–18). He insists *tuchē* and the orator's nature play an inextricable role in rhetoric, whose field encompasses, and so is shaped by, the indeterminate ("interminable") character of logos. Isocrates would wholeheartedly endorse Bambrough's view that a practical problem can never be solved by a "Q.E.D." Instead, its solution requires a fluid and appropriate response to a particular *kairos*.

Bambrough's analysis, however, is flawed. He neglects to note that the very criticism he brings against the "ship-of-state" passage was given by Plato himself in both the *Laches* and the *Charmides*. In the former, Nicias makes it clear that techne, as exemplified by the physician, can do no more than diagnose the means toward the production of health and disease and knows nothing about which the physician *should* produce (see 195c). In the *Charmides*, Socrates points out again and again that techne as the model for knowledge prohibits the kind of self-reflection needed to make a consideration of ends possible. Finally, this sort of insight concerning the limits of techne is manifestly alive even in book 1 of the *Republic*: the arguments against Polemarchus show that if techne is the model of justice, justice cannot be knowledge. This is so for the very reason Bambrough cites with regard to the ship of state: techne, exemplified by boxing, is value-neutral (see 333e); it can be used for good or ill. In sum, Plato understands, rather than commits, "the Platonic error."

Assume both Bambrough and Isocrates are right concerning logos/political activity: since it is indeterminate it cannot become the subject matter of a rigorous techne. Bambrough in no way proves that Plato fails to grasp this point. Instead, he conceives of Plato as somehow victimized by his own analogies: "[T]hese analogies were very influential in shaping or directing Plato's thought" (189). Indeed, "Plato was led" (188) by them to the basic doctrines of his political philosophy.

This is odd. Might not Plato, like any writer in full command of his language, be using the analogy instead of being used by it? Is Bambrough justified in reducing the ship-of-state image to a single, seriously intended, analogical assertion: as the techne of piloting is to the ship, so justice is to the city? Is it necessary to suppose that Plato was in thrall to this assertion simply because he had his character Socrates utter the image suggesting it? No. There is another way of explaining Socrates' use of the ship of state at this juncture of the *Republic*, and this is to take its *dramatic* context into account.

After pronouncing that philosophers must rule in order for the perfectly just city to come into being (473d), Socrates begins to describe the philosopher. Adeimantus, his interlocutor at the moment, finds each of Socrates' particular points convincing, but remains unconvinced by the general thesis that philosophers can and should rule cities. This is because he is skeptical about actual philosophers: those who are serious and stay with it for a long time, he thinks, become "quite queer, not to say completely vicious; while the ones who seem perfectly decent, do nevertheless suffer at least one consequence of the practice [Socrates is] praising—they become useless to the cities" (487d).

How, then, can philosophers become rulers if in reality they are either queer or useless to the cities? This is the context in which the "ship-of-state" image is found; it is specifically designed to convince Adeimantus he is being wrongheaded (487e). As such, it, and the techne analogy implicit in it, perform a role much like that found in the *Laches*. There (184e) Socrates uses it to persuade Lysimachus that it would be foolish to entrust the question, How can arete be taught? to the votes of a majority and better to seek someone knowledgeable. Here the analogy urges Adeimantus to continue the discussion, to value the pursuit of knowledge and philosophy. Its usage, in short, is *protreptic*. The image does employ techne as the model of knowledge. But, as always, the reader must be cautious in inferring from this that, as Bambrough thinks, Plato invokes the analogy strictly as a framework for a theoretical project.

Techne is the kind of knowledge most easily recognized. It is paradigmatic of knowledge issuing in useful results. When on a ship, we invariably prefer to have it sailed by a technically proficient pilot. Nobody sane would recommend that questions about piloting be decided randomly or put up for a vote, since this is an activity we agree can, and therefore should, be governed by knowledge. Thus when Socrates uses techne in the image, he has an effective way of reminding the nonphilosophical Adeimantus that, in some areas, knowledge is unambiguously capable of making useful decisions. Perhaps, then, its role in the ruling of a city should be seriously considered. With the techne analogy Socrates persuades Adeimantus that knowledge is good and should be sought, that is, the philosophical project is coherent and should be practiced. His doing so does not require the reader to attribute to Plato the belief that techne is the exclusive, or even the best, model of knowledge. Only if the analogy is analyzed in isolation from its dramatic context, as has regularly been done by practitioners of the SAT, will such a view seem compelling.

Wisdom in the *Euthydemus*

The previous sections have disclosed at least three tasks to which Socrates puts the techne analogy:

1. *Critique.* Socrates forces Laches and Nicias to explicate their definitions of courage—"intelligent endurance" and "knowledge of what is to be feared and what is to be dared"—in comprehensible and familiar terms. He does the same with Euthyphro's definition of piety, "*therapeia* to the gods," and Critias's definition of *sōphrosunē*, "self-knowledge." These are all promising notions that, in an important sense, are never refuted. Instead, Socrates shows that these definitions fail *if* techne is the operative model of knowledge. Perhaps they fail *only if* this model is operative.

2. *Refutation.* This is a stronger version of (1). Polemarchus's definition of justice, "doing good to friends and harm to enemies," is shown to be flawed when techne is assumed as the model for justice as knowledge. So too is Thrasymachus's "justice is the advantage of the stronger."

3. *Protreptic.* In the *Laches* Socrates urges Lysimachus to seek someone knowledgeable in arete; he urges Adeimantus not to abandon the project of philosophy in the *Republic* (book 6).

In each of these dialogues, Socrates takes full advantage of the connotations of "techne" that are attractive and familiar to his interlocutors. Techne is ordinary knowledge attained by the recognizable expert; it is determinate, methodical, teachable, noncontroversial, authoritative, purposive, and generally issues in a useful result. Socrates' analogical arguments do not, however, necessarily imply that Plato holds a specific conception of moral knowledge. Precisely because it is familiar and recognizable, techne is a useful device for critique, refutation, and exhortation. Consequently, it is a reasonable place to initiate, but not necessarily to finish, an inquiry into the character of moral knowledge. Perhaps, like Solon and Sophocles, Plato has Socrates use techne as a contrast to the moral knowledge he seeks. Perhaps he is fully aware of the decisive limitations of the analogy, even while exploiting its positive features, and the purpose of the "early" dialogues may thus be to point toward a nontechnical conception of moral knowledge.

The third usage cited above, protreptic, is most fully exhibited in the *Euthydemus.* In a two-pronged argument, Socrates attempts, first, to demonstrate what heretofore has only been assumed: arete requires or simply is knowledge, or "wisdom." Second, he raises the "what is it?" question concerning such wisdom and in doing so directly confronts a key question of this book: is there a techne that knows how to *use* the results of the other technai? The doctor, as Nicias observes in the *Laches,* knows only how to produce health. He does not know whether he *should* in any given case use his knowledge—whether, for example, preventing death is always a good. Medicine, like boxing, is mute on such questions. Insofar as techne represents the paradigmatic form of knowledge, the question naturally arises, Is there a techne whose subject matter is "use" itself? Since "use" is the basis of, or equivalent to, the concept of "value," this question really asks, Is there a techne of arete? In the *Euthydemus,* Socrates directly confronts these issues when he treats "the kingly techne." His inquiry ends in aporia and so points yet again to a conception of nontechnical moral knowledge.

Many scholars, especially those offering a continuist version of the SAT, would disagree. For them, the aporia of the *Euthydemus* is a positive theoretical development preparing the way for later dialogues, particularly the *Republic* and the *Statesman.* Chance, reiterating views shared by Sprague and Shorey, argues thus:

> If an individual should "learn" and so fully "understand" this art . . .
> the art of virtue, so as to guarantee correctness in thought, speech,
> and action, then he would acquire the sought-after knowledge. . . .
> Moreover, if the possessor and user of this master science were to
> sit at the helm, guarding and controlling all things so as to render
> them useful . . . this blessed ruler would acquire the knowledge that
> in Plato's view can truly be called philosophy. . . . Although he
> reserves the full articulation of this conception for other dialogues,
> nevertheless in the *Euthydemus* Plato has roughly adumbrated this
> science.[54]

My thesis will be disputed from the discontinuist branch of the SAT as well. One could, for example, read the aporia of the *Euthydemus* as evidence of Plato's turn away from Socrates and the techne analogy. This is Reeve's strategy in explicating the aporiai of the *Republic*'s first book. As I did in arguing against him, in this section I show that the reasons adduced for the untenability of technical moral knowledge in the *Euthydemus* are isomorphic with the aporiai generated in earlier works. Socrates elaborates familiar objections to the techne model, ones intrinsic to Plato's conception of nontechnical knowledge.

Before turning to the *Euthydemus* itself, a final position needs mention. Vlastos describes this dialogue as "transitional" (i.e., late early or early middle). A basic difference between an early and a transitional work, on his account, is that in the former Socrates is engaged in elenctic activity, while in the latter he is not. "In the Elenctic dialogues Socrates$_E$'s method of philosophical investigation is adversative: he pursues moral truth by refuting theses defended by dissenting interlocutors. This ceases in the Transitionals: there he argues against theses proposed and opposed by himself."[55]

On the *Euthydemus*, Vlastos says this: "Here for the first time in Plato's corpus we see Socrates unloading his philosophizing on an interlocutor in the form of a protreptic discourse expounded in flagrantly non-elenctic fashion as virtual monologue . . . the elenchus has been jettisoned. . . . [For so] drastic a departure . . . we must hypothesize a profound change in Plato himself" (116–17). The principal cause of this change, of this liberation from elenctic moral philosophizing, was Plato's advanced study of mathematics (see 107–31).

Two rejoinders: First, in the *Euthydemus* Socrates does deliver what amounts to a protreptic monologue. As a result, if the elenchus is deemed the essential feature of Socratic philosophizing, then Plato does seem to have undergone a profound change. If, however, the techne question is taken to be central to the Socratic project, then there is no need to postulate such a change in the author. Simply put, this is because the treatment of techne presented in the *Euthydemus* is fundamentally similar to that found in the "earlier" dialogues.

Second, I dispute Vlastos's contention that only in the transitional and middle works does Plato show a great interest in mathematics. Recall a passage from the *Euthyphro*: Socrates is examining Euthyphro's statement "What the gods love is holy, and what they do not love is unholy" (7a). The problem is that the gods often disagree about what they love, and then become angry with one another. Socrates urges Euthyphro to specify what the gods disagree and get angry about: "My good man, disagreement about what creates hostility and anger? Look at it this way: if you and I disagree about number (*arithmos*), which [of two numbers] is larger, would the disagreement about this make us hostile and angry with one another, or would we settle it quickly by turning to calculation (*logismon*)" (7b6–c1).

Socrates elaborates: If we disagree about what is greater and what lesser, we quickly put our dispute to rest by turning to "measurement"

---

55. Vlastos 1991, 49. Page numbers in parentheses that follow refer to this book.

(*metrein:* 7c4); if our disagreement is about what is heavier and lighter, we turn to "weighing" (*histanai:* 7c7). Since each of these areas of potential dispute can be authoritatively adjudicated by a mathematical techne, disputants need not get angry with one another. This is in sharp contrast to disagreement about what is "right and wrong, fine and shameful, and good and bad" (7d).

Euthyphro 7b–c demonstrates that, for the early Plato, mathematics supplies a, perhaps *the*, paradigm case of clarity and distinctness. It does so because it supplies the best examples of authoritative technai. To prefigure an argument I elaborate in Chapter 3, consider another passage from the *Ion*. In examining Ion's claim to have the rhapsode's techne (530b3, 530c8) and to "expound" or "speak well" about Homer, Socrates asks whether he can speak equally well about other poets, such as Hesiod and Archilochus. Ion answers no. This puzzles Socrates, since Homer and Hesiod often address the same subject. Why is it, then, that Ion can "expound" only Homer's poetry and not Hesiod's? To illustrate the problem, Socrates offers the counterexample of arithmetic:

SOCRATES: So, my dear Ion, when many people are talking about number and one of them speaks best, I suppose there is someone who will be able to distinguish the man who speaks well?
ION: Yes, I'd say so.
SOCRATES: And will this same man be able to identify those who speak badly, or will it be someone else?
ION: The same man, I suppose.
SOCRATES: And this is the man who has the arithmetic techne, isn't it?
    (531d–e)

If someone possesses the arithmetic techne (531e3), he can identify those who speak well (correctly) and those who speak badly (incorrectly) about number. Socrates assumes Ion's claim to the rhapsodic techne is analogous. As a result, Ion should be able to identify and discuss not only those who speak well within his field, like Homer, but also those, like Hesiod, who do not.

In this passage arithmos again represents an area to be mastered by an expert who can authoritatively distinguish between right and wrong answers, and in turn good and bad speakers entering that area. *Ion* 531d–e suggests arithmetic is paradigmatic of this feature of techne. As a result, Vlastos's assertion that Socrates privileges mathematics and appreciates its power not until the *Euthydemus* (and the *Meno*) surely must be called into question.

The point is this: in the early dialogues, Socrates consistently calls upon mathematics to illustrate what a techne is. This is manifestly the case in the *Charmides*, where geometry and statics exemplify the basic subject/object structure of a techne. It is true in the *Ion,* the *Gorgias,* and the *Protagoras* as well (which is discussed in Chapter 3). In other words, and pace Vlastos, there is no need to postulate a dramatic change in, and thereby to construct an elaborate (and of course speculative) chronological story about, Plato's mind. Even in his early work, Plato appreciates and relies upon the fact that *mathematics illustrates a decisive feature of techne.* This is especially true in the *Euthydemus.* Its treatment of mathematics, techne, and moral knowledge harmonize with that found in the early dialogues. The absence of elenctic activity in this dialogue is thus best explained, not by recourse to a speculative account of Plato's putatively developing mind, but by the dramatic context in which Socrates finds himself.[56]

Plato's *Euthydemus* is strange. In it two old but inexperienced Sophists, the brothers Euthydemus and Dionysodorus, show off their "eristic" wares, that is, their ability to refute. They are, says Socrates, professional teachers of a "pancreatic techne" (272a5), knowledge of fighting the battle of words in the law courts. Their sophistic show consists of bombarding the audience with fallacies, many of them quite absurd. (Example: this dog is a father; this dog is yours; therefore, this dog is your father [see 298e].) The dialogue is loaded with wordplay, and throughout Socrates is transparently ironic in his praise of his sophistic competitors. For example, when they finish their exhibition, he says, "No one of those present could praise highly enough the argument and the two men, and they nearly died laughing and clapping with joy" (303b).

As a result of its almost farcical quality, commentators often feel constrained to begin their work on the *Euthydemus* by asking whether it is even serious enough to merit analysis.[57] The challenge for the commentator is then to extract enough serious material to justify the commentary. Typically the sophistical fallacies, which constitute about half of the work, have been taken as the most significant portion of the dialogue. Even if they are occasionally absurd, arguments concerning the nature of learning

---

56. This section relies heavily on Roochnik 1990. I am grateful to *Interpretation* for permission to reprint parts of this article. See also Roochnik 1994a for an elaboration of some of the following points concerning mathematics.

57. See, for example, Keulen 1971, 4–5.

(275d–77d) or the ambiguity of the verb "to be" (283b–e) or the issue of self-predication (300e–301c) are obviously of both historical and philosophical significance.[58]

Instead of focusing on the three eristic scenes (275d–277d, 283b–288b, 293b–303b), I concentrate on Socrates' two "protreptic" speeches (278e–283a and 288d–293a), which together compose a single argument. Many commentators have dismissed, simply paraphrased, or ignored this argument. Stewart, for example, describes it as an "extravagant induction" and "equivocal." Praechter characterizes it as essentially negative and "fruitless."[59] By contrast, on my reading, these speeches raise philosophical questions of the highest order. They do so because they center around the two basic terms of this entire study, "techne" and "arete."

Socrates' two speeches together form a continuous argument that is indeed quite serious. Just because it is protreptic, however, the argument is also intrinsically problematic. Protreptic, as explained by Socrates, is a form of argument designed to persuade its audience that "one ought to philosophize and care about arete" (275a6).[60] It invites its readers into the project of philosophy and promises, either implicitly or explicitly, great rewards. But in itself protreptic is incomplete: it only promises and does not deliver "what comes next."[61] It urges its audience to love wisdom but does not itself provide or clearly articulate its nature. As a result, protreptic encapsulates the most pressing questions raised by the "early" (and "transitional") dialogues: Do they contain a "positive" teaching? Can Socrates' promise of wisdom be fulfilled? Is there a theoretical doctrine, a techne, that actually does come next, or is Socratic protreptic merely promissory? Does Socrates only refute and exhort his interlocutors, or does he actually teach them?

There is indeed a positive dimension to the protreptic, but it is not technical. Socrates' protreptic argument *fails* to demonstrate conclusively why one ought to pursue wisdom and care about arete. This is largely because it is compelling only to those already leaning toward agreement with its conclusion. As such, does the protreptic undermine itself? After all, if arguments purporting to show that one ought to philosophize are themselves riddled with difficulty, then why should anyone philosophize?

58. See Roochnik 1990, 211–12, for elaboration.
59. See Stewart 1977 and Praechter 1932, 9.
60. For the sophistic correlate to protreptic, see Isocrates *To Nicocles* 57.1; *Evagoras* 77.1; *Antidosis* 60.4, 84.2, 86.2. See also Aristotle *Rhetoric* 1358b.
61. This phrase comes from *Cleitophon* 408d7. See Roochnik 1984 for a commentary.

While its conclusion is not universally or necessarily true, the protreptic does not undermine itself. Instead, these peculiar arguments are uniquely instructive. While not powerful enough to persuade everybody to philosophize (i.e., to demonstrate that philosophy is an unconditional universal good), they can yet be effective in urging someone like Cleinias, the young man who (along with the reader) is the target of Socrates' speeches and who, as his name suggests, is already "leaning" in that direction, to pursue philosophy.[62] Furthermore, they can teach him how to do so. For this reason, they will flesh out the suggestions made in the four earlier sections of this chapter regarding what nontechnical moral knowledge is.

In the prologue to the dialogue, the two Sophists make a mighty boast: "Arete, Socrates, is what we think we can transmit more finely and quickly than anybody else" (273d8–9). The first question Socrates poses is: "Are you able to make good only a man who is already convinced he should learn from you, or can you also teach the man who is not yet convinced, either because he does not believe that in general arete is teachable or that you two are teachers of it? Come on, is it the work of the same techne to persuade such a man that arete is teachable and that you are the ones from whom someone could best learn, or is this the work of some other techne?" (274d7–e5).

Dionysodorus answers: the same techne does these two different jobs. Socrates reformulates: "Therefore, Dionysodorus, of all men, you most finely encourage (or 'protrepticize,' *protrepsaite*, 275a1) others to pursue philosophy and to be concerned about arete?" (274a8–275a2). The Sophist agrees.

This passage attributes to teaching at least four distinct stages: (1) Before beginning a subject, a student must *first* be persuaded the subject can actually be taught. In a typical techne like geometry this is easily done. A prospective student can simply observe that those who took Geometry 101 in the fall and knew nothing of the subject can prove a host of theorems by the spring.

(2) The student must be persuaded the prospective teacher can actually teach the subject. For geometry, evidence of this is again easy to obtain. It can be determined that the teacher received a degree in mathematics and taught the students who took Geometry 101 the previous year.

Both (1) and (2) imply characteristics long associated with techne, that

---

62. In reading this manuscript, Jacob Howland noted that the name "Kleinias" comes from *klinein*, to lean.

is, teachability and certifiability. Plato reiterates these criteria in the *Laches.* To qualify as a *technitēs,* and as a teacher, the "professor" must have a "diploma" or be able to muster sufficient examples of the successful application of his techne. Techne is knowledge trusted and relied upon; it can be taught, and its teacher should be able to demonstrate competence.

(3) A third required preparatory stage, one only suggested by the passage, is that the student must be convinced that putting in the hours of study the subject demands is "worth it." The teacher must somehow persuade the student that, for example, geometry has value. A good teacher of a typical techne thus requires two separate capacities: mastery of the actual material to be taught and the ability to arouse interest in and commitment to the subject. The former, however, need not imply the latter: many who are knowledgeable in their professions are unable to inspire their students. This common problem discloses an important limitation of a techne: it is not self-reflexive and so in itself knows nothing of its own value. An expert shipbuilder, qua shipbuilder, can say nothing about why it is good to learn how to build ships.

(4) The final stage of instruction is, of course, communication of the actual course material.

This schema seems applicable to any ordinary techne. Arete, however, is an extraordinary subject whose teaching will disrupt the schema. First of all, it is hardly obvious that arete is an actual subject. There is no ready version of "Arete 101," and despite the advertisements of the Sophists, its teachers are not easily identified. How, then, does one persuade a student of its teachability? The student must be "protrepticized," exhorted to attempt and "care about" an extraordinary subject.

For most people, instruction in arete is left to the customs or institutions of the community: imitation of elders, obedience to civil law, and adherence to religious traditions are examples. To persuade someone to study arete as a distinct subject therefore requires the student to call into question familiar authorities. To be a serious candidate for such instruction, the student must be willing, *at the outset,* to question the nature of arete. But this is equivalent to commencing the study of arete itself. In other words, the initial protreptic stages 1 and 2 from above collapse into stage 4, the actual study of the subject.

The same collapse occurs even more dramatically with stages 3 and 4. How does a teacher convince a student that arete, assuming it can be taught, is worth studying? Only by arguing that knowledge of arete is valuable. But, as the phrase "is valuable" suggests, this argument can be made only by invoking the notion of arete itself. In other words, should a teacher try to persuade a student that arete is worth studying, that teacher would have to explain the value of the subject. But this explanation would be an actual lesson in arete. Again, there is no division between the protreptic preliminaries and the actual study itself.

The dilemma of commencing the study of arete thus echoes Meno's famous paradox. A student cannot learn arete unless he can be convinced it is both teachable and worth studying. But only the student *already* convinced of both is open to the possibility of being so persuaded. To explicate this dilemma, I deliberately exaggerate it: since the conviction that arete is teachable and worth studying is itself a component of being good, only somebody already good can be made good. To put it mildly, if this were true, it would limit the audience of Socratic protreptic. (Furthermore, it would do so in a fashion surprisingly similar to Isocrates' limitation of rhetoric to those who *already* have a good nature [see *Against the Sophists*, 14, and the section on Isocrates in Chapter 1]. This affinity between Platonic philosophy and rhetoric is crucial in Chapter 3.)

According to Dionysodorus, one and the same techne persuades a student (1) arete is teachable and (2) he and his brother can teach it (274e6). In a sense, he is right: because of the collapse of the various instructional stages just discussed, one and the same activity must both persuade the student to study and engage in the actual instruction of arete. In another sense, however, the Sophist is clearly unaware of the problems lurking within his answer. Since the study of arete is strange, can it become the subject matter of a techne (the most unstrange form of knowledge) of arete? If so, who are its teachers and why is it not regularly taught and with consistent success? If not, is there no knowledge of arete at all?

The first eristic scene commences when Euthydemus asks Cleinias, the promising youth who is the occasion for the entire dialogue (see 273a–c and 275a), "Of the following two groups, who are the ones who learn, those who are wise (*sophoi*) or those who are ignorant (*amatheis*)?" (275d). When Cleinias answers, "The wise," he is quickly refuted. He responds by answering, "The ignorant," and is refuted once again. As Socrates later explains (277e–278a), the Sophist here plays on the ambiguity of *manthanein*, which can mean either "to understand" (*sunienai*: 278a4) or "to learn something new": to expand upon knowledge presently possessed (a student who already knows his letters will understand a grammar lesson) or to acquire new knowledge (a student who does not know his letters can learn them). As such, the question can receive two different, and seemingly exclusive, answers. Given the first meaning of the verb, the answer is "the wise"; given the second, it is "the ignorant." Cleinias is befuddled.

This argument has occasioned much debate. It is not clear, for example, exactly where the force of the ambiguity falls. "Does the sophism depend upon an equivocation on *manthanein* . . . or on an equivocation on *sophoi* and *amatheis*?"[63] It is also possible that the fallacy is better described as "the one known traditionally as *a dicto secundum quid ad dictum simpliciter*. . . . This fallacy consists in taking absolutely what should be taken only accidentally, e.g., to go from 'knowing one's letters' to simply 'knowing.' "[64]

Since the focus here is on Socrates', and not the Sophists', arguments, I simply assert that some form of equivocation is going on. Still, whatever the exact status of the argument, its consequences are serious, for they require a calling into question of the very possibility of learning. If "the one who learns" cannot be identified, then the process of learning itself cannot be rationally explained, and it becomes legitimate to consider Meno's famous dilemma and ask whether learning is even possible.

After explaining the equivocation, Socrates seems to dismiss the Sophists' arguments:

> These are student games (*paidia*), and thus I tell you that these fellows are playing (*prospaizein*) with you—and I call this play (*paidian*) because even if someone should learn either many or all of such things as they teach, he would have no more knowledge of how things really are, but he would only be able to play with other men, tripping up and overturning them, by his use of the difference of names. They are like boys who take pleasure in pulling a chair away from people who are about to sit down and laugh when they see them sprawled upside down. You should think of what these fellows do as play. (278b1–c2)

Instead of just playing, Socrates urges the Sophists to fulfill their promise to engage in the serious work (*ta spoudaia*: 278c3) of protreptic. A series of dichotomies thus suggests itself. Sophistry is mere wordplay; it is concerned only with appearances and refutation and not with instruction

63. Hawtrey 1981, 58.
64. Sprague 1962, 6.

in how things really are; it is superficial, manipulative, and bad. By contrast, philosophy uses words to understand reality; it is serious, protreptic (or "dialectical"),[65] and good. While such comfortable dichotomies are attractive, they are not easily sustained. Despite their lack of perspicacity, the Sophists hold a potentially serious position. Whatever the exact status of the argument concerning learning, overcoming Meno's paradox is not easy. If the process of learning cannot in fact be rationally articulated and its possibility should therefore be called into question, then the verbal combat of sophistry, the manipulation of words whose goal is only to achieve victory in any given debate, *should* be taken very seriously. Since the use of language could promise no higher goal, that is, knowledge, there would be no reason not to become a Sophist.

This is exactly the point I made in Chapter 1 about Gorgias (and it applies to Protagoras as well). He weaves into his sophistical project a strand of skepticism. *On the Nonexistent,* as well as section 11 of "The Praise of Helen," does so explicitly. If there is but *doxa* and reliable episteme is not available, then the very function, indeed the essence, of logos is persuasion. If things in themselves cannot be known, then what remains for logos is the production of human *doxai.* In short, there is a coherent worldview backing up rhetoric: its skepticism warrants its commitment to the production of *doxa.*

For the *Euthydemus,* the key point is this: even if the Sophists who oppose Socrates are comic figures, their position is not a trivial counterpoint to the serious work of Socratic philosophy. It is possible to extract the sophistic view from its playful context, and the result is formidable. This becomes apparent in Socrates' first protreptic argument, whose conclusion—one ought to philosophize and care about arete—is, at the least, precarious. In other words, it does not obviously provide good reasons why Cleinias, the target of the protreptic, *should* accept the injunction to philosophize rather than join the sophistic camp. Indeed, Socrates' argument requires prior agreement with, and does not itself establish, at least one of its premises; and it is precisely this premise that the sophistic skepticism concerning learning would call into question.

The protreptic argument I extract from Socrates' questions and Cleinias's answers is this:

1. All human beings wish to do well (*eu prattein:* 278e6), that is, wish to be happy (*eudaimonein:* 280b6).

65. Sprague 1962, 3.

2. In order to do well, the possession of good things is required (279a2–3).
   a. A sample list of good things: wealth, health, physical beauty, good family, power and honor in one's community, temperance, justice, courage, wisdom (279a7–c3).
   b. Good fortune (*eutuchia:* 279c7) is a subsequent addition to the list. However, because "wisdom is good fortune" (279d6), the same item is actually listed twice.
3. To bring happiness, good things must benefit their possessor (280b7–8).
4. To benefit, good things must be used (280c1–d7).
5. To benefit, good things must be used correctly (280e3–4).
6. Correct use requires knowledge (*epistēmē:* 281b2).
7. All items on the sample list (2a) are actually neutral (281e3–4).
8. Conclusion: knowledge (or "good sense" [*phronēsis:* 281b6] or "wisdom" [*sophia*] or "intelligence" [*nous:* 281b7]) is the only intrinsic good and should be sought at any cost.

This is a classical protreptic argument, traces of which probably appear in Aristotle's *Protrepticus.*[66] Its conclusion—"[I]t is necessary to love wisdom (*philosophein:* 282d1)"—if seriously accepted, would demand a total commitment on the part of anyone who agreed. Unfortunately, the premises are stated in terms quite vague. A similar vagueness is found in the conclusion itself, where Socrates uses several words to describe the wisdom toward which the argument directs Cleinias, should he agree. Two related questions, What exactly is this wisdom? and How might Cleinias attain it? are thus left distressingly open.

Most important for my purposes, the principal examples Socrates uses to illustrate knowledge, or wisdom, come from the typical technai. It is not clear, however, whether these can actually provide an adequate theoretical model for the wisdom the argument exhorts Cleinias to seek.

The first premise contains a famous ambiguity in the phrase *eu prattein.* Does it mean "to do well" in the sense of being virtuous, or in the value-neutral sense of "to succeed"? Gifford says, "In its usual acceptation it would rather mean 'faring' well than 'acting well.'"[67] The reformulation the phrase receives, *eudaimonein,* typically but never quite adequately translated as "to be happy," only recapitulates the problem. It hardly

66. See Düring 1961, 19, and compare *Meno* 87e–89a.
67. Gifford 1909, 18. See also Hawtrey 1981, 20.

seems that all people wish to be virtuous. We may, however, all wish to succeed, that is, to attain what we deem to be worth attaining. *Eu prattein* covers both cases.

Its ambiguity, however, may not be vitiating. The first two premises express a basic and typically Socratic opinion about human behavior: all human beings desire what seems to be good. We make value judgments, pursue goals, attempt to move from here to there with an eye toward attaining what we want and deem, even if inarticulately, to be good (compare *Symposium* 206a). The argument assumes, and does not prove, free agency and the capacity for rational choice of what seems good. Even if vague and undefended, the assumption conforms with ordinary experience and observation.

Premise 2 implies that human action is inspired by *epithumia,* the desire for and consequent pursuit of objects, a notion again reflecting a broad and (to some) compelling perception of human behavior: people go after what they want, which is what they think is good.

I describe Socrates' list of good things as "sample" because its specific items are not themselves critical. What matters is only that such a list can be drawn. Its items (which have been accused of fluctuating "between the causes and constituents of success")[68] range widely from bodily beauty to justice. Still, in keeping with the kind of analysis made so far, the list is plausible: it signifies something basic about ordinary behavior. Each of us has a set of goals to energize our desires, a sample list of good things we think are worth pursuing.

To summarize: The assumptions initiating Socrates' protreptic argument are vague and questionable. Nevertheless, they express a plausible conception of human action as free and governed by rational choice. Unfortunately, more-serious problems with the argument are yet to come.

After placing wisdom on the list of sample goods, Socrates digresses, for he and Cleinias have left out "the greatest of good things . . . good fortune" (279c7). Socrates will not, however, add this to the list, because it would duplicate an item already present, namely, wisdom. By means of a series of examples, he explains. In the matter of flute playing, it is the skilled flautists who have the best fortune; in reading and writing letters, it is the writing masters; in warfare, it is the wise generals; in times of sickness, one would always prefer to try one's luck with the wise doctor. Soc-

---

68. Stewart 1977, 23.

rates generalizes: "Wisdom everywhere makes human beings have good fortune" (280a6).[69]

Why does Socrates digress? To focus attention on the character of techne. As described in Chapter 1, techne is knowledge that best overcomes, and enables its possessor to control, *tuchē* (see, for example, criterion 3, List 4). The pilot, for example, fares well, has good fortune, when facing the contingencies of the sea. But a familiar question looms: can wisdom, soon to be defined as knowing how to use things correctly and thus to bring happiness to the one who knows, be properly modeled by techne?

Premise 3 states that the good things on the sample list must benefit their possessor. This is true by definition and so adds little to the argument. Premise 4 does add something new: benefit requires that the good things be used. I may possess an apple, but it brings no nutritional benefit unless I eat it. A woman may have a great deal of money, but she would neither be benefited nor made happy by it unless she used (spent) it (280d). "Use" is the critical term because it refers to the process of bringing possessions into the human sphere of action, that is, of applying them in a value-laden manner.

Premise 5 elaborates this notion. Benefit requires that good things be not only used, but used "correctly" (*orthōs:* 280e3). If the item is used incorrectly the result is "bad" (*kakon:* 280e6). This premise is pivotal because it implies that the items of the sample list are neutral and can be used for good or ill. Even more important, it assumes that the use of an item can be understood as correct or incorrect. This assumption, however, is questionable. Are things like wealth and health not good but neutral? Can the use of these items be rationally evaluated as correct and for the good, or incorrect and for the bad? It is possible to accept the earlier premises but still answer no and reject premise 5. Indeed, this is precisely what Sophists such as Dionysodorus and Euthydemus would typically do. For them, human beings are free agents whose actions are motivated by some conception of what is good, for example, attaining political power in the Assembly. Without this assumption, their sophistry would become meaningless. They might not, however, agree that the good use of neutral items can be *known*. Their skepticism, as disclosed (perhaps) in the first eristic scene, prohibits them from doing so. As suggested above, the case for sophistry rests on the denial of objective knowledge.

---

69. Gifford (1909, 22) says of *eutuchia:* it means both "an accidental concurrence of favourable circumstances, and success resulting from the agent's judicious choice of means." Note the appearance of *eupragia* at 279e1.

Premise 5 of Socrates' protreptic argument assumes objective moral knowledge (of the correct or good use of a neutral object) is attainable. Socrates assumes, in other words, that we *can* answer the question, How should we live our lives and apply or use our possessions? From this assumption, he concludes that such answers *should* be sought. If Socrates' premises are granted, then knowledge of how to use one's possessions becomes the most desirable possession, for it is needed in order to be happy (which everybody wishes to be). Everyone, therefore, ought to seek knowledge of the correct use of neutral items. It is indeed "necessary to philosophize."

According to Socrates, an item like health is neither good nor bad, for it can be used well or badly. A strong body can beat up innocent weak bodies or build hospitals. Socrates assumes one of these applications of the body is and can be known as correct. But this assumption begs the crucial question. If correct use is a property belonging to neutral items, and if neutral items span the broad range suggested by the sample list, then knowledge of correct use *is* required for happiness. The conclusion is thus built into the premise: *if* correct use really exists, knowledge of it should be sought. But why assume the protasis? What if use is simply in the eyes of the beholder? What force does the protreptic then have? Can the living of a good life in fact be directed by knowledge? Perhaps so. This, however, is precisely what the argument should show, not assume.

As if to signal distress, the conclusion is stated in a flurry of different terms: *epistēmē* (281b2), *phronēsis* (281b6), *sophia* (281d6), and *nous* (281b7) are all used to label what should be sought. This terminological flux helps to raise the next problem with Socrates' argument: what exactly is this knowledge, assuming it exists, Cleinias is being exhorted to seek? Throughout the discussion, most clearly in the *eutuchia/sophia* digression (279c–280b), typical technai such as flute playing, reading and writing, piloting a ship, soldiering, and doctoring have been cited as examples of knowledge. Furthermore, carpentry provides the example of correct use to explicate premise 5 (see 281a). Should Cleinias then seek a typical techne, one whose subject matter is the good use of neutral items? The mere presence of so many technical examples would seem to suggest so. Such a conclusion, however, is premature. Socrates' example of carpentry shows why.

The carpenter knows how to use tools and wood (280c8–9) in the production of furniture (281a5). Socrates draws an analogy between the carpenter with his tools and a man with money. The carpenter uses his tools and wood knowledgeably (or technically) and is therefore benefited by them. Analogously, the man with money should use his wealth knowledgeably in order to be benefited and made happy by it (280d). "In the working and use (*chrēsis*) concerned with wood, is there anything other than the episteme of carpentry that effects the right use?" (281a2–4). The answer is no. Analogously, says Socrates, episteme should direct the possessor of items such as wealth toward the correct and therefore beneficial use of his possessions; toward, in a word, happiness.

There is, however, a problem with this analogy. There are two senses of "use." The carpenter knows how to use his tools and wood to build furniture. *But he does not know how to use the furniture.* The carpenter knows how to build a chair; but will the chair be used to seat someone comfortably at a symposium, or as an instrument for torturing a political prisoner? This second, value-laden sense of "use" would be required for "using" the neutral items on the sample list correctly and for the good. Of this, however, the carpenter qua *technitēs* knows nothing. Only in the first sense (using his tools correctly to produce the chair) is the carpenter knowledgeable.

This problem shows how difficult it is to identify what type of knowledge the target audience of the protreptic should seek. It cannot, for the reasons just stated, be an ordinary techne such as carpentry. But the examples of knowledge suggested have all been technai. What form of knowledge, then, will lead to happiness? The second part explicitly attempts to answer this question, to articulate the character of wisdom.

Socrates begins by restating his first conclusion: human beings should seek wisdom, that is, should philosophize (288d6–7). But what wisdom should we seek (see 289d9–10)? To elicit an answer, he suggests the knowledge of how to discover gold (or alchemy), that is, to produce wealth (288e6–289a5), medicine, and the ability to produce immortality (289b1). None, however, really brings happiness, for they do not know how to use their results.[70] An immortal life, even one supplied with endless wealth, can still be wretched.

The type of knowledge needed to be happy, therefore, is one in which knowing how to produce is combined with knowing how to use what is produced (289b4–7), in which the making is united with the using (*chrōmenē*) techne (289c2).[71] Clearly, the sense of "use" here is not technical but value-laden. As a result, this is *the* techne we have been looking for,

---

70. "Episteme" is used at 288d8, 288d9, 289a1, 289a4, 289b1, 289b4. "Techne" returns at 289c4.

71. For the "using techne," see *Republic* 601c, *Phaedrus* 274e, and Aristotle's *Physics* 194b.

the one to constitute wisdom and bring happiness, the one lurking as a tantalizing possibility ever since Solon first raised his doubts about the relationship between techne and human happiness. But what exactly is this techne? Can its structure be articulated? The search begins.

Because ordinary technai, exemplified by instrument making, know only how to make but not how to use their results, they fail the test. Socrates then enthusiastically asks, "By the gods, what if we should learn the techne of making speeches (*logopoiikēn*)? Is this what is required to make us happy?" (289c6–9). Cleinias answers no. This techne, he says, suffers the same split as any other: it is possible for speech makers not to know how to use their speeches (289d).

Socrates expresses disappointment at the failure of *logopoiikē*. On the one hand, he is being ironic, for "speech making" immediately connotes the work of men like the very Sophists against whom he is arguing (see 304–6; compare *Phaedrus* 257c). On the other hand, his disappointment hints at something more positive: "logos" is surely part of the right answer to the question at hand, What knowledge can make us happy? Wisdom, a logos of how to use all objects of desire, a comprehensive account of what is good in the human or moral sphere, is needed for happiness. But what is wisdom? Socrates offers the general's techne (*stratēgikē:* 290b1) as a possible candidate, apparently because the general knows how to command, organize, and in this sense "use" the various technicians under his sway. In other words, the general seems to have a "second-order" art. From my earlier discussion of the *Charmides,* however, the intrinsic problems within the conception of a second-order techne are now familiar. If they are not, Cleinias immediately begins to raise them.

The general's techne, he says, is a kind of hunting (290b5). Therefore, just as the hunter of game hands over his catch to a cook, so the general hunts and acquires cities and "then hands them over to the political men, for [the generals] themselves do not know how to use that which they hunt" (290d2–3). In fact, Cleinias gives a quite detailed description of this type of knowledge:

> No part of hunting itself covers more than chasing and overcoming. And when the hunter overcomes what he is chasing, he is not able to use (*chrēsthai*) it. Instead, hunters and fishermen hand over their catch to cooks. Analogously, geometers and astronomers and mathematicians (for these are also hunters, since none of them make their diagrams; they discover what is), since they themselves do not know how to use these things but only how to catch them, hand

them over to those men accomplished in dialectic so that they can use what these hunters have discovered—at least they can use however many of their discoveries that are not entirely senseless. (290b7–c6)

This is an impressive little speech, for it succinctly presents an entire conception of techne. As if to signal its remarkable character, Plato couches it in an extraordinary dramatic context: he has Crito interrupt Socrates' narration to ask whether young Cleinias was actually the speaker (290e1). This is a good question: how did a mere boy learn about dialectic? Socrates claims not to recall who the speaker was; perhaps it was the older Ctessipus. Even more mysteriously he adds, "Good Crito, perhaps one of the higher beings (tōn kreittonōn) was present and uttered these things" (291a3–4).

Such mystery is, I think, unparalleled in the dialogues. It is reminiscent, however, of Laches' statement that "unless . . . he is a god," no one can possess the knowledge that is courage (196a), and Socrates' remark in the *Charmides* that "a great man" is needed to determine which, if any, human activities are genuinely self-reflexive (168e). In other words, these three passages each project an extraordinary conception of knowledge, one whose subject matter would be use/value. In each case the knowledge is not identified, and Socrates attributes it only to a "higher being."

The dramatic tension ushered in by Crito's interruption highlights the fecundity of Cleinias's succinct epistemological proposal. Diagram 1, although somewhat awkward, at the same time schematizes Cleinias's remarks and a conception figuring prominently in several other dialogues (see Appendix 3). First, it discloses two basic forms of techne, the productive and the "acquisitive." The former, such as carpentry and pottery, are "ordinary" and, as suggested early in Chapter 1, constitute the original meaning of techne. The latter is itself divided into two parts, the second of which is couched in metaphorical terms: the acquisition of nonliving beings represents, I suggest, what the Eleatic Stranger describes in the *Sophist*, what Aristotle calls "theoretical knowledge," that is, knowledge that simply apprehends ("hunts") and does not construct or even alter its object.[72] As Socrates puts it, the geometers, astronomers, and mathematicians discover rather than make their objects.

A mathematical techne, such as geometry, "hands over" its "catch" to

72. See *Sophist* 291c1–7 and Rosen 1983, 91–92.

Diagram 1

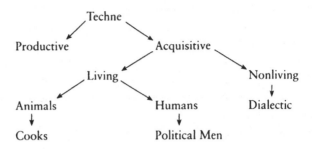

the dialectician. Dialectic in this passage seems to refer to some form of meta-mathematics, for example, the study of "number itself." It is not possible, given the single mention of "dialectic," to determine what exactly Plato means here. At best, the passage seems to posit some form of theoretical knowledge "higher" than ordinary mathematics.[73]

Analogous to the geometer, who hands over theoretical entities to the dialectician for study, is the "hunter of men," that is, the general, who hands over his acquisitions to the "political men," (290d2) who presumably have the political techne, the very one "we were seeking and the cause of correct acting in the city. And just (*atechnōs*) as Aeschylus says, it alone would sit at the helm of the city, steering everything and commanding everything and making everything useful" (291c10–d3).

This knowledge, the putative goal toward which the protreptic urges, is also called "the kingly techne" (291b5 and 291d7).[74] With this "discovery," the serious work of protreptic seems done, for the knowledge Socrates has been exhorting Cleinias to seek, the wisdom to comprehend arete and make him happy, has been identified: it is the kingly techne, a second-order "art" or knowledge of how to use all neutral items, including human beings. In the *Euthydemus* Plato, it seems, has named the long-sought-for moral knowledge and prefigured, even if clumsily, the famous Aristotelian tripartition of episteme into a theoretical (or "acquisitive"), a productive, and finally a "practical" branch, that is, an "architectonic" techne that "determines which of the epistemai are to be present in the cities, and what kinds of knowledge each of the citizens should learn, and up to what point" (*Nicomachean Ethics* 1094b).

73. See Klein 1968, 21–49.
74. Compare *Memorabilia* 4.2.2 and *Statesman* 305c–e.

Unfortunately, crippling objections are soon brought against this third, architectonic form of knowledge.

When he and his mysterious interlocutor reconsider the kingly techne, Socrates tells Crito, "We were totally ridiculous, just like children running after birds" (291b1–2). Why? Because the attempt to elucidate the structure and specific subject matter of this knowledge leads to aporia. First, they agree that the kingly and the political techne are the same. To it "the general's techne and all the rest hand over the results (*erga*) of which they are the producers (*dēmiourgoi*) for it to rule on the grounds that it alone knows how to use them" (291c7–9). Again, this is an immensely hopeful epistemic prospect. But what result does the kingly techne itself produce (291e1)? Spokesmen for medicine (291e5) or farming (291e8), for example, can identify the results of their knowledge (health or food from the earth). If the kingly techne is analogous, its spokesman should be able to do the same. But this Crito at least cannot do (292a6).

Because the kingly techne is assumed to be beneficial, Socrates next asks, "Isn't it necessary it supply us with some good?" (292a11). Since the first protreptic argument established that "nothing else is good except knowledge" (291b1–2), the results one would typically point to when considering this techne, such as wealth for the citizens, freedom, and the absence of factionalism, are "neither good nor bad." Only if it can make the citizens wise (or good or happy) can this techne be counted truly beneficial (292b4–c1). Once again, however, this description fails to satisfy, for Socrates next asks a question reminiscent of the *Charmides:* In what specific sense will the kingly techne make men good? Will it make all men good in all things? Since knowledge is the sole good, will it provide all forms of knowledge, including shoemaking, carpentry, and the rest (292c6–9)?

This line of inquiry concludes in failure: *no determinate ergon can be identified for the kingly techne.* As the first protreptic argument shows, it cannot issue in an ordinary result; if it did, that result would end up being classified a neutral item. The only knowledge, therefore, it can provide, is "*of itself*" (292d3–4). This obscure formulation is not explained further. (I return to it shortly.)

Socrates tries a last time to describe the kingly techne: it makes other men good (292d5–6). But, he asks, those men who are made good will be good with respect to what? The answer: only in making other men good. Of course, this is no real answer, for the question, Good with respect to what? would resurface. The basic problem, again reminiscent of the aporia of the *Charmides,* concerns the proper object of the kingly techne, the search for which is described as "labyrinthine" (291b7). Every time Socrates thinks he has found a way out (it makes the citizens wise, it makes them good), the demand for specification (wise in what? good with respect to what?) amazes him again.

This extraordinary section closes with Socrates saying, "Corinthus, son of Zeus, the situation is exactly (*atechnōs*) as I was describing it: we are still far, if not farther, from knowing what that knowledge is that will make us happy" (292e3–5). (For evidence that Socrates again is punning with *atechnōs*, see Appendix 2.)

This confession of a serious theoretical aporia (292e6) is expressed playfully. "The Scholiast on the passage relates that when Corinth had sent ambassadors to Megara to complain of their revolt, one argument advanced was that the mythical founder 'Corinthus, son of Zeus,' would be aggrieved if they failed to exact condign punishment. The proverb came to be used of boastful repetitions of the same story."[75] The story here is indeed repetitious: techne is the model of wisdom, and aporia is the result. Socrates professes to be drowning in the "third wave" of the argument (293a3), and he calls upon the two old Sophists to save him. This is ludicrous, for of all men they surely can provide no relief.

Problems plague Socrates' protreptic. The premises of its first stage are questionable. Even if they are granted, his conclusion—it is necessary to philosophize in order to be happy—is jeopardized by its obscurity. Just what is the wisdom we are exhorted to pursue? This obscurity is amplified by Socrates' second speech: the very notion of a kingly or second-order techne is problematic. How, then, can the target audience, which is exhorted to pursue wisdom, even begin its quest? Does the protreptic thus undermine itself? If so, the *Euthydemus* would have to be counted as truly bizarre: the Socratic protreptic would really be "apotreptic"; it would turn people away from the pursuit of wisdom. On this reading, Socrates, the serious protrepticizer who accuses the Sophists of wordplay, fails to give good reasons why we should pursue philosophy rather than sophistry.

Socrates' arguments end in an aporia from which he needs rescue. His is not, however, a failure, because these very arguments provide guidance in how to perform the rescue operation. Cleinias and, more important, we readers are being called upon to respond to the aporia that Socrates has created for us. We are being called upon to philosophize.

The serious question raised by the *Euthydemus* is twofold: What is the

---

75. Gifford 1909. Neither he nor Hawtrey nor Chance comments on *atechnōs*.

wisdom that will make us happy, and is it a techne whose subject matter is arete? As such, the *Euthydemus* recalls the pattern basic to the "early" dialogues. Socrates asks, "What is virtue X?" and then in his examination assumes, first, that virtue is inextricably linked to knowledge and that, second, this knowledge is best modeled by a techne. In the *Euthydemus,* however, Socrates actually argues that arete, the highest good, is knowledge, and challenges the second assumption by raising questions concerning the "using techne." Is there a techne whose subject matter is the correct and beneficial application of neutral items in the moral domain? Is there a techne to make its possessor happy? The answer appears to be no.

The epistemic lesson of the *Euthydemus,* then, is that knowledge of arete, or wisdom, cannot be strictly analogous to a techne. This is because the latter has a determinate subject matter or result. Medicine studies health; farming studies the production of crops. There is no analogous subject of the putative kingly techne. Apparently this is because the good use of neutral items is indeterminate. Socrates presents no explicit argument here (292c–293) why this is the case. Perhaps it is because the items on the sample list, namely, the objects typically deemed good by human beings, are themselves indeterminate. The question of their correct use does not allow for a determinate answer and so does not constitute a stable epistemological entity. This is why Socrates and his mysterious interlocutor, "one of the higher beings," repeatedly fail to identify a specific object of the kingly techne. Consequently, *if* techne is the only form of knowledge, there can be no knowledge of arete, and Socratic protreptic can not be distinguished from sophistry.

There is, however, a thread to lead us out of this labyrinth: a conception of nontechnical knowledge.[76] To begin, recall Socrates' obscure description of the kingly techne. It has, he says, itself as an object. Note the similarity between this formulation and Socrates' description of his entire search for wisdom: "When we reached the kingly techne and were examining it, to see if this techne was the one that supplied and produced *eudaimonia,* it was just as if we had fallen into a labyrinth: when we thought we reached the end, we twisted around again and appeared to be again at the very beginning of our search and just as much in need as we were when we began searching" (291b4–c2).

Why is this search circular? The premises of the argument stipulate that

---

76. Another possible thread is Gaiser's thesis that the dialogues are exoteric exhortations to wisdom, while the positive teaching is esoteric.

the kingly techne must supply something good. But what is this? Given the results of the first protreptic argument, the answer must be knowledge. But knowledge of what? Of what is good. But the good is knowledge: hence, the circularity. The kingly techne, which we know is not ordinary, is then described: "It is necessary that it be a producer (*dēmiourgos*) of no result, either good or bad; instead, it must transmit no knowledge other than that of itself" (292d1–4).

Possessors of typical technai study and then teach about (or produce) a distinct object. The doctor teaches about the workings of the human body, the carpenter about the production of furniture from wood. Techne (or episteme) is linear; it is *tinos,* of something specific other than itself. Is there an analogous object of the kingly techne? One is tempted to answer, Yes, it is arete. But this is not quite right. Recall the conclusion of Socrates' first protreptic: wisdom must be sought. This means that the knowledge Socrates has is not of arete per se; he knows only *that knowledge of arete should be sought.* When this knowledge is transmitted to students, they do not know arete per se; instead, they are equipped *only* to exhort others to seek it.

This is strange. Those who learn their Socratic lesson well know nothing other than how to exhort others to love wisdom. Their wisdom is manifested in their knowledge that wisdom is lovable. Protreptic teaches the student how to protrepticize. Like the labyrinthine aporia, it is circular; in other words, it has no object distinct from itself.

Socrates exhorts his listeners to pursue arete and to philosophize. Such an exhortation, however, appeals only to those already persuaded that wisdom is worth seeking. In this sense, Socrates does not teach his students anything. His protreptic goes nowhere, for he is able to speak effectively only to those already protrepticized. As argued above, the implicit premises of his argument—human beings are free and rational agents; the correct/good use of neutral items can be known—are undefended. Acceptance of the conclusion—it is necessary to philosophize—therefore requires a predisposition to accept the premises and to commence the search for objective knowledge. In other words, only those already philosophical can be persuaded to philosophize.

Socrates' accomplishment is nonetheless significant. He reinforces and explicates a desire present in his audience. To clarify, imagine listening to Socrates' first protreptic argument. Its conclusion takes the form of an imperative (which I paraphrase): turn away from your typical concerns; care about arete and pursue wisdom! The audience can respond in at least

three ways. (1) They can reject such an exhortation by dogmatically denying they need any help. (2) They can object to it and demand reasons why
they should follow such advice. (3) They can heed the argument's imperative.

Options 2 and 3, however, are similar: those asking for reasons why are,
like those in (3), philosophizing.[77] The argument itself, however, fails to
provide conclusive reasons why they should philosophize. As such, it cannot be said to produce (rationally) a new disposition to philosophize in the
target audience. What then does protreptic accomplish? It provides an occasion, as well as guidance in how, to philosophize. It addresses someone
like Cleinias, who is already "leaning" toward knowledge, and encourages
him to consummate this desire. Furthermore, the argument teaches him
how to do so. In particular, it points him toward nontechnical knowledge.

Techne is the pivot around which the protreptic turns. As "one of the
higher beings" explains, it provides a conceptual framework with which
ordinary knowledge can be classified and extraordinary knowledge con-
trasted. This framework allows someone like Cleinias to know where he
stands, to understand what is required to consummate his desire for the
knowledge of how to use neutral items correctly, that is, for the wisdom to
make him happy. What Cleinias really wants is extraordinary, that is, nontechnical, knowledge possessed (perhaps) by "one of the higher beings" (or
"a great man" or "a god").

Socrates does not identify this wisdom, and so his protreptic is aporetic,
even maddening. But it is not without result. This is because in itself it
represents a nontrivial form of knowledge. If the protreptic premises are
granted, the typical objects of desire (for wealth and beauty and other
items on the sample list) are neutral and not good. *If* knowledge of the
correct use of these neutral items is possible—which it admittedly may not
be—then it is also desirable as the condition for happiness. The target
audience of the protreptic, however, *already* leans toward such knowledge.
Therefore, at least implicitly, they grant the protasis. In this manner the
protreptic directs the desires latent in the target audience; it shows how the
nontraditional and potentially alienating or damaging desire for wisdom
can be transformed into a coherent activity leading to a happier life.

To reiterate: Socrates fails to prove philosophy is an unconditional
good. The imperative "It is necessary to philosophize" is not legitimately
universal or categorical. In particular, it would not bind those joining Eu-

---

77. For a classic protreptic move, see Düring 1961, 44.

thydemus and Dionysodorus in rejecting premises 5 and 6 (correct use is an objective property of neutral things and can be learned). Philosophy, then, is only conditionally good, and the imperative expressed as the conclusion of the argument should be hypothetical. *If* one is predisposed to philosophize and to question the traditional purveyors of arete, then one must philosophize in order to be happy.

Of course, this sounds tautologous. In fact, however, it is a crucial lesson for someone like Cleinias. By virtue of his openness to Socratic protreptic, Cleinias has called into question the traditional meaning of arete. Because he is no longer anchored in the familiar norms of his community, he is at risk. He may well become "lost"; he may become a revolutionary or a tyrant, a nihilist or a Sophist. To avoid such disastrous pitfalls, Cleinias needs to aim for what belongs to "one of the higher beings." He needs philosophy and the telos of wisdom.

The key point is this: *protreptic itself manifests nontechnical knowledge.* It does not have a determinate object distinct from itself. Its object is itself, for it is the knowledge of the desire to know arete. Other technai make discernible progress. One can move from ignorance of carpentry to skill by studying with a master. This is why the ordinary technai are easily recognized and usually admired. The progress in the study of arete is not analogous. Only one who already knows can be taught. But knows what? Knows that knowledge of arete is desirable. This, however, is the conclusion of Socrates' argument. As such, the protreptic discloses, or even instantiates, nontechnical knowledge, for it represents self-knowledge, knowledge of one's desires.

Cleinias, the target of Socrates' protreptic, has been present throughout, presumably listening with care. But we, the readers, whether we identify with Cleinias or not, do not know whether he will become a philosopher. Because this question is left open, the dialogue imitates, rather than abstractly describes, the protreptic moment. As such, an interpretive indeterminacy infects the *Euthydemus:* has the Socratic protreptic been effective? The reader does not, indeed cannot, know. By incorporating such dramatic tension, by including within itself such indeterminacy, the *Euthydemus* expresses nontechnical knowledge. This is knowledge whose epistemic content, unlike a $techne_1$, is indeterminate and cannot be systematically divided and then taught. Unlike a $techne_2$, it cannot be "packaged" and then sold for a high tuition fee. Instead, this is knowledge alive in the moment of dialogue.

Proponents of the SAT of course would disagree. They take various stands on the aporia of the *Euthydemus*. A "continuist" like Sprague reads it as a statement or outline of a theoretical project because it shows "Plato's awareness of the major difficulties bound to be encountered in the delineation of the second-order arts."[78] Sprague's Plato progressively moves closer to the solution of these difficulties and by the time of the *Republic* and *Statesman* actually consummates the promise of a second-order political art. This story is flawed, for it does not take into sufficient account the intrinsic difficulties of a second-order techne.

A discontinuist like Irwin also reads the aporia as evidence of Plato's awareness of these difficulties. He describes the Plato of the *Euthydemus* as putting forth "a superordinate science . . . needed to use other sciences' products. . . . A kingly, ruling science is required." But in doing so Plato "shows the problems in making [the craft analogy] useful" and so begins his gradual liberation from Socrates and the techne analogy.[79] Like Sprague, Irwin assumes the early Plato was seeking a rigorous moral theory. Unlike the continuists' Plato, however, Irwin's "transitional" Plato junked the techne analogy for not meeting up to sufficiently rigorous criteria.

My own reading is this: the *Euthydemus* is one of several dialogues pointing toward nontechnical knowledge. I do not come to the early dialogues with the assumption animating the SAT, that from the outset Plato aspired to a technical moral theory. Instead, I find Plato as ever exploring, through the lens of techne, the nature of the extraordinary moral knowledge he seeks. Nontechnical moral knowledge, which would make us happy, is not a theory. It is a Doric harmony of word and deed, a way of life spent seeking wisdom and urging others to do the same. It is a life spent turning a searching eye inward and therefore turning away from the external objects that become the subject matters of the ordinary technai.

If my argument is plausible, a major problem looms. What I attribute to Plato begins to seem distressingly similar to his putative archenemy, sophistic rhetoric. In *Against the Sophists,* for example, Isocrates also rejects $techne_1$ as a model for knowledge; he continually qualifies his pedagogic prowess and insists the content of his teaching can only be communicated through intensive personal interaction between a naturally gifted student and his teacher. His is a thoroughly value-laden enterprise, and, like Socra-

78. Sprague 1976, 53.
79. Irwin 1977, 76.

tes, he exhorts his listeners to pursue arete. He even describes his own subject as *philosophia*.[80] What, then, differentiates Platonic nontechnical knowledge from Isocratean rhetoric?

However qualified his claim may be, however studiously he avoids actually using the word "techne" to describe his own profession (see Appendix 4), Isocrates, simply because he hangs a shingle, founds a school, and charges tuition, implicitly professes a techne (albeit a techne$_2$). By contrast, Socrates accepts no payment, has no techne. Indeed, he does not claim even to possess a techne$_2$. Instead, he wanders the streets, picking up conversations where he happens to find them. He urges his interlocutors to pursue philosophy. This takes knowledge, not an abstract techne like arithmetic but a knowledge of how to direct a single individual to desire wisdom. Plato shows Socrates at work in his dialogues. And these, in and of themselves, represent his nontechnical knowledge.[81]

This is as yet unclear. I turn next to a discussion of the *Gorgias* and the *Protagoras*, two dialogues in which "philosophy v. rhetoric" takes center stage. This old quarrel, when viewed through the lens of the techne question, discloses much about the nontechnical knowledge toward which the first two chapters of this book have been pointing.

---

80. See Schiappa (1993), who discusses not only the word *philosophia* in Isocrates but also how to distinguish it from "Philosophy."

81. An obvious question: but did Plato not found a school and, in this sense, hang a shingle? The actual character of the Academy is not obvious: see Mueller 1992.

CHAPTER THREE

IS RHETORIC A TECHNE? THE PLATONIC VIEW

Philosophy v. Rhetoric: The *Gorgias*

My interpretation of the techne analogy bears a significant cost, for the nontechnical conception of moral knowledge I ascribe to Plato veers perilously close to that which the philosopher is traditionally assumed to despise: rhetoric.[1] Consider these points of similarity:

(1) In *Against the Sophists*, Isocrates explicates his understanding of rhetorical education through a *via negativa;* he contrasts his teaching with a *tetagmenē* techne such as orthography. Rhetoric is precisely *not* analogous to such a rigid form of knowledge. In Chapter 2, I argue that Socrates' use of the techne analogy is designed to communicate a similar lesson: if moral knowledge is assumed to be strictly analogous to a techne, arete cannot be knowledge. Since this conclusion is unacceptable, moral knowledge is not analogous to a techne.

Because of the distinction between a $techne_1$ and a $techne_2$ developed in Chapter 1, these negative assertions concerning Isocrates and Plato are not entirely informative. While rhetoric as conceived by Isocrates is not the former, it may well be the latter (i.e., a stochastic form of knowledge).

---

1. My use of "v." in the title to this section is a nod to Stanley Fish (1990). Some of the material in this section is elaborated in Roochnik 1994b.

Quintilian certainly thinks so. Unlike Isocrates, he unambiguously describes rhetoric as an *ars*. He does, however, repeatedly qualify this claim by distancing himself from the *artium scriptores,* the writers of the manuals who reduce rhetoric to a series of formulae and definitions. Even if rhetoric is not a strict compendium of elements and the rules for their synthesis, it is nonetheless a distinct and marketable discipline, with its own professors and high tuition fees.

A similar ambiguity may also apply to Plato. Perhaps, even while rejecting the model of a techne₁, he too conceives of a stochastic form of moral knowledge. This chapter, however, will show why this is not the case.

(2) Because it is not a strict techne, the teaching of rhetoric is precarious, even problematic. Although his curriculum does include a fixed portion (the *ideai* [16]), Isocrates' student must already have a "manly and intuitive (*doxastikēs*) soul" (17) in order to perform the "creative" work of forging appropriate and effective responses to specific occasions. This ability, essential to the good orator, cannot be taught, at least not in a formal sense. The student with a good nature must develop (and pay for) a personal relationship with his teacher, who functions as a *paradeigma* (18) able to impress upon him the sensitivity needed to speak well.

A similar conclusion emerges from the *Euthydemus.* Arete can only be taught to someone already predisposed to learn it, that is, someone good. Philosophy, then, seems infected with the same kind of problem as rhetoric. Neither is a techne₁, the paradigm of linear, stable, hence teachable knowledge. Neither can be reduced to a manual or set of rules. Like Isocrates, Socrates demands a personal dialogue with his students, and in the *Apology* (23b1) he describes himself as a *paradeigma* who somehow effects his listeners through an intense personal encounter.

(3) Rhetoric is, to cite Quintilian (who elaborates Protagorean and Isocratean themes), a "practical" art: "[I]t is with action that [rhetoric's] practice is chiefly and most frequently concerned, let us call it an active . . . art" (2.18.5). Rhetoric, because it is not an abstract body of knowledge, can only be fully exhibited in actual practice. In this sense, it is like the Doric harmony praised in Plato's *Laches,* which, I have argued, is an important clue to what nontechnical knowledge is for Plato.

(4) Rhetoric, at least the segment of its tradition running from Isocrates to Quintilian, is value-laden. Even though Isocrates hedges by saying, "[L]et no one think I am saying that justice is teachable," he nonetheless asserts, "[T]he practice of political logoi can more than anything else stimulate and exercise such qualities of character" (21). He praises virtue and

denies rhetoric is merely a collection of devices with which to persuade. His own orations are exhortations for good living. Quintilian is overt on this point: for him the good orator *must* be a good man (12.1–5). Since rhetoric (at least in its own self-estimation) is *not* a value-neutral set of persuasive techniques, what differentiates it from the Socratic quest for moral knowledge?[2]

(5) The good rhetor must be sensitive to the *kairos*, the particular occasion to which he must respond appropriately. As I have frequently noted, because he writes dialogues, Plato places Socrates into highly particularized dramatic situations. Socrates must respond to the specific needs and demands of a Thrasymachus or Euthyphro or Lysimachus, each of whose characters is expertly drawn by Plato. Socrates' ability to do so well is reflective of his nontechnical knowledge. If so, is Socrates simply a good rhetor?

(6) Socrates *uses* the techne analogy for critique, refutation, and exhortation. Does this mean he uses it rhetorically, that is, to address specific interlocutors in terms appropriate to their specific circumstances? Is Socrates, then, an orator at work, aiming only to clarify, refute, and exhort? Or is he a philosopher engaged in the project of attaining the contextless Truth?

Plato's preoccupation with rhetoric is manifest. He devotes the *Protagoras* and the *Gorgias* to well-known Sophists, and rhetoric is present as a force to be reckoned with in numerous other works. This is because, as stated in Chapter 1, rhetoric is the first discipline to claim technical mastery over the field to which Socrates himself is devoted: arete, logos-as-action, the good life. As a result, the Sophists are Socrates' prime competitors and "philosophy v. rhetoric" is *the* battle he is eager to fight. Even so, the standard story—with Plato as the mortal enemy of rhetoric, to which he diametrically opposes philosophy—is greatly oversimplified. Plato's near obsession with rhetoric is fueled not only by the desire to combat an enemy but also by the distressing possibility that the enemy is not too different from himself.

In this chapter I use the techne question as a lens through which to examine the old quarrel between philosophy and rhetoric. Through it, I elucidate the basic terms of this debate and, most important, extract what ultimately is at stake in it. "Philosophy v. rhetoric" is a fundamental dispute, for it concerns precisely the questions animating this entire book: To

2. See Schiappa 1993.

what extent can human life, the realm of politics and public speeches, of praxis and logos, be known? Can it be rendered fixed and determinate? Can anything in this world of human affairs be counted upon? Is the political world analogous to the alphabet, which, as the subject matter of orthography, is the paradigm of reliable and systematic knowledge? Can human life be stabilized such that secure and technical knowledge of what is best about it can be attained?

The Platonic philosopher and the rhetorician indeed disagree, but their positions are surprisingly close. The techne question helps me articulate the structure of this dispute and in doing so illuminates the nature of the nontechnical knowledge central to the Platonic project.

Socrates v. Gorgias and Polus

The question, Is rhetoric a techne? has had a long and tenacious life. It was debated continuously throughout antiquity, from Plato's *Gorgias* and Isocrates' *Against the Sophists* (both written around 385 B.C.E.)[3] through the works of Cicero, Quintilian, Philodemus, and Sextus Empiricus. It was satirized by Lucian and discussed at great length by Aristides.[4] It has figured prominently as recently as 1988, in Vickers's *In Defense of Rhetoric*. The question has been pivotal in shaping the millennia-old battle between philosophy and rhetoric. Its *locus classicus* is in the *Gorgias,* where Socrates describes rhetoric as but an *empeiria* and *tribē,* an empirical knack producing gratification and pleasure (462a). Like cooking, it is a species of "flattery" and therefore has no "share in what is admirable" (463a): Rhetoric "seems to me, Gorgias, not to be a technical practice (*epitēdeuma technikon*), but instead a quality of an intuitive and manly soul, one that is clever by nature in dealing with human beings. In general, I call it flattery" (463a).

To explain, Socrates offers the scheme shown in Diagram 2. Socrates asserts, but does not prove, that body and psyche each have an inherently good condition (*euexia:* 464a2) that can be securely known and attained.

---

3. The exact dates of these works is of course difficult to ascertain. In this case, chronology is potentially interesting because it bears directly on the question, did the *Gorgias* influence *Against the Sophists,* or is it the other way around? Jaeger (1967, 302) views the latter as a response to the former, which he believes was composed between 395 and 390. Dodds (1966, 24–27) dates the *Gorgias* to 387–385 and *Against the Sophists* to 390. Ledger (1989) dates the *Gorgias* to 386.

4. See Lucian, "The Parasite," and Aristides, "In Defense of Oratory."

Four technai, medicine and gymnastics for the body, and justice and legislation for the psyche, ascertain the good condition of their objects and help
them attain it. The pairs, medicine/justice and gymnastics/legislation, differ
because the former correct deficiencies and return their objects to their
euexia, while the latter nurture and create abidingly good conditions. In
contrast to these genuine technai, flattery "perceives, I do not say it knows
but that it guesses (*stochasmenē*), there are four branches [of techne],
which always exercise their objects, namely, the body and the soul, toward
what is best, and then it [flattery] divides the parts, pretending it is that
which it has insinuated itself into. It does not care at all for what is best,
but it always hunts out foolishness by saying what is most pleasant, and it
deceives those who are foolish by making it seem as if it is the most valuable thing of all" (464c–d).

Diagram 2

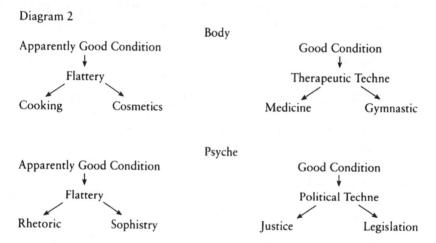

A cook, for example, may pretend he is a doctor by describing a cookie
as good for the stomach. The cookie is delicious and hard to resist. Since
the cook merely gratifies his audience without contributing to the actual
excellence of their bodies, he is like the rhetorician.[5]

This scheme can be expressed "geometrically": as cosmetics is to gymnastics, so sophistry is to legislation, and as cooking is to medicine, so
rhetoric is to justice (465c). With such a scheme in place, Socrates condemns the forms of flattery as shameful: "Flattery, I call it, and I state that
such a thing is shameful, Polus—for I'm saying this to you—because it

5. As Irwin (1979, 134) points out, "But surely Socrates is wrong to say that cookery
pretends to offer healthy food."

guesses what is pleasant without the best. And I say that it is not a techne, but an *empeiria*, because it gives no account (*logos*) of the things it applies, what sort of nature they are, and so it cannot state the cause (*aitia*) of each thing. I refuse to call anything irrational (*alogon*) a techne" (465a).

The intent of the passage seems obvious, namely, to condemn rhetoric, and the basic terms of "philosophy v. rhetoric" thus appear set. However, although the Socratic charge can be compressed into a single statement— rhetoric is not a techne—its particulars are surprisingly complex. First, exactly why, according to Socrates, is rhetoric shameful? Because it is not a techne. But why is it not? Because it guesses at what is pleasant and does not know the good condition of the psyche. But where does the emphasis in the charge lie? On the fact that rhetoric aims for the pleasant without the good, or on its being stochastic, that is, epistemically deficient? Even the first sentence of the passage cited above is ambiguous: rhetoric is shameful because it "guesses" (*stochazetai*) at what is pleasant without the good. But is it shameful because it guesses, or because its end is pleasure and not the good?

In other words, the attack on rhetoric comprises both an epistemic and ethical prong.[6] There is, however, no obvious connection between the two prongs. The latter part of the passage (465a6–8) seems strictly epistemic (and quite Aristotelian: see *Metaphysics* 1.1). The various branches of flattery are not technai, because they cannot give a logos of the *aitia*. Does this inability make rhetoric shameful? It does not, for if it did, everything nontechnical would be shameful. A child's ability to walk, for example, is hardly to be blamed for not being a techne. Why, then, does rhetoric's nontechnical status render it shameful? Presumably because the rhetorician, unlike the child, dissembles: he *pretends* to possess a techne while in fact having but an "image" (*eidōlon*: 463d2) of it.

Second, rhetoric is condemned on ethical grounds for aiming at the pleasant rather than the good. But is this in itself a matter for blame? Only given certain assumptions. If, for example, the rhetor aims *only* for pleasure, and if pleasure is totally divorced from the good, then he could be fairly blamed. But if "what is pleasantest over all is also best over all," then "if the rhetor aims at what is pleasantest, will he not aim at what is

---

6. The two prongs of Socrates' objection to rhetoric are encapsulated in the standard Stoic definition of a techne (as reported by Sextus Emiricus *Against the Professors* 2.10 and cited in Chapter 1): "Every techne is a body [*sustēma*] consisting of items of knowledge which are mutually cohesive and having reference to one of the ends which are useful in life." The translation is from Barnes 1986, 5.

best over all?"[7] In other words, Socrates does not make it clear why aiming for pleasure is in itself shameful.

Third, Socrates seems to assume that *because* rhetoric aims for the pleasant rather than the good, it cannot be a techne. But why? Why can there not be a techne of cooking or cosmetics whose goal is pleasure? Such a goal would be quite different from those of medicine or gymnastics, but why can the cook or "cosmetologist" not apply real knowledge in performing their tasks?[8]

Fourth, all the technai in Socrates' scheme aim for the "good condition" of their objects. But the good condition of the body, the goal and epistemic content of medicine and gymnastics, seems quite different from that of the psyche, the goal of legislation and justice. Medicine is concerned with the proper *functioning* of a determinate entity, the body, and unconcerned with whether the well-functioning body is used to perform just or unjust actions (see 456d). Because it ministers to the good condition of the body only in this technical sense, it is value-neutral. By contrast, the good condition of the psyche, and therefore the technai of justice and legislation, are by definition value-laden. Why, then, is the single word *euexia* used to label two apparently different conceptions? Does Socrates assume values are a matter of fact and straightforwardly knowable? Does he think the good condition of the psyche is, like the body, fixed and stable and thus apprehensible by a techne? Or, conversely, does he conceive of every techne, even the one aiming only for the proper but value-neutral functioning of the body, as somehow aiming for the good?[9]

Fifth, as Dodds points out, there is no place in Socrates' scheme for the individual psyche.[10] This is puzzling, since the individual psyche would seem to be the natural correlate to the individual body. A question must thus be asked: even if the good condition of the political psyche, or the polis, is determinate and hence apprehensible by a techne, is this true of the individual psyche as well? If so, would this putative techne whose subject matter is the good condition of the individual psyche be equivalent to philosophy? Or is the individual psyche somehow indeterminate and thus ineligible as subject matter of a techne?

7. Irwin 1979, 135.
8. See Aristotle *Nicomachean Ethics* 1152b18 for this point.
9. See Hemmenway 1993 for this position. Note also *Republic* 444e1, where Socrates defines arete as a *euexia*. This passage of course would provide support for the SAT. My reasons for disagreeing with it are presented in the fourth section of Chapter 2, in particular my discussion of Warren.
10. Dodds 1966, 227.

A related problem is raised by Hall: if "justice" and "legislation" were moral technai, then their subject matter, the excellence of the psyche, would have to be like the body or the subject matter of any other techne; it would have to be construed as passive and ready to be "informed" by the work of the *technitēs*. But surely a moral psyche must be active rather than passive.[11]

There is an implicit resolution to several of these problems. Assume (as Socrates does at *Philebus* 27e) that pleasure is inherently indeterminate. This might be true in two senses. First, people experience pleasure in an indefinite and unpredictable variety of ways; second, pleasure and pain form a continuum that always admits of the "more and the less" (*Philebus* 24a). Pleasure thus offers no fixed, stable, and epistemically reliable standard at which to aim. Assume further that a techne is a rigorous form of knowledge with a determinate subject matter. If so, there can be no techne of or aiming for pleasure, and if rhetoric indeed aims to produce pleasure, it cannot be a techne.[12] (This point is made explicit later in the dialogue when Socrates describes flattery as "irrational" because it fails to "differentiate" [*diarithmēsamenē*: 501a7] or "to reckon by number." In other words, flattery, because it is concerned with the indeterminacy of pleasure, cannot make determinate distinctions.)

Such an implicit resolution, even if accurate, is only partial. It may explain why there cannot be a techne of pleasure, but not why aiming for pleasure is shameful. Again, presumably the reason flattery in general and rhetoric in particular are shameful is that they *pretend* to be technai when in fact, because of the indeterminate nature of the subject matter (i.e., pleasure), they are not. However, as I next show (in the *Gorgias* at least), rhetoric and its representatives initiate no such dissembling: it is none other than Socrates himself who, in the course of debating both Polus and Gorgias, invites, indeed pressures, them to describe rhetoric as a techne.

Consider one of the most striking but least commented-upon features of the *Gorgias:* while Socrates denies that rhetoric is a techne in his argument against Polus, he asserts the opposite while debating Gorgias. In fact, rhetoric's being a techne is an essential assumption of the entire confrontation between the famous rhetorician and the philosopher. This becomes clear at

11. Hall 1971.
12. Dodds (1966, 229) makes this point: the pleasant, he says, is not "in each case rationally determinable." So too does Gosling (1975, 153): "[T]hey [*emperiai* like rhetoric] fail to be technai because no general account can be (or at least is) given of what pleases people, and so there are no general canons for ensuring success." Also, note the *aei* at 464d2.

the outset of the dialogue, when Callicles invites Socrates to listen to one of Gorgias's famous displays. Socrates responds, "I want to find out from him what (*ti estin*) the power of the man's techne is and what it is he professes and teaches" (447c). As was typical in the dialogues discussed in Chapter 2, *Socrates* supposes his interlocutor either has or is speaking about a techne.

Callicles is confident that Gorgias can answer Socrates' question; after all, the great rhetorician says he can answer "every" (*hapanta:* 447c7) question. With such a brag, the principal issue of the dialogue is broached. Gorgias can answer every question; presumably his field of expertise, or subject matter, is, precisely as Quintilian will later describe it, "everything" and as such is indeterminate. Socrates, however, refuses to allow the rhetorician's boast to go untested. He instructs his proxy Chaerephon to ask Polus, Gorgias' student, "who he [Gorgias] is." Chaerephon does not understand the question. Socrates explains by analogy: if you were to ask a shoemaker who he is, he would answer "a shoemaker."

Chaerephon dutifully inquires, "If Gorgias happened to be knowledgeable (*epistēmōn*) about the techne in which his brother Herodicus is knowledgeable, what would we rightly call him?" (448b4–5). The answer is "a doctor." If he were knowledgeable in the techne of Aristophon, he would be called a painter. In what analogous techne, asks Chaerephon, is Gorgias knowledgeable, and what should he thus be called?

This question, *which governs the entire argument with Gorgias,* is generated by the analogy "As a typical techne is to its subject matter, so is rhetoric to some X." Medicine, for example, has a specific subject matter, the health of the body, which determines what it is and renders it unique among the technai. Socrates' strategy is clear. He wants to pry Gorgias away from his extraordinarily broad self-description by forcing him to identify a particular subject matter. Toward this end he repeatedly asks variations on the question, *peri ti?* ("about what is rhetoric?") (449d1).

Gorgias's first answer is, It is about "speeches" (*logoi:* 449e1). Socrates immediately objects: gymnastics and medicine are also about speeches, speeches about disease and the good condition of bodies. "And this is true of the rest of the technai, Gorgias. Each of them is about those speeches which happen to be about the subject matter of their techne" (450b). Gorgias must try again. Unlike the other technai, he insists, rhetoric is not a craft with a distinct product (*cheirourgēma:* 450b7). Instead, its whole activity and efficacy is "through logoi" alone (450b9). To borrow Aristotelian terminology: rhetoric is a "theoretical," rather than a productive, techne (see Appendix 3 for a full discussion of this distinction). Gorgias's move, however, fails to specify the unique features of rhetoric, for other technai, notably mathematics, also are a matter of pure logos (450d).

Gorgias next proposes that rhetoric is "about the greatest and most excellent of human affairs" (451d7). This too is inadequate, says Socrates, for all technai seem to evaluate themselves as positively as Gorgias evaluates rhetoric. The doctor, for example, thinks health is the greatest good. Simply by virtue of having chosen to pursue a certain field, every technitēs, it seems, is disposed to evaluate himself and his work positively. Gorgias's description of rhetoric, therefore, is neither precise nor unique (452a–c).

These exchanges show how vigorously the rhetorician resists delimiting his subject matter. As he conceives it, his ability is unrestricted, and his power embraces within it all other powers. He is able, for example, to persuade the sick patient to take his medicine, a feat even the technically proficient physician cannot perform (456a–c). As such, rhetoric seems to be (says Socrates) "something daimonic" (456a6). But if rhetoric has this daimonic power to talk about everything to everyone, how can rhetoric be a techne and be taught? The technitēs is an expert, and no one can be an expert in or teacher of everything.

In response to Socrates' insistent demand to specify in what sense rhetoric is valuable (which is a variant on the question, peri ti?), Gorgias says it is the "capacity to persuade with speeches either judges in the law courts or statesmen in the council chamber or citizens assembling in the assembly or in any political gathering" (452e1–4).

This is a reasonably sharp definition: the subject matter of rhetoric would, on the basis of this passage, be "political persuasion." Socrates, however, reformulates: "Rhetoric," he says, "is the producer (dēmiourgos) of persuasion" (453a2). The alteration is significant. Gorgias himself had restricted the realm of persuasion to the political, but Socrates, even though he had pressed for just such restriction, widens the definition to encompass all forms of persuasion. Gorgias, perhaps unwittingly, agrees to the reformulation. As a result, Socrates can repeat his ceaseless refrain: about what in particular is rhetoric persuasive (453c1)? After all, every techne can teach, and since teaching is a form of persuasion, all technai persuade. "Producer of persuasion" fails, and Gorgias must try again.

"Rhetoric," he says, "is persuasion concerning the just and the unjust" (454b7). This is the crucial response, and it reveals, I think, the reason why Socrates dismissed the previous definition, "political persuasion," by changing it to "producer of persuasion": he was pushing Gorgias away from the former because he could refute the latter on the grounds of inde-terminacy. When Gorgias tries again at 454b7, he includes the words "just and unjust" and thereby invokes precisely the terms Socrates wishes him to. He has claimed to be a teacher of arete (a claim the historical Gorgias may well have avoided). Socrates summarizes: "Rhetoric stands in relation to the just and the unjust, and the shameful and the fine, and the good and the bad, as [the physician does] to health, and as the rest of the technai do to their objects" (459d1–3).

This summary proves disastrous for Gorgias because he had already characterized rhetoric as a typical techne like wrestling, whose teacher says nothing about the good or bad use (*chrēsthai*: 456d2) of the knowledge he imparts to his students. In fact, the technically proficient wrestler/rhetori-cian might well strike his "father or mother." In other words, Gorgias's characterization of rhetoric as use- or value-neutral at 456d directly con-tradicts his claim to know arete at 459d.

Polus objects to Socrates' handling of his teacher. Gorgias, he says, was *shamed* into granting that "the rhetorical man" both knows and teaches what is just and fine and good (461b), and through this was led to contra-dict himself. In other words, if Gorgias had resisted making the claim to teach arete, he could have saved himself from refutation. In a formal sense, Polus's diagnosis is accurate, for Gorgias's assertion about arete (at 460a) led him to contradict his earlier description of rhetoric as value-neutral. But Polus has not grasped the real cause of Gorgias's demise, which is Socrates' use of the analogy "As medicine is to the health of the human body, so rhetoric is to a comparably determinate X." In other words, the presupposition that *rhetoric is a techne* is essential to the refutation of Gorgias. This is strange because the opposite assumption—*rhetoric is not a techne*—dominates the refutation of Polus. Which is it? If the latter, what conclusion can be drawn about the argument against Gorgias, which presupposes the former?

Perhaps the Socrates/Gorgias debate constitutes a *reductio ad absurdum*. From his initial assumption of rhetoric as a techne, Socrates generates a contradiction. This leads to a negation of the assumption, which negation then becomes the first premise Socrates uses in his argument against Polus (as well as his sincere belief).[13] While plausible, this reading does not quite account for the dialogue. First, even if the assertion that rhetoric is a techne is eventually rejected, it nonetheless remains essential to the refuta-

13. I owe this formulation to Francisco Gonzalez.

tion of Gorgias. As a result, if rhetoric proves not to be a techne, then the refutation would have to be retroactively voided. Second, the interpretation of the two arguments as a *reductio* does not fully account for the beginning of the dialogue, where Socrates badgers Gorgias to formulate his conception of rhetoric in terms of techne. To reiterate: this is Socrates' doing, not the rhetorician's.

But why would Socrates foist what he takes to be a false statement— rhetoric is a techne—on his opponent? The obvious answer is *In order to refute him*. Socrates demands of Gorgias, who boasts of being able to answer "every" question, that he explicate rhetoric as a techne with a specific subject matter. Doing this forces the rhetorician to identify precisely what it is he professes to know. Once this identification is made, Socrates can then examine and evaluate it. At the very least, then, it is immensely helpful to the philosopher *if* the rhetorician professes to have a techne. If he does, Socrates can refer to the specific subject matter about which he professes technical expertise ("the just and the fine and the good": 461b) and invoke it as a standard by which to measure and then refute the general claim to teach rhetoric.

Socrates' strategy is effective in revealing how unreflective Gorgias actually is. Since a typical techne is value-neutral, and since techne is both the most familiar form of knowledge and the one regularly claimed by the rhetorician who charges tuition, Socrates shows that Gorgias has failed to consider the great challenge implied by the twin claims of being able to teach arete and of having a techne.

By using the techne analogy against Gorgias, Socrates seems to invite the rhetorician to make a false statement, and to do so because it is to his dialectical advantage. When arguing against Polus, he follows a different strategy. Simply put, Socrates speaks differently to different people. Does he wield the techne analogy, then, as a rhetorical device? If so, the line between Platonic philosophy and rhetoric would be difficult to draw indeed.

A possible way of drawing this line is available to proponents of the standard account of techne. On this reading, the philosopher aspires to transform knowledge of the human good into a techne and thereby render human affairs rationally controllable. By contrast, the rhetorician affirms, or even celebrates, the indeterminate, the contingent and the unpredictable. Like an open hand, he welcomes all comers and applauds all the many goods embraced by all the many human beings; he is willing to talk

about everything. The philosopher is like the closed fist, grasping firmly—
that is, technically—his conceptual content, namely, *the* determinate good.[14]

But to ask the question central to Chapter 2, does Plato actually recommend that moral knowledge be transformed into a techne? If so, this is
hardly obvious from the *Gorgias*. First, as evinced by his conversation
with Gorgias, Socrates is not quite firm even on the question, Is rhetoric a
techne? If philosophy is (or should be) a techne, then it should be able to
identify the form of flattery that imitates it. The carpenter will unambiguously describe a child playing with a hammer as "nontechnical." But
against Gorgias, Socrates does not make an analogous denunciation of
rhetoric.

Second, there is the absence of the individual psyche on Socrates' geometrical scheme depicting the forms of flattery. If philosophy were a
techne, perhaps this is what its subject matter would be. The absence of
the individual psyche, therefore, may be designed to cause the reader to
wonder whether it can in fact be stabilized or rendered sufficiently determinate to become the subject matter of a techne. (This question is ad-
dressed in my discussion of Callicles below.) Perhaps this is true as well for
the psyche "writ large," that is, the polis. Even if it is present on the
scheme as the subject matter of legislation and justice, there is the tacit and
problematic characterization of the good condition of the political psyche
as being as stable, and hence as straightforwardly apprehensible, as the
health of the body (i.e., a moral *euexia* is analogous to a technical one).

Third, in an important sense Socrates is similar to Gorgias. While
Gorgias offers to field, and presumably answer, all questions, Socrates
spends his days wandering the agora, asking all sorts of questions. It is,
quite simply, very difficult to identify Socrates' determinate field of expertise. It is, as his interlocutors well know, difficult to force him to give
straightforward answers even to the questions he himself poses (such as, Is
rhetoric a techne?). And what else is a techne if not a series of answers?

Considerations such as these, as well as the arguments of Chapter 2,
argue against the position that (1) Plato conceived of moral knowledge as
analogous to a techne and (2) this conception is *the* critical difference between him and the rhetorician. At the same time, however, my argument
might seem to fly in the face of Socrates' startling assertion at 521d: "I
think I am one of the few Athenians, if not the only one, who really attempts (*epicheirein*) the political techne."

14. This famous image is Zeno's and is cited by Quintilian at 2.20.7.

Two responses: Socrates does not say he actually possesses a techne; he only "attempts" one.[15] Even if techne were to function as a kind of ideal at which the philosopher aims, "to aim for" is not the same as "to achieve." Second, perhaps Socrates' assertion is itself a kind of *reductio*. After all, Socrates is anything but an obviously political or technical man. As such, if he, of all people, attempts the political techne, perhaps this is good evidence of its being impossible. As Callicles puts it, Socrates spends his days "whispering in a corner with three or four lads" (485d) instead of fighting in the Assembly for the views he champions. His whispers tend to be questions rather than answers, and so, unlike the typical *technitēs*, Socrates hangs no shingle, has no students, and, most notably, *accepts no tuition*. If Socrates were to possess a techne, it would be unlike any discussed in Chapter 1.

Socrates on the Goodness of Determinacy

A single concept has lurked behind Socrates' refutations of Polus and Gorgias: determinacy. The scheme used against Polus, for example, concerns pleasure. Since it is the goal of rhetoric, and since it is indeterminate, rhetoric cannot be a techne. It is precisely this basic feature of a techne—namely, it must master a determinate subject matter—that Socrates exploits in using the analogy against Gorgias. There he attempts to identify and thus make refutable the rhetorician's otherwise vague, and hence irrefutable, claim to teach the "daimonic" power of all powers. In both cases, Socrates puts the notion of techne, and therefore its foundational concept, determinacy, to good use. Specifically, he uses it to refute his opponents.

There is another sense in which the philosopher finds the techne analogy useful. Against Polus, Socrates draws a geometrical scheme—as cooking is to medicine, so rhetoric is to justice—not only to locate rhetoric but also to denigrate it by giving it a dismal place in a hierarchy. By doing so, and in much the same way as he does with the "divided line" of the *Republic,* he exhorts his listeners to seek what is higher. In other words, Socrates uses the analogy in the *Gorgias* in the same two basic ways in which he does in "earlier" dialogues, namely, to *refute* the claim of the rhetorician to have a techne, and to *exhort* the uncommitted listener to seek knowledge of the good. Neither use necessarily implies that the philosopher himself possesses a techne with a determinate subject matter. Instead—and

15. However, *epicheirein* can also be translated as "undertake."

this is the crucial point—they imply only his belief that determinacy, the notion undergirding his use of the techne analogy, is useful and good.

The rhetoricians' view of determinacy is an exact counterpoint. If Socrates praises determinacy while denying the possession of a determinate body of knowledge, they praise indeterminacy while simultaneously hanging their shingles. Gorgias and Quintilian, for example, boast of their ability to talk about everything. Gorgias emphasizes the pivotal role of *doxa*. Isocrates insists his curriculum cannot be fixed, because of the primacy of the *kairos*, the contingent moment to which the good speaker must appropriately respond. The rhetoricians typically require some measure of democratic openness and free speech to ply their trade. They affirm contingency and change and tailor speeches to their specific circumstances.[16] In this manner, they advocate the open hand of indeterminacy. In sharp contrast, however, they claim a specific expertise allowing them to teach students and, very significantly, charge tuition. In other words, even if stochastic, rhetoric is nonetheless a techne, the paradigmatic form of teachable, marketable knowledge.

Again: how can the indeterminate "everything" of which rhetoric speaks be sufficiently delimited to function as the subject matter of a legitimate and teachable techne? This fundamental epistemic problem inevitably haunts the rhetoricians whenever they reflect upon the nature of their own expertise. Such epistemic self-reflection, however, is not frequent. Unlike the philosopher, whose head is in the clouds, that is, for whom reflection is a way of life, the rhetorician is a "practical" thinker largely involved either in the making of actual speeches to be delivered in the Assembly and courts, or in the direct and methodical presentation of subject matter. For the rhetoricians, then, the techne question, precisely because it is atypical, is uniquely revealing (at least in the eyes of the philosopher): when addressing it they are forced to ask, *what is* this knowledge they present methodically and that allows them to speak well? As a result, the techne question functions as a lens through which to glimpse the epistemic self-conception of rhetoric. And as I noted in Chapter 1, the glimpse is revealing. Rhetoric, either (in Isocrates' case) by vacillating or (in Quintilian's case) by qualifying the claim to a techne, conceives of human logos/praxis as dominated by the unpredictability of the *kairos*. While indeterminate in this sense, logos/praxis is not unintelligible, for even if there are no systematic rules, there are nonetheless informal "rules of thumb." Even if his

16. A fine description of rhetoric in these terms can be found in Fish 1990.

subject is not *tetagmenē*, it is possible for Isocrates *somehow* to teach, make an impression on a young student, and mold and train him to become a good speaker and a decent citizen. The rhetoricians claim a techne, even if, as in Isocrates, that claim is ambiguous or, as with Quintilian, that techne is a techne₂. Again, this they do simply upon hanging their "shingle," starting a school, or being "invited" to teach students for a fee.

Socrates, by contrast, *claims no techne*. He has no school. He charges no tuition, for he professes no knowledge whose value can be numerically fixed. Unlike the rhetoricians, he lives in the midst of indeterminacy, walking the streets, haunting the gyms, picking up conversations as they happen along. Simultaneously, however, he praises determinacy and evaluates it positively. He seems animated by the goal of rigorous knowledge when he asks his many variations of the *ti esti* or the *peri ti* questions. When he describes himself as one of the few Athenians, if not the only Athenian, to "attempt" the political techne, he seems to posit it as an ideal of some sort. There is thus a basic tension surrounding Socrates' stance toward techne. To explain, I return to an old theme.

Plato wrote dialogues. As a drama, that is, an imitation of characters both speaking and acting, a dialogue is infused with irremediable particularity. Socrates does not, for example, offer a straight theoretical refutation of rhetoric. Instead, he argues against Gorgias at a very specific time and place, and when doing so he assumes rhetoric is a techne. When shifting to Polus, a different strategy is required. Because the dialogue is written thus, the reader can never extract any single argument Socrates makes and then declare it "Platonic." The argument may well be tailored to meet the dialogical needs generated by the particular context in which it is spoken.

Socrates' positive evaluations of determinacy, clarity, intelligibility, and techne are inextricably situated within the contingencies of the dialogical context from which they emerge. From within such turmoil, the philosopher frequently makes techne look good and seems to offer it as the goal of his inquiry. But Plato never allows this goal to be completely actualized nor even to be pursued in isolation from the dialogue. Simply put, he never writes a treatise, or a "Techne." He never has his Socrates found a school or charge tuition. Even if Plato himself did both (although the latter is not clear), he wrote only dialogues.[17]

---

17. See Mueller 1992. See also Hyland 1968 for an excellent discussion of why Plato wrote dialogues.

This is yet vague. To explain, I return to those lines in the *Euthyphro* in which Socrates examines Euthyphro's definition of piety: "What the gods love is holy, and what they do not love is unholy" (7a). The problem with this definition is that often the gods disagree about what they love, and then become angry with one another as a result. Socrates asks Euthyphro to specify what it is that the gods disagree about and that then causes their anger: "My good man, disagreement about what creates hostility and anger? Look at it this way: if you and I disagree about number (*arithmos*), which [of two numbers] is larger, would the disagreement about this make us hostile and angry with one another, or would we settle it quickly by turning to calculation (*logismon*)?" (7b6–c1).

Socrates elaborates. If there is disagreement about what is greater or lesser, or heavier or lighter, the disputes end quickly by turning to "measurement" (*metrein:* 7c4) or "statics" (*histanai:* 7c7). By contrast, when disagreement is about "right and wrong, fine and shameful, and good and bad," that is, about moral values, there is real trouble, since for these no satisfactory solution seems forthcoming and hostility between disputants is therefore likely (7d1–5). As possible objects of inquiry, then, arithmos and morality seem fundamentally different.

But what exactly does "arithmos" mean? In ordinary Greek, the word means both "number" and "counting," and the former is never severed from the latter. As Nussbaum explains, "The most general sense of arithmos in ordinary Greek of the fifth century would be that of an ordered plurality or its members, a countable system or its countable parts."[18] In Klein's words, a number is "a definite number of definite things."[19] For this reason, neither zero nor one were generally considered to be arithmoi.

The *Euthyphro* passage shows Plato following ordinary usage. When Socrates offers the case of two people disagreeing *peri arithmou*, he must imagine them disagreeing about, for example, how many olive trees there are in a field. If you say "fifty" and I say "forty," we need not get angry, for we can unambiguously count the trees.

There is another sense in which the passage shows Plato to be traditional in his understanding of arithmos: he appreciates its unique knowability. As Nussbaum puts it, "[F]rom the earliest texts (and fifth-century texts are fully consistent with these) we see the use of arithmos to mean that which is counted and a close association between . . . numerability

18. Nussbaum 1979, 90.
19. Klein 1968, 46.

and knowability."[20] (Recall Prometheus's praise of arithmos as "wisdom above all other" and my discussion of this statement in Chapter 1.) What is noteworthy about the passage, of course, is the contrast drawn between the epistemic reliability of number and, presumably, the precariousness of morality.[21] Unfortunately, by itself the passage tells little about Plato's view of exactly how the two poles constituting this contrast—arithmos and morality—relate to one another. Should the former serve as a model for the latter? Presumably it should, although it is far from clear exactly what this means.

To elaborate, consider again a passage from the *Ion,* another early dialogue. In examining Ion's claim to have the rhapsode's techne (530b3, 530c8) and thereby to "expound" or "speak well" about Homer, Socrates asks whether he can speak equally well about other poets, such as Hesiod and Archilochus. Ion answers no. This puzzles Socrates, since Homer and Hesiod often address the same subject. How, then, can Ion expound only Homer's poetry and not Hesiod's? To illustrate the problem, Socrates offers the counterexample of arithmetic:

SOCRATES: So, my dear Ion, when many people are talking about number and one of them speaks best, I suppose there is someone who will be able to distinguish the man who speaks well?

ION: Yes, I'd say so.

SOCRATES: And will this same man be able to identify those who speak badly, or will it be someone else?

ION: The same man, I suppose.

SOCRATES: And this is the man who has the arithmetic techne, isn't it?
(531d12–e4)

To reiterate a point made earlier: If someone possesses the arithmetic techne (531e3), he can identify those who speak well, that is, correctly, and those who speak badly, that is, incorrectly, about number. Socrates

20. Nussbaum 1979, 91.

21. The *Euthyphro* passage thus shows Plato to be aware of the sort of distinction Aristotle later draws between ethics and mathematics. Because of the nature of its subject matter, the former cannot achieve as high a degree of precision (*to akribes*) as the latter. Ethics cannot be rendered completely apodictic, as can mathematics, because the human good is residually indeterminate. As a result, "It is characteristic of an educated man to seek after just that degree of precision that the nature of the subject matter admits. For it seems to be equally [inappropriate] to accept merely persuasive talk from a mathematician and to demand a demonstration from a rhetor" (*Nicomachean Ethics* 1094b25–27). (The subject matter of rhetoric overlaps that of ethics.)

assumes Ion's claim to the rhapsodic techne is analogous. As a result, Ion should be able to identify and discuss not only those who speak well within his field, like Homer, but also those, like Hesiod, who do not.

In this passage arithmos represents a field to be mastered by an expert who can authoritatively distinguish between right and wrong answers. Arithmetic, it seems, is paradigmatic of this feature of techne. (Socrates also cites medicine at 531e9.) This should recall the discussion in Chapter 2 concerning the close bond Plato conceives between mathematics and techne. At *Charmides* 166a3–7, for example, "calculation," which is about the odd and the even and their "relation to each other," is said to be paradigmatic of the basic subject/object structure of a techne. (Socrates also mentions statics at 166b1.) A similar move is made in the *Gorgias*. When demonstrating that rhetoric is far from unique in being "through logos," Socrates divides the technai into a productive and a "logical" branch (450b9). He relies on arithmetic, calculation, and geometry to illustrate the latter.

Socrates invokes arithmetic and geometry as paradigms in the following passage as well:

> Suppose someone asked me . . . "Socrates, what is the arithmetic techne?" I would say to him, as you just now did to me, that it is one of those which have their effect through logos. And suppose he went on to ask, "With what is its logos concerned?" I should say, With the odd and even numbers, whatever may chance to be the amount of each. And if he asked again, "What techne is it that you call calculation?" I should say that this is also one of those which achieve their whole effect by logos. And if he proceeded also to ask, "With what is it concerned?" I should say, in the manner of those who draft amendments in the Assembly, that in all respects calculation corresponds with arithmetic, for both are concerned with the same thing, the odd and the even; but that they differ to this extent, that calculation considers the numerical values of odd and even numbers not merely in themselves but in relation to each other. (451b7–c5)[22]

Once again, mathematics exemplifies two decisive and related features of the technai: (1) they have a basic subject/object structure in which the

---

22. My translation here largely follows that by Lamb (Cambridge, Mass.: Harvard University Press, Loeb Classical Library, 1974).

object, or subject matter, is different from the subject; (2) this object can be clearly delineated and thereby distinguished from other such objects. (Socrates also uses the example of astronomy at 451c5–10.) This entire line of thought is, I propose, encapsulated by a remark Socrates makes in the *Republic:* "The lowly business . . . of distinguishing the one, the two, and the three. I mean by this, succinctly, number [*arithmos*] and calculation. Or isn't it the case with them that every kind of [techne] and [episteme] is compelled to participate in them?" (522c5–9).

Socrates does not explain in what exact sense every techne must participate in arithmos. Is every techne some version of applied mathematics? Perhaps. But this statement could also be taken in a more general, almost metaphorical sense. On this reading, a techne must have a determinate subject matter, some *one* area of expertise. And arithmos is the paradigm case and indeed what makes possible determinacy. The key point is this: since techne, which Socrates so regularly invokes in his examinations, plays so large a role in the "early" dialogues, and since mathematics is crucial in articulating what a techne is, mathematics is correspondingly significant in the "early" dialogues.

One more point: because of the strong relationship between arithmos and techne, it is clear that for Plato a techne is a $techne_1$, whose hallmark has long been its affiliation with mathematics (see List 4, criterion 7, and List 6, criterion 8, in Chapter 1).

To summarize: Socrates calls upon the goodness of arithmos.[23] It is clear, stable, and epistemically reliable. We can count on it, and it represents a realm in which agreement is prior to hostility. It is (in some unspecified way) the basis of techne, which, as the most accessible example of authoritative knowledge, Socrates regularly puts to good use both to refute and exhort his listeners. This very positive evaluation of mathematics, and therefore of both determinacy and techne, is crucial in differentiating philosophy from rhetoric, for the latter, though it calls itself a techne, is generally neutral or negative concerning these "technical" qualities. (This remark is elaborated in the following section.)

And yet, there is an unmistakable tension in Plato's dialogues. Even while his Socrates relies on arithmos and techne and thereby claims their goodness, he regularly exposes their limitations, that is, their use-neutrality and lack of self-reflection. Furthermore, even when praising techne, he inevitably does so in the midst of a dialogical *kairos* injecting his speeches

23. See Roochnik 1994a.

with an irremediable measure of indeterminacy. Plato himself offers no theories, writes no "Techne." Instead, he places his Socrates into a carefully crafted dramatic context from within which he praises the contextless goodness of arithmos and techne. To amplify, I turn to Callicles.

Socrates v. Callicles

Nowhere does the goodness of mathematics emerge more powerfully than in Socrates' extended discussion with Callicles in the *Gorgias*. Callicles is the favored interlocutor of this dialogue because, Socrates says, he possesses three characteristics: knowledge, goodwill, and frankness (487a2–3). Callicles, in turn, even describes himself as a brother to Socrates (see the citation from Euripides' *Antiope* at 484e4–7). Like Socrates, he is a lover: he loves the son of Pyrilampes, Demos, as well as the Athenian people, or *dēmos* (481d) (i.e., political power). Socrates in turn loves Alcibiades and wisdom. Like the philosopher's, Callicles' desires are powerful, his intelligence is acute, and his firmness real. Like Socrates, he conceives of a sharp distinction between *nomos* and *phusis* and, as a consequence, between the many and the few. For these reasons, Socrates says to him, "Know well that if you agree with me concerning the things my soul opines, then these things themselves are true" (486e5–6).

In one critical way Callicles differs from Gorgias and Polus, the previous two interlocutors who were each rather easily handled by Socrates: *he does not claim a techne.* Unlike them he is not a professor of rhetoric, for he only practices what they teach. Because of their professional "shingle," Polus and Gorgias implicitly limit the scope of their expertise. Even if they brag about the breadth of their ability, the fact is they are professors of rhetoric, not of music or mathematics.[24] By contrast, Callicles suffers no such limitation, for he professes no techne. Indeed, he seems to hold it in contempt. This becomes clear in the following exchange he has with Socrates.

Callicles has asserted his principle of *pleonexia* (483c2): the "superior should take by force what belongs to the inferior, the better should rule the worse, and the more worthy have a greater share than the less worthy" (488b). Not surprisingly, Socrates insists the critical terms in this assertion—"more worthy," "better," "superior"—be clarified. Callicles obliges

24. This sort of delimitation becomes problematic with a Sophist such as Hippias. See de Romilly 1992, 114–16.

by reducing them to "more intelligent" (*phronimōterous:* 489e8). Socrates, however, remains unsatisfied and demands again that "intelligent" be clarified. To press Callicles, he invokes the techne analogy. When it comes to food and drink, doctors are more intelligent than laypersons, and so should have more. When it comes to clothes, the weaver is more intelligent, and so should have more; to shoes, the cobbler; to land, the farmer. The question Socrates tries to foist upon Callicles is, With respect to what particular field is your version of the intelligent man, that is, the one who should have more, more intelligent? (490b–e).

Callicles, however, is able to resist Socrates. Unlike Laches, whose definition of courage ("intelligent endurance") uses the same critical term as does Callicles, and who is then faced with a similar line of Socratic questioning (*Laches* 192d–193d), Callicles simply does not allow Socrates to wield the analogy against him. He complains, "By the Gods, you simply (*atechnōs*) do not stop speaking about shoemakers, fullers, cooks, and doctors, as if our discussion were about them" (491a).

Callicles is right: Socrates does talk continually about shoemakers, fullers, cooks, and doctors, about men who possess a techne. (And he indeed does so *atechnōs:* see Appendix 2.) In sharp contrast to Socrates' other interlocutors, he decries such talk as "nonsense" (490e4), for he refuses to accord to techne the kind of goodness implied by Socrates' frequent use of the analogy. For example, when Socrates likens him to an "engineer" (*mekanopoios*), Callicles objects. He despises "the techne of that man" and would refuse to allow his child to marry into the family of a *technitēs* (512c1–7). His scorn can of course be attributed to "the contempt generally felt by the Greeks for 'banausic' occupations."[25] Callicles' attitude toward techne, however, tokens a much deeper objection.

Callicles' ambition is grand, and so he is driven beyond the limitations implied by a techne. He is a *pleonektēs,* who continually demands to have more than his fair share and is willing to take advantage of others to get what he wants (483c). Unlike Gorgias and Polus he does not limit himself even to the "daimonic" subject of rhetoric. He wants instead to exploit rhetoric, use it for his own advantage. Callicles rejects limits, wants nothing bounded, and contemptuously describes Socrates' mode of argumentation as "small" and "narrow" (497c1). In one sense he is again quite right: Socrates repeatedly invokes the techne analogy, and a techne is narrow

25. Dodds 1966, 349.

insofar as its subject matter is limited (compare Hippias's similar remark at *Hippias Minor* 369b).

Socrates criticizes Callicles for his rejection of limits and his inability to restrain himself; he accuses him of lacking *sōphrosunē*. Callicles agrees. For him, a *sōphrōn* man is a "simpleton" (491e2); "the man living correctly should allow his desires to be as great as possible and not restrain them" (491e8–492a3). In short, Callicles' desires are those of a potential tyrant. His love of political power, his brutal honesty about the weakness of the many, and his disregard for convention make him a genuinely dangerous character, one whom Socrates feels obligated to combat in public. But how is a man such as this to be combated?

Without rehearsing all the many details, I simply assert that Socrates attempts to reform Callicles by offering him a vision of an orderly and knowable whole. In other words, he follows the advice Aristotle will later give: the only effective cure for tyrannical desires is philosophy (see *Politics* 1267a). The man who strives always for more than his fair share and is willing to trample those beneath him to meet his indefinitely expanding desires can only be reformed by "sublimation," by having his sights turned away from the political realm to the "largest" or highest of all possible objects, the whole itself. Only the love of wisdom can adequately replace the tyrant's desire for unlimited power, for only it can satisfy at a higher level.

Whether Aristotle's advice is sound or not, Socrates seems to be following some version of it when he says:

> The wise men tell us, Callicles, that heaven and earth and the gods and men are held together in community and friendship, orderliness, moderation and justice; and, my friend, for these reasons they call the whole a cosmos rather than a chaos or a realm of unrestraint. You, it seems to me, do not pay attention to these things, even though you are wise, but the fact that geometrical equality has great power among both the gods and men has eluded you. You hold that pleonexia is what one ought to practice, for you disregard geometry. (507e6–508a8)[26]

Socrates urges Callicles to replace his chaotic striving for political power with a vision of an orderly cosmos, a world "geometric" and intelligible.

---

26. Compare Aristotle on geometric proportion, *Nicomachean Ethics* 1331b12–1332b17 and *Politics* 1301b30–39.

What is striking about this passage is the causal relationship (note the *gar* at 508a8) posited between Callicles' neglect of geometry and his moral failing, that is, his advocacy of pleonexia. Geometry, it seems, can be therapeutic, instrumental in the shaping of character and perhaps even in the reform of a potential tyrant. As Irwin rightly notes, Socrates' "mere reference to geometrical equality leaves many unanswered questions," for he does not explain how geometry can turn its students around, from pleonexia to *sōphrosunē*.[27] A digression might help. I turn briefly to the *Republic*.

After having presented the image of the cave, Socrates asks Glaucon: "Do you want us now to consider in what way such men [philosophers] will come into being and how one will lead them up to the light, just as some men are said to have gone from Hades up to the gods? . . . Then, as it seems, this wouldn't be the twirling of a shell but the turning (*periagōgē*) of a soul around from a day that is like night to the true day; it is that ascent to what *is* which we shall truly affirm to be philosophy" (521c).[28]

Socrates next asks what study facilitates this turning of the soul away from becoming and toward being. The answer: calculation and counting (*arithmein*: 522e2).[29] But how does counting turn the soul around? Socrates explains by discussing sensation. Some sensations appear to be self-contradictory. When looking at three fingers on a single hand, the middle seems both larger and smaller. Reflection clarifies this appearance by disclosing that in fact the middle is larger than the smallest finger, and smaller than the largest. In this case, the intellect has been "summoned" in order to stabilize a seeming contradiction (523b–524e).

The most obvious way the intellect is summoned to do its work is by measuring and counting. By first separating the three fingers and conceiving of them as discrete individuals and then measuring them to determine they are, respectively, two, three, and four inches long, the potentially discordant appearance of the middle finger as both larger and smaller will, by being explained, be dissolved.

In this very ordinary act of counting, the soul is invited to turn around. *Arithmein* is always a counting of items, of units. If I count three fingers

27. Irwin 1979, 226.
28. I follow the translation of Bloom (New York: Basic, 1968).
29. I move from geometry in the *Gorgias* to arithmetic in the *Republic* without commenting on the difference between the two, because my basic point holds for both: as mathematical technai, both have determinate subject matters that can be apprehended methodically and unequivocally. In general, Plato seems more interested in geometry, perhaps because both its methodology and results were more highly developed and prominent during his lifetime.

on my hand, each finger functions as just such a unit. But the number "three" can also be used to count three toes on my foot. The same number is invoked to count different sensible items: a toe is not a finger; indeed, even each of the three fingers is different from the other two. In the act of counting, however, the number, the count, treats each finger as an equal unit. As Klein puts it, "[W]henever we are engaged in counting, we substitute—as a matter of course, even if we are not aware of what we are doing—for the varied and always 'unequal' visible things to be counted 'pure' invisible units which in no way differ from each other."[30]

In other words, even in the vulgar count of ordinary people (see *Philebus* 56d5), a purely intelligible, formal, and stable entity is invoked: the number. Simply to count, then, is informative: it reminds us that intelligible stability can and does intervene in human experience, that there is something, even amidst the "barbaric bog" (533d2) of human life, on which we can count. In this sense, arithmos turns the soul around, away from becoming and toward being. It is an invitation to shift one's sights, away from the sensible and toward the intelligible. Counting, the most ordinary of intellectual acts, "leads the soul powerfully upward" (525d6); it inspires us to reconsider the very nature of our experience by supplying us with both the material to think about and some ideal at which to aim.[31]

In short, arithmos is good. To say this, however, is to locate it within a practical, human context and to invoke a nonarithmetical standard. Arithmos is good because it turns souls around, leads them to *sōphrosunē*, makes them *care* about something beyond the immediate testimony of the senses. By offering an inkling of formal perfection, it promises a genuine alternative to the tyrannical desires of a *pleonektēs* such as Callicles. Arithmos is remedial, therapeutic, and good.

So too is techne. Recall *Republic* 522c5–9: "The lowly business . . . of distinguishing the one, the two, and the three. I mean by this, succinctly, number [*arithmos*] and calculation. Or isn't it the case with them that every kind of [techne] and [episteme] is compelled to participate in them?" Because of their intimate relationship, many of the same characteristics I have just attributed to arithmos will apply to techne as well.

Techne is the critical notion Socrates uses in so many of his dialogues. With it he refutes and exhorts. To succeed, he requires agreement that

30. Klein 1975, 117.
31. As Whitehead (1971, 674) puts it, "Our existence is invigorated by conceptual ideals, transforming vague perceptions. . . . Here we find the essential clue which relates mathematics to the study of the good."

techne itself is good, an assumption operative once techne is invoked as a familiar and welcome model of knowledge (albeit one that is limited because ignorant of its own good use; its goodness is, in other words, conditional). Without securing agreement on this, he could not have refuted Gorgias. Nor could he have demonstrated the incompleteness of Critias's and Laches' otherwise promising definitions of courage and sōphrosunē ("intelligent endurance" and "self-knowledge"). He could not have persuaded Lysimachus to abandon the principle of majority rule when seeking answers to moral questions, or Thrasymachus that justice is not the advantage of the stronger.

All of these arguments hinge on granting the goodness of techne. Should the interlocutor agree to this, he is committed to the notion that knowledge is good and not equivalent, either in kind or value, to opinion. It further implies that he thinks determinacy, clarity, precision, and arithmetic stability, the hallmarks of techne, are desirable. Should the interlocutor agree to these assertions, he will be refuted by Socrates, for his own views cannot measure up to these standards. Once refuted, he becomes open to the exhortation to seek moral knowledge, that is, to become philosophical.

But what happens if the interlocutor does not acknowledge the goodness of techne? This is precisely what occurs in "Socrates v. Callicles." *Because he claimed a techne, Gorgias was refuted.* Callicles, however, is not a professional teacher and so does not hesitate to reject the goodness of techne (as he does of geometry). *This renders him immune to Socratic attack,* for he no longer shares a basic assumption with the philosopher. Dialogue between them becomes impossible. Socrates repeatedly tries to convince Callicles of the goodness of techne, dangling this notion before him like a lure. But Callicles resists.

For Socrates self-rule is superior to ruling others, and sōphrosunē superior to pleonexia (491d). Callicles, however, denigrates those who are sōphrōn as simpletons and, in obedience to the principle of mē kolazein (492a1), chooses not to restrain or control his desires. Socrates uses various strategies to dislodge him from this position. First, he tells the myth of the jars (493a–494a), but this makes no impression on Callicles. Socrates tries to shame him, by comparing Callicles to the *charadrios*, the urinating bird, and then the catamite (494b–e). This too fails, for Callicles, unlike Gorgias and Polus, seems impervious to shame. Finally, Socrates formulates his opponent's position as a form of hedonism and asks Callicles whether the pleasant and the good are the same. Callicles assents (495a), and the stage is set for Socrates to go to work.

His strategy is to shatter the strict identity between the pleasant and the good. First, he states that the good and the bad are opposites and therefore cannot occur simultaneously; by contrast, pleasure and pain can occur simultaneously; therefore, pleasure is not the good, and pain not the bad (495a–497d). Second, he reminds Callicles that fools and cowards can feel pleasure as much as those who are intelligent or brave; cowards and fools are bad; therefore, the presence of pleasure cannot be a mark of those who are good (497d–499b).

At this point Callicles makes an admission crucial in refuting any form of hedonism: he acknowledges a distinction between good and bad pleasures (499b). Not surprisingly, Socrates presses for specification. A good pleasure, he offers, is beneficial. In turn, a beneficial pleasure is "useful" (*chrēstas*) and does some good. Socrates then asks: "Is it in the power of every man to select what sort of pleasures are good and what sort are bad? Or is a man who is *technikos* required to do this in each case?" (500a4–6).

Callicles agrees: the technical man is needed to distinguish good and bad pleasures. At this point, Socrates recalls the scheme he used against Polus. The various forms of flattery are concerned only with pleasure, not the good; they are ignorant of the *aitia* and altogether "irrational" (*alogos*). In a striking phrase, Socrates describes flattery as "having failed to differentiate by number" (*diarithmēsamenē*: 501a7). In other words, flatterers do not count, because they cannot divide their subject matter, pleasure, into distinct, stable units comparable to one another. As a result, they are "utterly nontechnical" (*komidē atechnōs*: 501a4). By contrast, the true technai can count the difference between and hence "know what is good and what is bad" (500b3).

Socrates asks whether Callicles will accept such a distinction: "Now consider first whether you think this has been sufficiently explained, and that of those sorts of pursuits that concern the psyche, some are technical (*technikai*) and have forethought for what is best for the psyche, while others denigrate such activity and consider only the pleasure of the psyche" (501b).

Callicles agrees, but *only*, he says, in order to gratify, that is, give pleasure to, Gorgias (501c8). This is a good move on his part, for with it he remains faithful to his own hedonistic principles and still allows the conversation to continue (which Gorgias had earlier urged him to do: see 497b). Presumably, Callicles on his own would have lapsed into the indeterminacy of silence and refused to talk with Socrates. But for whatever halfhearted reason, he does agree to distinguish flattery and techne and

acknowledges the latter as superior to the former. This admission is required for Socrates to proceed, for with it he can denounce rhetoric as a
pleasure-seeking, irrational form of flattery that does no more than pander
to its audience.

Callicles dissents. Some rhetors, he thinks, have actually made the city
better (503a). Socrates disagrees: he knows of no rhetor who actually has
met this description. Callicles assures Socrates that if he were to seek properly, he would find one (503d3). Though he agrees to try, Socrates first
explains whom he is looking for:

> The good man, the one who aims for what is best when he says
> what he says, will not say anything at random; instead, he will keep
> his eye on something. Just as each of all the other craftsmen (*dēmi-
> ourgoi*), with an eye to their own function (*ergon*), applies the mea-
> sures he applies, not at random but selecting them in order to get
> the thing he is making to acquire a particular form (*eidos*). For
> example, if you consider the painters, or the house-builders, or the
> ship-builders or all the rest of the craftsmen, you will see that each
> of them arranges into some order whatever it is that he arranges,
> and that he forces each element to be appropriate (*prepon*) and
> fitting with one another, until he has put together everything into a
> whole work that has been ordered (*tetagmenon*) and composed.
> (503e)[32]

The "craftsman" aims to inform the material upon which he works, and
everything he does is guided by what he "keeps his eye on," namely, the
model or preconception he plans to actualize. He fits together his materials, forces them (*prosanangkazei*) to play their appropriate roles in the
orderly whole that is the final work. This work, whether a painting or a
house or a ship, is the result of the craftsman's discipline and ability to
subordinate the various elements with which he works to the determinate
form dictating where and how they fit. As a consequence, order and regularity (*taxis* and *kosmos*) become the standards of a good piece of work.

The same principle applies, says Socrates, to our bodies, the ministering
technai of which are medicine and gymnastics. If there is order and regularity in a body, it is excellent and strong. So too for the psyche: if it has
order, it attains the virtues of justice and *sōphrosunē* (504d). To these,

---

32. The text is corrupt. I follow Dodds 1966 and borrow his translation. Note well *prepon*
and *tetagmenon*, two terms prominent in Isocrates' *Against the Sophists*.

therefore, the "technical and good rhetor" (*technikos te kai agathos*: 504d6) must look in working with his material, the citizens of the polis whom he must force into an orderly whole. Given the strictures of the analogy, the good rhetor must therefore discipline and correct the desires of himself and his citizens. Callicles' principle of *mē kolazein* has thus been fundamentally challenged (505c).

Socrates uses the analogy (as housebuilding is to wood, so technical rhetoric is to the citizens of the polis) both to refute and to exhort Callicles. He attempts to steer him away from his tyrannical desires by showing him that *if* he accepts techne as an appropriate model, he must keep his eye on and be willing to subordinate his desires to the "form" of justice and *sōphrosunē*. Is he, then, postulating a moral techne? Probably not, because the assumptions undergirding the analogy (if it is taken literally) are untenable, a fact that, I suggest, Plato understands full well.

First, the analogy conceives of citizens as *hulē*, inert matter waiting only to be "informed" by the activity of the technical rhetor, who keeps his eye on the determinate forms of justice and *sōphrosunē* and can then actualize them in his population. At the least, this is problematic: surely becoming good is a moral change requiring the citizen himself to be active and responsible, rather than passive and inert. Hall makes this point well: "The moral paradox in the *Gorgias* stems from the assumption that moral individuals are self-determined. . . . Yet these moral beings are 'created' by the art of politics and the practisers of that art much as any object is created by its appropriate techne." He goes on: "[I]t is paradoxical that an individual who contributes nothing to the attainment of his morality and who is completely 'shaped' by an external agent is . . . moral."[33]

Hall is right when about the *Gorgias* he concludes "it shows implicitly the impossibility of patterning a theory of the moral education of the individual along the lines of a techne."[34] In other words, the notion of a moral techne is so intrinsically problematic that, despite his offer to Callicles of a "moral technician," Socrates probably does not consider it to be a realistic possibility. Hall's explanation why Plato has Socrates use what is manifestly an inappropriate paradigm is less satisfying. For him, the *Gorgias* is a transitional dialogue in which the maturing Plato criticizes his earlier doctrines in which he *did* conceive of moral knowledge as strictly analo-

33. Hall 1971, 203, 204.
34. Hall 1971, 216. Jacob Howland, when reading this book in manuscript, noted that in the Myth of Er (*Republic* 619b–c) the citizen who is virtuous by habit, that is, is passive, is eager to become a tyrant.

gous to a techne (i.e., *did not* understand the problematic consequences of the analogy).

There is, however, for at least two reasons, no need to postulate an elaborate chronological thesis to explain Socrates' use of the analogy. First, as "early" as the *Charmides*, Plato clearly understands why the psyche is not an appropriate subject matter of a typical techne. Far from being passive, it has the power of self-reflection. As a result, knowledge of it must be "strange," that is, nontechnical. Second, even if the analogy implies a paradox, as Hall rightly argues, Socrates' use of it can be explained internally, that is, on dialogical grounds, without recourse to a speculative account of Plato's developing intelligence. On my reading, Socrates offers the analogy to Callicles for much the same reason he used it to exhort Lysimachus. Techne is *the* obvious exemplar of valuable knowledge. Socrates wants to persuade Callicles of its goodness and that he should seek something like a techne when it comes to morality. He wants to curb Callicles' prodigious appetites and offers him a vision of stability and intelligibility to tempt him. His doing so need not imply that moral knowledge is strictly analogous to a techne, only that it is knowledge and that it is good (albeit conditionally). Callicles has yet to be persuaded of either proposition, and Socrates is in the midst of a desperate attempt to change his mind.

Finally, however, what is most striking about Socrates' attempt is its *failure*. It is precisely at the moment when Socrates calls upon the techne analogy to exhort him that Callicles simply drops out of the discussion. As he reminds Socrates, he has only been conversing "for the sake of Gorgias" (505c6). He describes Socrates as overbearing (*biaios:* 505d4). He is right. Socrates tries to force rhetoric into a preestablished mold, one assuming techne (specifically, a techne$_1$) is a good and useful model with which to conceive political life. Callicles lapses into the indeterminacy of silence, and so Socrates is forced, from 505e to 509c, to speak virtually alone.

In its own way, Callicles' silence, his refusal to play Socrates' game, makes good sense: it tokens his awareness that the philosopher's strategy requires agreement on two assumptions: (1) techne and flattery are different, and (2) the former is better than the latter. Despite the occasional lip service Callicles pays to both statements, he in fact rejects them. He does so because, it seems, he realizes that accepting them would lead to refutation. To reiterate: acknowledgment of the goodness of techne is required if the interlocutor is to be led to the Socratic conclusion that moral knowledge is desirable. Callicles is not refutable. He is a man of indeterminacy from start to finish. His powerful desires expand indefinitely, and he wishes neither to control them nor to claim a techne for himself.

Socrates is somewhere in between the indeterminacy of Callicles and the determinacy of the technai he praises and exploits in his analogical arguments. He does not have a techne, but he does claim to be one of few Athenians to "attempt the political techne" (521d). He, like the craftsman, keeps his eye on something (*apoblepōn pros ti*); he looks toward a vision of order and regularity. This is not to say, however, he is, or even desires himself to become, a *technitēs*. There are good reasons, in fact, to think this an impossible task. As mentioned, the human psyche is not a kind of *hulē*, a passive object to be treated as a recipient of technical action. Furthermore, it is not obvious that there is an *eidos* of the human psyche apprehensible with technical precision.[35] Indeed, the very presence of Callicles challenges these contentions. He is erotic, spirited, ever in motion toward conquest. He is alive, and his desires are unleashed. He cannot be refuted by Socrates, and thereby shows how, in some sense at least, the psyche is indeterminate.

From 506c to 519d Socrates, who earlier had prohibited Gorgias from giving a long speech (449b), gives one himself (interrupted only a few times by Callicles). In it he reiterates several of the themes just discussed: he praises *sōphrosunē* and justice, the practice of which leads to *eudaimonia* (507a). He describes the orderliness of the cosmos and the therapeutic power of geometric equality (508a). He explains why doing wrong is worse than suffering it (508c). But, he asks, how does a man avoid doing wrong? He must have some *dunamis* (509d). At the mention of this word ("power!"), Callicles' interest is piqued, and he is again drawn back into the conversation.

But Socrates is there to frustrate him; he says, "We should provide ourselves with some power and techne in order not to do wrong" (510a3–4; see also 409e1). The reader feels Callicles' palpable dismay as "techne" invades the conversation yet again. Nonetheless, Socrates, who seems never to give up on his difficult friend, presses forward: "What is the techne of preventing us from suffering wrong?" (510a6–7). Is it that of a tyrant or ruler? On this note, Callicles is happy to agree. To avoid suffering wrong, he thinks, one need only imitate and flatter the tyrant. But to do this is to do wrong, which is what the tyrant does. How, then, can one

---

35. This is the major theme of Griswold 1986b.

avoid doing wrong? Will not the tyrant simply put to death the man who contravenes him by doing right? Probably, says Callicles. But, asks Socrates, does Callicles imply that the goal of a decent man is to live as long as possible and to practice only those technai, including rhetoric, which save him from risk? Yes, says Callicles.[36] But if this is the case, then rhetoric is on a par with swimming and piloting, two mundane technai useful in saving lives.

Socrates is again trying to shame Callicles, first by saying he values mere survival and then by showing him that this puts him on the same level as the technai he despises (512c). He urges Callicles to desire what is good and, yet again, returns to his basic theme: a genuine techne, unlike a form of flattery, aims for the good and not merely the pleasant (513d–e). The purpose of the political/moral techne, then, would be the production of decent citizens. But who has such a techne? If the city were interviewing candidates concerning the building of a wall or arsenal or temple, it would first ask if they understood the techne (514b). Second, it would ask if each candidate could show any previous works to substantiate his claim to being qualified. Could he point to a past *ergon* or teacher with whom he apprenticed (514b–c)?

With this example Socrates returns to a familiar theme: the certifiability of a *technitēs*. If the techne analogy holds, then Callicles, who wants political power, must offer analogous documentation to demonstrate he is qualified to rule the city. He should be able to point to other men he has made better (515a–b). Callicles is peeved: "You love to pick fights, Socrates" (515b3). Socrates disagrees. Since the techne analogy is in effect, he only wants Callicles to document his ability to rule. This will not be easy to do. After all, Pericles, Cimon, Miltiades, and Themistocles would each have failed this test (515c–516e). Socrates is forced once more to conclude pessimistically: "Our previous logoi were true, it seems, in that we know no good man who has practiced the political things in this city" (517a).

As we have seen again and again, this whole line of argument hinges on the single assumption of there being a political techne, an assumption to which Callicles yielded insincerely and which, as argued above, is intrinsically problematic. Still, it is the key to the entire dialogue. As Socrates puts it at 517c: "In these logoi you and I are doing something ridiculous. For during the whole time that we have been conversing, we have ever

---

36. Note that at 511c rhetoric is again treated as a techne.

been circling around the same point (*eis to auto*) and misunderstanding what each other was saying" (517c5–7).[37]

The "same point," around which the conversation *revolves,* is the assumption that techne is not flattery, that it is good and an appropriate notion through which to consider political/ethical life. Without it, Socrates cannot refute Callicles. And indeed, finally he cannot, for Callicles simply will not bite at the lure Socrates dangles before him: the vision of an orderly whole in which techne is good. As if to signal the failure of the techne analogy, Socrates ends his dialogue with a myth, the story of judgment in the afterworld. But this becomes just another failed attempt to reform Callicles, to encourage him to turn around.

Philosophy v. Rhetoric: The *Protagoras*

Socrates knows how to refute the (professional/technical) rhetoricians, at least those who choose to argue with him, and to exhort those who will listen to him, two tasks he typically performs by means of the techne analogy. He understands the limits of his ability to persuade a Callicles, a man not sharing his conviction in the goodness of arithmos. He requires personal interaction and human connection in order to teach, and what he knows is communicated in the very dialogical interactions he himself engineers. The Socratic endeavor is by nature precarious, since the dialogues themselves frequently end in aporia or, as in the case of the *Gorgias,* with failure. Is Socrates, then, a rhetorician?

He is not, precisely because he evaluates arithmos, as well as the concept of techne it makes possible, positively and lets it shed light on his quest for moral knowledge. At the same time, however, he denies having a techne, hangs no shingle, and so earns no money. This intricate balance of almost opposites, this dialectical interplay between techne and *kairos* lying at the heart of the dialogues, is what makes Socrates' knowledge so alluring and yet so maddening.

I turn next to the *Protagoras* and many of these same themes. Once again, Socrates will use the techne analogy for the twin purposes of exhortation and critique. Once again, his commitment to the goodness of mathe-

37. For a similar confession of being "ridiculous," compare *Euthydemus* 291b. Another similarity is the circular nature of the argument in both dialogues.

matics will emerge as a salient feature to distinguish him from his sophistic competitor. Protagoras will prove to be a familiar figure to us, for his conception of sophistry will closely resemble that held by Isocrates. (By "Protagoras" I refer *only* to the character appearing in Plato's dialogue.) This will become most striking when Socrates asks him, What is the nature of your techne? The Sophist's answer will be ambiguous but, much like Isocrates', deliberately and artfully so.[38] Protagoras's response expresses a conception of rhetoric that, even while (perhaps just because) it answers "yes and no" to the techne question, is coherent and able to resist Socratic penetration. Again, watching Socrates confront this formidable opponent will clarify what differentiates philosophy from rhetoric and what constitutes the knowledge he himself possesses.

Does Protagoras Claim a Techne?

Young Hippocrates awakens Socrates before dawn.[39] He is thoroughly agitated by the exciting news he has come to announce: Protagoras has come to town! He desperately wants Socrates, with whom he is obviously intimate, to help him meet the famous Sophist. Socrates agrees, but not before he reports that he has known, for two days already, of Protagoras's arrival. Until Hippocrates asked him to, however, he showed no interest in visiting the Sophist (310b8–9). Presumably he reverses himself in order to accompany Hippocrates because of his close and seemingly paternal relationship with this boy. Hippocrates is wild with enthusiasm and therefore susceptible to the lures of the high-priced and famous teacher. Simply put, Socrates wants to protect him from Protagoras.

This, the prologue of the dialogue, sets the stage for all that follows. Even if couched in the most polite of terms, the *Protagoras* is adversarial in nature. It is an *agōn* between the philosopher and the Sophist for the soul of Hippocrates.

The initial step in inoculating the boy against Protagoras's wiles is to urge him to consider carefully what the Sophist actually teaches. To do this, Socrates says, "Tell me, Hippocrates, as you now endeavor to visit Protagoras and to pay him money as a fee for the services he will render to you, whom do you expect to visit, and who do you expect to become?" (311b2–5).

38. Because of the chronological proximity of the *Protagoras* and *Against the Sophists*, I am not sure which influenced which.
39. I discuss the *Protagoras* in Roochnik 1990, 51–63.

To clarify his question—which is strikingly similar to the one he instructed Chaerephon to ask Polus (*Gorgias* 447d1)—Socrates explains: If you were to visit Hippocrates the doctor, you would do so because he is what? A doctor. If you were to approach Polycleitus or Pheidias, whom would you be approaching? A sculptor. When studying with Protagoras, then, with whom are you studying? In other words, as Hippocrates is to medicine and Pheidias is to sculpture, so Protagoras is to X. What is X? Hippocrates is forced to answer—and (at the very moment the sun rises) he blushes as he does so—"sophistry" (311c–e).

But who is the Sophist? Hippocrates answers, "The one knowledgeable (*epistēmona*) about wise things" (312c6). Socrates criticizes (again in terms reminiscent of the *Gorgias*) by repeating the analogy: the painter also knows wise things, those used in the production of likenesses (312d2–3). Hippocrates' answer is unacceptable because, given the strictures of the analogy, it is insufficiently determinate. If the analogy between the painter and Sophist holds, then as the painter is to the production of likenesses, so the Sophist is to the production of a unique and identifiable X.

Hippocrates dutifully supplies a substitute for X: the Sophist produces clever speakers (312d6–7). His statement of course reflects the prominent role of the Sophist as teacher of rhetoric. Invoking the techne analogy, Socrates again objects: the master of the kithara can also make a student clever at speaking, speaking about the kithara. The Sophist can make the student clever at speaking about what? The X remains indeterminate (312d9–e5).

Hippocrates confesses to not knowing. By doing so, however, he reveals how successful Socrates' use of the analogy actually has been. The boy realizes his ignorance: he knows he does not know what the Sophist teaches. Unlike the other technai, the subject matter of sophistry is far from obvious. Inoculated by the analogy, that is, aware sophistry is not a typical techne, and therefore ready to demand a clear answer to the question, What exactly do you know? Hippocrates is prepared to confront Protagoras.

Immediately upon being introduced to Hippocrates, Protagoras launches into an encomium of the ancient lineage of his own profession: "I say that the sophistic techne is old" (316d3–4). Note that here Protagoras does *not* quite say he has a techne; he only describes the sophistic techne as old. Since Protagoras is widely known as a Sophist, a title he does not disavow, he may well seem here to be laying claim to the techne. Again, however, he does not make this unambiguous.

Protagoras next describes his ancient predecessors. They were dissemblers because they feared the opprobrium associated with sophistry. Among these older Sophists he includes Homer, Hesiod, Simonides, the prophets, the disciples of Orpheus and Mousaios, great trainers, athletes, and musicians (316d–e). One is tempted to respond by asking, Who isn't a Sophist? Recall that Hippocrates is no doubt listening eagerly to this exchange. By it he should be reminded of his predawn conversation, in which he learned how little he really knows about Protagoras. If all these famous men of the past were Sophists, then identifying sophistry is, at the least, problematic.

A pattern in Protagoras's self-description begins to emerge. By mentioning the ancient lineage of "the sophistic techne," Protagoras *seems* to claim a techne. However, by listing his motley crew of predecessors, he draws attention to the problematic status of sophistry itself. In short, he describes himself in a potentially contradictory manner: his sophistry is, and is not, a techne.

Such ambiguity should sound familiar, for in *Against the Sophists* Isocrates describes himself and his subject in analogously ambiguous terms. To understand, consider the possible motivations for Protagoras's and Isocrates' ambiguity on the techne question. The first is prudential (or rhetorical). As Cahn has argued, it is to Isocrates' advantage to distance himself from the *artium scriptores* by offering a unique product in a highly competitive market. In other words, by demonstrating the "impossibility of writing a handbook of rhetoric" (i.e., of showing rhetoric is not a techne$_1$), and by offering in its stead a "personalized educational program," Isocrates can "differentiate his school from the teaching of rhetoric that has come under suspicion."[40]

In addition to this marketing strategy, Isocrates also makes a substantial point when he hedges on the techne question: political logos is by nature dependent on the *kairos*, the contingent moment, to which the good orator must be able to respond appropriately, and there are no hard and fast rules on how to do this. Given this view of the nature of logos, indeed of political life itself, Isocrates' vacillation on the techne question makes good sense, that is, it adequately reflects the substantial nature of his subject matter. No, rhetoric is not a techne; its subject matter, the fluid changes of human life, does not allow it to be; but yes, of course rhetoric can be taught, albeit informally and precariously. Isocrates' genius is his ability to turn this vacillation into a coherent and attractive prospect.

40. Cahn 1989, 128, 132, 133.

Protagoras's motivation, at least at the outset, seems prudential. An *agōn* with Socrates is brewing, and techne is an effective weapon in Socrates' arsenal. Perhaps Protagoras, like Callicles, foresees the troublesome implications of making an explicit claim to a techne. If so, his hedge on the techne question may be designed to ward off Socratic refutation. But there will also be a substantial side to Protagoras's vacillation. Because of the nature of his subject matter, because of his conception of human political reality, he understands the inappropriateness of a strong techne claim. However, even if he does not profess a $techne_1$, he does hang a shingle and charges a famously hefty tuition fee. He must thus navigate the same Scylla and Charybdis as Isocrates: he must somehow locate himself between the strong but unsupportable claim to a $techne_1$ and the abandonment of his professional status.

Socrates, fearing Protagoras will launch into an extended oratorical display, interrupts by asking him what (*ti*), specifically, Hippocrates will gain from associating with him (318a3–4). The Sophist answers: Hippocrates will become better (318a6–9). Of course, such a response suffers from the same defect as did Hippocrates' earlier answer to Socrates' questions: it is insufficiently determinate and does not, therefore, adequately identify sophistry. If the boy were to associate with Zeuxippus, Socrates argues, he would get better with respect to (*pros*) painting. If he were to associate with Orthagoras, he would get better with respect to (*eis*) fluting. If he now associates with Protagoras, he will get better with respect to what? (318b5–d4).

As he has done so often with others, Socrates demands Protagoras formulate his profession of knowledge in terms dictated by the analogy (see also 348e). Like Callicles, however, Protagoras resists this strategy by making a disclaimer. Unlike the other Sophists, particularly Hippias, *he does not teach the technai*. These he illustrates with the telling examples of calculation, astronomy, geometry, and music (318e1–4). Instead of teaching such (mathematical) subjects, Protagoras satisfies his customers, instructs his students, by teaching them *only* what they came to him to learn:[41] "And this subject (*mathēma*) is good counsel concerning domestic affairs, how one can best (*arista*) manage one's household, and concerning political affairs, how one can be most capable/powerful (*dunatōtatos*) with respect to both acting and speaking in political affairs" (318e5–319a2).

---

41. For Isocrates on mathematics, see *Antidosis* 261–69. Note the lovely hedge: yes, mathematics is useful for practical life; but then again, it is not (263). See also *Panathenaicus* 26–29. Also, as Alex Mourelatos pointed out to me, the plural "technai" may refer to a more general sense of knowledge than the singular.

In this "advertisement" *mathēma*, "subject," replaces "techne." With this broader word, Protagoras distinguishes himself from Hippias by avoiding an explicit profession to teach a techne. Note the parallel structure of the sentence. There are two prepositional phrases beginning with *peri:* "concerning domestic affairs," "concerning political affairs." Each is followed by *hopōs*, which introduces a verb in the optative ("how one can . . . ," "how one can . . ."). But the first clause uses *arista*, related to "arete," while the second uses *dunatōtatos*, a more ambiguous word. (Indeed, it is difficult even to translate it. I offer "capable/powerful" for reasons to be explained shortly.) Protagoras teaches something about excellence concerning domestic affairs, but only how to become capable/powerful when it comes to political affairs. Domestic affairs are not spoken of in the remainder of the dialogue. So the question arises, does Protagoras only teach about *dunamis?*

In response to this advertisement, Socrates says, "You seem to me to mean the political techne and to promise to make men good citizens" (319a3–5). Protagoras enthusiastically agrees with Socrates' reformulation.

A typical Socratic move: it is he, not Protagoras, who formulates the Sophist's advertisement as a techne. In keeping with its most obvious connotation, Socrates interprets "techne" as productive, the product in this case being good citizens. Finally, note how it is not entirely clear with what part of the reformulation Protagoras agrees. Does he promise to make men good citizens *and* claim to possess the political techne? Or does he only agree to the first and not the second? If he agrees to the second, why does he not simply claim a techne instead of dancing around this question as he has consistently done to this point in the dialogue?

To summarize: Two critical ambiguities concerning Protagorean sophistry have surfaced. First, does he teach a techne or not? He seems to profess the sophistic techne at 316d3–4 (although he does not quite say so) and agrees that he teaches the political techne (although he may only agree that he makes men good citizens). But he also disavows teaching the technai (in particular, the mathematical technai). Second, does he teach a value-laden subject or not? He substitutes *dunatōtatos* for *arista* in his advertisement and thus seems to disavow teaching arete. But he also claims to make men good citizens.

Does Protagoras contradict himself? Not simply. Instead, because "techne" is a flexible term with at least two meanings, Protagoras can consistently deny teaching one sense of "techne," while he affirms another.

Specifically, he will deny teaching techne as defined by Socrates, namely, as rigorous knowledge of a determinate subject matter (which, as is now clear, is Socrates' basic understanding of the term). The knowledge he hopes to sell is not analogous to the mathematical disciplines or the specifically productive crafts. In short, *it is not a techne₁*. The Sophist must, however, profess to teach something; otherwise he would go out of business. Since "techne" is the paradigmatic form of teachable knowledge, Protagoras must, in some sense, lay claim to one.

After eliciting from Protagoras a claim to the political techne, Socrates attacks again by describing "this" as not teachable (319a10). Socrates uses two empirical arguments to support his contention. First, he recalls the behavior of the Athenians in their Assembly. When the issue is a teachable one, they consult an expert. If, for example, a ship is to be built, they consult the shipbuilder for advice and disregard the opinions of ordinary citizens. A layman, no matter how fine or rich or nobly born, is not an expert; his advice is therefore worthless, and so he is laughed down if he persists in telling the Assembly how to build a ship. In general, the Athenians behave this way when they believe the question at issue is "technical" (*en technē*: 319c8). By contrast, when the debate concerns matters of public policy, the opinions of all citizens are welcome. If, for example, the question is, *Should* the city build a ship? the Athenians assume there are no experts, and all are invited to speak (319b–c).

In sum, Athenian behavior suggests the *disanalogy* between techne and the making of public policy. Socrates' argument of course only reports the view of the Athenians. They conceive of public policy as a domain of values and ends, of arete, in which there are no experts. Presumably this is because arete is not a determinate subject, analogous to shipbuilding, in which someone can gain expertise and then become a teacher. If this is so, Protagoras is a fraud.

The Athenians cited by Socrates seem to believe not only (1) that arete and techne are disanalogous but (2) that techne is the paradigmatic mode of teachable knowledge. As a result, they (like Lysimachus in the *Laches*) decide questions of policy by the nonepistemic principle of majority rule. But does Socrates agree with them? We can be sure only of this: he *uses* their implicit views about techne to argue against Protagoras. What exactly this implies about his beliefs is more difficult to decipher. I have already argued that Socrates does agree with (1). He may, however, disagree with (2); in other words, he may well conceive of arete as teachable, albeit in some suitably nontechnical sense.

Socrates uses a second empirical argument against Protagoras's (ambiguous) claim to the political techne. Good fathers frequently fail to transmit arete (319e2) to their sons. In technical subjects in which teachers are readily available, like horse riding, spelling, or mathematics, fathers regularly succeed in educating their sons. But, as most parents know, teaching excellence is a precarious operation at which even those with the best intentions frequently fail (compare *Meno* 93c–94c). Because "techne" implies the possibility of reliable transmission, arete is not one. Again, the further conclusion—arete is unteachable—only follows if techne is identical to knowledge.

Rather than merely indicate what the Athenians think, Socrates, in his own voice, makes this observation concerning the failure of fathers to teach excellence. If he intends this as a serious point, he must believe that he can recognize excellence when he sees it: how else would he be able to detect its absence?

The adversarial context in which Socrates forces Protagoras to present his views is now set. The Sophist must respond to the accusation of having no techne to sell. To do so, he must explain how the knowledge he professes is analogous to techne in the Socratic sense, that is, knowledge, best exemplified by mathematics or by specifically productive technai, of a determinate subject matter. Protagoras's response to the Socratic attack is his "long story" (320d–328c). In it he systematically vacillates on the nature of what he teaches. He does so, however, not because of faulty logic or carelessness. Instead, the long story is the Sophist's deliberate, and brilliant, attempt to disguise his *mathēma*. He wants to gloss it with the appearance of being a techne, without having to accept the consequences following from such a claim. (To see the similarities to Isocrates, consult Appendix 4.)

"Techne" first appears in Protagoras's story in the phrase *tēn entechnon sophian* (321d1), "technical intelligence." Epimetheus was in charge of distributing among the animals the various *dunameis*, "powers" (a word related to the *dunatōtatos* of Protagoras's advertisement), that allowed them to survive. But Epimetheus neglected the human race. Unlike the birds, who were given wings, and the wolves, who were given thick hides, humans were naked, unshod, bedless, weaponless, and had no means to protect and save themselves. Prometheus, attempting to correct his thoughtless brother's error, intervened. He stole technical intelligence, along with fire, from Athena and Hephaestus. This provided humans with *sophia*, "intelligence," for the maintenance of life (321d4).

"Technical intelligence" here refers to a general intellectual ability to maintain life, and it leads to building tools, houses, agriculture, and so forth. It is, to reformulate twice, the "fiery (*empouron*) techne" (321e2), the ability to use fire to build tools, or the "productive (*demiourgikē*) techne" (322b3). It is similar to the broad powers Aeschylus describes in his *Prometheus Bound*. It is, to quote Nussbaum again, "a deliberate application of human intelligence to some part of the world, yielding some control over *tuchē*."[42]

Human being, in Protagoras's story, is by nature technical. But what exactly does this mean? Is techne at this stage analogous to, say, geometry or painting? No. "Techne" here, in all three of its formulations, tokens a very general ability. Only when it is specifically refined, when the fiery techne is rendered determinate through the establishment of a particular subject matter and its attendant standards, goals, and procedures, does a typical techne arise. At this stage of the story, therefore, the theme is really "proto-techne," the natural ability that is prior to the systematic acquisition and transmission of knowledge.

"Proto-techne" grants us a portion of divinity. It makes us like gods, specifically Athena and Hephaestus. By it we construct altars and statues (i.e., organized religion), "speech and words," houses, clothing, shoes, beds, and food (322a3–8). In short, it is the basis of all cultural phenomena. Man, for Protagoras, is man the maker. Language, religion, the polis: none of these is "natural" in the sense of formally existing before human activity. They are all made by human beings, and for one reason only: survival, the guiding principle of the Protagorean story. As such, religion, language, and the polis are analogous to the bird's wings and the wolf's thick skin: they are attributes of the human species that are best comprehended by their contribution to our survival.

Can proto-techne be taught? No. After having been transmitted by Prometheus it is a general ability waiting to be actualized. What can be taught are the systematic refinements of this ability, but at this stage of his story Protagoras does not mention these. Later, however, these, the "typical technai," somehow have filtered into his developmental account. Hermes, for example, asks if he should distribute "respect and right" (*aidōs* and *dikē*) in the same manner by which the technai "have been distributed" (322c5). The use of the perfect tense indicates that at some point there was a transition from proto-techne to the specific technai. How this transition was effected is not explained.

42. Nussbaum 1986, 95.

This omission reveals again the subtlety of Protagoras's story. He makes proto-techne paramount in the human quest for survival. By doing so he creates an expectation in his listeners: they expect the technai to be a significant dimension of human activity. Protagoras does not disappoint, for he says quite clearly at 322c5 that Hermes has *already* distributed the technai. He, however, is silent on what exactly these were and how they arose. The listeners' expectation, therefore, is only minimally fulfilled, for essential details are left out. This suits Protagoras's intentions perfectly. In order to maintain his status as a teacher, he wants the audience to associate him with techne. At the same time, for reasons to become apparent below, he resists the claim to a determinate, or typical, techne. Exactly as in his story, he does not supply those essential details concerning his *mathēma* needed to fit his claim into the strictures demanded by Socrates' use of the analogy.

As noted above, *poleis* are produced by proto-techne for the purpose of survival (322b6). *Poleis* does not here mean "cities"; instead, it refers to primitive communities in which humans gather together to protect themselves from the stronger animals. But these *poleis* do not function well. The war against the animals is being lost, and survival threatened, because humans do each other wrong on account of not having the political techne (322b5–8). This time Zeus intervenes. He sends Hermes to humanity with "respect" and "right," so that *philia,* the bonds of communal solidarity, might be forged among human beings.

Hermes asks whether these two gifts should be distributed in the same way as were the technai (322c5). Zeus answers no. The technai are distributed only to a few who then administer to the needs of many citizens. One doctor, for example, treats many patients. But *aidōs* and *dikē,* the primitive constituents of political life, are distributed to all and hence are *disanalogous* to the typical technai. With this move Protagoras echoes Socrates' earlier observation of the Athenians in their Assembly. But Protagoras's is not a total disanalogy. If it were, then the Sophist, whose subject is somehow political, would no longer be able to hang his shingle and advertise his teaching. Protagoras's strategy, therefore, is to describe his *mathēma* in a carefully ambiguous manner. On the one hand, he denies the analogy between it and techne; on the other, he affirms it at certain strategic moments in order to give his *mathēma* the veneer of epistemic credibility.

Consider, for example, the use of the phrase "political techne" at 322b5 and 322b8. Both contexts are negative: primitive humanity did not have it.

This is why primitive communities failed. Later in the story communities are said to succeed. The listener is thus invited to infer that humanity gained the political techne. In fact, however, Protagoras never quite says this. Instead, he says that *aidōs* and *dikē* were distributed to all. Once again, the listener is invited to infer that *aidōs* and *dikē* are equivalent to the political techne. Soon the phrase "political arete" replaces *aidōs* and *dikē* (322e2–3). Then "arete" alone comes to the fore (323a3). The listener is led to believe that "arete" is synonymous with "political techne," and indeed scholars regularly make this claim.[43] *But Protagoras himself does not,* and for good reason. Techne, in the strict, Socratic sense, is knowledge of a determinate, fixed object. Protagoras does not want to make just this claim. On the other hand, he must maintain his *mathēma* is teachable and worth paying for, and so he invites his listeners to infer the presence of the political techne in his developmental account as a basic possibility in human life.

Protagoras uses a rather unusual phrase at 322d7. When there is a debate about "political arete," all can enter. By contrast, when the debate is about the *aretē tektonikē,* the "carpenter's arete," few can participate. The more expected phrase here would have been *technē tektonikē.*[44] The effect of this strange substitution is, again, to invite the listeners to assimilate "techne" and "arete." Protagoras wants his audience to think he has the former, whose domain is the latter. He does not, however, want to make the analogy between the two explicit, and so he never actually admits the political techne exists or that he has it.

All human beings, says Protagoras, must participate in the political *aretai*, in justice and *sōphrosunē* (323a1–2).[45] To reiterate: this implies the disanalogy between techne and political life, since the former is available only to a few experts. There is another point of disanalogy: "In the other *aretai*, just as you describe, if someone says he is a good flautist, or good with respect to any other techne that he isn't good at, they either laugh at him or get angry" (323a7–b1).

If a man cannot play the flute, he would be mad to say he could. After all, once a flute is put into his hands and he is asked to play, he will

43. See Taylor 1976, 85.

44. See Adkins 1973, 6, for a discussion of this point. This entire essay discusses the "vagueness of 'aretē' and 'techne'" (10) and reaches a conclusion somewhat similar to my own.

45. *Sōphrosunē* and *dikaiosunē* have replaced *aidōs* and *dikē* at 323a1–2. On this, see Loenen 1940, 26.

quickly be exposed as a fraud. It is a straightforward matter to establish
clear criteria to determine whether someone possesses this techne or not.
By contrast, concerning "justice and the rest of the political arete"
(323b1), it is madness *not* to dissemble. Since justice is constitutive of the
human community, to deny possessing it would amount to a denunciation
of one's humanity. Therefore, if someone is unjust, he should dissemble.
And he may well succeed: it is extremely difficult to establish criteria by
which to identify who is just. It is, by contrast, a reasonably straightforward matter to agree on who is a good flutist.

Note again how "aretai" is used instead of the expected "technai" at
323a8. Protagoras, even in a single sentence whose purport seems to be to
contrast the two, deliberately blends them. Taylor and Guthrie, for example, read "aretai" as equivalent to "technai" and so translate it as "skills."
Lombardo and Bell render it as "art."⁴⁶ In so doing, each falls victim to the
Sophist's rhetoric. Protagoras wants the listener to associate the two terms,
for he wants customers to whom he can teach arete. And yet he does not
want the analogy to be strict, and so he avoids "techne" itself. Finally, we
can see why. It would be madness for Protagoras to claim the ability to
play the flute; Socrates would put one into his hands and ask him to play.
Analogously, if Protagoras were to claim a political techne with a determinate subject matter, that is, justice, Socrates would put the political analogue of the flute into Protagoras's hands in order to expose his ignorance
(which is just what he does with Gorgias). Protagoras is too crafty to allow
Socrates to pin him down in this fashion. Therefore, he systematically vacillates on the analogy between his *mathēma* and techne.

From 323c to 326e, Protagoras raises two empirical arguments to coun-
ter Socrates' earlier objections. First, he observes that men punish others in
matters they think are a consequence of "practice and exercise and instruction" (326d6–7). They do not, for example, punish someone for being
small. Since men do punish others for political wrongdoing, they must
believe political arete is teachable. This argument, like Socrates' point
about the Athenians, only shows what men think. Its intention, however,
is unmistakable: at this juncture, Protagoras wants to draw the analogy
between arete and techne in order to suggest the teachability of the former
(and therefore the legitimacy of his own enterprise).

46. Taylor (1976, 15) translates "In the case of the other skills." Guthrie (1956, 54) translates "In specialized skills." Lombardo and Bell (1992) translate "arts."

In response to the Socratic objection concerning the failure of fathers to transmit arete to their sons, Protagoras observes that many fathers send their sons to schools in the belief that there they will learn—from the poets, for example—about good men. Furthermore, according to the fathers, the city itself teaches the boys by means of its laws (325c–326d) (compare *Apology* 24e). Again, even if this only reports what fathers believe about the education of their sons, it nonetheless discloses Protagoras's purpose, namely, to promote the analogy between arete and techne.

Protagoras, however, must yet confront Socrates' objection: why do fathers often fail to transmit arete? Carpenters do not often fail to transmit their knowledge of carpentry. Protagoras argues next for the natural variation of human aptitudes. If everyone were taught to play the flute, only a few would excel, for only some have musical natures (327b9). Analogously, some have natural aptitude for arete, while others do not. But this seems to contradict an earlier statement: the universal distribution of *aidōs* and *dikē* was a requirement for the coming into being of political life. Protagoras resolves the tension thus: all human beings have some capacity for and so can be taught some measure, however small, of arete. Since aptitude is naturally various, some, like Protagoras, learn better than others and can become teachers.

To elaborate, Protagoras offers a comparison with a child's learning to speak Greek. A boy learns how to speak simply by being around adults, all of whom may be counted as teachers in this sense. A true expert in the art of language, however, can perfect the child's capacity in a uniquely thorough fashion. So too with arete (328a–b).

Protagoras's analysis of his student clientele jibes almost perfectly with Isocrates'. Some students, Isocrates says, are by nature good speakers, and these he can educate. Those who are naturally inferior he cannot make excellent. He can, however, at least help them to improve, however slightly. In short, both Isocrates and Protagoras superbly accomplish a dual purpose: they maximize their possible clientele—everyone can learn a little virtue, can be made a little better speaker—while simultaneously explaining why their educational programs are suitable only for those few who are already talented.

To summarize: When claiming his *mathēma* is teachable, Protagoras accedes to Socrates' techne analogy. His arguments based on punishment, on fathers' efforts to educate their sons, and on natural aptitude are meant to show the similarities between it and a techne. By making proto-techne pivotal in his developmental story, by actually smuggling the typical technai into the story at 322c5, and by suggesting that the political techne makes political life possible, he implicitly invites the reader to draw the analogy between his sophistry and techne.

But Protagoras is far too clever to push the analogy too far. He realizes his subject is not determinate in the sense acceptable to Socrates; he is not going to allow Socrates to put the political analogue of the flute into his hands. He therefore explicitly contrasts his teaching with the technai; the latter belong to a few experts, while his subject potentially belongs to all. This is parallel to his earlier statement that, in contrast to Hippias, he does not teach the technai, specifically the mathematical ones. He disanalogizes further: in the other technai it is prudent to admit one's ignorance, while in political matters it is prudent to lie.

To summarize again: Protagoras's long speech closely resembles the vacillation on the techne question found in Isocrates' *Against the Sophists*. Both are motivated to avoid a hard claim to a techne$_1$ for prudential reasons: Isocrates to distinguish himself from his rhetorical competitors, the *artium scriptores*, Protagoras to avoid falling prey to Socrates' refutative maneuvers. The vacillation in both thinkers is also motivated by substantial reasons, by the demands made by the content of their subjects. For Isocrates political logos is dominated by the *kairos*. Because the domain of his "expertise" is the contingent and indeterminate realm of political life, his answer to the techne question is "yes and no." No, not in the ordinary sense: rhetoric is not a techne$_1$; but yes, since it is something he can teach and for which he can legitimately charge tuition. In sum, for Isocrates rhetoric is a techne$_2$, a stochastic techne.

Protagoras holds a similar view. To clarify: recall his "advertisement" in which he professes to make his student *dunatōtatos* in political affairs. As mentioned above, it is difficult even to translate this word. "Capable" has a vaguely positive ring to it; the politically capable man is, presumably, not only an able member of the polis, but a responsible member as well. Levi, however, overtranslates when he renders 319a1–2 as "how to excel in speech and action." He does so because he sympathetically views the Sophist as holding "an absolute ethical standard," one based upon the social nature of human being (which, in turn, is outlined in Protagoras's long story). According to Levi, the function of the Protagorean rhetor is to replace "the less perfect by better laws," that is, those more conducive to the production of social harmony. For him, the Sophist is a traditionalist reflecting the basic sensibility of the Greek polis and aiming to instruct the young in a responsible fashion.[47]

Nussbaum holds a similar view. She paraphrases rather than translates 319a1–2. "Protagoras' announced goal is, through his techne, to make 'human beings good citizens,' teaching them good deliberation both about their household and about the affairs of the city."[48] Nussbaum's Protagoras "provides, in [his] general account of human nature and needs, some universally fixed points with reference to which we could assess competing social conceptions" (104).

The primary "point" to which Nussbaum refers is the same as the one noted by Levi: the social nature of humanity as expressed in the long story.[49] Recall that Prometheus stole fire, that is, technical intelligence, in order to promote the survival of the species. Zeus, in turn, distributed *aidōs* and *dikē* to all. The social life and survival of humanity are, presumably, very good things. Protagoras, then, professes to be able to teach young men how to become contributing members to a healthy community. He can "make the already well-trained young person more aware of the nature and interrelationships of his ethical commitments." Such a claim, however, is "modest" because it largely "leaves our original problems more or less where it found them, making small advances in clarity and self-understanding. [Protagoras] can claim to teach a techne that increases our control over *tuchē;* but the internality and plurality of its ends, and the absence of any quantitative measure, seem to leave his art lacking in precision" (104, 105).

By noting the absence of a quantitative measure and precision in Protagoras's "art," Nussbaum captures the sense in which the Sophist's *mathēma* is really a techne$_2$. She is quite right in describing Protagoras's claim as "modest" (although, like Isocrates, Protagoras charges an immodestly high tuition fee), for admission of epistemic limitation is an important feature of a techne$_2$ (see Chapter 1, List 7).

However coherent Protagoras's epistemic project may be, however appealing in its (Isocratean) modesty, Socrates clearly finds it unsatisfying. Simply put, he *wants* more. He wants, for example, an answer to the *ti esti,* the what-is-it, question. The answer to, say, "What is courage?"

47. Levi 1940, 287, 302.

48. Nussbaum 1986, 103. Since I quote extensively from this work, henceforth I put page references in parentheses in the text.

49. Moser 1966, 113: Protagoras wants to engender "beliefs which are conducive to social harmony."

would be a definition. In other words, Socrates wants definition/determinacy, presumably because he thinks it good. This desire is reflected in both his equation of a techne with a techne$_1$ and his use of the techne analogy. The latter is isomorphic with the what-is-it (as well as the who-is-he) questions, which frame so many of the dialogues. Because Socrates conceives of techne as techne$_1$, once he extracts from an opponent, say Gorgias, a knowledge claim analogous to a techne, it becomes legitimate to demand from him a distinct answer to the question, *Peri ti,* "about what," is your knowledge? Both the analogy and the *ti* questions, then, disclose much about Socrates' epistemic ambitions. By rejecting techne$_2$, he manifests his "immodest" desire for intellectual stability, for formal perfection. This, by contrast, the rhetoricians (as well as their contemporary admirers such as Nussbaum and Fish) are too "modest" to demand. Protagoras, for example, pointedly denies teaching arithmetic, astronomy, and geometry, that is, the quintessentially determinate forms of knowledge (318e). In a parallel fashion, he refuses to give a specific account of the subject matter of his teaching, and he dodges Socrates' techne analogy. What he professes is to help his students—presumably through exercise, imitation, informal instruction (and probably a small measure of formal instruction as well)—become "capable" in the affairs of the city. But what exactly does this mean? He does not, because he cannot, say.

Like Isocrates, Protagoras expresses himself by coherently, even elegantly, vacillating on the techne question. On the one hand, his *mathēma* must be a techne. It can, after all, be packaged and taught. But, no, it is not really a techne (at least not a techne$_1$), for it cannot be taught, at least not as a formal discipline, nor can its subject matter be rigorously defined. Rhetoric, the ability to become capable in the city, requires "perception of ultimate particulars," a unique sensitivity to the amorphous character of political life. If a student already has this sensitivity, his abilities can be refined and systematized by the appropriate teacher. If he does not, he can only be marginally improved. What markedly cannot happen is what does occur in the teaching of arithmetic and spelling, namely, the linear, measurable progress of systematic learning.

The coherence of Protagoras's self-description is tokened by the dramatic fact that *it works.* Like Callicles, he does not allow himself to be pinned by the techne analogy. As a result, immediately after the Sophist has delivered his great speech, Socrates is forced to change strategy. He abruptly shifts course and begins a new discussion concerning the unity of arete (329c). The analogy has failed to work its magic, for the opponent has refused to grant him two basic assumptions, those concerning the goodness of techne and the singular appropriateness of a techne$_1$.

For Protagoras, the unity-of-arete issue is easy: it is one, but has several "parts" (329d). In my discussion of the *Laches* in Chapter 2, I noted the connection between this issue and the techne question. Since a techne must have a determinate subject matter able to be divided into discrete parts (see List 8 in Chapter 1), it follows that if arete is an atomic unity, it cannot become such a subject matter. I will not, however, pursue this notoriously controversial issue any further. Instead, I simply repeat that, by broaching it, Socrates has changed direction significantly. He does so because, as the dramatic prologue clearly shows, his main purpose in this dialogue is to refute Protagoras for the benefit of Hippocrates. Since the techne analogy has not done the job, he tries something else.

Although the *Protagoras* is hugely complex, I concentrate, as I have consistently done throughout this book, only on the techne question. Most relevant for this chapter, then, is the end of the dialogue, when Socrates announces, with seeming enthusiasm, an entirely new concept: the measuring (*metrētikē*) techne. This passage has long provoked commentators to ask, Does Socrates claim this new techne for himself? Does he advocate it as a serious theoretical proposal? Nussbaum and other proponents of the SAT think so. I do not.

Does Socrates Claim a Techne?

Nussbaum reads the *Protagoras* as an *agōn* between the Protagorean and the Socratic conceptions of techne. Both are "practical," but the former is "qualitative, plural in its ends, and [is one] in which the art activities themselves constitute the end . . . such a techne seems unlikely to yield the precision and control that would be yielded by an art with a single, quantitatively measurable, external goal." In my terminology, Nussbaum is describing a techne$_2$ and rightly so, for Protagoras's artful vacillation on the techne question bespeaks his commitment, like Isocrates', to just this kind of stochastic knowledge. Nussbaum's Socrates, by contrast, "finds this insufficient. We must go further, be more thoroughly scientific, if we are to 'save our lives'" (99). According to Nussbaum, Socrates' measuring techne is thus a serious and sincerely held theoretical model of practical knowledge.

> Haven't we seen that the power of appearance leads us astray and throws us into confusion, so that in our actions and our choices

between things both great and small we are constantly accepting and rejecting the same things, whereas the techne of measurement would have canceled the effect of the appearance, and by revealing the truth would have caused the soul to live in peace and quiet abiding in the truth, thus saving our life? Faced with these considerations, would human beings agree that it is the techne of measurement that saves our lives, or some other techne?

Measurement, he agreed. (356d–e)[50]

And what will be measured? Units of pleasure. Socrates (who seems to be speaking for the many) had earlier stated, "To the extent that something is pleasant, is it not according to this good?" (351c). On Nussbaum's reading, Socrates seriously maintains pleasure as the good and therefore proposes a techne to calculate the respective weights of competing pleasures in order to guide ethical decision making. Her interpretation, however, is controversial. The hedonism of the *Protagoras* is one of the great riddles of the Platonic corpus, since nowhere else does Socrates identify the pleasant with the good. Indeed, in other dialogues he argues forcefully against such a view.[51] As Adam says, none of the other dialogues "contains an ethical theory so difficult to reconcile with ordinary Platonic teaching."[52]

Nussbaum's solution to the riddle is this: Plato's principal concern in the *Protagoras* is not with hedonism per se. Instead, his real goal is to quantify the realm of value in order to make goodness a suitable matter of technical calculation. To accomplish this he must transform goodness into a determinate entity capable of being divided into homogeneous, and thus measurable, units. Pleasure is, for the young Plato, a first attempt, a *"pro tempore"* (112) candidate for such a unit. The older Plato later abandons it, but, by contrast, the project of an ethical techne, the rational control of human experience and the "de-fragilizing" of goodness, remains a defining feature of Platonic philosophy throughout most of his career.

Socrates does indeed invoke a techne$_1$, exemplified by measurement and arithmetic, in this passage. And yet even if he speaks glowingly about the measuring techne, Socrates does so *ironically* and in the form of a *reductio ad absurdum*. Nussbaum, in short, is dead wrong.

In disputing Nussbaum on the *Protagoras* I am not alone. As Vlastos

50. I follow Nussbaum's translation (1986, 109).
51. See *Gorgias* 495d; *Republic* 505b, 509a; *Phaedo* 64d.
52. Adam 1971, ix.

puts it, "[T]he majority of commentators have held that [hedonism] is not Socrates' own position, but the 'unconscious hedonism of the average person.'"[53] He here is citing A. E. Taylor, who argues thus: Socrates is trying to show that even from the point of view of those who consider pleasure and the good to be identical, goodness can be demonstrated to be knowledge of some sort (which, as discussed in Chapter 2, is an essential Socratic assumption). This hedonism can be described as "unconscious" and "average" because it reflects a typical and thoughtless account of decision making. Most people, when asked why they had chosen X over Y would say they wanted the result X would bring, that X would feel better than Y. Socrates, according to Taylor, is trying to convince "the average man that, on his own assumptions, goodness is a matter of right calculation" and that while he might superficially believe he is acting simply according to the desire for pleasure, he is, in fact, deciding on the basis of an implicit calculation, namely, that X will feel better than Y.[54] Even hedonism, apparently a nonepistemic explanation of ethical decision making, requires a calculus to produce maximum pleasure. If hedonism, apparently the worst, that is, least epistemic, case, implies the "measuring techne" (356d4), a kind of knowledge, then a fortiori all other accounts of ethical decision making must similarly implicate knowledge, and the fundamental Platonic conjunction of excellence and knowledge is secured.

The minority position, championed by Nussbaum, interprets hedonism as a view actually, although temporarily, belonging to the young Plato. I side with the majority: instead of representing his own view, the hedonism announced by Socrates belongs indeed to the "average person." In this dialogue, however, that person is very specific: *it is Hippocrates*. Recall the prologue: Socrates had known of Protagoras's arrival for two days, but had expressed no interest in visiting him. He consents to go to Callias's house *only* because of his desire to protect his young friend from the lures of sophistry. And, as Plato makes clear when he has Hippocrates tell Socrates about his nocturnal adventures, the boy sorely needs protection.

> It was during the evening, after I had gotten in very late from Oenoe. For, you see, my slave Satyros had run away. And of course I was going to tell you that I was going to chase him, but I forgot on account of some other matter. When I came home and we had our dinner and were about to retire, my brother told me that Pro-

53. Vlastos 1956, xl.
54. Taylor 1926, 260.

tagoras had arrived. Right away I tried to come to you, but then it
seemed to me too late at night. But as soon as sleep had gotten rid
of my fatigue, I got up at once and came over here. (320c2–d2)

Hippocrates recounts his late night in Oenoe, an Attic deme. He was
searching for his lost slave Satyros. "Oenoe" is derived from *oinos,*
"wine," and Satyros is related to "satyr," the companion of Dionysus. In
other words, Hippocrates had been on a binge in "wineville." When he
returned home and learned of Protagoras's arrival, he could not muster the
wherewithal to act upon this valuable piece of information. Why not? He
says it was because it was too late at night. This explanation, however, is
highly implausible, since Hippocrates has already shown himself to be indifferent to the hour: he has just aroused Socrates well before dawn! After
having been out drinking, he returned home, learned that Protagoras was
in town, wanted very much to go to Socrates, but was unable to do so
because he was drunk. He napped instead.[55]

There is obviously no way of proving that the sequence of dramatic
events occurred as I sketch them. My appeal instead is to a carefully
crafted dramatic scene and to the simple assumption that Plato included
such minute details (especially the naming of a slave) for a reason. If I am
correct, then Socrates' entire encounter with Protagoras must be interpreted in light of his relationship to Hippocrates. The boy is in need. He is
lazy; he wishes simply to pay a fee and be made wise, rather than engage
in any difficult course of study himself (310d6). He wants someone else,
Socrates, to enlist Protagoras's aid for him. He is impetuous, undisciplined,
immoderate, and perhaps given to drunkenness. He is, one might say, a
fledgling hedonist, someone whose deeds bespeak the inarticulate belief
that pleasure is the good. Socrates' strategy against Protagoras is shaped
by his desire to exhort Hippocrates to change his ways, to reexamine the
notion that pleasure is the good and to pursue knowledge instead.

I read Socrates' invocation of the "measuring techne" as a dialectical
device meant to address Hippocrates on terms familiar to him. Even if one
identifies, as the boy seems to, pleasure with the good, one can be led to
the conclusion that knowledge, specifically calculation, is required. And
calculation, as a form of knowledge, tokens, perhaps even breeds, a kind
of *sōphrosunē.* To the stability and precision of arithmos the calculator
must submit.

55. See Roochnik 1988.

Socrates thus introduces the measuring techne for the purpose of exhortation. As such, its presence in the dialogue does not commit Plato to a technical or scientific conception of practical knowledge, for the only proposition it implies is that practical knowledge should be sought.

Nussbaum states, "It is only with the aid of the hedonistic assumption that Socrates is able to reach the conclusion that he clearly claims as his own" (111). But how does she know what conclusion Socrates would claim as his own, since he is responding to the contingencies of a specific dramatic situation? Surely the "measuring techne" passage itself cannot warrant her confidence, for as with all uses of the techne analogy this one is interpretively indeterminate. Instead, what propels Nussbaum is precisely the Nietzschean conception of Plato as a theoretical optimist eager to transform the "fragile" world of human goodness into bloodless units amenable to rational calculation.

There is no evidence that Socrates possesses the art of measurement he appears to advocate. At one point he says, "We will consider later what this techne and episteme are" (357b5–6). What needs explaining, therefore, is why he extols this techne but does not disclose it. Is Plato withholding his knowledge from others? Or is he alluding to his plans for future research? As a good chronologist, Nussbaum opts for the latter, and of course her answer is possible. But her position presupposes access to the putative development of Plato's psyche. By contrast, my view takes its bearings from what Socrates *does* with the analogy. And this is to show Hippocrates that knowledge is desirable. By citing the measuring techne, Socrates advocates the goodness of determinacy. It is good to measure, to count. This is in sharp and deliberate contrast to Protagoras's earlier expression of contempt for the mathematical technai (see 318e). What the Sophist offers is a techne$_2$, an indeterminate set of rules of thumb offering guidance on how to become "capable" in the affairs of the city. For Socrates, this is not good enough. In response, he holds out the measuring techne as a lure for Hippocrates, offering him—as he did with Callicles—a framework in which the search for knowledge, and not pleasure, makes good sense.

CHAPTER FOUR

WHAT DOES SOCRATES KNOW?

The Strangeness of Socratic Knowledge

What does Socrates know? That moral knowledge is good and should be sought and that, as a result, philosophy is superior to the power politicking of a Callicles. The knowledge he seeks, however, is neither a $techne_1$ nor a $techne_2$: not the former because its subject matter is not a determinate entity analogous to arithmos or the alphabet and therefore capable of being divided into discrete parts and then systematically taught; not a $techne_2$, the very notion of which is, even if tenable, epistemically unsatisfying. Even if it earns him no tuition fee, he knows his search for moral knowledge, that is, his version of "philosophy," is better than the *philosophia* offered by Isocrates, whose epistemic claim, mirrored in Plato's character Protagoras, is, because it is not a $techne_1$, too "modest." Still, the Sophist professes a techne, and so he is simultaneously too assertive as well. He hangs a "shingle" advertising himself as a professional teacher of logos/arete. Doing so, he treads on Socratic turf, and the philosopher, in response, pits himself against the rhetorician in public debate.

Socrates, however, is himself manifestly rhetorical. He knows how to refute, how to embarrass, how to exhort others to philosophize. He is superbly responsive to the dramatic *kairos* in which he finds himself. Almost paradoxically, he understands that arithmos and $techne_1$ are good, *even if* they are themselves use- or value-neutral and hence inappropriate as models of moral knowledge.

In short, Socratic knowledge is strange.[1] One of its most perplexing features is how often Socrates denies having knowledge at all. In this section, I examine this famous denial, using it as yet another clue in my exploration of the nontechnical character of Socratic knowledge.

My task in what follows will, in the minds of many Plato scholars, be associated with the work of Vlastos, who was long fascinated by what he, echoing Alcibiades, called Socrates' "strangeness," his *atopia*.[2] Much of his last work was spent in the attempt to decipher it and articulate its philosophical implications. In this section I take my bearings, but finally diverge sharply, from Vlastos's much-discussed interpretation.

There are four components constituting, for Vlastos, the basis of Socratic strangeness: (1) his use of irony; (2) his regular disavowal of knowledge; (3) his less frequent but no less serious claims to having knowledge; (4) his utter commitment to moral, as opposed to metaphysical or epistemological, philosophy.

Socrates is strange because, first, the practice of irony—"the use of words to express something other than, and especially the opposite of, [their] literal meaning"—constructs a mask behind which lives "a mysterious, enigmatic figure, a man nobody knows."[3] To speak covered by such a mask is quite simply a strange thing to do. Second, (2) seems to contradict (3) and make (4) unintelligible. How can someone who professes ignorance also coherently lay claim to knowledge and, furthermore, describe moral knowledge as a valuable possession? Throughout his writings, Vlastos concentrated on this cluster of problems, the solution to which he found in irony.

According to Vlastos, Socrates practices complex irony, a mode of speaking, indeed of living, defined as follows: "In 'complex' irony what is said both is and isn't what is meant: its surface content is meant to be true in one sense, false in another."[4] When, for example, Socrates says to Alcibiades, "I love you," he both means and does not mean it. He does not intend this sentence to convey the message of a typical Greek pederast. Instead, he means it in his own, unique sense, namely, that he loves Alcibiades' soul.[5]

1. Barnabas (1986) takes up, but does not go far with, this theme.
2. Vlastos 1991, 1. See also Roochnik 1995.
3. Vlastos 1991, 21, 37.
4. Vlastos 1991, 31.
5. Vlastos 1991, 41. Regrettably, Vlastos never cites the discussion of "complex irony" in Hyland 1988.

For Vlastos, Socratic irony, even if involving concealment, is free from the intention to deceive. It is educational, for it is riddling and forces us readers, as well as Socrates' interlocutors, to "puzzle out for ourselves" what it could mean.[6] The most significant instance of complex irony is Socrates' "disavowal of knowledge." On the one hand, he says, "I am aware of being wise in nothing, great or small."[7] Nevertheless, "he speaks and lives, serenely confident that he has a goodly stock of [knowledge] . . . And he implies as much in what he says."[8]

This apparent paradox is at the heart of Socratic "strangeness," and Vlastos rightly declares, "To keep faith with Socrates' strangeness some way has to be found to save both the assertion of his ignorance and the implied negation."[9]

The way Vlastos has found is a distinction between two kinds of knowledge. When Socrates states, "I do not know," he both means and does not mean what he says. Socrates does not have certain, infallible "knowledge-C," whose rigor is on a par with that regularly attained in mathematics. But he does have the radically weaker "knowledge-E," elenctic knowledge whose content is true moral propositions and that is supported by Socrates' various analyses of the beliefs held by his interlocutors. Since the supporting reasons for elenctic knowledge are provided by those arguments Socrates actually engages in and that are therefore contingent, and since elenchus "is a human process, a contest, whose outcome is drastically affected by the skill and drive of the contestants," there is always a "security gap between the Socratic thesis and its supporting reasons." As a result, Socratic knowledge "is full of gaps, unanswered questions; it is surrounded and invaded by unresolved perplexity."[10]

Vlastos uses this distinction to reconcile Socrates' disavowal of knowledge with his several direct claims to having knowledge: "When [Socrates] says he knows something he is referring to knowledge-E; when he says he knows nothing—absolutely nothing, 'great or small'—he refers to knowledge-C."[11]

Even granting, as I would, the legitimacy of Vlastos's notion of complex irony and his reliance on two meanings of "knowledge" operative in the early dialogues, his account is incomplete.[12] This is because throughout his

6. Vlastos 1991, 44.
7. *Apology* 21b, cited in Vlastos 1985, 5.
8. Vlastos 1991, 3.
9. Vlastos 1991, 3.
10. Vlastos 1985, 18–19.
11. Vlastos 1985, 20.
12. By contrast, Lesher (1987) thinks the whole project is ill conceived.

works he is silent about the pivotal term shaping the conception of moral knowledge the early dialogues express: "techne." This word occurs with striking frequency in just those dialogues with which Vlastos is most concerned. For example, during Socrates' argument with Gorgias in the *Gorgias* (447b–461a), it can be found forty-five times in only fourteen Stephanus pages (see Appendix 1). But the index of *Socrates: Ironist and Moral Philosopher* lists but two pages under the heading "techne," and on both the comments are passing.[13] Even in his extended criticism of Terence Irwin, whose instrumentalist interpretation of Socrates' moral theory largely depends on a specific reading of the "craft [techne] analogy," Vlastos says only this: "Consider the 'craft analogy' to which Irwin appeals again and again in support of the instrumentalist thesis. I would argue that his confidence that the analogy has this implication is misplaced. For though Socrates certainly wants moral knowledge to be in some respect like that of carpenters . . . he knows that it is radically different in others."[14]

For all the reasons discussed in Chapters 2 and 3, this criticism is right on the mark. Vlastos, however, never supplies the full interpretation of Socrates' use of "techne" his criticism of Irwin would seem to require. His silence is all the more puzzling because, as Woodruff has shown, Vlastos's own analysis of Socrates' disavowal of knowledge can be readily formulated in terms of techne. Briefly put, Woodruff's thesis is that "expert knowledge"—his rendition of "techne"—"is what Socrates means to disavow" and "nonexpert knowledge" is what Socrates in fact has. The latter would include "the knowledge that he, Socrates, is not an expert . . . the moral truth that it is bad to disobey one's superior," and, finally, the results of Socrates' elenctic examinations. "The elenchus thus exposes what you believe in the last analysis, and simply treats this sort of belief, without apology, as non-expert knowledge."[15]

One purpose of Chapters 2 and 3 was to show how that moral knowledge may be like a techne, but only to the extent it is knowledge, useful and desirable. Irwin's strict reading of the analogy to delineate a technical conception of moral knowledge is thus neither necessary nor plausible. It is entirely possible that Plato has his Socrates use the analogy in a negative fashion and for protreptic reasons: to *point* to a nontechnical conception of moral knowledge and urge his readers to consider what it would be.

13. Vlastos 1991, 174, 240.
14. Vlastos 1978, 233.
15. Woodruff 1992, 66, 78, 81.

This view is in keeping with Woodruff's thesis and, implicitly at least, with Vlastos's as well.

By focusing too narrowly on the elenchus, Vlastos lost sight of the techne question. Shifting interpretive focus back to techne has several advantages. First, it mitigates the severity of the "turn" Vlastos attributes to Plato. For him, the Socrates$_E$ of the early dialogues is fundamentally different from the Socrates$_M$ of the later works. The early dialogues, he argues, consistently show Socrates engaged in elenctic activity, whereas transitional and middle dialogues do not. "In the Elenctic Dialogues Socrates$_E$'s method of philosophical investigation is adversative: he pursues moral truth by refuting theses defended by dissenting interlocutors. This ceases in the Transitionals: there he argues against theses proposed and opposed by himself."[16]

Consider the *Euthydemus,* a "transitional" dialogue. "Here for the first time in Plato's corpus we see Socrates unloading his philosophizing on an interlocutor in the form of a protreptic discourse expounded in flagrantly non-elenctic fashion as a virtual monologue . . . the elenchus has been jettisoned." For so "drastic a departure . . . we must hypothesize a profound change in Plato himself."[17] The major cause of this change, this liberation from the elenctic moral philosophizing of the historical Socrates, is Plato's advanced study of mathematics.[18]

The Socrates of the *Euthydemus* does seem to behave otherwise than the main speaker of the *Charmides, Laches,* or *Euthyphro.* He does deliver what amounts to a protreptic monologue. As a result, *if* the elenchus is deemed essential, then Plato would appear to have undergone a profound change. If, however, the techne question, and not the elenchus, is taken to be essentially informative concerning the Platonic project, then the shift is not as drastic. This is because the doctrine concerning techne presented in the *Euthydemus* is similar to that found in the *Laches* and *Charmides.* All three dialogues, as I argued in Chapter 2, point to nontechnical knowledge. As such, even though there is no extended elenchus in the *Euthydemus* as there is in the *Charmides,* the similarities between the dialogues outweigh their differences, and, on this score at least, there is no need to postulate a dramatic change in the mind of their author.

If the reader's focus is on the techne question, the early Plato no longer appears as an exclusively moral philosopher who "maintains epistemologi-

16. Vlastos 1991, 49.
17. Vlastos 1991, 116–17.
18. See Vlastos 1991, 107–31.

cal innocence, methodological naïveté,"[19] and the maturing Plato need not
be described as having been decisively changed by his study of advanced
mathematics. This is because the early dialogues demonstrate an acute
awareness of the epistemic character and the limits of techne. Most important, they manifest a deep understanding of the most significant philosophical concept attending the techne question, namely, determinacy, a concept
figuring prominently in both epistemology and metaphysics. I argued this
in terms of the *Euthyphro,* the *Ion,* the *Gorgias,* where the goodness of
arithmos is pivotal. Recall that in the *Gorgias* and *Charmides* mathematics
is the decisive example used to illustrate the technai (see Appendix 3 for
elaboration). The relationship between mathematics and techne, as well as
the importance of that relationship, is succinctly explained at *Republic*
522b–c. In sum, throughout these works the level of reflection on the
nature of mathematical, hence technical, knowledge is serious and mature.
As a result, Vlastos's story of Plato's "deep, long plunge into mathematical
studies" and of his turn away from exclusive concern with moral philosophy is questionable.[20] There is thus no need to postulate a dramatic shift in
the putatively developing mind of Plato, a move that, however carefully
marshaled is its evidence, is irremediably speculative.[21]

The following statement from the *Apology* is pivotal for Vlastos: "But
to do injustice (*adikein*) and disobey my superior, god or man, this I *know*
to be evil (*kakon*) and base (*aischron*)" (29b6–7). Vlastos comments:
"This single text, if given its full weight, would suffice to show that Socrates claims knowledge of a moral truth."[22] In "Socrates' Disavowal of
Knowledge" and again in a lengthy note to his last book, he collects several such knowledge claims and asks how they are compatible with the
more famous and emphatic disavowals of knowledge.[23] Once again, his
strategy is a simple and sensible way to attack the problem of Socratic
knowledge. But once again, Vlastos's story is incomplete: he does not take
into account a cluster of Socrates' most direct and significant claims to
knowledge, two of which occur in the *Symposium* and the *Meno.* This is,
of course, because he considers these middle dialogues, whose author has
radically changed his views (although, when it suits him, as it does when

19. Vlastos 1983, 53.
20. Vlastos 1991, 118.
21. For a brief history of the chronological interpretation of the dialogues, see Tigerstedt
1977. For an excellent critique of the contemporary approach to chronology, see Howland
1991.
22. Vlastos 1985, 7.
23. Vlastos 1985; 1991, 236–42.

discussing irony itself, Vlastos himself is not averse to citing the *Symposium:* see 1991, 33). In fact, the middle-dialogue claims are compatible with those found in earlier works, for both sets of dialogues manifest a consistent preoccupation with a single cluster of issues that are best illuminated by the techne question.

The most striking of the Socratic knowledge claims *not* discussed by Vlastos is *Symposium* 177d8: "I say that I know nothing other than the erotic things (*ta erōtika*)."

For someone already convinced of the general efficacy of Vlastos's strategy, this statement should be alluring, since it both asserts and denies the possession of knowledge. On the one hand, Socrates knows the "erotic things"; on the other, he knows nothing else. A highly schematic summary of Socrates' teaching on eros in the *Symposium* (expressed through the persona of Diotima) is this: eros is a capacity to enter into relationships with objects. To love is to love something (199d). Furthermore, what is loved is something lacked (200b). Following upon the awareness that an object is lacked comes the counting of the object as good; once deemed good, the object is loved and pursued. Since these various "moments" (lack, awareness of lack, deeming what is lacked good, striving to overcome the lack) underlie all human desires and activities, it is fair to say (following Hyland) that human beings are essentially erotic.[24] Therefore, Socrates' claim to know "the erotic things," is tantamount to saying he knows something fundamental about human beings. To reformulate: he has what is described in the *Charmides* as "self-knowledge."

Symposium 177d8 elaborates Socrates' famous self-description in the *Apology:* "What kind of wisdom is this? Perhaps that which is human wisdom, for perhaps I really am wise in this wisdom" (20e1). "Human wisdom" is knowledge of "the erotic things" characterizing being human. Like all forms of knowledge, this one is conditioned by the nature of its subject matter. Eros is not a stable and determinate entity; instead, it is the capacity to enter into relationships with an indeterminate array of objects. As such, knowledge of *ta erōtika* cannot be a rigorous, systematically teachable techne.[25] Instead, it is an understanding of what it means to be in

---

24. This view of eros has been best explained in Hyland 1981.

25. Nehamas and Woodruff (1989) badly mistranslate *ta erōtika* as "the art of love." I note, however, that in the *Phaedrus* Socrates suggests he has the erotic techne (257a8). In the *Theaetetus* he claims to have the techne belonging to the midwife (149a). Even if these passages, like *Gorgias* 521d, appear to token a Socratic techne, a proper understanding of their dramatic context would show that this is not so. Griswold (1986) demonstrates this point exceedingly well concerning the *Phaedrus*.

a constant state of striving for objects. For these reasons, "human wisdom," like self-knowledge in the *Charmides,* is *atopos;* it is strange. Literally, it is knowledge somehow out or bereft of *topos,* "place." Since the very notion of place implies "boundary," and since the bounded is the determinate, if eros is indeterminate, it cannot have a place.

Socrates (or Diotima) puts this point in mythic terms when telling the story of the birth of Eros. Born from Resource and Poverty and sharing characteristics of both, Eros is forever *metaxu,* "in between," not only resource and poverty but the mortal and the divine (203b–c). Finally, as developed in the "ascent passage" (210a–212a), eros is in between the object striven for, whether it is a beautiful body or soul or institution or "Beauty Itself," and the subject striving to attain that object. It has no place of its own.

As such, eros cannot be sufficiently stabilized to become a properly specific subject matter of a techne. Still, it is possible to gain knowledge of it: human wisdom is the nontechnical knowledge of the essential incompleteness, and consequent need to strive for desired objects, characterizing the human psyche.

Another passage from the *Apology* expresses this point. Like 29b, it is critical to Vlastos, who describes it as the "clearest statement" of Socrates' disavowal of knowledge: "For I am aware of being wise in nothing, great or small" (21b2–5).[26] Because it figures so prominently in his reading, Vlastos cites this line thrice in his last book. At one point he changes the translation slightly: "For I am not aware of being wise in anything, great or small."[27] At another he paraphrases: "[Socrates] *asserts* that he has no knowledge, none whatever, not a smidgin of it, 'no wisdom, great or small.'"[28]

As the paraphrase may suggest, Vlastos's translation is problematic, for 21b2–5 could also be rendered: "For I am aware of being wise neither with respect to something great nor with respect to something small." The significant difference between this translation and Vlastos's is in the latter's placement of a comma (which is absent in the Greek). This allows Vlastos to paraphrase the line by saying Socrates "has no knowledge, none whatever." My translation allows for the possibility that, even if he is wise neither with respect to something great nor with respect to something

26. Vlastos 1991, 82.
27. Vlastos 1991, 82.
28. Vlastos 1991, 3; see also 1991, 239.

small, Socrates might still be wise: with respect to something in-between. And this would be eros.[29]

Socrates' knowledge of the erotic things helps resolve a perplexity of long standing. In his famous assertion of human wisdom he seems to say, "I know that I do not know," and thus to contradict himself. In fact, he does *not* quite say this. As Vlastos has argued,[30] the statement, "I know that I do not know," is neither identical to nor necessarily implied by the actual lines uttered by Socrates: "I am not aware (*sunoida*) of being wise in anything, great or small" (*Apology* 21b) and "As for me, I have no knowledge, nor do I think I have any" (*Apology* 21d).

If, however, the meaning of the first "know" is different from the second, then it is possible Socrates does mean he "knows that he does not know," and yet does not contradict himself. What if Socrates' nontechnical knowledge of eros stands behind the first "know," while techne is behind the second? If so, he knows, in a nontechnical sense, that he does not have a techne. Knowledge of eros requires acknowledgment of ignorance, for eros itself is always an incompleteness. It is not a stable entity but a striving for objects not possessed. It is a force, a "great *daimon* in between the divine and the mortal" (*Symposium* 202e). Knowing it, therefore, cannot be a matter of a techne; instead, it is an awareness of the incompleteness of all activities.

Socrates' knowledge of his own ignorance sends him on his philosophical quest and is the precondition for his most notorious utterance: the question. If a man knows he is ignorant and desires to be otherwise, he will ask a question. For this reason, knowledge of eros, understood as knowledge of ignorance, helps to explicate another passage of great importance to Vlastos, *Gorgias* 505e4–5: "I think we should be contentiously eager (*philonikōs*) to know what is true and what is false about the things we discuss."[31]

Vlastos asks, How can Socrates contend eagerly for knowledge of what is true if, after decades of searching, he "remained convinced that he still knew *nothing*"?[32] Knowledge of eros again supplies an answer. Since eros is a striving for what is lacking, and since it is constitutive of human activity, to be human is to strive. If knowledge is lacking, and if someone is

---

29. Fortunately, my argument does not hinge on this speculation.
30. Vlastos 1991, 82.
31. Cited in Vlastos 1985, 6.
32. Vlastos 1985, 6.

aware of the lack, then there will be a striving for knowledge. Since knowledge, at least in the form of a rigorous moral techne, is always lacking, Plato would agree with the opening line of Aristotle's *Metaphysics:* "All human beings by nature desire to know."

Socrates expresses this belief at *Gorgias* 505e4–5 by his use of the word *philonikōs,* literally meaning "with love of victory." Knowledge is a prize, the search for which is an erotic quest. The love of knowledge—or philosophy—is a consequence of the essentially erotic character of human nature. In other words, to know the erotic things is to know knowledge should be sought. It is equivalent to knowing the goodness of philosophy. It is, to cite the most famous of Socrates' assertions, to know "the unexamined life is not worth living for a human being" (*Apology* 38a5–6).

To return to *Apology* 29b, Vlastos's pivotal text: knowledge of eros offers a basis for the claim it expresses, which can be paraphrased (using somewhat different translations), "I know that it is bad (*kakon*) and shameful (*aischron*) to do wrong (*adikein*) and not obey my superior." This is equivalent to "I know it is good (*agathos*) and fine (*kalon*) to do right."

Vlastos fails to analyze sufficiently the actual content of this statement. Socrates identifies those people who do right as better than those who do not. In this sense, his assertion of knowing it is "good and fine" to do right is equivalent to claiming a moral truth. But *Apology* 29b does not address what doing right actually is. Socrates only says it is better than doing wrong. Doing right is something people should care about, should consider "fine" (*kalon*) and try to do. In other words, Socrates describes a basic desire (for doing what is right). *Apology* 29b is a statement about what one should feel: it is "shameful" (*aischron*) to do wrong. Therefore, one *should* feel shame when one does wrong. Socrates knows what people should feel, what they should care about. He knows some people are better than others, not because of what they specifically do, but because of what they care about and try to do.

As highly as he regards this passage, Vlastos actually understates its importance. The *Apology* both begins and ends in a disavowal of knowledge. Its first sentence contains the words, "I do not know" (17a), and its last expresses the same thought by stating that only a god would know whether Socrates or the jurors will be going to a better place (42a). As a quick count of Stephanus pages shows, 29b is the center of the dialogue. This small textual device is meant to underscore the intensity of the statement. Socrates knows it is good to desire what is right.

This may seem obvious, and so the knowledge expressed at *Apology* 29b may be counted trivial. But it is not. Consider Polus in the *Gorgias*. He agrees with Socrates that to do wrong is more shameful than to suffer it. He does not agree, however, that if X is more shameful than Y, it is worse than Y, for he believes doing wrong is better than suffering it. He is willing, in other words, to splinter what Socrates believes are two firmly bonded couples: the fine and the good, and the bad and the shameful (474c). Eventually Socrates refutes Polus's view (which is then taken up and reformulated in much more powerful terms by Callicles). Initially, however, Polus affirms the opposite of what Socrates claims to know: it is reasonable and right to desire what is shameful.

Polus, like Callicles, neither cares about nor desires what he should. But how does Socrates *know* this? By understanding the erotic nature of the human psyche. To explain, I examine two final passages, both from the *Meno*.

After having gone through his experiment with the slave boy in order to overcome Meno's paradox, Socrates concludes with an account of "recollection." Since human beings can recollect here on earth what they knew in a previous life, it is, pace Meno, both possible and desirable to attempt to (re)acquire knowledge (*Meno* 85c–86b). To cap this story, Socrates says, "On the one hand, I cannot be confident about most of the remarks I have made on behalf of my logos; but that by believing we should inquire into matters we do not know, we shall be better and braver and less lazy than if we believe that we are neither able nor should inquire about what we do not know—about this, I would do battle, so far as I am able, in both word and deed" (*Meno* 86b).

This is strange. Searching for knowledge, it seems, should be counted a good even if the "proof" of the possibility of such a search, namely, the recollection story, is not persuasive. We shall be braver and more energetic, more committed to a way of living, if we believe what we cannot prove.

Socrates' assertion here fits with the analysis above. Given its erotic nature, the human psyche ever strives for what it lacks. Knowing *ta erotika*, therefore, is equivalent to "human wisdom" concerning the essential incompleteness of human striving and knowledge. Socrates knows he does not know. Exactly as he states here in the *Meno*, he knows his "theory of recollection" is not a technically compelling proof. (Indeed, it is a story, and not a theory at all.) Still, because of the nature of eros, searching for knowledge is an essentially human activity. Socrates is committed to the proposition "The unexamined life is not worth living for a human being," even if he cannot prove that examination can actually culminate in learning.

What is most striking about *Meno* 86b is its elevation of "practice" over "theory." Even in the absence of a real theory, a techne, one *should* believe learning is possible, because of the practical consequences of holding such a belief. While admitting his ignorance, that is, his failure to arrive at a techne, Socrates nonetheless knows a certain kind of life, one engaged in the quest for knowledge, is worth living. All the claims analyzed to this point, those from the *Apology, Gorgias,* and *Symposium,* would lead to this same conclusion. (As would my earlier discussion of the "Doric harmony" in the *Laches.*) Because of his human wisdom, his knowledge of eros, Socrates knows how to live: in the active striving for knowledge. He knows what to urge others to do: philosophize.

Later in the *Meno* Socrates states, "True opinion is no worse a guide to action than wisdom" (97b). He also says, "I speak as one who does not know but only conjectures (*eikazōn*). Still, that correct opinion is something different from knowledge does not seem to me to be a matter of conjecture but something I would claim to know. I would claim this about few things, but I would include this among those that I know" (*Meno* 98b).

Knowledge is distinct from true or right opinion. But how does Socrates know this? Perhaps, like his assertion at 86b, it is a matter of practical conviction. Or perhaps the claim here at 98b is known by means of an indirect proof: without the distinction between right opinion and knowledge, there would be no pressing need to search for knowledge to replace opinion. But this would be is absurd, for there *is* a pressing need: eros is a great *daimon*. It presses us, pushes us forward to seek what we do not have. And we do not have knowledge.

Socrates knows *ta erōtika*. Plato expresses this not by means of an abstract techne. Instead, he writes richly nuanced dramas peopled with characters of great variety. Figures like Lysimachus, Laches, and Hippocrates are initially indifferent to philosophy and the quest for knowledge. As a result, they are potentially easy prey for professionals, such as Protagoras, whose instruction is for sale. Socrates wants to energize them, exhort them to be critical and pursue knowledge. He does so by means of the techne analogy. But why does he do so? Because shifting their focus would improve their lives, make them better. But how does he know this is better? Because he knows *ta erōtika*.

Characters like Euthyphro and Polemarchus are confident they understand arete. Such confidence is ill conceived and potentially disastrous. Euthyphro, for one, is enthused with his own righteousness and is on the verge of accusing his father of murder. As often noted, great harm has been committed under the banner of virtue. Socrates needs to shatter Euthyphro's confidence, make him aware of what he does not know and, in turn, persuade him to philosophize. He uses the techne analogy to do so. It is not clear whether he succeeds. Euthyphro leaves the court without having filed his suit, but the reader can only guess where he will be tomorrow.

Professional teachers like Thrasymachus, Gorgias, Protagoras, and Polus are trapped by their own claims. On the one hand, they are rhetoricians, affirming, like Thrasymachus, the relativity, hence the indeterminacy, of value judgments. On the other hand, they hang a shingle boasting their expertise. Socrates exploits this tension and, with varying degrees of success, attacks with the techne analogy.

Callicles is a genuinely erotic man. Passionately driven to achieve political power, he wants no truck with techne, has no liking of geometry and hence no patience with Socrates. He cannot be refuted. His is an eros without limits, veering toward tyranny. Socrates beckons him with a vision of an orderly, knowable world, one that would satisfy his hunger. But Callicles does not bite. And Socrates must speak alone.

Socrates understands his interlocutors, knows what is appropriate to say to them. In this sense, then, the early Platonic dialogues express knowledge of, rather than theorize about, eros. Because they are dramas, they are the superb, even if strange, vehicles for the expression of nontechnical knowledge.

To return to Vlastos: his use of complex irony, as well as his bifurcation of knowledge into two distinct kinds, as the means of understanding Socrates' disavowal of and claims to knowledge is a fruitful approach to the early dialogues. His singular identification of Socrates with the elenchus is, however, too constricting. Many of Vlastos's best insights can be preserved if the view of Socrates is shifted away from the elenchus and toward his use of the term and concept of techne. Once such a shift is made, there is less need to postulate a radical transition between the early and middle dialogues, for both, as philosophical dramas, hinge on the issue of nontechnical knowledge. As a result, it is legitimate to invoke the claims Socrates makes in the *Symposium* and the *Meno* and to relate them to the earlier dialogues. Doing so helps to articulate Socratic strangeness, for especially the claim to knowing the erotic things elucidates what it is Socrates knows and how this knowledge is compatible with his repeated assertions of ignorance.

On this reading, Socrates is a philosophically consistent character who, whether he appears in an early or a middle dialogue, is primarily concerned with, and indeed knows, the erotic things; who has human wisdom; who knows he does not know; who acknowledges he cannot prove knowledge is possible, but nonetheless is convinced that life without examination is not worth living for a human being.

The Platonic Version of Nontechnical Knowledge

I conclude by approaching the issue of nontechnical knowledge from an entirely different direction. Diagram 3 schematizes much of the argument offered in this book (and then some). This diagram represents a pattern of argumentation found regularly in the early dialogues. Socrates asks his interlocutor either, What is X?—X being a specific virtue—or, About what is your techne? if the character being questioned has made a strong knowledge claim. Sometimes, as with Gorgias and Protagoras, he simply asks, "Who is he?" and expects the answer to be given in terms of the opponent's expertise. All these "*ti*-questions," (*ti esti, peri ti, tis esti, eis ti, pros ti*) require a definition or a specified subject as their answer. As such, they reflect a philosophical commitment to determinacy, which is assumed to be a reasonable and appropriate epistemic goal.

An example of the *ti esti:* Socrates asks Laches, What is courage? Laches willingly responds, Intelligent endurance. At this moment, then, an assumption binds both parties: *ti esti* is a reasonable question both to ask and attempt to answer. In turn, this means, as stated above, that the determinacy implied by the *ti* is an appropriate epistemic goal. After Laches proposes an answer, Socrates examines it. He does so through the techne analogy; that is, he assumes (and Laches agrees) that the "intelligence" implicated in the definition is like a techne. This assumption, as I showed in the *Laches* section of Chapter 2, is what brings the definition down. Nevertheless, the assumption that techne—even if ultimately it fails to provide a satisfying model for intelligent endurance—is somehow a reasonable goal of the inquiry (and in this sense is good) is operative.

The diagram shows the connection between arithmos and techne. Since

Diagram 3

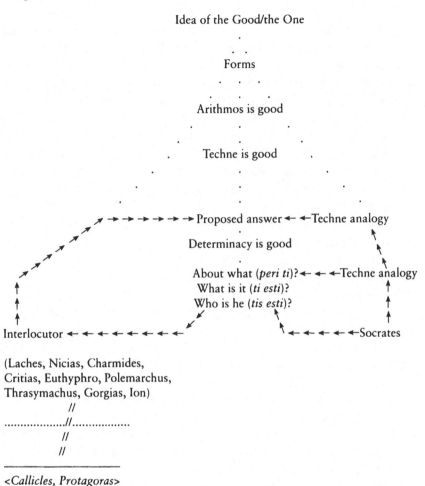

Idea of the Good/the One

Forms

Arithmos is good

Techne is good

→ → → → → → Proposed answer ← ← Techne analogy

Determinacy is good

About what (*peri ti*)? ← ← ← Techne analogy
What is it (*ti esti*)?
Who is he (*tis esti*)?

Interlocutor ← ← ← ← ← ← ← ←   ← ← ← ← ← Socrates

(Laches, Nicias, Charmides,
Critias, Euthyphro, Polemarchus,
Thrasymachus, Gorgias, Ion)
                //
................//..................
                //
                //
_____

<Callicles, Protagoras>

the former is the basis of latter, the assumption of the goodness of techne implies the goodness of arithmos as well.

When an interlocutor, such as Gorgias or Protagoras (or Ion: see Appendix 1), professes expertise and the ability to teach, Socrates requires him to explicate his claim via the terms of the analogy. If Gorgias can teach, he must, says Socrates, have a techne. If so, he is required to specify, as clearly as can the mathematician or the painter, with respect to what (*eis* or *pros ti*) he is expert. Once Gorgias agrees to the analogy, he too is committed to the assumption of the goodness of techne and the determinacy it presupposes (a presupposition that ultimately works against him).

I have included at the top of the diagram the Forms and at its pinnacle the Idea of the Good, which I identify with the One.[33] Since they have not been discussed in any previous section of this book, I include them here only to make a suggestion. Plato's concern with the Forms in his middle dialogues and with the Idea of the Good in book 6 of the *Republic* is fully compatible with his asking *ti esti?* and *peri ti?* as well as his use of the techne analogy, in the early dialogues. The two *ti* questions and the analogy imply the goodness of determinacy. If the Forms themselves are conceived as the structures making intelligibility and determinacy possible, a clear connection is forged between "early" and "middle" Plato.

Woodruff makes this point: "Here is the main bridge from early Plato's theory of Techne to later Plato's theory of Forms: if you have a techne, you know the essential nature of your product; essential natures will turn out in the middle dialogues to be Forms."[34] Since techne is not restricted to production, Woodruff's "product" is not quite accurate. Still, he is right: techne implies a knowable *ti* as a subject matter to be mastered by the *technitēs*. It is "*ti*-ness" that, perhaps, the Forms are meant to explain and make possible.

The Idea of the Good is the Idea of Ideas, and it is, I think, the One. I offer no answer to the notoriously vexing questions about the relationship between the Forms and numbers or about the exact sense in which the Good is the One. Again, I only suggest a point of continuity between the early and middle/late Plato: if the Idea of the Good is conceived as the One, it is, as Aristotle says about the One (*Metaphysics* 1021a10), the principle, the *archē*, of arithmos, and not a number itself. It makes counting possible, but it itself cannot be counted. To count is to count units, and the One, because it is unit itself making possible all other units, cannot itself be counted. (Like the sun, it cannot be directly seen, but only makes visible that upon which it shines.)

If the One is the principle of arithmos, it is also the principle of determinacy, for to be a knowable X is to be a unit, a unified something, a *ti*. Since a techne requires a definite subject matter, and since both *peri ti* and *ti esti* imply determinacy, ultimately the One is the condition of the possibility of basic Socratic questions, the asking of which is central to his philosophizing. In this sense, then, One is the Good.

One purpose of Diagram 3 is to show how, simply by agreeing to *try* to

33. See Hirschberger 1932, 312.
34. Woodruff 1992, 98.

answer the Socratic *ti esti* or to abide by the techne analogy, the interlocutor makes a series of increasingly strong commitments: to the goodness, relevance, and appropriateness of determinacy and therefore of (Platonic) philosophy—perhaps ultimately to the Forms as the final objects of philosophical inquiry. As I have argued throughout, Socrates badly needs his interlocutor to make this initial move in order to proceed with his various refutations/exhortations. If he fails to secure agreement, the dialogue collapses. This pattern is most vividly expressed in "Socrates v. Callicles" in the *Gorgias*. Because Socrates cannot convince Callicles to abide by the rules of the techne analogy, Callicles having not sufficiently absorbed the lesson of "geometrical equality," there is no common ground between the two. Callicles remains unmoved by the philosopher's attempt at rehabilitation, and Socrates ends up talking to himself.

In a similar fashion, Protagoras artfully dodges the analogy in the *Protagoras* and so also remains undefeated (until the end of the dialogue at least). Because neither Callicles nor Protagoras ever fully buys into the Socratic assumptions, they are not implicated in the hierarchical conception shown in the diagram. They are not committed to the goodness of arithmos. They are immune to Socratic rhetoric, operating as they seem to do in an inviolate space of their own. Simply put, they are not, and perhaps cannot be, refuted.

The diagram is meant to capture the "upward" orientation, the movement toward transcendence, so characteristic of Platonism. But it adds an important qualification: the upward mobility toward the Forms is contingent upon the interlocutor's agreeing to the first moves of the Socratic examination. If the interlocutor agrees to answer the *ti esti* or the *peri ti*, if he assumes the legitimacy of the techne analogy, he makes commitments that eventually will be used against him. Gorgias, for example, agrees rhetoric is like a techne. Doing so forces him eventually to contradict himself: techne is not only value/use-neutral, he says, but it also has justice as its subject matter.

Or consider Meno. He begins the dialogue by asking Socrates whether arete is teachable. In response, Socrates insists he answer a prior question: what is arete? Meno quickly replies, "But that's not hard to answer, Socrates." He then proceeds to list a series of particular examples. The excellence of man is political activity: of a woman, managing the house; and so forth (71e). Socrates is indignant: Meno is not supposed to list particulars but to answer *ti esti* and thereby drive toward a single definition to cover all the particulars he has in mind. Meno eventually succumbs, that is, plays Socrates' game, but it was fully within his rights to refuse to do so. In other words, because he writes a dialogue, Plato offers his reader the opportunity to imagine Meno challenging the appropriateness of Socrates' questions. Once, however, Meno does venture possible answers, he is committed to a view that eventually will lead him into self-contradiction.

By contrast, Callicles and Protagoras are surds, intransigent opponents immune to Socratic rhetoric. They distort the otherwise beautiful symmetry of the diagram. And they are crucial to an understanding of the nontechnical knowledge present in the dialogues. The diagram represents not the structure of reality but the patterns of argumentation and hence the belief system of Socrates and his interlocutors. *If* the opponents agree with Socrates in his initial assumptions, then "higher" assumptions are entailed. But if they disagree—as Callicles and Protagoras do—then the project is derailed from the start. That the project can be so derailed means it is dependent upon the character, the desires, of the opponent. And these desires are, of course, contingent. The diagram, in short, represents not an ontological scheme but *ta erōtika*.

Like the rhetorician, Socrates knows how to talk to various people. There are those, like Hippocrates and Polemarchus, he can exhort and win over. They gladly buy into the techne analogy and begin the ascent represented in the diagram. (To what level of the ascent they rise, the reader of course cannot know.) By contrast, Protagoras, like Isocrates, prefers to play his own game. The various *ti* questions neither spark his imagination nor spur him on toward Socratic questioning. He is content, instead, to remain on the level of a techne$_2$, with an informal "knowledge" of what one needs to say in order to become *dunatōtatos* in the city. He is, as Nussbaum aptly puts it, a "jolly conservative" who does not share Socratic ambition. Why not? He is just not that sort of person. He is content with his shingle and the tuition it generates.

Socrates finds the Protagorean shingle, that is, his techne$_2$, unsatisfying: it represents the failure to wonder about and pursue the nature of its own presuppositions. A techne, whether 1 or 2, requires some measure of determinacy. But what is this, and what is its "cause"? What makes determinacy possible? What unifies our experience, our logoi, our political actions? What is beauty itself?

These questions the Socratic—the active, erotically charged—psyche asks, driving itself upward, pursuing the foundations of its own assumptions. By contrast, the Protagorean/Isocratean version of rhetoric "modestly" keeps its gaze aimed at rules of thumb rather than rules, examples rather than definitions, particulars rather than universals.

Moral knowledge, human wisdom, for Plato is not a techne, because the human realm is acutely infected by the inflections and contingencies of human eros.

Diagram 3 schematizes, inadequately of course, what the early dialogues teach. This teaching is not technical. Instead, it requires a dialogue or drama for its full expression. To capture adequately the contingency, the instability, the risk of interruption and failure characterizing the erotic ascent, a drama, an imitation of characters at work, is needed. Callicles and Protagoras, drawn so well by their author, must be there. So too must Laches, who candidly tells of his *philonikia*, his philosophical desire and his courage to pursue it. We, the readers, bear witness to the dramatic possibilities the diagram only abstractly represents. It is possible to go upward, to affirm techne and move toward the Ideas. It is also possible to rest content without beginning the ascent at all.

What brings the dialogues to life, what makes them alluring and maddening, perplexing and ever subject to reinterpretation, is that Socrates thinks techne is good, yet does not himself have one. Indeed, even while having his Socrates so regularly invoke it in his many analogical arguments, Plato adduces good reasons why techne cannot model moral knowledge. Techne is ordinary knowledge, the kind we typically recognize, rely upon, certify, and reward. As such, it simply is not strange enough to treat the erotic complexities of human moral life. The dialogues themselves, however, within which "techne" so stubbornly reappears, are extraordinary. As Socrates praises the beauty of formal knowledge and calls upon the technai for examples, he himself is located within the informal mess of human life. As he invokes techne to exhort his interlocutors to seek knowledge, he himself is no *technitēs*.

APPENDIX 1:
THE APPEARANCES
OF "TECHNE"

"Techne" is used, in all its inflections, 675 times in the dialogues.[1] In addition, there are 187 occurrences of words derived from (or including) it. Many of these are adjectival, including *technikos*, "technical," "knowledgeable"; *technikōteros* and *technikōtatos*, which are the comparative and superlative forms of *technikos*; and *homotechnos*, "of the same techne." *Atechnōs*, an adverbial derivative, is frequent (and important), and is treated separately in Appendix 2. Table 1 charts the rate of frequency per Stephanus page with which "techne" appears in the early dialogues.[2] Recall that, according to Vlastos, these are *Apology, Charmides, Crito, Euthyphro, Gorgias, Hippias Minor, Ion, Laches, Protagoras,* and book 1 of the *Republic*. Vlastos categorizes *Euthydemus, Hippias Major, Lysis,* and *Meno* as "transitional." The dialogues treated in Table 1 are listed in the order with which they were discussed in the body of the book.

Table 1 shows how frequently the word is used during refutations, specifically when Socrates works against those Sophists who claim, or are asked (pressured) to claim (by Socrates), a techne. This pattern is striking in the first scene of the *Gorgias* (447–61). Socrates refutes Gorgias's

1. This figure is based upon a character search performed on *Thesaurus Linguae Graecae,* which includes all the dialogues, even those considered spurious.
2. Page numbers have been rounded off slightly.

Table 1: The Frequency of "Techne" and Its Derivatives

Laches: 23 pages

"Techne"	Derivatives	
185e11	185a1 :	*technikos*
186c5	185b2 :	*technikōtatos*
193b10	b11:	*technikos*
c10	d9 :	*technikos*
195b9	e4 :	*technikos*
	e8 :	*technikōterous*
	187a1 :	*homotechnoi*

Frequency: 5/23 = .23 (with derivatives: 12/23 = .52)

Charmides: 23 pages

"Techne"	Derivatives	
161e7	171c8 :	*homotechnon*
e7	173c1 :	*technikōs*
165d5		
e6		
e8		
171c6		
174e4		
175a1		
a4		

Frequency: 9/23 = .39 (with derivatives: 11/23 = .48)

Euthyphro: 13 pages

"Techne"	Derivatives	
11d4	14e3 :	*technikon*
d6	15b10:	*technikōterous*
14e6		

Frequency: 3/13 = .23 (with derivatives: 5/13 = .38)

Republic, book 1: 27 pages

"Techne"	Derivatives
332c7	
c12	
d2	

Table 1: *Continued*

Republic, book 1: 27 pages

"Techne"	Derivatives
341d3	
d7	
d10	
e4	
e7	
342a1	
a3	
a5	
a6	
a6	
b3	
b4	
b5	
c4	
c5	
c8	
c9	
346a2	
c2	
c10	
d1	
d8	
e4	
347a1	
a3	

Frequency: 28/27 = 1.04

Euthydemus: 36 pages

"Techne"	Derivatives
272a5	303e5 : *technikōs*
272e4	
282d8	
285b4	
288a5	
289c2	
c7	
d6	
d9	
e3	
e5	

Table 1: *Continued*

Euthydemus: 36 pages

"Techne"	Derivatives
290a7	
b1	
b5	
d5	
291a8	
b5	
c5	
c7	
d7	
e8	
295e2	

Frequency: 22/36 = .61 (with derivatives: 23/36 = .64)

Gorgias: 80 pages

"Techne"	Derivatives		
447c2	455b5	:	*technikōtaton*
448b5	463a7	:	*technikon*
b12	500a6	:	*technikou*
c2	a6	:	*technikou*
c4	501b4	:	*technikai*
c6	504d6	:	*technikos*
c9			
e3			
e3			
e7			
449a1			
a4			
c9			
450a7			
b2			
b3			
b6			
c1			
c4			
c7			
c9			
d4			
d7			

Table 1: *Continued*

Gorgias: 80 pages

"Techne"	Derivatives
451a4	
a8	
b1	
b5	
452a5	
a8	
b3	
c7	
453a1	
d8	
e1	
454a2	
a9	
455c4	
456b5	
c7	
457a1	
a2	
b6	
459b7	
c4	
d3(end of "Socrates v. Gorgias")	
462b6	
b11	
d8	
d9	
463b3	
b4	
464b3	
465a2	
a5	
467a1	
477e7(end of "Socrates v. Polus")	
486b5	
500b5	
b5	
e5	
503d1	
506d7	
509e1	

Table 1: *Continued*

Gorgias: 80 pages

"Techne"	Derivatives
510a4	
a6	
511b9	
e4	
512c4	
d6	
513a8	
514b1	
e6	
517e4	
e7	
518a3	
520d11	
521d7(end of "Socrates v. Callicles")	

Frequency: 77/80 = .96 (with derivatives: 83/80 = 1.04)

Protagoras: 53 pages

"Techne"	Derivatives
312b3	319a8 : *technēma* ("technical thing")
315a5	321d1 : *entechnon* ("technical")
316d4	e1 : *ephilotechneitēn* ("they loved techne")
e5	327b1 : *technēmatōn*
317c2	328a2 : *cheirotechnōn* ("craftsmen/technicians")
318e1	a5 : *homotechnoi*
e2	
319a4	
c8	
321e2	
322a6	
b3	
b5	
b8	
c5	
d4	
323a9	
328a3	
348e6	
351a7	

Table 1: *Continued*

Protagoras: 53 pages

"Techne"	Derivatives
356d4	
e4	
357a2	
b4	
b5	

Frequency: 25/53 = .47 (with derivatives: 31/53 = .59)

boasts concerning rhetoric. "Techne" occurs 45 times in this passage, for a frequency of 3.2 per page. When the role of interlocutor shifts to Polus, a student of Gorgias with a lesser claim to make for himself, the frequency drops to 0.6 per page. When the role of interlocutor shifts to Callicles, who asserts no professional expertise at all, the frequency drops to 0.4. There is thus a direct proportion between the strength of the epistemic assertion of the interlocutor and the frequency of the word.

In *Protagoras* 314c–320c, while Socrates examines Protagoras, "techne" appears 1.33 times per page. Not surprisingly, in Protagoras's great speech (320d–328d), the frequency is also high, 1.11, for in this passage, as Chapter 3 showed, the Sophist attempts to give his audience the impression that he has a techne to sell (without making an explicit claim; compare Isocrates' strategy as analyzed in Appendix 4).

In book 1 of the *Republic,* during the exchange between Socrates and Polemarchus (331d–336b), the frequency is 0.6 per page. But when the role of interlocutor shifts to the professional rhetorician Thrasymachus (336b–354c), it rises to 1.39. (In books 2–10, the frequency is 0.18.) Again, the relationship between frequency and the strength of the claim made by Socrates' opponent is direct.

In the *Laches, Charmides,* and *Euthyphro,* Socrates exposes the weaknesses in various definitions of specific virtues. In each case, the rate of appearance is consistent.

Of all the dialogues, the *Ion* has the second highest frequency: 3.0 per page. In this work, discussed briefly in Chapter 2, Socrates argues against a rhapsode using terms similar to those invoked in his attack on the rhetoricians. Indeed, because he professes to know "what sorts of things it is fitting (*prepei*) for a man to say and what for a woman, and what kinds of things it is fitting for a slave and what for a freeman, and for one who is ruled and for one who is a ruler" (*Ion*, 540b), the rhapsode is much like the rhetorician.

The entire dialogue is framed by the techne analogy. For example, Socrates' first argument against Ion (531a–533b) proceeds thus: If X has a techne about Y, then X ought to know Y, the specific subject of which he is a master, thoroughly. Therefore, if A and B both speak about and make claims to knowing Y, and if A does so well but B poorly, then X should be able to evaluate and discuss critically both A and B. Recall that Socrates' example of a *technitēs* in this passage is the arithmetician. So, if Greta has mastered the arithmetical techne, and if Jan and Dean both talk about numbers, Jan well and Dean poorly, then Greta ought to be able to speak well about, evaluate, comment upon, be clever about, both Jan and Dean.

Ion fails this test. His subject matter is poetry, and yet he can speak only about Homer and not, for example, Hesiod. In fact, when any poet other than Homer is discussed, Ion "simply (*atechnōs*) dozes off" (532c2). Because techne grants its possessor total mastery of his field and thus should enable him to evaluate anyone venturing into it, Ion has been shown to be *atechnōs*, without a techne.

The highest frequency of all, at 4.0 per page, is found in the *Cleitophon*. This is a perplexing dialogue because in it Cleitophon examines Socrates and does so via the techne analogy. Eventually Cleitophon concludes that, because Socrates can exhibit no techne whose subject matter is justice, he would prefer to study with the rhetorician Thrasymachus. As Blits has argued, Cleitophon comes to Socrates assuming the identity of knowledge and techne.[3] Because Socrates fails to provide the secure answers and teachable system he craves, Cleitophon rejects him. His rejection is defensible only if techne actually is the best model of moral knowledge, a proposition this book has argued is false. Even if false, however, it is widely believed (by both ancients and moderns) that techne *is* the best, most accessible and obvious, model of knowledge. On the one hand, then, Cleitophon is quite similar to contemporary proponents of the SAT: he believes techne is the paradigm of or even equivalent to knowledge. It is because he realizes Socrates has no techne that he rejects him. Plato wrote this dialogue, I propose, to display a primary consequence of assuming moral knowledge must be strictly analogous to a techne: namely, the rejection of philosophy itself.

During the four pages of the *Hippias Minor* (365d–369b) in which Socrates refutes Hippias's contention that the truthful Achilles is superior to

3. Blits 1985.

the "wily" Odysseus, he argues thus: If Hippias has knowledge of calculation, geometry, or astronomy, he can, unlike the ignorant man, lie know-
ingly. Therefore, the true man is also the false man. The argument is based on
the value-neutrality of the mathematical technai in which Hippias specializes,
and "techne" is used four times in four pages. As I argued in Chapter 2's
section on book 1 of the *Republic,* this argument leaves open the possibility
that a true man who possesses a form of value-laden knowledge, that is, one
disanalogous with the technai, would not coincide with the false man.

This refutation serves the larger purpose of exposing Hippias's weaknesses. He is the most technically adept of all the Sophists (368b2 and
Protagoras 318e) and so boasts, like Gorgias, of being able to answer any
question (363d). His epistemic claim is huge, and Socrates uses the techne
analogy to cut him down to size.

In the final argument of the *Hippias Minor* (371–76), Socrates argues
on behalf of an apparently paradoxical thesis: "it is in the nature of the
good man to do injustice voluntarily, and of the bad man to do it involuntarily"; that is, "he who voluntarily errs and does disgraceful and unjust
acts, if there is such a man, would be no other than the good man" (376b).
The techne analogy is instrumental here (and "techne" is used three times
between 375b and 376a). If justice is knowledge (375e), and if knowledge
is best exemplified by technai such as medicine, music, "and all the rest
that are technical (*kata tas technas*)," then, since the technai are use-neutral, that is, can be used for good or bad, the person with techne can
voluntarily do what is bad. (In Chapter 2's section on the *Republic,* this
argument was compared to the *reductio* of Polemarchus's definition of
justice.) As a result, *if* justice were a techne, then the good man would do
injustice involuntarily. Since the good man does not do injustice voluntarily, justice is not a techne. It is, however, knowledge.

In the *Meno* Socrates converses with Anytus (90b–94e), a man convinced he knows what arete is. In this passage Socrates argues that if arete
were knowledge, it would be teachable (89e). At this point, the analogy
comes to the fore: if we wanted Meno to become a good physician, we
would send him to be instructed by expert physicians who claim (*anti-
poioumenos*) the techne and charge a fee for teaching it (90c–d). If we
wanted him to become a cobbler, we would send him to professional cob-
blers. If we wanted him to become a flautist, he would go to those who
profess the techne and charge a fee for teaching it (90e1). And so it is with
"the rest" (90c5), that is, with the other technai.

To whom, then, should we send Meno to become excellent? The only
possible candidates are the Sophists, for they alone boast arete as their

area of expertise and charge tuition for instruction. Since Anytus despises the Sophists (91b), he cannot identify a single teacher of arete. Instead, he advises a young man interested in learning arete simply to approach any "gentleman" in the city for instruction (92e). This highly democratic and civic-minded answer contradicts the very notion of a techne, which implies an expert who is "comparatively rare" (see criterion 4, List 1, in Chapter 1; also compare *Apology* 24e).

Socrates launches into a denunciation of famous "gentlemen" of the past (much as he does in *Gorgias* 515c–516e). Themistocles taught his son horsemanship (*hippikē*), but the boy did not become excellent in other matters. Pericles taught his sons how to excel in music and gymnastics "and whatever else is embraced by the term 'techne'" (94b), but they turned out to be wretches. In short, the teaching of arete and the technai are disanalogous. Identifying an expert in the technai and then teaching them is a straightforward task; doing so with arete is deeply problematic. (Against the view of Woodruff, who argues that the *Meno* is a "transitional" dialogue, with a different teaching altogether concerning techne, this negative lesson—moral knowledge is not a techne—is held in common with "early" works.)[4]

That "techne" appears in the *Meno only* when Socrates is examining Anytus can thus be explained precisely by Anytus's unreflective overconfidence concerning the knowledge of excellence. For him, the teaching of arete is a simple matter, easily done by anyone in the city. Socrates punctures this confidence. He has no need to deflate Meno himself, who, after all, is the proponent of the paradox that learning by inquiry is impossible.

I observe (but only in passing, since it is a later dialogue) that in the *Phaedrus* "techne" is used 48 times between 260 and 274 (3.4 times per page). This section is devoted to refuting Lysias's claim to having "a techne of speeches." It is also interesting to note that the only dialogues in which "techne" does not appear are the *Crito, Lysis,* and *Parmenides.* In the first two works, Socrates converses with men or boys with whom he is manifestly friendly and who make virtually no knowledge claim.

In sum, the rate of frequency of "techne" varies in proportion to the strength of the epistemic assertion held by Socrates' opponent. "Techne" makes its most notable and regular appearance, not when Socrates is offering a positive model of moral knowledge, but when, by means of the analogy, he is showing an opponent that he does *not* know what he thinks he knows.

4. Woodruff 1992.

The results of Table 1 might be thought to lend support to some sort of chronological thesis. One might, for example, argue that because "techne" is used 1.04 times per page in book 1 of the *Republic* but then drops to 0.18 in books 2–10, the first book was written earlier, when Plato was still in thrall to a technical conception of moral knowledge. A better explanation for the change in frequency is that after book 1 Socrates is no longer actively refuting an opponent: he is working jointly with Glaucon and Adeimantus in the construction of a city in speech. Furthermore, the frequency rates of later dialogues (*Theaetetus*, 0.28; *Sophist*, 1.0; *Statesman*, 1.46) are similar to those found in earlier works. On the techne question, there is good reason to think Plato changed neither his mind nor his vocabulary.

The second principal task to which Socrates puts the techne analogy is exhortation. The distinction between refutation and exhortation, however, is not rigid. When, for example, Socrates refutes an opponent by exposing his failure to fulfill the criteria demanded by the techne analogy, he simultaneously exhorts his audience to demand a rigorous form of moral knowledge and become reflective about what sort of (nontechnical) knowledge this might be.

In the *Laches*, Socrates exhorts Lysimachus to seek moral knowledge (184e–185e). In this one page, "techne" is used once, but adjectival derivatives appear six times, and "techne" clearly is the cornerstone of Socrates' protreptic speech. (*Crito* 47b is a similar scene.)

The scene between Socrates and Hippocrates in the *Protagoras* (311b–314c) is manifestly protreptic. In it "techne" is found but once. The notion, however, is present in Socrates' formulation of an analogy between the Sophist (whom Hippocrates hopes to visit) and the physician (311b), sculptor (311c), "language master" (*grammatistos*), expert lyre player, and trainer, each of whom has a techne (312b3). With the analogy Socrates exhorts the boy to think carefully about what it is the Sophist knows, teaches, and sells.

As argued in my discussion of the *Protagoras* in Chapter 3, Socrates' discussion of the "measuring techne" is protreptic. "Techne" appears five times during this passage (356c–357c).

"Techne" in the *Euthydemus* is concentrated in Socrates' second protreptic speech (288c–292c), in which he attempts to characterize the wisdom that is arete. In this passage the frequency is 4.0 per page. The only other occasions on which the word appears are when spoken by Socrates to characterize or examine his sophistic opponents (272a5, 274e5, 285b4, 288a5, 295e2).

The following outline reformulates the results of Table 1. In it are listed the major appearances of the techne analogy and the uses to which it is put. I include some dialogues that have not been discussed in the previous chapters, as well those usages of the techne analogy in which the word itself does not appear. This table is neither precise nor exhaustive; its strokes are too broad. It is meant to summarize much (but not all) of the textual data accumulated in this book.

Usages of the Techne Analogy

I. The analogy used for refutation
 A. Definitions of individual virtues
  1. *Laches* 192d–193d: Laches' definition of courage
  2. *Laches* 195a–c: Nicias's definition of courage
  3. *Charmides* 165c–176d: Critias's definition of *sōphrosunē*
  4. *Euthyphro* 13a–14b: Euthyphro's definition of piety
  5. *Republic* 332d–334c: Polemarchus's definition of justice
  6. *Republic* 341c–343a: Thrasymachus's definition of justice
 B. General knowledge claims
  1. *Gorgias* 447–61: Gorgias's profession of the rhetorical techne
  2. *Protagoras* 318a–320c: Protagoras's profession of the so-phistic techne
  3. *Ion* 531b–533d: Ion's claim to the rhapsodic techne
  4. *Euthydemus* 291b–293a: Ctessipus's claim for the kingly techne[5]
  5. *Amatores* 134d–135a: The unnamed lovers' definition of philosophy
  6. *Cleitophon* 409a–410e: Socrates' claim to teach justice
  7. *Hippias Minor* 365d–369b, 371–76: Hippias's status as the most technically proficient Sophist
II. The analogy used for exhortation (all spoken by Socrates)
  1. *Crito* 46c–47d: Socrates exhorts Crito to seek knowledge
  2. *Laches* 184e–185e: Lysimachus not to rely on majority rule when it comes to arete, but to seek moral knowledge
  3. *Euthydemus* 288–92: Cleinias to seek wisdom
  4. *Protagoras* 311b–313a: Hippocrates to consider what it is that Protagoras teaches
  5. *Theages* 123b–124c: Theages to clarify his conception of wisdom
  6. *Alcibiades* I, 106c–109a: Alcibiades to clarify in what sense he wishes to advise the Athenians

5. It is unclear who the speaker here is.

APPENDIX 2: THE
APPEARANCES OF
ATECHNŌS

The perispomenon adverb ἀτεχνῶς, derived (according to Liddell, Scott, and Jones) from ἀτεχνής, is an Atticism common in the Greek of Plato and Aristophanes.[1] While it is prominent in these two authors, it is absent from the works of the tragedians and the orators, and thus appears to be colloquial in tone. Thesleff specifically includes it as a "marker" of Plato's colloquial style.[2] Its most typical meaning is "really, simply, utterly, literally," and a scholium on Aristophanes' *Plutus* 109 lists *alēthōs, pantelōs, kathapax,* and *heni logoi* as synonyms. Obviously it is closely related to the paroxytone ἀτέχνως, derived from ἄτεχνος, and another scholium on the same line explains that the word with this accentuation means "without techne" and occurs "if someone speaks or acts contrary to (*para*) techne."[3]

In the Platonic dialogues, ἀτεχνῶς occurs seventy-five times. This appendix shows that Plato intended to exploit the etymological connection between it and "techne." When "really, simply, utterly," are used to translate it, the English contains no more than a colorless adverb. This may

1. This appendix appeared in an earlier form as Roochnik 1987. I thank the editors of *Phoenix,* the journal of the Classical Association of Canada, for permission to reprint portions of it.
2. Thesleff 1967, 86.
3. Koster 1960, 34.

have been the way this word was heard in actual conversation, and it is the way it is used in Aristophanes, but the philosophical significance and extreme frequence of "techne" in the dialogues strongly suggest the word is meant to be a pun.[4]

Plato frequently intended ἀτεχνῶς to have a dual meaning. In such passages not only does it mean "really, utterly, simply," it also means "without techne," or "artlessly" (ἀτέχνως). For Plato himself, who used no written accentuation, there obviously would have been no visible difference between these two words. This fact naturally increases the probability that he intended ΑΤΕΧΝΩΣ to be ambiguous.

In Burnet's edition ἀτέχνως is found only three times. In these passages, companion terms in the sentence establish the meaning, and therefore fix the accentuation, of the word. For example, Phaedo 100d3–4 reads, "haplōs kai ἀτέχνως kai isōs euēthōs." In the Sophist we find, "eikēi de ἀτέχνως" (225c1). Later (225c7), entechnon forms a direct contrast to ἀτέχνως and so makes the choice of accentuation straightforward. A passage from the Gorgias is slightly more problematic (as Dodds, but not Burnet, notes in his apparatus).[5] The phrase is "komidēi ἀτέχνως" (501a4: "quite unscientifically," according to Dodds). At 501a6 alogos seems to be a parallel term, and so again the choice of accent is straightforward.

The passages listed in Table 2 below are quite different. In them, the choice of the perispomenon accentuation seems quite plausible. In other words, ἀτεχνῶς in these passages does seem to be only a mild intensifying adverb. It is precisely in situations such as these, however, that Plato is punning.

To prove an ancient author is punning is often quite difficult, since it requires attributing to him an intention not made explicit in the text. Some puns, however, can be easily identified. For example, there is little doubt that Plato puns on the meaning of Polus's name, "colt," in Gorgias 463e2. The use of tokos, "interest" and "offspring," in Republic 507a2–5 is a well-known case of a single word whose two meanings are both invoked in an elaborate dual metaphor.

The situation is more problematic when the word in question is colloquial, because it would seem that common words are most likely to be used unreflectively. This, however, is a dangerous assumption to apply to

4. ἀτεχνῶς is used in the following passages in Aristophanes: Acharnians 37, Clouds 408, 425, 439, 453, 1174; Wasps 772, 810; Peace 199, 206; Birds 60, 820; Frogs 106; Plutus 109, 362. Once again, this list has been generated by Thesaurus Linguae Graecae.
5. See Dodds 1966, 147.

the dialogues. Plato is an extraordinarily careful writer, and the reader should examine virtually every word in the text, even the most colloquial, and seek to determinate its role. In the case of ἀτεχνῶς, the several synonyms available to Plato, and its obvious affiliation with "techne," make it prima facie a good candidate for a pun.

According to several scholars, ἀτεχνῶς has two functions in the dialogues: (1) To signal an allusion to or quotation of a proverbial saying. Tarrant states, "A further clue to a few semi-proverbs may perhaps be found. Plato frequently uses certain phrases of emphasis to point to the applicability of some figure or turn of language. The chief of these are ἀτεχνῶς . . ."[6] (2) To indicate a comparison or simile. As Shorey puts it, "ἀτεχνῶς . . . marks the application (often ironic or emphatic) of an image."[7] It is precisely in the midst of these usages (which I term "quotation" and "comparison") that Plato is punning.

Consider the *Ion*. Poets, Socrates says, produce their works, not by techne, but by inspiration. As evidence, he cites Tynnichus the Chalcidian. This man had never produced a single poem worth mention, until one day he somehow composed a paean considered to be among the most beautiful. What he had written was "simply (ἀτεχνῶς), just as he himself said, an 'invention of the Muses'" (534d8).

Tarrant is surely right: ἀτεχνῶς here indicates the citation of a "semi-proverb." As such it does not appear to carry much weight in the sentence and "simply" is a reasonable translation. Examination of the context, however, reveals the dual meaning of the word. The entire dialogue concerns the relationship between techne and poetry (and the activity of the rhapsode). Forms of "techne" are used often in the near vicinity of 534d8: 533d1, e6; 534b8, c5, c6. Indeed, as mentioned in Appendix 1, in the twelve Stephanus pages of the *Ion* there are thirty-seven occurrences of the noun. Socrates is specifically arguing that the poets write *aneu technēs*. Therefore, it is hard to imagine him not punning at 534d8. If this were not a pun, Plato would have to be accused of a rather gross literary insensitivity. It would be comparable to an author's writing—in a treatise on parenthood in which the phrase "a parent" is used three times per page— "He is apparently a father," and being unaware of the pun he has made. Such artlessness would be utterly uncharacteristic of Plato.

6. Tarrant 1946, 114.
7. Shorey 1926, 78. Aristotle only uses ἀτεχνῶς in order to express comparison. See *Nicomachean Ethics* 1102b18, *On the Generation of Animals* 731a21, 743b22, and *On Sophistical Refutations* 172a34.

The situation is similar, if not quite as marked, at *Euthydemus* 291d1. Socrates describes the "kingly techne." To it, he suggests, the other technai must hand over their *erga* to be used properly. The kingly techne is "the cause of correct acting in the city. And just (ἀτεχνῶς) as Aeschylus says, it alone would sit at the helm of the city, steering everything and commanding everything and making everything useful." The "line" that Socrates paraphrases is from Aeschylus's *Seven Against Thebes*, and so Gifford is correct: ἀτεχνῶς is used here in "quoting a proverbial saying."[8] The context, however, strongly suggests a pun.

As I argue in my discussion of the *Euthydemus* in Chapter 2, this section of the *Euthydemus* principally concerns the conceptual difficulties attending the "using" or "kingly" techne. Because techne is the model of moral knowledge in Socrates' protreptic, the attempt to identify moral knowledge fails. As in the *Ion* 534d8, "techne" is found numerous times within the immediate vicinity of *Euthydemus* 291d1: 290a7, b1, b5; 291a8, b5, c5, c7, d7. Clearly, "techne" should be foremost in the mind of the attentive reader, and ἀτεχνῶς should also be heard as ἀτέχνως. Because it is intrinsically difficult, if not impossible, the kingly techne sits ἀτέχνως at the helm of the city, that is, does not exist.

An example of the second acknowledged usage of the adverb, namely, to mark a comparison, is found at *Phaedo* 90c4. A man, Socrates says, becomes a misologist when he has unrealistic expectations of other men and so is terribly disappointed when they fail him. Misanthropy arises on account of trusting others "without techne" (89d5, 89e5). So too with misology: it arises when someone "without the techne concerning logoi" (90b7) naïvely expects speeches to be true and is then frustrated and embittered when examination finds them lacking. Such a man despairs of the efficacy of logos itself and believes that "all things simply (ἀτεχνῶς), as in the Euripus, twist up and down and never stay put for any time" (90c4–6).

Shortly after this line Socrates describes the misologist as not blaming his own *atechnia* (90d3), but the logoi themselves, for his disappointment. Thus, the context makes it almost unmistakable that Plato here puns.

At *Laches* 188d6, ἀτεχνῶς is used to form a metaphor, and while this passage is not as clearly a pun as the *Phaedo* citation, it is suggestive nonetheless. Laches describes his ambivalence toward logoi. He is impressed by the man who "practices what he preaches," but when a speaker's deeds fail to live up to his words, Laches is appalled. He demands that the

8. Gifford 1909, 43.

Table 2: ἀτεχνῶς in the Dialogues

Euthyphro	Cratylus	Symposium	Lovers	Gorgias	Republic
3a7 C	395e1 C	173d5 C	136a7 A	486c1 A	349a6 C
5c7 A	396a2 C	179b1 Q		491a1 A	419a10 C
	402a5 Q	192e7 A	*Charmides*	494d1 A	432a2 A
Apology	440c8 C	198c2 Q	154b8 Q	525c6 A	443d6 C
17d3 A		214b2 C			473c7 C
18c7 A	*Theaetetus*	217c7 C	*Laches*	*Meno*	548a9 C
18d6 C	151c6 A		187b3 Q	80a3 C	563c5 Q
26e8 A	161a7 A	*Phaedrus*	188d6		
30e2 C	179e6 A	230c7 C		*Ion*	*Laws*
35d4 A		242a7 A	*Euthydemus*	532c2 A	677d8 A
	Sophist		271c6 A	534d8 Q	732e5 C
Phaedo	246a8 A	*Alcibiades* I	273e7 C	541e7 C	790e1 C
82e1 A	255d6 A	116e3 C	291d1 Q		793b6 C
90c4 C		123a1 Q	292e3 Q	*Menexenus*	819b3 A
103a8 A	*Statesman*		303e1 A	249b7 A	840d2 A
116a6 C	277b7 C	*Alcibiades* II			858a8 C
	288a1 A	146e5 C	*Protagoras*	*Cleitophon*	923a3 Q
	294c5 A		326d1 C	408c3 C	952e2 C
	303c8 C		352b8 C		

Note: A = attribution; C = comparison; Q = quotation.

speaker and his speeches be in harmony. When they are, a man becomes truly musical, for he has tuned himself "simply (ἀτεχνῶς) in the Doric mode, not the Ionian." Here the word intensifies the metaphor. As I argued when discussing the *Laches* in Chapter 2, however, Laches' praise of the Doric harmony is an important clue to what nontechnical knowledge is. If this is correct, then the odds of 188d6 being a pun are considerable.

There is a third function of ἀτεχνῶς, one less specific, but more important, than the two well-known usages of comparison and quotation. I term it "attribution," and it is best explicated by citing again *Ion* 532c2. Ion is uninterested in all poets other than Homer. Whenever someone discusses any other poet, "I simply (ἀτεχνῶς) doze off" (532c2). Ion's drowsiness is sure evidence he has no techne. Thus, when he falls asleep during a reading of Archilochus or Hesiod, he ἀτέχνως dozes. Reading the sentence in this manner, an adjective derived from the adverb can be "attributed" to the subject of the verb. The sentence means, "I, who am without a techne, simply doze off."

In four lines of the *Apology* (17d3, 18d6, 30e2, 35d4), Socrates uses ἀτεχνῶς in a manner that invites readers to attribute ἄτεχνος to himself. At 17d3, for example, he says, "I am simply (ἀτεχνῶς) a stranger to this form of [legal] dialect." In other words, he does not have the rhetorical techne. He explicitly disassociates himself from Evenus who, at least in Callias's eyes, does seem to have the techne of educating the youth in arete (20c1). The *Apology* is the only dialogue in which ἀτεχνῶς is used more frequently than "techne" itself (6:2). This makes good sense if we think of the word as a pun and a Socratic self-attribution.

Many more examples could be cited and analyzed. In lieu of this, Table 2 lists all occurrences of ἀτεχνῶς, with a rough indication of how each word is used. Before closing this section, I return to the beginning of this book, the epigraph of its introduction: "By the gods, you simply (ἀτεχνῶς) do not stop speaking about shoemakers, fullers, cooks, and doctors, as if our discussion were about them" (Callicles to Socrates, *Gorgias* 491a).

Callicles, as I argued in Chapter 3, is the privileged interlocutor of the dialogue and, in several crucial instances, is strikingly insightful. This passage shows one of them. Socrates indeed talks continually about shoemakers, fullers, cooks, and doctors, in short, about men who possess a techne. And he does so ἀτέχνως, without possessing a techne himself.

APPENDIX 3:
THE DIVISION
PASSAGES

Borrowing terminology from Aristotle, I will reformulate the thesis of this book. Aristotle divides the *epistemai* into three branches: the theoretical, productive, and practical. As this appendix demonstrates, Plato divides the technai in a similar manner and probably influenced Aristotle on this issue. There is, however, one crucial difference between them: Plato's is a *bi*partition, not a *tri*partition. It offers no correlate to what Aristotle calls "practical knowledge." This textual fact is not meant to signal the impossibility of moral knowledge. Instead, it reiterates its strangeness, its *atopia:* as the diagrams below show, there is no *topos* into which moral knowledge can fit.

Appendix 3 provides further documentation of another thesis: for Plato, techne is equivalent to techne₁. It is either productive or theoretical, and the latter is both exemplified by and conceptually related to mathematics. In both branches the subject matter is determinate, a high level of expertise is achieved by the *technitēs,* and the subject is straightforwardly teachable.

In *Metaphysics* 6, Aristotle says physics is a form of "theoretical knowledge" (*theorētikē epistēmē*) that, because of the nature of its subject matter, is neither practical (*praktikē*) nor productive (*poiētikē*). Physics studies "a certain kind of being" that has its *archē,* its originative source, of change and rest in itself. In productive knowledge the object studied, namely, the thing produced, finds its originative source outside of itself, in the human producer. Practical knowledge studies things done or doable (*ta prakta*). What exactly this means is not here specified except by saying that their *archē* is in the one doing, in rational choice, which again is distinctly human (*Metaphysics* 1025b19–24).

In addition to physics, the theoretical forms of knowledge include mathematics and theology (*Metaphysics* 1026a19). Each studies objects whose *archai* are nonhuman and cannot "hold otherwise" (*Nicomachean Ethics* 1139a9), that is, are necessary. By contrast, practical and productive knowledge study human reality, which is contingent (*Nicomachean Ethics* 1140a1).

The implications of this split between theoretical and practical/productive knowledge are several. Practical knowledge cannot achieve as high a level of precision as, say, mathematics. This is because the subject matter of the latter is the necessary realm of abstract magnitude, while that of the former is the human world of contingent actions. Therefore, "it is equally uneducated to accept merely probable conclusions from a mathematician as it is to demand rigorous demonstrations from a rhetorician" (*Nicomachean Ethics* 1094b25–27). (The purview of rhetoric, as indicated in my discussion of Sophocles' *Antigone* in Chapter 1, is similar to that of ethics.)

The goal of practical knowledge is not simply to know but to act: "The end of theoretical [episteme] is the truth while that of practical [episteme] is action" (*Metaphysics* 993b22; see also *Nicomachean Ethics* 1103b26–30). Again, the basis of this difference is the object studied. Practical knowledge takes up for study the human agent himself, that is, the contingent world of praxis. As a result, it is possible for the student of "ethics" to revise himself as an agent as a result of his studies. Practical knowledge can "have great weight for life and, just as archers taking aim, would we not better attain what is right?" (*Nicomachean Ethics* 1094a22–24). By contrast, the study of physics is about objects—the movement of the heavens, for example—impervious to human effort. Since they are fixed, their study is for the sake of *theōria* alone.

For my purposes, the salient feature of Aristotle's tripartition is its inclusion of practical knowledge. Aristotle conceives of ethics/politics as a self-contained discipline, capable of being "written" in a single book. Despite his repeated insistence that ethics cannot be as precise as mathematics and that its goal is not merely knowledge but action, ethics/politics is nonetheless similar to mathematics or physics; it is a subject matter of a specific Aristotelian treatise. In other words, for Aristotle, practical knowledge is a techne$_2$. Aristotle would reject this description because for him "techne" labels only productive knowledge (see *Nicomachean Ethics* 6.4). Nevertheless, his sense of practical knowledge is analogous to what the Hippocratic physicians, Isocrates, and Alexander of Aphrodisias put forward in articulating their sense of stochastic techne (see "The Hippocratic Writings" in Chapter 1).

By contrast, Plato regularly offers a bifurcation of the technai, in which there is a theoretical and a productive branch. *He offers no place for a practical techne.*

The diagrams below are meant to corroborate this thesis. They use Aristotelian terms. If Plato does use a labeling term it is also included (in parentheses). Prominent examples used in the dialogues to illustrate each kind of techne also follow in parentheses. Finally, passages from several late dialogues are included. Since the argument of this book is restricted to the early dialogues, this is meant only to suggest that, on the question of a practical techne, Plato was consistent throughout his career.

Diagram 4: *Charmides* 165c–166b

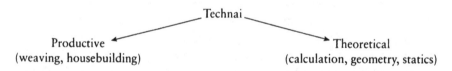

Technai

Productive   Theoretical
(weaving, housebuilding)   (calculation, geometry, statics)

In the *Charmides* Socrates examines Critias's definition of *sōphrosunē* as self-knowledge (see Chapter 2). "If *sōphrosunē* is some sort of knowing, it is clear that it would be an episteme and of something. Right?" (165c5–6). Medicine is the episteme of health, housebuilding of houses. Since "it would be similar in the rest of the technai" (165d4–5), self-knowledge must analogously be about a particular *ti,* a determinate object other than the knowledge itself.

Critias objects: Socrates has falsely homogenized the technai, for they are not all productive like medicine or weaving. He cites calculation and geometry as counterexamples. Socrates grants the objection, but insists calculation and weaving share one crucial feature: they are about a determinate object other than themselves. Calculation is about the odd and the even, statics about the heavy and the light (166a–b). Socrates' comments imply two kinds of technai: in Aristotelian terms, the productive and the theoretical, with the latter exemplified by mathematics.

Diagram 5: *Gorgias* 450b–d

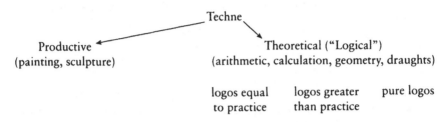

Techne

Productive   Theoretical ("Logical")
(painting, sculpture)   (arithmetic, calculation, geometry, draughts)

logos equal   logos greater   pure logos
to practice   than practice

In the *Gorgias* Socrates forces Gorgias, via the techne analogy, to specify the subject matter of rhetoric, that is, to specify what it is about. Gorgias first replies, "about logoi." Socrates objects: medicine is about those logoi concerning health, gymnastic about those concerning the good and bad condition of our bodies, "and the rest of the technai are similar." Each is a logos of its own subject matter. Gorgias rebuts: unlike the other technai, rhetoric is concerned with logos alone and so has no *cheirourgēma,* no tangible product. Socrates counters with Diagram 5.[1] Its basic stroke, as in Diagram 4, is between the productive and the theoretical, which is again exemplified by mathematics. The schema in the *Gorgias* is more complex than that depicted in Diagram 4, because Socrates suggests that productive techne can be divided into two branches: those having no part in logos and those requiring a little (though this is not shown on Diagram 5). And he divides the theoretical branch into three kinds: those achieving almost their whole purpose through logos and thus requiring either no or little *ergon.* It is here that he cites arithmetic, calculation, geometry, and draughts. Nonetheless, the initial division is the same as in the *Charmides.*

In the *Euthydemus* Socrates begins his second protreptic speech with the conclusion of his first: one must seek wisdom, that is, philosophize, in order to become happy (288d). But what is this wisdom one must seek? To specify, he cites examples of typical technai that "know how to make something" (289a6). These, however, cannot supply a model for wisdom, because they do not know how to *use* what they make. In them, the "making techne" and the "using (*chrōmenē*) techne" are distinct (289c2).

This remark seems to raise the hope of there being a branch in the division for a using, that is, a practical, techne. As shown in Chapter 2, how-

---

1. Dodds (1966, 197) rightly describes *Gorgias* 450b–d as a *diaeresis* of techne and refers to *Charmides, Statesman,* and *Philebus* for comparable passages. Although he should have used "productive," he claims, as do I, that these texts presage "Aristotle's distinction between practical and theoretical technai."

Diagram 6: *Euthydemus* 288d–290d

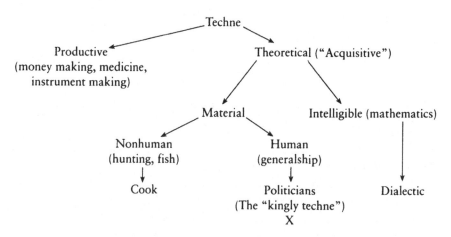

ever, this hope is dashed by Socrates' critical examination of the "kingly techne" (291c–292e). Socrates begins by offering generalship, *stratēgikē* (290b1), as a plausible candidate for the using techne. Cleinias objects: *stratēgikē* is the art of hunting human beings (290b5). Once a general acquires other people, however, he does not know how to use them; instead, like huntsmen, who hand over their catch to those who will cook it, generals hand their catch over to others, to the "politicians" (290d2), to be used. So too do the geometers, astronomers, and calculators—all of whom are metaphorical hunters, that is, they acquire, or discover, and do not produce their epistemic results. These mathematical huntsmen hand over their results to the "dialecticians," who do know how to use them. "Use" in this context does not carry a practical connotation, but refers instead to some sort of meta-mathematical analysis.

Here a slot seems to have opened for the "kingly techne." Finally, however, it is rejected; the search for its subject matter ends in aporia, and so this type of knowledge remains unspecified and thus unacceptable. Therefore, Diagram 6, summarizing the kinds of techne alluded to in this complex passage, has but its two initial branches.

The first stroke of the division passage in the *Euthydemus*, between productive and acquisitive, is echoed in the *Sophist,* a late dialogue (see Diagram 7). The Eleatic Stranger plans to discuss the Sophist, statesman, and philosopher (217a). Are they the same or, as their names suggest, three different kinds of men? To explicate the method he will employ, the Stranger first performs an exemplary division on the "angler." He is a

Diagram 7: *Sophist* 218e–219d

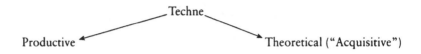

technitēs (219a3), but the analysis soon shifts away from the man to the techne itself. The Stranger begins thus: "But of all the technai there are just two forms" (219a6). Of these, the first is exemplified "when someone leads anything that was not at first existent into being; we say that the one leading produces and that which is led is produced" (219b4). The examples the Stranger chooses here are somewhat problematic: agriculture, animal husbandry, the putting together of tools, and the techne of imitation (*mimētikē*), all of which can be construed as *poiētikē* (219b11). By contrast, the second branch of the division covers "the entire class of learning (*to mathēmatikon*) and that of gaining knowledge and money making and fighting and hunting. Since none of these produces anything but only coerces by word or deed things that are and have become or prevents others from coercing them, it would be appropriate, on account of this, that a certain techne be called acquisitive (*ktētikē*)" (219c1–7).

This passage renders explicit what is metaphorical in the *Euthydemus*: nonproductive forms of techne are "acquisitive" and hence conform to the description of Aristotle's theoretical episteme. Of acquisitive/theoretical techne the Stranger provides no examples, but *to mathēmatikon*, which here probably means learning in general, at least suggests its more particular meaning, namely, mathematics. As a result, Diagram 7 is parallel to the previous diagrams: the basic cut is between the theoretical and the productive, with mathematical technai taking the lead in the latter category. (This first stroke is retained in six of the eight divisions that follow in the dialogue.) Again, there is no slot open for what Aristotle would term practical knowledge.

In the *Statesman*, one might well expect to find room for a practical techne, for its subject is precisely the statesman's knowledge. The Eleatic Stranger takes up, and perhaps resuscitates, the "kingly techne" broached but finally rendered aporetic in the *Euthydemus*. As a result, proponents of the continuist branch of the SAT (notably Sprague) have relied on the *Statesman* to argue that late in his career Plato not only continued to advo-

Diagram 8: *Statesman* 258b–260b

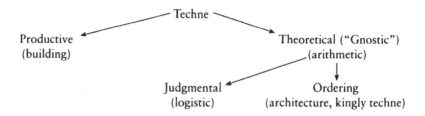

cate but significantly developed his notion of a moral/political techne.[2] The division passage of the *Statesman,* however, is ambiguous and does not necessarily support such a thesis.

The Stranger begins by asking whether the statesman has an episteme or not, and then shifts his focus to the epistemai themselves (258b). In a passage reminiscent of *Gorgias* 450, he describes "arithmetic and other technai that are akin to it" (258d4–5) as "bereft of any praxis; they only supply knowledge" (258d4–6). (This line justifies the description of the passage as a division of the technai, for it shows that even late in his career Plato employed "episteme" and "techne" as virtual synonyms.) In other words, this branch of the division is what Aristotle would term theoretical knowledge, again exemplified best by *arithmetikē.*

The second branch is productive: "the technai that concern carpentry and handicraft in general and possess episteme that is innately related to practice; with its aid [these technai] make bodies come to be that previously were not" (258d8–e2). The Stranger then offers two labels, *praktikē* and *gnōstikē* (258e5). It is obvious, however, that the former refers to production.

The discussion moves to the statesman. A man will rightly be called a king if he has the kingly episteme (259b1). But what is this? "This indeed is clear, that for preserving his power the king can do little in general with his hands or his entire body, compared with the intelligence and strength of his soul" (259c6–9). Therefore, the king's knowledge is more akin to the "gnostic," or theoretical, branch of the technai. But this branch requires further division. Calculation (*logistikē*), for example, is gnostic, and its work is solely "judging" (*krinai:* 259e6) the different kinds of number. Architecture, by contrast, does more: it gives orders to various workmen

2. Sprague 1976.

in the building of a house. There are thus a "judgmental" and an "ordering" (260a10) branch of gnostic techne. The former is clearly theoretical; its possessor is like a "spectator" (*theatēn*: 260c2), a word with the same root as Aristotle's *theōretikē*.

Again, it may appear as if the kingly techne, by virtue of being classified as an ordering, rather than a judging, form of gnostic knowledge is indeed a correlate to Aristotle's practical knowledge. Aristotle describes the highest good as the object of *politikē*, which, because it gives orders to the citizens (especially concerning which epistemai they are to study), is *architektonikē* (*Nicomachean Ethics* 1094a20–b10). Sprague's argument that in the *Statesman* a slot is opened for a practical, ordering techne is thus plausible. It might seem that the "kingly techne," so perplexing in the *Euthydemus*, is here rehabilitated.

Fortunately, this book does not require a full interpretation of the *Statesman*. I would simply advise caution. Aristotle talks about that form of practical knowledge which is architectonic. By contrast, in this division passage the Eleatic Stranger talks about forms of knowledge that, like architecture, are about building. In other words, the emphasis in the *Statesman* is on production. This is even more apparent when the simile characterizing the statesman's knowledge emerges later in the dialogue: the statesman's techne is like weaving (279b). In short, the second cut of the division, between judging and ordering, recapitulates what occurs in the first: the split between theory and production.

Whether Diagram 8 does or does not allow for practical knowledge, one pattern is now clear: in exemplifying the theoretical branch of techne, Plato consistently relies on mathematics. Further elaboration comes from the *Republic*. At *Republic* 522c, a line already cited twice in this book, Socrates notes the centrality of mathematics in the constitution of a techne: "Isn't it the case concerning these [counting and calculation] that every techne and episteme is forced to participate in them?" (522c). What "participate" (*metokos gignesthai*: 522c8) means is not obvious. Later, however, Socrates amplifies. In specifying the curriculum for his guardians, he insists they study mathematics, "not after the fashion of private men, but to stay with it until they come to the contemplation of the nature of numbers with intellect itself, not practicing it for the sake of buying and selling like merchants or tradesmen, but for war and for ease of turning the soul itself around from becoming to truth and being" (525c1–6).

All technai, this passage suggests, are somehow mathematical, but some—those of the private men who, for example, buy and sell—are ap-

Diagram 9: *Republic* 522b–525c

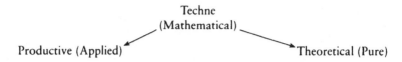

Techne
(Mathematical)

Productive (Applied)   Theoretical (Pure)

plied. The merchant knows some arithmetic, and so calculates how much profit he can make from a sale. By contrast, the "pure" number theorist studies the nature of the odd and even themselves.

Diagram 9 is not an obvious parallel to the previous ones, for there is no mention of production, nor is "techne" used to label the "theoretical" branch. (It is, however, used to label the "applied" branch: in the "divided-line" passage, that mode of thought proceeding from "mathematical objects" back down to sensible things, is described as "the technai" [511c6].) Nonetheless, implicit within the passage is a broad division into two different forms of knowledge: one analogous to what Aristotle calls theoretical episteme and that studies reality for the sake of knowledge; the other somehow making use of mathematical knowledge in its everyday interaction with the sensible world.

This passage thus confirms a basic feature of Platonic techne: it relies on mathematics. Even productive techne is somehow mathematical, at least insofar as its unit of study, for example, building ships, is a single object. This view is expanded in another late dialogue, the *Philebus* (see Diagram 10).

Socrates debates Protarchus concerning the respective merits of knowledge, his choice for the Good, and pleasure, Protarchus's favorite. The condition of the debate is that both candidates be submitted to the same treatment, namely, division into their kinds (14a). After working through pleasure, Socrates confronts the epistemai. He begins clearly enough: one branch of episteme is productive (*dēmiourgikon*), and one about "education and support" (58d1–3). This first stroke seems to divide knowledge into theoretical and productive branches. As Socrates proceeds, however, ambiguity arises. He next states, "In all the manual technai (*cheirotechnikai*) we notice, first of all, if one part is more closely connected to episteme and another is less so, if one part is considered more pure and another less pure" (55d5–8).

Socrates does not explain whether by "manual technai" he refers only to the productive branch of the original division. Instead, he begins talking about mathematics: "if arithmetic, measurement, and statics were taken

Diagram 10: *Philebus* 55d–58a

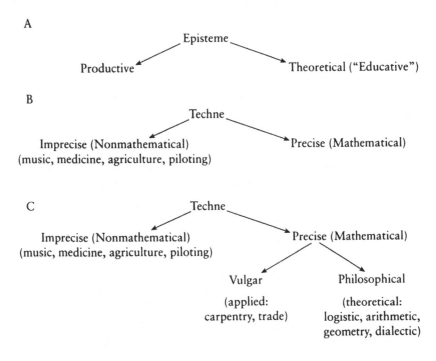

away from all the technai, what would remain would be, so to speak, worthless" (55e). What would be left would be conjecture, experience (*empeiria*), "knack" (*tribē*), and guessing (*stochastikē*). Here Socrates speaks not only of productive knowledge but of "all technai." He proceeds: "So let us divide the so-called technai into two kinds: those which resemble music and have less precision (*akribeia*) in their works, and those which, like building, have more" (56c). What determines whether a techne has less or more precision is whether it is less or more mathematical. Building (*tektonikē*: 56b4) is, for example, more precise, "more technical" (*technikōteran*: 56b6), than music because it uses more instruments (the ruler, the chalk-line, etc.) to make measurements (although at 17d–e music is used to illustrate dialectic). The division seems to be as shown in Diagram 10B.

Socrates refines the division further. Some technai are "most precise" (*akribestatas*: 56c8): arithmetic is the prime example. Arithmetic itself, however, can be divided, for there are two kinds of it: the vulgar and the philosophical. Protarchus does not understand, and so Socrates explains.

There are two types of units counted by the two types of arithmetic: the pure, or intelligible, and the sensible. One may count two oxen or simply consider the properties of the number two. The builder and the trader (see *Republic* 525c) each use mathematical technai, but since their counts are of sensible units (yards of lumber, dollars), that is, since they apply what they know about mathematics to the sensible world, their counts are vulgar ("of the many"). For each branch of mathematics, then, there seems to be an applied and "philosophical," that is, theoretical, branch. The division appears as depicted in Diagram 10C. The right branch of this division is parallel to the division depicted in Diagram 9. Socrates drops the left branch; indeed, it seems eventually to cease to be treated as part of techne at all. (Recall that at 56c, Socrates speaks of the "so-called" technai, a phrase that may mean that these are so "imprecise," so lacking in any participation in mathematics, as to be merely a matter of *empeiria*.) Eventually, dialectic is added as the culmination of the "philosophical" technai (57e—although it is called a *dunamis* at 57e8). Diagram 10C now is significantly similar to Diagram 6.

The *Philebus* is extraordinarily complicated, and the diagrams oversimplify. Still, they support two theses: For Plato, techne is either theoretical or productive; *both* are techne₁ because both are constituted by mathematics. Dialectic is a form of theoretical reflection upon mathematics; productive techne is the ordinary intercourse of human beings, who are able to count, with the sensible world.

The *Philebus*, I note in closing, offers the most sustained reflection on another theme basic to this book: the goodness of arithmos, of determinacy (*to peras*). Socrates develops this theme at length in his account of the one and the many, as well as the determinate and the indeterminate (during his explication of his "method": 16b5). Without broaching the difficulties of this passage, suffice it to say that Socrates' method is a kind of counting, and this, he says, is somehow at the basis of techne (16c2). Furthermore, in his account of the "four genera" (23c–28b), determinacy is explicitly associated with the good. As a result, techne is good.

In sum, the *Philebus*, a late dialogue, seems consistent with many of the most basic patterns recorded in the body of this book. In it Socrates allows for theoretical and productive techne and associates both with mathematics. He counts techne, and the arithmos making it possible, as something good. Furthermore, like the "early" works, the *Philebus* is concerned with the good life. The question of this dialogue is, What sort of life should we lead, that of pleasure or of philosophy? Even if a practical techne is not forthcoming, it is critical, in curbing the appetites of the hedonist, to aim for rigorous knowledge, to praise the goodness of techne, and to understand the goodness of *to peras*.[3]

3. Philebus himself should, like Callicles, be counted as someone who rejects Socrates' most basic assumptions, chooses not to participate in the discussion, and hence cannot be refuted.

APPENDIX 4:
ISOCRATES ON TECHNE

Chapter 3 showed that Plato's Protagoras systematically vacillates on the techne question. In doing so, he imitates Isocrates, who, in *Against the Sophists*, repeatedly responds, "on the one hand (*men*), yes; on the other hand (*de*), no," to the techne question. In both cases, the vacillation is purposive and artful; its goal is to give voice to the precarious form of knowledge that is rhetoric conceived as a techne₂. On the one hand, Protagoras has an epistemic package to sell and wants his audience to think of him as a *technitēs*; on the other hand, he refuses to make the kind of determinate claim favored by the *artium scriptores* and easily refutable by Socrates.

In Appendix 4 I have collected a series of passages from Isocrates' *Antidosis* in order to show how consistently he employs this strategy. Like Plato's Protagoras, he wants his readers to associate him with techne. On the other hand, he wishes to distance himself from the typical practitioners of rhetoric, who do conceive of their subject as a mechanically teachable and stable form of knowledge.[1] As a result, he never actually claims to possess a techne.

I demonstrate this by charting a persistent mistranslation in the standard English version of Isocrates' *Antidosis*, that by George Norlin.[2] Norlin repeatedly uses the phrases "art of discourse" or "art of words." The paral-

---

1. See Cahn 1989.
2. In *Isocrates*, vol. 2. (Cambridge, Mass.: Loeb Classical Library, 1982). References are to section numbers.

lel phrase in Greek, *technē tōn logōn,* is, however, *never used by Isocrates.* Norlin's rendition is not a simple mistranslation; it is instead the product of an artful strategy used by Isocrates to create an expectation in his reader. Consider the following seven passages from Norlin's *Antidosis:*

(1) Section 180: "In my treatment of the *art of discourse* (*tēs tōn logōn paideias*), I desire, like the genealogists, to start at the beginning." *Paideia* is simply not *technē;* thus, Mathieu's "l'éducation oratoire" is obviously more literal.[3]

(2) Section 231: "In fact, however, you will find that among our public men who are living today or who have but lately passed away those who give most study to the *art of words* (*tous pleistēn epimeleian tōn logōn poioumenous*) are the best of the statesmen." Like *paideia, epimeleia* is more flexible than "techne." Men of the past, like Solon, who cared most about and pursued logoi accomplished the most good for their city. Did they actually "study" the "art" of rhetoric? Pace Norlin, Isocrates does not say.

(3) Section 235: "And of these men [the great men of the past] who carried out such great enterprises not one neglected the *art of discourse* (*oudeis logōn ēmelēsen*)." Here there is not even a noun to which Norlin's "art" corresponds.[4] The great men of the past took great pains when it came to logoi. This is an ambiguous statement, for the extension of "logos" for Isocrates is so wide. As the famous passage in *Nicocles* 6 shows (repeated in *Antidosis*), it embraces virtually all of human culture.

(4) Section 253: "We ought, therefore, to think of the *art of discourse* (*peri tōn logōn*) just as we think of the other arts (*tōn allōn*)." Norlin's supplementation of the Greek here is plausible because just before this remark (251–52) Isocrates presented the following argument: If a man inherited a large fortune and then used his wealth to achieve vicious ends, no one would blame his father, who originally accumulated the wealth; blameworthy is the son, who used it badly. Similarly, when it comes to men who have "mastered the art of war" (*hoplamachein mathontes*) or of boxing or pancration, we blame the students, and not the teachers, if they use what they have learned to achieve despicable ends. Presumably, this is because techne (with which episteme is here synonymous) can be used for good or ill.

Clearly, then, when Isocrates uses the phrase *peri tōn allōn* in section

---

3. Isocrates, *Discours,* ed. and trans. G. Mathieu (Paris: Societé d'Edition "Les Belles Lettres," 1943).

4. Mathieu also mistranslates: "l'art de la parole."

253, he has in mind what Norlin says he does, that is, "the other arts," like boxing and pancration. But note what Isocrates does not say. While, on the one hand, he seems to associate rhetoric with "the other arts," he does not explicitly say rhetoric is a techne. Instead, he merely urges us to think about logoi the way that we think about the other technai. This, I propose, is Isocrates' intention here: he wants his reader to expect rhetoric to be like the other technai. But he avoids making the unqualified assertion that it actually is one, and he himself *never* uses the phrase *technē tōn logōn* to name what it is he teaches.[5]

(5) Section 258: "But why should we be surprised at him [Lysimachus] when even among the professors of disputation there are some who talk no less abusively of the *art of speaking* (*peri tōn logōn*) on general and useful themes." These disputatious abusers are not, Isocrates says, ignorant of the power (*dunamin*) of logoi; instead, as Norlin puts it, "they think that by decrying this *art* they will enhance the standing of their own." Again, Norlin has imported the word "art"; in Greek there is only the pronoun *toutous*, whose antecedent is *logoi*. As such, Norlin's translation is really an interpretation: he is convinced rhetoric is a techne and therefore ignores Isocrates' own, much more circumspect formulations.

(6) Section 277: "It follows, then, that the power to speak well and think right will reward the man who approaches the *art of discourse* (*pros tous logous*) with love of wisdom and love of honour."

(7) Section 292: "[I]t is well that in all activities, and most of all in the *art of speaking* (*tōn logōn*), credit is won, not by gifts of fortune, but by efforts of study (*epimeleias*)."

As in (4), Isocrates here offers a comparison between what he teaches and "all activities" (*tōn allōn hapantōn*). Again, he is trying to create an association, and an accompanying expectation, in the reader's mind. Norlin's translation, with its persistent inclusion of "art," gives voice to it perfectly.

Isocrates launches his strategy of associating rhetoric with techne at section 178: "I shall try as best I can to explain what is the nature of this education, what is its power, what of the other arts it is akin to, what benefit it is to its devotees, and what claims I make for it."

What Isocrates teaches is "akin to" (*homoieidēs*) the other technai. This is not, however, to say rhetoric itself is techne. It may be like the other technai insofar as it is knowledge and thus teachable; but it might not be

---

5. This is a conclusion supported by a *Thesaurus Linguae Graecae* search.

"technical" knowledge and thus might not be teachable in the same fashion as they. (The section on Isocrates in Chapter 1 shows this is the crucial point Isocrates makes in *Against the Sophists*.) The passage in section 178, then, invites the reader to think of rhetoric as a techne, but does not explicitly assert it is one.

A similar move is found at section 189. After discussing the classic triad of nature, education, and practice in sections 187–88, Isocrates says, "Now these observations apply to any and all the arts (*technōn*). If anyone, ignoring the other arts, were to ask me which of these factors has the greatest power in the education of an orator I should answer that natural ability is paramount and comes before all else."[6]

Again, note Isocrates' care: what he has said about nature, education, and practice applies to the technai; it also applies to *tōn logōn paideia*. Such a similarity does not imply identity, however. Perhaps rhetoric is like the technai in some respects, but unlike it in others.

Isocrates continues his effort to persuade his reader that rhetoric is like a techne at section 202. In responding to those who would criticize him because they think education is incapable of genuinely improving men's ability to speak and handle political affairs (197), Isocrates says this:

> And yet how can we fail to deny intelligence to those who have the effrontery to demand powers which are not found in the recognized arts (*technōn*) of this which they declare is not an *art* and who expect greater advantages to come from an *art* in which they do not believe than from arts which they regard as thoroughly perfected? Men of intelligence ought not to form contrary judgements about similar things, nor refuse to recognize a discipline (*paideian*) which accomplishes the same results as most of the arts (*technōn*).

Norlin again mistranslates by twice adding the word "art" when *technē* does not appear. (The two instances are italicized above.) Isocrates complains that his critics demand more from rhetoric than they do from the recognized *technai*. This seems to contradict their assertion that rhetoric is not an art at all. Isocrates, however, does not quite say what Norlin thinks him to, namely, "of this which they declare is not an art." Instead, he only uses pronouns: "of this which they declare is not [*hēn ouk einai phasi*]." He does not say, "of greater advantages to come from an art in which they

6. See Shorey 1909.

do not believe"; he only uses a participial phrase, *para tēs apistoumenēs*, "from that in which they do not believe."

Again, Isocrates dangles a temptation in front of his reader with a beautifully elusive sentence. He encourages the reader to reconstruct the meaning of the sentence thus: my critics think rhetoric is not an art, but they expect more from it than they do from other arts; therefore, rhetoric must be an art. But he studiously avoids actually using "techne" to speak about what it is he teaches, while at the same time trying to associate what he teaches with the arts.

The same strategy emerges at sections 205–6:

> Furthermore, this also will be agreed to by all men, namely, that in all the arts (*technōn*) and crafts (*cheirourgiōn*) we regard those as the most skilled (*technikōtatous*) who turn out pupils who all work as far as possible in the same manner. Now it will be seen that this is the case with philosophy. For all who have been under a true and intelligent guide will be found to have a power of speech so similar that it is evident to everyone that they have shared the same training. And yet, had not a common habit and a common technique of training (*diatribēs technikēs*) been instilled into them, it is inconceivable that they should have taken on this likeness.

This is as close as Isocrates comes to describing his education in "philosophy" (by which he means rhetoric) as an art. Again, however, note how circumlocutious he is. Isocrates' students and those of the recognized arts are similarly equipped. This invites the implication that rhetoric is a techne. But he does not say this. Instead, his students had a "technique of training." Obviously, then, Norlin is not simply wrong in so frequently adding the word "art" in his translations: the teaching of rhetoric *is* similar to a techne. As he notes in *Against the Sophists*, there is a fixed and stable (*tetagmenē*) dimension of his program. But, yet again, this is not quite the same as saying rhetoric is a techne.

If he is circumlocutious when describing his own subject in positive terms, Isocrates can be extremely straightforward when making an epistemic denial:

> For since it is not in the nature of man to attain a science (*epistēmē*) by the possession of which we can know positively what we should do or what we should say, in the next resort I hold that man to be

wise who is able by his powers of conjecture to arrive generally at the best course. (271)

I consider that the kind of art (*technen*) which can implant honesty and justice in deprave natures has never existed. (274)

These denials, which were conceived originally in *Against the Sophists*, must be juxtaposed with the positive associations made on behalf of rhetoric in *Antidosis* 178, 189, 203, and 205–6. In other words, Isocrates wants his rhetoric to be some sort of teachable knowledge, but at the same time not to be held to the rigorous standards of a typical, *tetagmenē* techne.

The cumulative picture is this: what is most important in the training of a rhetor is the student's nature. But a good nature alone will not suffice. Practice will help greatly (see 189–91). What, then, remains the role of education? This is precisely where the passages discussed above begin. In them Isocrates gives voice to the precarious form of knowledge that is his morally charged, but difficult to communicate, sense of rhetoric. Isocrates, then, offers a techne$_2$, a kind of teachable knowledge that makes none of the hard and fast claims of a techne$_1$.

As the *Protagoras* shows, Plato understands this form of knowledge, and even has some sympathy for it. (His own conception of moral knowledge is, after all, also not a techne$_1$.) Finally, however, he rejects it. It simply is not satisfying.

REFERENCES

Secondary Resources

Adam, J. 1971. Introduction to Plato's *Protagoras,* edited by J. Adam. New Rochelle, N.Y.: Caratzas Publishing, 1971.

Adkins, A. 1973. "Arete, Techne, Democracy, and Sophists." *Journal of Hellenic Studies* 93:3–12.

Allen, J. 1989. "Failure and Expertise in the Ancient Conception of an Art." Distributed by the Society for Ancient Greek Philosophy, April.

Anhalt, E. 1993. *Solon the Singer.* Lanham, Md.: Rowman & Littlefield.

Annas, J. 1981. *An Introduction to Plato's Republic.* New York: Oxford University Press.

Bambrough, R. 1971. "Plato's Political Analogies." In *Plato II,* edited by G. Vlastos, 187–205. New York: Doubleday.

Barnabas, M. 1986. "The Strangeness of Socrates." *Philosophical Investigations* 9:89–110.

Barnes, J. 1986. "Is Rhetoric an Art." *Discourse Analysis Group Newsletter* (of the University of Calgary) 2:2–22.

Barwick, K. 1963. "Das Problem des Isokratischen Techne." *Philologus* 107:275–95.

Benson, H., ed. 1992. *Essays on the Philosophy of Socrates.* New York: Oxford University Press.

Blits, J. 1985. "Socratic Teaching and Justice: Plato's *Cleitophon.*" *Interpretation* 13:321–334.

Bloom, A. 1968. "Interpretive Essay." In *The Republic of Plato,* translated by A. Bloom. New York: Basic.

Blümner, H. 1912. *Technologies und Terminologie: Der Gewerbe und Künste bei Griechen und Römern*. Leipzig: Teubner.

Bolkestein, H. 1958. *Economic Life in Greece's Golden Age*. Leiden: Brill.

Brumbaugh, R. S. 1973. "Knowledge as Skill and Used Information: Hippias." In *Philosophical Themes in Modern Education*, edited by R. Brumbaugh, 25–35. Boston: Houghton Mifflin.

———. 1976. "Plato's Relation to the Arts and Crafts." In *Facets of Plato's Philosophy*, edited by W. Werkmeister, 40–52. Amsterdam: Van Gorcum.

Burnet, J. 1967. *Platonis Opera*. New York: Oxford University Press.

Cahn, M. 1989. "Reading Rhetoric Rhetorically." *Rhetorica* 7:121–44.

———. 1993. "Six Tropes of Disciplinary Self-Constitution." In *The Recovery of Rhetoric*, edited by R. Roberts. Charlottesville: University of Virginia Press.

Cambiano, G. 1971. *Platone e le techniche*. Turin: Einaudi.

Chance, T. 1992. *Plato's Euthydemus: Analysis of What Is and What Is Not Philosophy*. Berkeley and Los Angeles: University of California Press.

Cole, Thomas. 1991. *The Origins of Rhetoric in Ancient Greece*. Baltimore: Johns Hopkins University Press.

Coolidge, F. 1993. "The Relation of Medicine to *Sōphrosunē*." *Ancient Philosophy* 13:23–36.

Cunliffe, R. 1963. *A Lexicon of Homeric Dialect*. Norman: University of Oklahoma Press.

de Romilly, J. 1975. *Magic and Rhetoric in Ancient Greece*. Cambridge: Cambridge University Press.

———. 1992. *The Great Sophists in Periclean Athens*. Oxford: Clarendon.

Detienne, M., and J.-P. Vernant. 1978. *Cunning Intelligence in Greek Culture and Society*. Translated by J. Lloyd. Atlantic Highlands, N.J.: Harvester Press.

Dodds, E. 1966. Introduction and commentary to Plato's *Gorgias*, edited by E. Dodds. New York: Oxford University Press.

Dunne, J. 1993. *Back to the Rough Ground: Phronesis and Techne in Modern Philosophy and Aristotle*. Notre Dame, Ind.: University of Notre Dame Press.

Düring, I. 1961. *Aristotle's Protrepticus: An Attempt at Reconstruction*. Göteborg: Institute of Classical Studies.

Dyson, M. 1974. "Some Problems Concerning Knowledge in Plato's *Charmides*." *Phronesis* 19:102–11.

Edelstein, L. 1952. "The Relation of Ancient Philosophy to Medicine." *Bulletin of the History of Medicine* 26:299–316.

———. 1967. *Ancient Medicine: Selected Papers of Ludwig Edelstein*. Baltimore: Johns Hopkins University Press.

Finley, M. 1978. *The World of Odysseus*. New York: Viking.

Fish, S. 1990. *Doing What Comes Naturally*. Durham, N.C.: Duke University Press.

Frede, M. 1985. Introduction to Galen's *Three Treatises on the Nature of Science*, edited by M. Frede. Indianapolis: Hackett, 1985.

Führmann, M. 1960. *Das Systematische Lehrbuch*. Göttingen: Vandenhoeck.

Gifford, E. 1909. Commentary on *The Euthydemus of Plato*. New York: Oxford University Press.

Gomperz, T. 1910. *Die Apologie der Heilkunst.* Leipzig: Von Veit.

Gosling, J. 1975. Commentary to Plato's *Philebus.* Edited by J. Gosling. New York: Oxford University Press.

Gould, C. 1987. "Socratic Intellectualism and the Problem of Courage." *History of Philosophy Quarterly* 4:265–79.

Gould, J. 1955. *The Development of Plato's Ethics.* New York: Russell.

Graham, D. 1991. "Socrates, the Craft Analogy, and Science." *Apeiron* 24:1–24.

Greene, W. 1963. *Moira: Fate, Good, and Evil in Greek Thought.* New York: Harper & Row.

Griswold, C. 1986a. "Philosophy, Education, and Courage in Plato's *Laches. Interpretation* 14:177–93.

———. 1986b. *Self-Knowledge in Plato's Phaedrus.* New Haven: Yale University Press.

———. 1988. *Platonic Readings, Platonic Writings.* New York: Routledge.

Hall, R. 1971. "Techne and Morality in the *Gorgias.*" In *Essays in Ancient Greek Philosophy,* vol. 1, edited by J. Anton and G. Kustas, 202–18. Albany: State University of New York Press.

Harris, W. 1989. *Ancient Literacy.* Cambridge, Mass.: Harvard University Press.

Hawtrey, R. 1981. *Commentary on Plato's Euthydemus.* Philadelphia: American Philosophical Society.

Heath, T. 1981. *A History of Greek Mathematics.* New York: Dover.

Heidegger, M. 1977. *The Question Concerning Technology.* Translated by W. Lovitt. New York: Harper.

Heinimann, F. 1961. "Eine vorplatonische Theorie der Techne." *Museum Helveticum* 18:105–30.

Hemmenway, S. 1993. "The Techne-Analogy in Socrates' Healthy City." Paper presented to the Society for Ancient Greek Philosophy, New York, October.

Heyde, D. 1963. "Zur Geschichte des Wortes 'Technik,'" *Humanismus und Technik* 9:25–43.

Hinks, D. 1940. "Tisias and Corax and the Invention of Rhetoric." *Classical Quarterly* 34:61–69.

Hirschberger, J. 1932. *Die Phronesis in der Philosophie Platons vor dem Staate.* Leipzig: Dieterich'sche.

Howland, J. 1991. "Re-Reading Plato: The Problem of Platonic Chronology." *Phoenix* 45:189–214.

———. 1993. *The Republic: The Odyssey of Philosophy.* New York: Twayne.

Huffman, C. 1988. "The Role of Number in Philolaus's Philosophy." *Phronesis* 33:1–29.

Hyland, D. 1968. "Why Plato Wrote Dialogues." *Philosophy and Rhetoric* 1:38–50.

———. 1981. *The Virtue of Philosophy.* Athens, Ohio: University of Ohio Press.

———. 1988. "Taking the Longer Road: Irony in Plato's *Republic.*" *Revue de Metaphysique et Morale* 3.

Irwin, T. 1977. *Plato's Moral Theory.* Oxford: Clarendon Press.

———. 1979. *Plato's Gorgias.* New York: Oxford University Press.

Isnardi Parente, M. 1966. *Techne.* Florence: La Nuova Italia.

Jaeger, W. 1967. *Paideia: The Ideals of Greek Culture.* Translated by G. Highet. Oxford: Oxford University Press.

Jones, W. 1956. Introduction to *Hippocrates,* vol. 1, translated by W. Jones. Cambridge, Mass.: Harvard University Press, Loeb Classical Library.

Joos, P. 1955. *Tuche, Phusis, Techne.* Winterthur: Keller.

Kahn, C. 1986. "Plato's Methodology in the *Laches.*" *International Review of Philosophy* 9.

Kato, M. 1986. *Techne und Philosophie bei Platon.* Frankfurt: Peter Lang.

Kennedy, G. 1963. *The Art of Persuasion in Greece.* Princeton: Princeton University Press.

Keulen, H. 1971. *Untersuchungen zu Platons Euthydem.* Wiesbaden: O. Harrassowitz.

Klein, J. 1968. *Greek Mathematical Thought and the Origin of Algebra.* Cambridge, Mass..: MIT Press.

———. 1975. *A Commentary on Plato's Meno.* Chapel Hill: University of North Carolina Press.

Klosko, G. 1981. "The Technical Conception of Virtue." *Journal of the History of Philosophy* 19:95–102.

Koster, W. 1960. *Scholia in Aristophanem.* Groningen: Wolters-Noordhoff.

Krämer, H. 1959. *Arete bei Platon und Aristoteles.* Heidelberg: Carl Winter.

Kraut, R., ed. 1992. *The Cambridge Companion to Plato.* Cambridge: Cambridge University Press.

Kübe, J. 1969. *Techne und Arete.* Berlin: DeGruyter.

Kühn, J. 1956. *System- und Methodenprobleme in Corpus Hippocraticum.* Wiesbaden: Franz Steiner.

Kurz, D. 1970. *Akribeia: Das Ideal der Exaktheit bei den Griechen bis Aristoteles.* Göppingen: Alfred Kümmerle.

Larson, M. 1979. *The Rise of Professionalism.* Berkeley and Los Angeles: University of California Press.

Ledger, G. 1989. *Re-Counting Plato.* Oxford: Clarendon Press.

Lesher, J. 1987. "Socrates' Disavowal of Knowledge." *Journal of the History of Philosophy* 25:275–88.

Lesses, G. 1982. "Virtue as Techne in the Early Dialogues." *Southwest Philosophical Studies* 13:93–100.

Levi, A. 1940. "The Ethical and Social Thought of Protagoras." *Mind* 49:285–305.

Lidov, J. 1983. "The Meaning of Idea in Isocrates." *La Parola del Passato* 38:273–87.

Lloyd, G. 1963. "Who Is Attacked in *On Ancient Medicine?*" *Phronesis* 8:108–26.

———. 1987. *Revolutions of Wisdom.* Cambridge: Cambridge University Press.

Loenen, D. 1940. *Protagoras and the Greek Community.* Amsterdam: Swets & Zeitlinger.

Lyons, J. 1967. *Structural Semantics: An Analysis of Part of the Vocabulary of Plato.* Oxford: Blackwell.

MacDowell, D. 1982. Introduction and notes to Gorgias's *Encomium of Helen.* Bristol: Bristol Classical Press.

Marrou, H. 1956. *A History of Education in Antiquity.* Translated by G. Lamb. New York: Mentor.

McPherran, M. 1992. "Socratic Piety in the *Euthyphro.*" In *Essays on the Philosophy of Socrates,* edited by H. Benson. New York: Oxford University Press.

Moser, S., and G. Kustas. 1966. "A Comment on the Relativism of Protagoras." *Phoenix* 20:110–18.

Mueller, I. 1992. "Mathematical Method and Philosophical Truth." In *The Cambridge Companion to Plato,* ed. R. Kraut. Cambridge: Cambridge University Press.

Murakawa, K. 1957. "Demiurgos." *Historia* 6:385–415.

Nietzsche, F. 1967. *The Birth of Tragedy.* Translated by W. Kaufmann. New York: Vintage.

Nussbaum, M. 1979. "Eleatic Conventionalism and Philolaus on the Conditions of Thought." *Harvard Studies in Classical Philology* 83:63–108.

———. 1986. *The Fragility of Goodness.* Cambridge: Cambridge University Press.

O'Brien, M. 1963. "The Unity of the *Laches.*" *Yale Classical Studies* 18:135–45.

———. 1967. *The Socratic Paradoxes and the Greek Mind.* Chapel Hill: University of North Carolina Press.

Orwin, C. 1982. "The Case Against Socrates: Plato's *Cleitophon.*" *Canadian Journal of Political Science* 15:741–53.

Parry, R. 1983. "The Craft of Justice." *Canadian Journal of Philosophy,* supp. 9:19–38.

Penner, T. 1992a. "Socrates and the Early Dialogues." In *The Cambridge Companion to Plato,* ed. R. Kraut. Cambridge: Cambridge University Press.

———. 1992b. "The Unity of Virtue." In *Essays on the Philosophy of Socrates,* edited by H. Benson. New York: Oxford University Press.

———. 1992c. "What Laches and Nicias Miss." *Ancient Philosophy* 12:1–29.

Pokorny, J. 1967. *Indogermanisches Etymologisches Wörterbuch.* Bern: Francke.

Praechter, K. 1932. "Platon und Euthydemus." *Philologus* 87:121–35.

Radermacher, L. 1951. *Artium Scriptores.* Vienna: Rohrer.

Reeve, C. 1988. *Philosopher-Kings.* Princeton: Princeton University Press.

Roochnik, D. 1984. "The Riddle of the *Cleitophon.*" *Ancient Philosophy* 4:132–45.

———. 1986. "Socrates' Use of the Techne-Analogy." *Journal of the History of Philosophy* 24:295–310.

———. 1987. "Plato's Use of Atechnos." *Phoenix* 41:255–63.

———. 1988. "The Tragic Philosopher: A Critique of Martha Nussbaum." *Ancient Philosophy* 8:285–95.

———. 1990. "The Serious Play of Plato's *Euthydemus.*" *Interpretation* 18:211–33.

———. 1991. *The Tragedy of Reason.* New York: Routledge.

———. 1992. "Stanley Fish and the Old Quarrel Between Rhetoric and Philosophy." *Critical Review* 5:225–46.

———. 1994a. "The Goodness of *Arithmos.*" *American Journal of Philology* 115:543–63.

———. 1994b. "Is Rhetoric an Art?" *Rhetorica* 12:127–54.

———. 1995. "Socratic Ignorance as Complex Irony." *Arethusa* 28:39–52.

Rosen, S. 1983. *Plato's Sophist.* New Haven: Yale University Press.

Salkever, S. 1994. "Plato on Practices: The Technai and the Socratic Question in *Republic I.*" In *Proceedings of the Boston Area Colloquium in Ancient Philosophy,* vol. 7, edited by J. Cleary. Lanham, Md.: University Press of America.

Schaerer, R. 1930. *Episteme et Techne: Études sur les notions de connaissance et d'art d'Homère à Platon.* Lausanne.

Schiappa, E. 1993. "Isocrates and Canons." Distributed by the Society for Ancient Greek Philosophy, December.

Schmid, W. 1992. *On Manly Courage: A Study of Plato's Laches.* Evanston, Ill.: Southern Illinois Press.

Searle, J. 1993. "Rationality and Realism: What Is at Stake?" *Daedalus* 122:55–84.

Segal, C. 1986. *Interpreting Greek Tragedy.* Ithaca: Cornell University Press.

Shorey, P. 1909. "Phusis, Meletē, Epistēmē." *TAPA* 40:185–201.

———. 1926. Commentary to Plato's *Republic.* Cambridge, Mass.: Harvard University Press, Loeb Classical Library.

———. 1968. *The Unity of Plato's Thought.* New York: Archon Books.

Sprague, R. 1962. *Plato's Use of Fallacy.* New York: Barnes & Noble.

———, ed. 1972. *The Older Sophists.* Columbia, S.C.: University of South Carolina Press.

———. 1976. *Plato's Philosopher King.* Columbia, S.C.: University of South Carolina Press.

Starr, P. 1982. *The Social Transformation of American Medicine.* New York: Basic.

Stewart, M. 1977. "Plato's Sophistry." *Aristotelian Society,* suppl. vol. 51.

Tarrant, D. 1946. "Colloquialisms, Semi-Proverbs, and Word-Play in Plato." *Classical Quarterly* 40:109–17.

Taylor, A. E. 1926. *Plato.* London: Metheun.

Taylor, C. 1976. Commentary to Plato's *Protagoras.* Oxford: Clarendon.

Thesleff, H. 1967. "Studies in the Style of Plato." *Acta Philosophica Fennica* 20:75–88.

Thomas, R. 1989. *Oral Tradition and Written Record in Classical Athens.* Cambridge: Cambridge University Press.

Thomsen, D. 1990. *Techne als Metapher und als Begriff der sittlichen Einsicht.* Freiburg: Karl Alber.

Tigerstedt, E. N. 1977. *Interpreting Plato.* Stockholm: Almqvist & Wiksell.

Tiles, J. 1984. "Techne and Moral Expertise." *Philosophy* 59:49–66.

Versenyi, L. 1963. *Socratic Humanism.* New Haven: Yale University Press.

Vickers, B. 1988. *In Defense of Rhetoric.* New York: Oxford University Press.

Vlastos, G. 1956. Introduction to Plato's *Protagoras.* Indianapolis: Bobbs-Merrill.

———. 1973. *Platonic Studies.* Princeton: Princeton University Press.

———. 1978. "The Virtuous and the Happy." *Times Literary Supplement,* 24 February, 230–33.

———. 1983. "The Socratic Elenchus." *Oxford Studies in Ancient Philosophy* 1:27–58.

———. 1985. "Socrates' Disavowal of Knowledge." *Philosophical Quarterly* 35:1–31.

———. 1991. *Socrates: Ironist and Moral Philosopher.* Ithaca: Cornell University Press.

Wadia, P. 1986. "The Notion of Techne in Plato." *Philosophical Studies* 31:148–58.

Warren, E. 1985. "Plato's Refutation of Thrasymachus: The Craft Argument." Distributed by the Society for Ancient Greek Philosophy, December.

———. 1989. "The Craft Argument: An Analogy?" In *Essays in Ancient Greek Philosophy III: Plato,* edited by J. Anton and A. Preus. Albany: State University of New York Press.

Wehrli, F. 1951. "Der Arztvergleich bei Platon." *Museum Helveticum* 8:177–84.

Weiss, R. 1992. "*Ho Agathos* as *Ho Dunatos* in the *Hippias Minor.*" In *Essays on the Philosophy of Socrates,* edited by H. Benson. New York: Oxford University Press.

West, M., ed. 1980. *Delectus ex Iambis et Elegis Graecis.* Oxford: Clarendon Press.

Whitehead, A. 1971. *The Philosophy of Alfred North Whitehead.* Lasalle, Ill.: Open Court.

Woodruff, P. 1992. "Plato's Early Theory of Knowledge." In *Essays on the Philosophy of Socrates,* edited by H. Benson. New York: Oxford University Press.

Primary Resources

Aeschylus
Prometheus Bound. Translated by C. Herrington and J. Scully. New York: Oxford University Press, 1989.

Anaximenes
Rhetorica ad Alexandrum. Translated by H. Rackham. Cambridge, Mass.: Harvard University Press, Loeb Classical Library, 1936. (Listed by Harvard University Press under "Aristotle.")

Aristides
Aristides. Vol. 1, *In Defense of Oratory.* Translated by C. Behr. Cambridge, Mass.: Harvard University Press, Loeb Classical Library, 1973.

Aristotle
Protrepticus. Edited by I. Düring. Göteborg: Institute of Classical Studies, 1961.

Galen
Three Treatises on the Nature of Science. Edited by M. Frede. Indianapolis: Hackett, 1985.

Gorgias
The Encomium of Helen. Edited by D. MacDowell. Bristol: Bristol Classical Press, 1982.

Hippocrates
Hippocrates. Vol. 1. Translated by W. Jones. Cambridge, Mass.: Harvard University Press, Loeb Classical Library, 1956.

Homer
Homer's Odyssey. Edited by W. Merry. New York: Oxford University Press, 1966.
The Iliad of Homer. Translated by R. Lattimore. New York: Harper & Row, 1975.

The Iliad of Homer. Edited by M. Willcock. London: Macmillan, 1978.
The Odyssey of Homer. Translated by R. Lattimore. New York: Harper & Row, 1979.
Isocrates
  Discours. Vol. 2. Edited by G. Mathieu. Paris: Societé d'Edition "Les Belles Lettres," 1943.
  Isocrates. Vol. 2. Translated by G. Norlin. Cambridge, Mass.: Harvard University Press, Loeb Classical Library, 1982.
Longinus
  On the Sublime. Translated by W. Roberts. New York: Garland, 1987.
Lucian
  Lucian. Vol. 3. Translated by A. Harmon. Cambridge, Mass.: Harvard University Press, Loeb Classical Library, 1960.
Philodemus
  The Rhetorica of Philodemus. Translated by H. Hubbell. New Haven: Connecticut Academy of Arts and Sciences, 1920.
  Volumina Rhetorica. Edited by S. Sudhaus. Leipzig: Teubner, 1892.
Plato
  Charmides. Translated by W. Lamb. In *Plato*, vol. 8. Cambridge, Mass.: Harvard University Press, Loeb Classical Library, 1974.
  The Euthydemus of Plato. Edited by E. Gifford. New York: Oxford University Press, 1909.
  Gorgias. Edited by E. Dodds. New York: Oxford University Press, 1966.
  Philebus. Edited by J. Gosling. New York: Oxford University Press, 1975.
  Plato's Protagoras. Edited by G. Vlastos. Indianapolis: Bobbs-Merrill, 1956.
  Platonis Opera. Edited by J. Burnet. New York: Oxford University Press, 1967.
  Protagoras. Edited by J. Adam. New Rochelle, N.Y.: Caratzas Publishing, 1971.
  Protagoras. Translated by W. Guthrie. New York: Penguin, 1956.
  Protagoras. Translated by S. Lombardo and K. Bell. Indianapolis: Hackett, 1992.
  Protagoras. Translated by C. Taylor. Oxford: Clarendon, 1976.
  The Republic of Plato. Translated by A. Bloom. New York: Basic, 1968.
  Republic. Edited by P. Shorey. Cambridge, Mass.: Harvard University Press, Loeb Classical Library, 1926.
  Symposium. Translated by A. Nehamas and P. Woodruff. Indianapolis: Hackett, 1989.
Quintilian
  The Institutio Oratoria of Quintilian. Vol. 1. Translated by H. Butler. Cambridge, Mass.: Harvard University Press, Loeb Classical Library, 1989.
Sextus Empiricus
  Philosophical Works. Vol. 4, *Against the Professors*. Translated by R. Bury. Cambridge, Mass.: Harvard University Press, Loeb Classical Library, 1947.
Varro, Marcus Terentius
  On Agriculture. Translated by W. Hooper. Cambridge, Mass.: Harvard University Press, Loeb Classical Library, 1934.

INDEX

Printed in the United States
205046BV00001B/311/A

Made in the USA
Monee, IL
22 March 2021